PRINCIPLES OF EMERGENT REALISM

A Monograph in

MODERN CONCEPTS OF PHILOSOPHY

Series Editor

MARVIN FARBER

State University of New York at Buffalo
Buffalo, New York

PRINCIPLES OF EMERGENT REALISM

Philosophical Essays
by Roy Wood Sellars

Compiled and Edited by

W. PRESTON WARREN

*Department of Philosophy
Bucknell University
Lewisburg, Pennsylvania*

WARREN H. GREEN, INC.
St. Louis, Missouri, U.S.A.

Published by

WARREN H. GREEN, INC.
10 South Brentwood Blvd.
St. Louis, Missouri 63105, U.S.A.

All rights reserved

© 1970, by WARREN H. GREEN, INC.

Library of Congress Catalog Card No. 70-96993

Printed in the United States of America

Foreword

At the request of Professor Preston Warren, I am writing a brief Foreword to his careful study of the development of my philosophical position.

I have been fortunate in two things at least. I have had a long time to reflect on basic points in my theses, some sixty years in fact. And these theses have lent themselves to clarification and development. They were, it would seem, what I call *neglected alternatives* which were constantly bypassed by my contemporaries. They did not see how they could be fitted together. That was my job and I found considerable stimulus in integrating these parameters.

These were essentially three in number, though they involved enlargements as in my theory of value and what I call agential causality, or man as a causal agent. I early tried to show that valuation is a different operation from cognition, as such, and had different ingredients and criteria. I do not see how man could be an agent without this dimension in his life. The inorganic sciences, quite naturally, neglected it. They were concerned essentially with description and laws. And the idea of evolution came late and was not much meditated on. I think I was one of the first to stress levels of causality. That was in my *Evolutionary Naturalism* (1921), though I had suggested the idea earlier.

But, to come back to the three parameters which I sought to integrate. These were, first, a realistic analysis of perceiving which showed that sensations were not terminal but operationally used in sensuous thinking of the stimulating object. I also held that *knowing* was a development preceded by sensory guidance, as in animal life. The second parameter was the mind-body question. Here I early developed a double-knowledge approach, being very skeptical of Cartesian dualism. This fitted in with my theory of perceiving which had made sensations integral to the act of perceiving and not terminal. I thought of perceiving as a mind-brain activity under external control but involving what I called directed response. This made possible a new kind of direct realism different from the presentational realism of the new realists. Things are responded to selectively and sensuously thought. My idea that guidance preceded explicit cognizing fitted in here. Man's color sense was probably developed in his arboreal state and enabled him to discriminate better.

The third parameter was that of the evolutionary approach to human life and experience. I think I was one of the earliest to stress emergent novelty. At least, Lloyd Morgan so believed, though American philosophers have given me small credit. I am really rather puzzled by this treatment. Certainly, after the thirties, American thinkers looked abroad for their paradigms. And I fear that Europeans were both clamorous and ignorant of American thought. As I recall it, young American thinkers were fed with the notion that there had been some sort of stalement here. May I be permitted to say that I have always kept my eye on problems rather than on slogans and fashions. The University of Notre Dame Press brought out a book of mine in the spring of 1969 devoted to reflections on American philosophy.

Now the reader can see that I succeeded in integrating these paramenters. My analysis of perceiving not only gave me a direct realism but also fitted in with the natural idea that sensations arise in the cerebral centers connected with the sense-organs. It is a curious fact that Dewey, Woodbridge, and Brand Blanshard rejected such location as involving a *subcutaneous mind* focussed on brain-events. Lovejoy, likewise, made fun of the "under-the-hat" theory of mind. No one seems to have paid much attention to my analysis of perceiving as responsively directed and using sensation in guidance and sensuous thinking. But do we not look at the things which attract our attention and reach out to them, guided by the sensations they arouse? My view fits in more with modern information theory. Science is now developing artificial types of sensors. But, of course, our sense-organs are still basic. As nearly as I can make out, the above men seem to have thought of perceiving as a sort of apprehension, and it could only apprehend the brain if there it was. I had a quite different idea of perceiving. I thought of it as a rather complex guided act in which sensations were used as controlled sources of information. I called this a non-apprehensional view of perceiving. I stress a from-and-to circuit. Strange as it may seem for such brilliant men as the new realists, they had the belief that external things are somehow just presented. That is, they transformed Hume's sense-impressions into presented objects. The only alternative they could think of was that of Locke's subjective ideas with its blocked attempt to get to the outer world. Montague insisted that I was in this situation. This was in his *Story of American Realism*. And, it was widely accepted.

Professor Warren makes it quite clear that mine is a referential realism which avoids the whole traditional gambit of starting with sensations, or sense-data, removing them from their operational context and trying to infer an external world from them. I pointed this out once to Russell but he did not understand what I was driving at. Instead of perceiving, he stressed *percepts*. I have sometimes felt that among philosophers, as such, it was almost a case of Sellars against the world. I suppose something like that sometimes happens. Biologists, like Ritter of California and Herrick of Chicago, got in touch with me, and I have had a long standing relationship with psychologists. I have always been thankful that my son, Wilfrid, grasped my point and developed it technically against logical positivism. And I am glad that Farber, Warren, and Melchert are defending realistic naturalism against neglect and misunderstandings.

What, then, is critical realism? It is an explication of what takes place in perceiving and develops a different stance than presentationalism, realistic or phenomenalistic, and from traditional representationalism. In contrast to these, it emphasizes the referential framework of perceiving and regards sensations as used in the act as guiding and informational. It is, in this sense, a direct realism. In the strict sense we never *intuit* material things but achieve knowledge about them. Transcendence is, thus, an affair of directed reference and fed-in information. It is only in this fashion that our human minds get to the stars. As Professor Warren points out, there is no mysterious, cognitive relation.

Let me turn now to the status of the sensory *qualia* used in perceiving. They seem mysterious to us since we have learned to think the material world in terms of abstract knowledge-about qualified by lapses into naive, presentational realism. As I see them, they are translations in the sensory centers by the brain of the stimuli forwarded to them. We become aware of them and use them in guidance and in cognizing. I do not see how this could have been done otherwise.

Perhaps, as Sir Russell Brain suggested, we can learn more about the *conditions* of their emergence. But it must be remembered that we cannot *intuit* their neural setting. Here, and here alone, do we participate in nature. The panpsychist makes much of this but he is weak in epistemology. I think this holds of Whitehead.

A word now about truth. Professor Warren has, I think, brought out sufficiently my analysis of truth as evidenced knowledge-about. To say that a statement is true is to endorse it with evidence given. The only element of correspondence is the informational base. It has long been realized that we cannot compare the statement with the state of affairs it is about. My direct realism avoids this traditional dilemma. The coherence theory of idealism stresses a logical test within knowledge. Pragmatism is a kind of compromise stressing working within experience. It has no clear epistemology. If we accept a statement as true, we regard it as a case of knowledge. The essential thing is to get the correct framework.

It will be recalled that I stressed evolutionary levels of causality. This rejects mere Newtonianism. I think the self emerges in the focus of control. Hence I speak of agential causality. Hence, I agree with the psychotherapists, like Rollo May, that self-awareness and reflective deliberation are important. Erich Fromm and Karen Horney should also be included along with May—and indeed Sigmund Freud. There is no pushbutton "free-will" but capacity to judge and work out standards. Wisdom is something to be acquired. I do not think our so-called statesmen have too much of it. It requires compassion and imagination. They seem to me second-raters. They can, of course, destroy the world. What a pity!

But this Foreword must not be too long. Nevertheless, I must say something about the transition from the world as perceived to the world as *described* as a result of scientific methods and instruments. It is still the perceivable world but this is not explored. The first step in the transition was that of the insights of Galileo and Newton. Inertia and mass were first discovered as testable concepts. Measurement and the behavior of bodies were stressed. The law of falling bodies is an example. The law of gravitation is another. Combining proportions in chemistry is still another. New instruments were invented and applied. One should read the history of science. I can find nothing epistemologically or ontologically puzzling. But philosophy was stymied in the mechanism of perceiving and the mind-body problem. I am not too much awed when I am told that a certain philosopher is also a mathematician or a physicist. I know something about these subjects and I know that curious philosophies were worked out by Mach, Eddington, and Jeans. So I sit tight and continue to analyze my parameters. Let Europe send its latest fashions from logical positivism to existentialism. I have not found in them anything as basic as critical realism and evolutionary naturalism.

These things sort themselves out in the long run. I want to thank Professor Warren for his great care in tracing my development and studying my period. I do think it was somewhat neglected.

ROY WOOD SELLARS

Introduction

I

Philosophical Contributions

It is my privilege in this volume to present a philosopher who has been far too little studied. One of the reasons for this is that a documented record of the growth and direction of his philosophy has not been available in any single work, despite the epochal findings of certain single works (notably *Critical Realism, Evolutionary Naturalism,* and *The Philosophy of Physical Realism*).

This factor of cumulative achievement, which we are documenting, is of course something quite in addition to certain unphilosophical facts, e.g., that philosophers divide into encampments, and those presumably most independent thinkers of the assumedly independent younger generations use the approach to philosophy via already established names. The role of historical geography in this is not unimportant. "Civilization," wrote Whitehead, "haunts the borders of waterways," and Whitehead believed that in his time the center of civilization had passed from Europe to the eastern seaboard of the United States.

The Great Lakes also are water fronts, but not the historical or most characteristic entrance ways to the United States. Hence major contributors to American and world thought may get short shrift unless they happen to be content to bask in the rays of sharply differentiated thinkers, such as Dewey, Santayana, Whitehead, Carnap, Sartre, or Heidegger. McGilvary was an exception and typically, his objective relativism proved a blind alley. As Russell said of behaviorism: it was so absurd, only a philosopher could have thought of it.

Roy Wood Sellars has not been in quest of striking absurdities, but basic solutions to basic problems: above all, that of our knowledge of the physical world (in the midst of which we find ourselves not as subjects versus objects but as active living beings who relate themselves to other entities for survival, achievement, or any of the many purposes of complex organisms). The reality of the physical is, of course, not merely taken for granted by doers in contrast to sheer perceivers; it is a prime governing principle of organic behavior. One would expect, therefore, that an adequate epistemology would find an integral place for such an essential, operational principle. David Hume bowed to it in his recognition of the requirements of action and the common life. The pragmatists have stressed action and the common life without a basic realism of the physical. Professor Sellars addressed himself to a continuing quest of such an adequate, functional realism.

Nine of his contributions stand out. 1) Originator of the concept of critical realism two years before the New Realists published their *Program and First Platform*;[1] giver of the name to the movement; consistent developer of critical realism as an unequivocal realism; it is not surprising that he should sometimes write as though his version of critical realism were definitive. I think it not presumptuous indeed to propose that the time has come to acknowledge him as the authentic expositor of critical realism, to think of him as the Professor of Critical Realism (or "Mr. Critical Realism," in the vernacular), and to hold that any treatment of critical realism which stops short of Sellars' most developed conceptions is derelict.

Others have their assumed realisms along with their epistemologies, yet never succeed in bringing the two into full jointure with each other. Santayana is the most candid in acknowledging a leap of intellectual faith from the intuition of essences to the referral of essences to things. Lovejoy's supplementation of an "intentionalist" critical realism with what Lewis Feuer calls a

[1] Edwin B. Holt, *et al.*: "Program and First Platform of Six Realists," *Journal of Philosophy*, VII (1910), hereinafter referred to as *JP*.

psychoanalytic realism is a comparable leap from cognition. D. C. Macintosh comes closer to showing that we have knowledge of external objects with his conception of "perception in a complex;" memory, imagination, reasoning may all enter into perception. That perception is built around behavioral reference, feedback, and increasing refinement of the conceptions essential to perception is not, however, developed by Macintosh. The development of a direct referential theory of perception is Sellars' most crucial achievement and is the key to the import of his other contributions. This is therefore contribution 2).

Sellars has not only clarified the jointure between the psychological subject and external entities. He has also brought epistemology into full relation with ontology, and ontology into full jointure with science and the world of ordinary human activities. His deprecation of "metaphysics" as a covering term for both ontology and cosmology is illustrative. A term meaning 'beyond physics' lends itself to the view that ontology deals with a reality that is beyond physical nature. For Sellars, ontology concerns the nature of physical organisms in a physical world, and, of course, the overall nature of this world, and its relations to the whole spectrum of values. His is not, therefore, simply a logical or quasi-logical system suspended in a largely intellectual world. It is full philosophy, firmly grounded in our physical world.

3) His *Evolutionary Naturalism* (1922), on the basis of which his theories of perception—and of mind—became possible, was conceived by 1909. Twice at least he writes of talking with Bergson in that year about the possibilities of an emergent naturalism.[2] Bergson, in turn, referred him to Driesch with whom he studied. His articles in 1919, 1920, and 1921 on Evolutionary Naturalism and his book in 1922 under that title antecede the work on emergent evolution by Samuel Alexander and Lloyd Morgan. Sellars visited Alexander in England in 1922, and it was the latter who called Morgan's attention to Sellars' *Evolutionary Naturalism*. Morgan, in turn, added an appendix

---

[2] "Existentialism, Realistic Empiricism, and Materialism," in *Philosophy and Phenomenological Research*, XXV (1965), 316, hereinafter referred to as *PPR*. "Panpsychism or Evolutionary Naturalism," in *Philosophy of Science*, XXVII (1960), 335.

on Sellars' cosmology to his *Emergent Evolution.* "Mine," said Sellars, "was more naturalistic." Nature he held to be dynamic, self-organizing, and productive, among other things, of complex organisms with capacities for thought, feeling, values and agential causality.

4) Sellars postulates a physical theory of mind and articulates 5) a double knowledge approach to the mind-body problem. It was in opposition to James Mark Baldwin's three progressions in the relation of mind and body that Sellars, in the summer of 1906, proposed and elaborated "A Fourth Progression . . ." At Baldwin's invitation, he published it in the *Psychological Review.* His concern with this question extended to a good dozen articles and chapters of which three are epochally important: "Evolutionary Naturalism and the Mind-Body Problem" (1919), "The Double Knowledge Approach to the Mind-Body Problem" (1923), and the "Analytic Approach to the Mind-Body Problem (1938). In his *Critical Realism* (1916) he had already demonstrated that mind is not *ipso facto* alien to the physical. This was his first espousal of what he came to designate "the neglected alternative."

His other contributions include

6) A distinctive amendment to the correspondence theory of truth. Correspondence has been conceived in an essentially pictorial sense and criticized as an unfeasible test of truth. But the tests of truth are really tests of knowledge: empirical, predictive, coherent (with established thought as well as with itself). Knowledge, therefore, is the primary category and correspondence is an implication of knowledge: it is a description adequately relevant to its purposes.

7) An empirically realistic functional theory of value. He distinguishes valuation from cognition and defines values in terms of appraised roles of objects in the human economy[3]— broadly conceived. He contrasts his theory with that of Urban,

---

[3] See Sellars' articles: "Cognition and Valuation," *Philosophical Review,* XXXV, 124-144, hereinafter referred to as *PR;* "Can a Reformed Materialism do Justice to Values?" *Ethics,* LV, 28-45; "In What Sense do Value Judgments and Moral Judgments have Objective Import?" *PPR,* XXVIII, 1-16.

Perry, Parker, Dewey, the emotivists, and others.[4] In his recognition of the role of human desires and interests in the determination of value, Sellars has affinities with Parker and Perry. In his emphases on appraisal or assessment, in distinguishing kinds and degrees of value, he has kinship with Dewey. In his stress on the functions of any and every type of factor or entity, he ties his theory in with common activities and experience. Yet he leaves the way open for uncommon roles of factors in both personal and social life: ideals, principles, high aspirations, objects of loyalty (persons and causes). Their actual import for man's life and culture needs constant, factual assessing. In his stress on the objective side of the value equation, indeed, he offers a theory which is both more realistic and more roundly oriented than that of any of the notable theorists from whom he distinguishes his view. His emphasis is on principles growing out of situations. That he might need some supplementation from depth psychology does not gainsay his basic position or the relative adequacy of his "alternative."

8) A democratic social realism. In both social philosophy and philosophy of religion, Sellars has been an American pioneer. His *Next Step in Democracy* (1916) accompanied a course on a critical Examination of Socialism, begun in 1914 or 1915.[5] He distinguished three stages in the development of socialism, of which Marxism was the second and a kind of Fabian gradualistic social realism the third. Well prior to the Russian revolution Sellars was concerned for the public as well as the private "sector." He began writing in this area as an undergraduate in 1902, with an article on the "Reinterpretation of Democracy."[6] Awareness of social, contra purely individual, reality was found to be clearly discriminated in recent American history. Always a philosopher and never an agitator, Sellars has labored on the clarification of social objectives and insisted that these must not

---

[4] *Ibid.*: Cf. especially "In What Sense do Value Judgments and Moral Judgments have Objective Import?"

[5] Evidence of the offering of this course first appears in the University of Michigan Catalogue for 1915, but the 1914 Catalogue was missing from the shelves of the main library.

[6] In the University of Michigan *Inlander*.

be lost from view through present obstacles and complications. Sellars, who had started as a child emigrant from Canada, has always been transnational in outlook. He was critical, therefore, of all nationalists and factionalists: Churchill, Truman, Johnson. The objective import of value judgments is basic to his social theory, and the *moral quality* of democracy is fundamental.

9) Naturalistic humanism in religion. His *Next Step in Religion* (1918),[7] two years after his *Next Step in Democracy*, gained him recognition as "Next Step" Sellars. This was the first book-length American publication on naturalistic humanism in religion and was selected by the New York critic Hunecker as one of the two best books of the year. (The other was Conrad's *Arrow of Gold*.) In 1928, Sellars published *Religion Coming of Age*, and early in the 1930s drafted a "Humanistic Manifesto," which was signed by the editor of the *New Humanist*, by John Dewey, and by many others. The mellowing and deepening of his humanism belongs especially to the last three decades.

While neither Sellars' social realism nor his naturalistic humanism are alternatives neglected by thinkers of the 60's, they are indeed far from receiving general acceptance. Sellars' espousal of these outlooks must, moreover, be put in the context of decades in which they were far more neglected than they are now.

Whether these types of "neglected alternative" are all parts of one alternative or so-many different alternatives, they are certainly, in Norman Melchert's phrasing, intricately meshed.[8] Sellars' epistemology and ontology—on the basis of which he derives his value theory, social philosophy, and philosophy of religion—are developed in continuous interrelation with each other. His is a whole philosophy for which epistemology and ontology are reciprocally fundamental.

Most comparable to Charles Peirce in originality, Sellars has thus contributed a really notable number of essential concepts. Both Andrew Reck and Marten ten Hoor indeed quote Sellars' distinguished idealist colleague DeWitt Parker—that "no American

---

[7] New York, Macmillan Co.
[8] Norman Melchert: *Realism, Materialism, and the Mind.* Springfield, Thomas, 1968, 198.

has done more persistent and original thinking on the fundamental philosophical problems in the last thirty years or so than my colleague Professor Sellars."⁹ Healthy longevity and the open fruitfulness of his concepts has enabled him to develop them adequately. Developments in science have contributed to this adequacy. Yet he has also been continuously alert to the need for enrichment of basic conceptions from the socio-moral and/or spiritual life of man.

II

Biographical

Roy Wood Sellars was born in Seaforth, Ontario, in 1880, the son of Ford Wylis Sellars and Mary Stalker Sellars. In *Contemporary American Philosophy* (1930), he relates that his father, who had been a school teacher, attended the University of Michigan Medical School and became a physician in 1882, after the birth of all three of his children. Forced to find a place where a practice would come quickly, he chose Pinnebog, in the thumb between Lake Huron and Saginaw Bay, in northern Michigan.

"Here," states Sellars, "my companions were farmers' boys. It was a simple life in its way, but one that would lead a sensitive and self-conscious boy to much introspection and meditation. Of philosophy, I knew little as yet except the name, though I read Carlyle and Emerson assiduously. My father was almost a zealot in his insistence upon education, and I owe him much for his stimulation of my interest in history and science. His library was literally the only one in the whole neighbourhood, and consisted largely of the books dating from his days as a schoolmaster. As I grew older, we used to talk together in his office about medicine. It is an interesting coincidence that I, who have stood in this country for naturalism, realism, and humanism in a rather aggressive fashion, should have been

---

[9] Reck: *Op. cit.* 208; ten Hoor, "Humanism as a Religion," *PPR*, XV (1954), 82; DeWitt Parker "Some Comments on 'Reformed Materialism and Intrinsic Endurance'," *PR*, July, 1944.

brought up in this atmosphere. I recall this small point of agreement with Aristotle with pride."

At seventeen, Roy attended Ferris Institute at Big Rapids, Michigan, to prepare himself for the University. He did so in one year. Both Woodbridge Ferris, Principal of the school (later, Governor of Michigan) and Mrs. Ferris, treated him as a protege, encouraging him to use their private library.

Roy taught in public school one year, for the experience, before entering the University of Michigan. He arrived at the University in 1899, with "a large amount of self-education" mingled with his schooling. In his sophomore year, he states, "I started my work in philosophy. Here I came under the influence of Wenley, Lloyd, and Rebec." They "awakened me intellectually," he continues, and "gave me perspective." In conversation, Roy said that Wenley regarded him as his ablest student but could not, later, stand his naturalism. Another teacher who affected him "in many ways was Craig . . . head of the Semitics department."[10] Here especially was the beginning of his culturally humanistic approach to religion.

A year at Hartford Theological Seminary introduced him to, among other things, Arabic. Then, a year as Fellow of the University of Wisconsin brought contacts with Sharp and Bode, with both of whom he had productive exchanges and from whom he secured further references. He was also brought in close contact with social liberalism and humanism—of which we shall take further note later.

Returning to the University of Michigan in 1905, as Instructor in Philosophy, Roy continued his studies: 1) with J. Mark Baldwin at the University of Chicago in the summer of 1906, and 2) in 1909 in France and Germany. "I had two long talks with Bergson," he wrote in "Existentialism, Realistic Empiricism, and Materialism,"[11] and was "bold enough to outline the idea of emergence in contrast to his more vitalistic stance. He suggested that I study under Driesch at Heidelberg, which I did."

What stands out from Sellars' work and associations with

---

[10] Adams, G. P., and Montague, W. P.: *Contemporary American Philosophy*, New York, Macmillan, II (1930) 262.

[11] *PPR*, XXV, 315.

philosophers is that he was almost from the start his own intellectual man, never an adherent of anyone. He differed with Baldwin on the mind-body problem, and Baldwin was big enough to publish Sellars' "Fourth Progression in the Relation of Mind and Body." His dissertation on Scientific Concepts involved the exploration of the work of Mach, Avenarius, Pearson, and James Ward. It was Ward's *Naturalism and Agnosticism* that provoked his most creative early efforts, and Sellars came through with an emergent naturalism and functional realism, well ahead of other proponents. He collaborated with six officially "critical realists," but would not accept their impasse. Hence his persistent analysis of the referential nature of perceiving.

Sellars is a most notable instance of a philosopher who has breasted the currents and winds of doctrine, developed and refined his philosophy vis-a-vis the issues that tended to become academically fashionable. In the twenties, behaviorism had gained an imposing vogue, though it had that vogue much earlier for Sellars. (He had roomed in the same house as the psychologist John Shepard when he first began teaching at the University of Michigan). In the thirties Carnap's logical empiricism became the intellectual fashion. Meantime "naturalism" was becoming sharply demarked as a purely methodological viewpoint, while phenomenology and existentialism were also gaining ground as imports from Europe. Independent American thought seemed to be losing rather than gaining status. Sellars wondered whether it was philosophy or intellectual colonialism that was current, but he sharpened his concepts and viewpoint by means of these whetstones.

We shall present more of Professor Sellar's biography in the Introductions to the several groups of essays, particularly in the Parts on the Development of his Referential Physical Realism and on his Social Philosophy.

He has indeed had recognitions: Vice President of the Eastern Division of the American Philosophical Association, 1918; President of the Western Division of the American Philosophical Association,1923; Reader of a paper on "The Double Knowledge Approach to the Mind-Body Problem" to the British Aristotelian

Society in 1922. His *Critical Realism* (1916) gained him a place in the second edition of Woodbridge Riley's *American Thought* (1923) and his subsequent work is shown in its factual historical context in Victor E. Harlow's *Bibliography and Genetic Study of American Realism* (1930). Moreover, as related immediately below, recent histories of philosophy by Werkmeister, Blau, and Reck give Sellars a prominent place in the development of American philosophy. And in 1954, *Philosophy and Phenomenological Research* devoted an issue to his philosophy.

Historians of philosophy have recently indeed begun to catch up with the distinctive and developmental character of Sellars' philosophy. W. H. Werkmeister was the first, in his *History of Philosophical Ideas in the United States*, to trace Sellars' thought systematically from its formulation in *Critical Realism* to his writings in the late forties.[12] In 1952, Joseph Blau followed with a portrayal of the profundity and originality of Sellars' work.[13] Most recently, in 1964, Andrew Reck singled out Sellars as one of ten real notables in recent American philosophy and carried his philosophy through his most recent writings, into the sixties.

This is indeed appropriate. Some of Sellars' most precise statements of his theories of perceptual knowledge and the levels of causality were published in the late fifties and early sixties, and his article "In What Sense do Human Values have Objective Import?" appeared in 1967, bringing his value theory up to the present. In 1968, he was editing his own social philosophy, and reformulating it for specific relevance to the present. This editor had supplements from him on social philosophy just prior to the submission of this manuscript to the publisher.

It seems time, therefore, for American philosophers to have a readier opportunity to give far more attention to the work of this basic philosopher, without neglecting the significant work of others.

---

[12] New York, Ronald Press, 1949, 446-494.
[13] *Men and Movements in American Philosophy*, New York, Prentice-Hall, 1952, 293ff.
[14] Reck: Ch. 7.

Acknowledgments

I. To Persons and Foundations

MY FOREMOST ACKNOWLEDGMENT is to Roy Wood Sellars. I have had the privilege of corresponding with him since he visited Bucknell University in 1963. I had known him previously as a philosopher with whom I had considerable affinity, but had not worked through the detail of his writings. Other active interests had side-tracked me from the more complete pursuit of an authentic realism. Roy Sellars brought me back to this issue. In 1965, I took the liberty of asking him whether anyone was working on a much needed anthology of his papers. In 1966, following the completion of another of his works, he invited me to edit a representative selection of his publications. I had already been assembling some of these for my classes, and it was a gratifying service to continue this work for the wider philosophical public.

Toward this objective, I have twice visited Professor Sellars: in April 1967 and June 1968. The latter visit encompassed a series of conversations scattered over four weeks. Professor Sellars has also kept me posted on his own continued work in rounding out his philosophical estate and has responded regularly to my inquiries. It has been a quite special privilege to have these associations with him and above all to attempt to put his work in a developmental context. In doing this, I hope that I have not in any sense played down either the substance or the import of his earlier works, which stand out historically as highly informed, realistically penetrating, and balanced, with a particularly significant developmental potential.

My second acknowledgment is to Professor Marvin Farber for endorsing this project and inviting me to present it in his series on MODERN CONCEPTS OF PHILOSOPHY. Professor Farber has expedited my work with queries and suggestions and by invaluable liaison with the publisher.

I am indebted similarly to Professor Sellars' noted son, Wilfrid Sellars, for his endorsements, counsel, and assistance. When I first talked with Wilfrid Sellars, it was on the question of a broader volume on American realisms. This project was interrupted by a collaborative study with colleagues at Bucknell. With R. W. Sellars' invitation to edit his papers, I turned back to realism, and resumed communicating with Wilfrid Sellars and others.

My indebtedness to Bucknell University has many facets, from personal encouragement by the President and Provost to the various services of the library, duplicating and secretarial offices, assistance of colleagues and students. Specifically, a grant awarded by the Bucknell University Research Committee enabled me to spend a full summer plus such other time as I could budget from my schedule as teacher and Chairman.

Three of my Bucknell associates are entitled to recognition for their assistance with the manuscript. The first of these is Mrs. Iva Weaver, departmental secretary, who has been almost literally my right hand in getting materials typed or duplicated and in checking sources and copy. The second is my instructional colleague in Philosophy, Dr. Joseph P. Fell, who has been one of my two notably competent editorial readers. The third is Miss Marilyn Maxwell, a major in philosophy, who did intensive work toward the editing of Part IV (on Professor Sellars' Philosophy of Values) in conjunction with a project in my course in Ethics.

The second of my editorial readers was Professor Norman Melchert of Lehigh University, author of *Realism, Materialism, and the Mind*—a study in Professor Sellars' philosophy. I am indebted to him for his very careful editing of my statements and for suggestions toward bettering the content and the structure of the manuscript.

My editorial efforts were further facilitated by a grant from the American Philosophical Society which supported my work in Ann Arbor during June, 1968.

II. To Publishers

The articles and excerpts of this book have been reprinted through the courtesy of the publishers. In the order in which publishers appear, acknowledgment is hereby made for permission to reprint the following articles, chapters, or excerpts:

To *Mind* for—
"Sensations as Guides to Perceiving," LXVIII (1959)

To *Philosophy and Phenomenological Research* for—
"Referential Transcendence," XXII (1961)
"In What Sense Do Value Judgments and Moral Judgments have Objective Import?" XXVII (1967)
"Bibliography of the Writings of Roy Wood Sellars," Gerald E. Meyers, ed., XV (1954)

To the *Philosophical Review* for—
"Causality and Substance," LII (1943)
"Epistemological Dualism versus Metaphysical Dualism," XXX (1921)
"A Re-examination of Critical Realism," XXXVIII (1929)
"Why Naturalism and not Materialism?" XXXVI (1927)
"An Analytic Approach to the Mind-Body Problem," XLVII (1938)
"Reformed Materialism and Intrinsic Endurance," LIII (1944)

To the *Psychological Review* for—
"A Fourth Progression in the Relation of Mind and Body," XIV (1907)
"An Important Antinomy," XV (1907)

To the *Journal of Philosophy Inc.* for—
"Consciousness and Conservation," V (1908)
"Critical Realism and Time Problem I," V (1908)
"Critical Realism and Time Problem II," V (1908)
"Is There a Cognitive Relation?" IX (1912)
"A Thing and Its Properties," XII (1915)
"Is Naturalism Enough?" XLI (1944)
" 'True' as Contextually Implying Correspondence," LVI (1959) with note from "A Correspondence Theory of Truth," XXXVIII (1941)
"Guided Causality, Using Reason and Free Will," LIV (1957)

To the Open Court Publishing Co., LaSalle, Ill., for excerpts from—
"The Status of the Categories," *The Monist*, XXX (1920)

To Williams & Wilkins for excerpts from—
Roy Wood Sellars, "A Clarification of Critical Realism," *Philosophy of Science*, 6:415-421, 1939.

To Editor of The Aristotelean Society for—
"The Double Knowledge Approach to the Mind-Body Problem," copyright 1923, The Aristotelean Society

To *Michigan Alumnus Quarterly Review* (now *The Michigan Quarterly Review*) for—
"The Quality of Democracy," XLVII (1942)
"Reason and Revolution," XLIX (1943)

To Russell and Russell Inc., New York, for excerpt from—
"Is Consciousness Alien to the Physical?" *Critical Realism* (1916); with new Preface, Russell and Russell (1969)
"The Natural and Status of Value," *The Philosophy of Physical Realism* (1932), augmented by two chapters, Russell and Russell (1966)

To The University of Chicago Press for—
"Can a Reformed Materialism do Justice to Values?" *Ethics: An International Journal of Social, Political and Legal Philosophy*, LIV (1944)

To *The Humanist* for—
"A Humanist Manifesto," *The New Humanist*, VI (1933)

To Beacon Press for—
An excerpt from "Accept the Universe as a Going Concern," in *Religious Liberals Reply* (1947)

Contents

	Page
Foreword	v
Introduction	xi
Acknowledgments	xxi

PART I

BASIC EXPLANATORY CONCEPTIONS

INTRODUCTION	3
Sensations as Guides to Perceiving	4
Referential Transcendence	17
Causality and Substance	27

PART II

THE DEVELOPMENT OF REFERENTIAL PHYSICAL REALISM

INTRODUCTION TO ESSAYS	51
In Quest of a Functionally Definitive Realism	64
Is There a Cognitive Relation?	75
A Thing and Its Properties	84
The Status of the Categories	97
Epistemological Dualism Vs. Metaphysical Dualism	101

	Page
A Re-examination of Critical Realism	112
A Clarification of Critical Realism	125
Why Naturalism and Not Materialism	131
Is Naturalism Enough?	140
Reformed Materialism and Intrinsic Endurance	150

PART III

THE MIND-BODY TEST CASE

INTRODUCTION TO THE ESSAYS	174
A Fourth Progression in the Relation of Mind and Body	176
Consciousness and Conservation	182
Is Consciousness Alien to the Physical	185
The Double-knowledge Approach to the Mind-Body Problem	188
An Analytic Approach to the Mind-Body Problem	202

PART IV

OTHER TESTS OF EMERGENT REALISM: THE THEORY OF TRUTH AND THE THEORY OF VALUE

INTRODUCTION	229
The Theory of Truth	232
"True" as Contextually Implying Correspondence	232
The Theory of Value	239
Can a Reformed Materialism Do Justice to Values?	239
In What Sense Do Value Judgments and Moral Judgments Have Objective Import?	256
Guided Causality, Using Reason, and "Free-Will"	261

PART V

OTHER TESTS OF EMERGENT REALISM: SOCIAL PHILOSOPHY AND PHILOSOPHY OF RELIGION

	Page
SOCIAL PHILOSOPHY	268
Introduction to Social Philosophy	268
Socialism and Democracy	277
Three Stages of Socialism	279
Reason and Revolution	289
The Quality of Democracy	293
Objectives and Priorities	301
Orientation in Social Philosophy	309
The Philosophy of Religion	312
Introduction to Philosophy of Religion	312
The Next Step in Religion (1918)	314
Naturalizing the Spiritual (1928)	321
A Humanist Manifesto (1933)	331
Cosmic Perspective	335
BIBLIOGRAPHY OF THE WRITINGS OF ROY WOOD SELLARS	335
BIBLIOGRAPHICAL SUPPLEMENT	342
Index	345

PRINCIPLES
OF
EMERGENT REALISM

SELECTED ABBREVIATIONS

BGS—(Victor E. Harlow) *Bibliography and Genetic Study of American Realism*
CR—*Critical Realism*
JP—*Journal of Philosophy*
PPP—*Principles and Problems of Philosophy*
PPR—*Philosophy and Phenomenological Research*
PR—*Philosophic Review*
RAP—*Reflections on American Philosophy from Within*
SPPH—*Social Perspectives and Political Horizons*
          unpublished MS

PART I

Basic Explanatory Conceptions

INTRODUCTION

THE BASIC DIFFERENCE between Sellars critical realism in the forties and fifties and his *Critical Realism* in 1916 is the well developed referential theory of perception in his later philosophy. This component not only gives precision to his epistemology, ontology, theories of truth and value, but is the principle of unity, completing the structure. It is the hub of the diverse facets of his philosophy, bringing together his analysis of categories with the practical sphere of discriminating activity and making possible a monistic conception of the brain-mind complex.

Sellars' physical realism in the forties differs from his physical realism of 1916 in being a well developed evolutionary, substantive materialism, with the distinction of levels of causality, especially the level of agential causality with all its functions and values. Man is here seen in his uniqueness yet in integral unity with the broad order of things.

We are electing, therefore, to begin with Sellars' later rather than earlier work: "Sensations as Guides to Perceiving" (1959) and "Referential Transcendence" (1961) on the issue of perceptual knowledge; "Causality and Substance" (1943) on the questions of cosmology and ontology." "Reformed Materialism and Intrinsic Endurance," at the end of Part II, could be read here also. We have placed it in Part II, on "The Development of Referential Physical Realism," because it is the culminating statement of Sellars' ontology. "Levels of Causality: the Emergence of Guidance and Reason in Nature," listed below, is a highly recommended supplemental essay.

The advantage of starting with Sellars' late formulations is that it helps to avoid preconceptions that interfere with recognition of developmental possibilities. The ease with which such preconceptions can be gained and maintained, I have suggested in an article on "The Mote in the Eye of the Critic of Critical Realism."* It would be easy indeed to pick up Sellars' *Critical Realism* (1916) or his "Epistemological Dualism versus Metaphysical Dualism" (1921) and to fail to distinguish important implicit components. The strands to be disentangled for later development are not self-announcing, while the later philosophy affords keys to essential differences between Sellars and his immediate contemporaries.

The distinction of stages and phases of development in Sellars' philosophy is the concern of Part II. Here we present the basic explanatory conceptions that have become clarified in the process of this development.

Supplementary readings include:

The Philosophy of Physical Realism, Macmillan, 1932; Russell and Russell, 1966.
"Causation and Perception," *PR*, LIII (1944), 634-556.
"Knowing and Knowledge," *PR*, V (1944-45), 341-344.
"Knowing Through Propositions," *PPR*, V (1944) 348-349.
"Materialism and Human Knowing," in *Philosophy for the Future* (R. W. Sellars, V. J. McGill and Marvin Farber, eds.) New York, Macmillan, 1949.
"Levels of Causality: The Emergence of Guidance and Reason in Nature," *PPR*, XX (1959), 1-16.
"American Realism: Perspective and Framework," in *Self, Religion, and Metaphysics*, Gerald Myers, editor, Macmillan, 1961.
"American Critical Realism and British Theories of Sense Perception," *Estratto Rivista Methods*, XIV (Nos. 55 and 56), 1962.
"Direct, Referential Realism," *Dialogue*, II, 2, 1963.

SENSATIONS AS GUIDES TO PERCEIVING**

> "Man, the conceptualist and linguist, lifts perceiving to the level of demonstrative and descriptive terms, in so doing arriving at explicit knowing."
> (p. 14 below)

Some forty years ago there was a movement in American

---

* *PPR*, XXVI, 35-50.
** *MIND*, Vol. 68, No. 269, pp. 2-9, 11-15.

philosophy called *critical realism*, which reached co-operative expression in a book, *Essays in Critical Realism*. It had two varieties, one of which stressed essences while the other thought in terms of concepts whose application in perceiving was guided by sensations. Both forms were *referential* rather than inferential in their outlook. That is, they thought of perceiving as involving a directed reference to physical things in an objective way, tied in with behaviour or action, rather than as being an affair of inference to them from sense-data. The aim was the establishment of a direct realism as against the Lockian tradition of an indirect, or representative, realism.

Not unnaturally, the essence-variety got the most attention—especially abroad—because of the prestige of Santayana and C. A. Strong. I belonged to the other group. Since I have had a long time to reflect on the problems involved and have, to my own satisfaction at least, clarified the issues, I thought it would be well to present my version of critical realism in its relation to modern biology and psychology and bring it to bear upon current controversion. It seems to me, for instance, to give a *framework* for the recent, linguistic approach without involving extreme behaviourism, as understood in England.[1]

American new realism was a form of presentational realism which, by a *tour-de-force*, more or less suggested by William James, gave objectivity to sensory presentations and rejected the category of the subjective. It was often called pan-objectivism and was associated with the kind of behaviourism which rejected any private stream of consciousness. Montague, who was one of the moving spirits, regarded it as a transformation of Humianism by giving an objective status to his sense-impressions.

R. B. Perry was, in many ways, the best expositor of this outlook. His form of philosophical behaviourism cut beneath Cartesian dualism by rejecting a subjective "consciousness." In this fashion, American new realism went further than English

---

[1] It may be of historical interest—to set the record right—to call attention to the fact that I gave the name to the movement, having started to call myself a critical realist in 1908 in a series of articles in the *Journal of Philosophy* and having published a book with that title in 1916. Durant Drake, the editor of the *Essays* carried through the adoption. Dawes Hicks used the term later and quite independently.

neo-realism with its transparent acts. Russell was intrigued by its rejection of "consciousness."

All this represented a gambit of a daring sort. I do not, myself, think it reflected as careful an anlysis of the perceptual experience as the critical realists were making. The line we took was that perceiving was a referential activity in which objects were characterized. Thus, I point denotatively to *this* chair before me and conceptually characterize it as brown, having four legs, etc. Knowing is, here, not a searchlight terminating on the presentational given but more of a propositional claim guided by sensory factors. It is this functional relation of sensations and cognitive claims which makes it *sense*-perception. But more about this later.

In this period of American philosophy, Cartesian dualism was being pretty generally attacked. I had rejected it in an article in the *Psychological Review* in 1907. This was in a controversial paper directed against Mark Baldwin under whom I had studied. Dewey swung from idealism—never favourable to Cartesian dualism—to a kind of biological experientalism. I do not think he was ever strong in epistemology which he thought was connected with Cartesian dualism. The psychologists were moving toward a sort of methodological behaviourism with reservations as to the standing of introspection. At Michigan, where we had a flourishing school of experimental, comparative psychologists, *Gestalt* ideas came increasingly into favour. I would speak of these psychologists as *Gestalt* behaviourists. That is, they took the organism as the unit and studied it in any available way. So far as rats were concerned, they could only observe experimentally controlled behaviour but they were ready to use *analogies* from the human level and even spoke of rats as *reasoning* when they met new situations and solved problems. Later, I came into contact with C. Judson Herrick, the distinguished comparative neural anatomist, who called himself a behaviourist but thinks of behaviourism as including mentation of different levels.

* * * * *

My referential view of sense-perception[1] allowed me to

---

[1] As far as I know, Miss Stebbing came nearest to this position in England. I could never see where C. D. Broad got his substance and causality to add to sense-data. He still seemed to begin with the data.

develop what I called a double-knowledge theory of the brain-mind. We can know it externally as the neurologist does and as its functioning is schematized by the student of behaviour who regards it as *par excellence,* the organ of behaviour. And each one can regard his personal experiencing as intrinsic to this functioning. This is the position taken by a neuro-surgeon, like Penfield, who tries to correlate his subject's descriptive comments with his surgical information. I was early led to speak of personal consciousness as a "natural isolate" which was experienced personally and could be correlated with the functioning of the brain as known *about* referentially.[2] This is my double-knowledge.

Now this signifies that epistemology can help to throw light upon the mind-body problem. After all, the philosopher should make use of his tools. But he should keep in touch with scientific developments.

Any knower has to start from his perceptual experience and its referential claims. There is *no* knower in general.

Thus we must come back to a study of the nature and conditions of perceptual experience, as our starting-point. The new realist simplified the issue by his presentationalism and his rejection of private consciousness (the subjective). The English neo-realist had his *act* of awareness left over but, so far as I could make out, did not pay very much attention to the mind-body problem. But the critical realist had before him the possibility that perceiving was a complex operation guided by sensations (personal) and terminating in behavioural and linguistic activities of a referential sort which could be objectively observed and communicated. Guided by my visual field, I point to *this* chair, walk towards it, make statements about it. What we call concepts have a close connection with both language and behaviour. But I take it to be fairly evident that, in sense-perception, this terminal complex is guided by sensations. It is *not* the sensations which are the objects of perception but the material things we are concerned with in behaviour and language, yet they function in the background. G. E. Moore was always

---

[2] Those who may be interested will find an account of this view in the *Aristotelian Society Proceedings* (1923).

bothered, I think, by this functional duplicity and worried over the question whether sense-data are parts of the surface of objects perceived. Now, as we shall see, the critical realist did not start with sense-data but with the objective reference and claims of perception; and he was open-minded as to the "how" of the operation. Perceiving seemed to him a referential operation tied in with behaviour and language. Thus to be knowledge *about;* and not a presentational *givenness* of the object. In short, a confirmable claim in terms of evidence, prediction, and successful fitting into conduct. The *complexity* of the perceptual operation is recognized, at the level of commonsense, by such terms as 'appears,' 'looks.' Psychology is apt to shift to visual fields as against the physical fields. But, in so doing, it tends to neglect the cognitive claim. It is the job of the philosopher to try to clarify the situation. But he needs an adequate epistemology as a point of departure.

But before I go further and examine perceiving as an achievement and its "how" or mechanism, I must say a few words about the climate of philosophy and its zigzag in the intervening years. There were slogans, proposals, logical accomplishments, a sort of ferment; but, so far as I could see, neglect of epistemology as a little *sinnlos* or the pronouncement that idealism and realism had reached a stalemate which should be politely recognized. Needless to say, I did not like it at all. But I was ready to welcome any technical advances. On the whole, I regard the linguistic development as an advance which fitted into my notion of objective reference. I describe linguistically what I am pointing at. Language is not tied up to *acquaintance* and special "proper names," as it tended to be with Russell. Gradually, the natural *context* and *use* of language was recognized. But, in my opinion, a corresponding epistemology had not been worked out. I shall try to show that critical realism offers the framework.

And so I say good-bye to logical positivism, phenomenalism, constructionism . . . On the whole, I think the English fell less for the magic of technical manipulation than did the Americans. And so I am going to connect up my story with the articles by Ryle, Ayer, Barnes and Hampshire in the volume entitled *Contemporary British Philosophy* which was sent to me for a brief review. Since I was a contributor to the American series of the thirties, my analysis may have historical interest. At least, it may call attention to a neglected possibility. Since phenomenalism seems to have shot its bolt, realism should come in for exploration again. Wilfrid Sellars used to tell me that the positivists were becoming realists but did not *like* the word. But now my friend, Feigl, calls himself a critical realist and declares that Schlick was much of that outlook before he came under the hypnotic influence of the Wittgenstein of the *Tractatus*.

I shall not give pagination references to the articles mentioned but concern myself with their purport. Ryle seems to be worried by the status and role of sensations; Ayer is defending direct realism against scepticism; Barnes stresses the factor of personal experience in perceiving—I think rightly; and Hampshire is concerned with the status of a bright spot on the horizon *which* we judge to be a ship, *which*, as I see it involves the role of sensory factors as guides in perceiving. What can the critical realist say about these points? In a way, I have already given my answer but I want to illuminate it by a detour. This will take up the so-called causal theory of perception which, historically, was the generator of the whole notion that we start, in perceiving, with sense-impressions, or sense-data, as isolated atoms and have the job of inferring external things something from them, something which both Berkeley and Hume saw could not be done. Unfortunately, instead of challenging the schematism (which, I shall try to show, had to wait for developments in modern biology and psychology) they resorted to subjective idealism, phenomenalism-*cum*-scepticism (however you wish to interpret Hume). . . .

Now the causal theory of perception was a theory of the "how" of perceiving which led philosophers down the garden path or . . . into a blind alley. It made our actual, perceptual beliefs untenable.

What was wrong? The model was *not* that of biology or modern psychology in which the *unit* is a *pattern* of stimulus *and* response integrated together or a sensori-motor circuit, as it is also called. Now the sensori-motor circuit is, in man and the higher animals, an open, or growing, one into the making of which *learning* enters. The correct formula is S-C-R. The stimulus gets its functional significance from its integration with R through C. The point is that there are levels of learning and integration. Centrally aroused processes, C, mediate between stimulus and response so that the stimulus becomes a *cue* to adjusted responses. It is important to stress such growth in the adequacy of responses to objects and situations, an affair of exploratory learning, as well as the fact that the stimulus is used according to this enlarged setting into which it plays. There has been a work of discrimination and interpretation going on. This is what I meant by saying that the whole pattern is the functional unit.

Now I do not think that I need to go into the technicalities of the present neuro-psychological view. Let it suffice to say that, as we pass up from the level of fairly fixed, sensori-motor patterns to those which permit modifications, we find this role played by cortical processes in building up responses under guidance, now very complex factors of guidance, which act as cues, or indications. What dominates the operation is the need, or motivation, of the percipient; and this is directed not so much at the stimulus, as at the object to which one is being alerted. The percipient is looking at something, listening to, exploring, feeling around. The stimulus is the *cue* to a directed and developed response, not, as a rule, something of moment for its own sake. But attention can be shifted to the sensations as in delayed responses; and this is very characteristic of man.

. . . I think it can be shown that this outlook does not, as the traditional one did, result in a model which frustrates objective perceiving as an achievement and shuts one into an awareness of sense-data as atomic facts from which one can escape only by a postulated, inferential act which seems to have no empirical base. Instead, the *how of* perceiving now supports, and throws light upon, the directed claims of perception, *as an achievement*. You cannot have an achievement without a mode in which it is accomplished. Neither science nor philosophy can be satisfied with the one without the other. Fortunately . . . the time is ripe for their linkage.

But, before I re-examine the modern, realistic movement

with its strong shift to the acceptance of *direct realism* as a starting-point, I want to bring out the point that the traditional model of the causal theory of perception was tied in with both an emphasis upon sense-data, as the primary objects, and with Cartesian dualism. I need not go into this in historical detail for it is too well known. The *scheme* was an impact upon the brain through the sense-organs and a consequential rise in the soul-mind of sensations which the soul-mind had the capacity to become aware of. Hume, of course, allowed this scheme to drop out of sight but he never quite accounted for awareness. But the point I want to make is that sensations were never linked up with response in a patterned way. The outlook was not biological but introspective and artificial. It was as though responses were so delayed, or ignored, that attention had shifted to sensations for their own sake. Their normal role as *cues* to learned patterns of response was disregarded. That was one of the great faults of traditional, introspective psychology which led to the revolt—carried to an extreme, at first—of behaviourism. The development of a solution of the mind-body problem which would free it from Cartesian dualism, emphasize patterns of the S-C-R type, and yet find a place for personal consciousness would take time. Personal consciousness would, of course, have to be localized in connection with the *alertedness* involved in the development and running off of patterns which are not automatic. Now an adequate epistemology would make for clarification here. But, unfortunately, philosophers were, on the whole, either still dominated by the schematism of the traditional model in some of its repercussions or inclined to adopt "behaviourism" as a way of escape from Cartesian dualism. The ingenuity exhibited was terrific. But it would seem that the period of second-thought is, at last, upon us.

 I am now ready to draw my conclusions and to show that critical realism had, in the main, the correct approach. The test will be epistemological, primarily, though I shall try to show that perception, as an achievement, fits in with the "how" of perceiving as studied by neurologists and psychologists, and with what I have long called the emergence, double-knowledge outlook on the mind-body problem. This latter is anti-Cartesian, behaviouristic, *in a broad sense,* but not reductive or blind to the facts of personal experience. It fits more into what I have called *Gestalt* behaviourism. What I have always been opposed to are Procrustean methods. I wanted to keep in mind the whole picture. I have often thought that philosophers missed the suggestions offered by developments in science. Analysis, *alone,* tends to be a case of trying to lift oneself by one's bootstraps. To solve problems one must make hypotheses and use insights, just as science does. . . . As my study of perceiving in its "how" and its achievement has, I believe, shown, philosophy has more than linguistic confusions to clear up. It must help to solve problems in cooperation with the sciences. And that is not speculation in the old sense.

. . . Russell, in his latest phase, has resorted to a causal approach founded on physics. Ayer Ernest Mach is, I think, quite right in his comment on it. My objection to it is that it did not probe the mechanism of perceiving itself. My friends told me that Russell had become a critical realist but that was only partially so. He had not pressed through an attack upon the epistemological problem, itself, and fell back on postulates.

* * * * *

I remember how the ingenious Hume, refusing the gambit of representationalism, suggested that we *take* sense-impressions to be things. But one problem was that of accounting for our *notion* of things. To me, it is clear that this *develops* in the setting of perceptual attitude, response and result. That is, we have to adjust ourselves to the things around us. Perceptual realism fits in with the biological setting in a way that subjective sensationalism does not. I seem to remember that Prichard worked this gambit of *taking* sensations to be things. But it will not do. What sensations do is to guide directed responses and to give *cues* for the location and description of things, co-ordinate with ourselves. . . .

Let me return now to Ryle. He is, as always, linguistically acute. And he does not want to be lost in the complexities of neurology and psychological, causal theory. And, in one sense, he is right. The epistemologist should reflect upon everyday distinctions and try to do justice to them. And Ryle does bring out the difference in the *framework* of perceiving and of noting sensations and feelings. But I think he is "stumped" because he has not worked out a clear theory of the constitution of perceiving with its reference and description, its external, existential concern and identifications, as against having sensations, tickles, feelings. He does not sufficiently see that, in *perception*, sensations function as guides and not as objects; while, in noting them for their own sakes, they become data of inspection. And he rightly sees that *pains* are not used as *cues* to external description in the way that heat sensations are. After all, the organism has many jobs to do. It has to withdraw, become aware of danger, take note of internal conditions, etc. It is this many-dimensional life, which philosophers should keep in mind. But I do think that clearing up the how and the achievement of veridical, referential claims should help to give the essential framework into which personal experiencings can fit both linguistically and as guides. Perceiving is not an impersonal matter. There must be a percipient.

Now I have argued that G. E. Moore did not have this empirical theory of perceiving, as a complex operation in which sensations *guide* the referential application of concepts, and that that is why he was so bothered by the question of the status of sense-data, . . . whether they were part of the surface of the object perceived. And, since he started with sense-data in the traditional way, he had to *prove*, in some affirmative fashion, the existence of the external world. There was the Kantian and Platonic background added for both Moore and Russell, as has recently been brought out by Morton White and Wilfrid Sellars. The critical realist did not try to prove the external world in this fashion. He did not have this kind of artificial problem.

These men were tremendously able. They simply did not have the reorientation necessary. I am convinced that my constant contacts with biologists and experimental, comparative psychologists helped me to work out this new orientation. That was a bit of luck.

My argument, in short, has been that philosophy got off to a bad start in the seventeenth century with the schematism of impact on sense-organs and brain, with terminal, mental states in the soul-mind, somehow given to inspection. The whole schematism is outmoded. The unit is the patterned, sensori-motor complex with interplay between the terms so that sensations guide response and response makes demands upon *discrimination* in sensations, an affair of learning. I could give chapter and verse for admirable, experimental work being done along these lines. A good summary is to be found in C. Judson Herrick's chapter on perception in his recent book, *The Evolution of Human Nature*.[1] I had the opportunity of talking it over with him in its first manuscript form. He has always been an enthusiastic Coghillian, that is, an advocate of the unified action of the organism as a whole as against fixed reflexes. Herrick has always been interested in philosophy. I think this helped him to avoid the retention of dualism, something Sherrington retained. The brain was the organ of behaviour but of a guided behaviour on which intelligence had leverage. He and I agreed on the role of learning as enlarging the stimulus-response circuit. The shift to this as the "open" unit which gave a *setting* to both stimulus and response represented the basic reorientation in the causal theory of perception. Thus we do not start with sense-data as mental units and puzzle as to their evidential connection with inferred objects. We find ourselves instead *right within* a developed, perceptual experience dominated by directed response and linguistically expressed in terms of demonstratives and descriptions. And yet sensory factors still operate in a guiding way and attention can be shifted to them. But the old tradition keeps philosophers still focused on sense-data as *isolated* givens from which, alone, perception starts. As we saw, Russell and the logical positivists—largely mathematicians and logicians—kept at this gambit until, in desperation, Russell, at least, shifted to physics as a point of departure. But, even then, perception tended to vanish into egocentric particulars somehow connected with the physical world. He had not really reorientated himself on perception. He did not see how perceiving is concerned with material things as referents. That is, this causal approach was still largely traditional. The organic *how* of actual perceiving was not explored.

---

[1] The University of Texas Press, 1956.

While the epistemologist has, for his main job, the establishment of a *direct realism* which puts man both actively and cognitively in touch with his world and turns him aside from the vagaries, or muddles, of phenomenalism, idealism and scepticism which bad empirical orientation (historically conditioned) had encouraged in the past, he must keep in touch with basic shifts in the newer sciences as well as in physics. It is a mistake to stress linguistic usage alone—valuable as that is as a check on absurdities inspired by bad starts—for one must solve problems in co-operation with the sciences.

Now all this leads me up, in conclusion, to the mind-body problem as pivotal. It will be recalled that Perry rejected the subjective and denied that the brain could be the seat of consciousness. He was influenced here by Bergson. He linked his pan-objectivistic presentationalism which was, as we saw, a kind of extroverted Humanism . . . with philosophical behaviourism. Now philosophical behaviourism—as against the *methodological behaviourism* of the psychologist, puzzled by introspection and the role of the brain—really reflects an inadequate epistemology. In its linguistic form, it expresses, often, an admirable study of words and sentences as tied in with behaviour. I, myself, have found Ryle extremely suggestive here. But what is the existential status of the concepts which *function* in verbal usage. Of course, they are not objects of inspectional intuition. Yet, surely, these meanings which declare themselves in both patterns of usage and patterns of behavioural response—so closely knit together—arise in that process of learning which the cortex furthers as it connects stimuli with behaviour. . . . But the existential locus of sensory qualia must also be worked out, if we are to escape dualism. And here we have a kind of knowledge which we can call experiencing or acquaintance with. And my thesis has always been that the *having* sensations connects up with this experiencing.

But where *are* the sensations? My answer is "in" the brain-mind as a feature of cerebral activity. They are "natural isolates" in that they and not their context are experienced. And they are features of cerebral activity which cannot be reached by external, perceptual knowledge about. The neurologist cannot *inspect* them in the brains he studies for *his* perceiving must be guided by his own sensory data. And the same is true of the behaviourist. The job is, then, that of adequate categorization of a unique situation, uninhibited by presuppositions of a dualistic sort. The Cartesian views of both mind and matter are outworn. Mind is not a substance but a guided activity leading to behaviour. Matter is not mere extension but something capable of high organization and levels of integrative functioning. And knowledge of neither is an affair of intuition. If we split them apart we get a *ghost* in the organism. The mind *is* the brain functioning (occurrently and dispositionally); and the self emerges as the focus of directional activities. Here we have a development of that *guided causality* which we have already noted in referential perception.

I think philosophy has a job of clarification to do here supplementary to that which the biological and psychological sciences are undertaking with no mean success. It is a pity that it has so long been thwarted by retention of antiquated, causal theories, such as those which arose in the seventeenth century, which led to the taking of sensations as terminal units. The actual *unit*, as we have noted, is sensori-motor with centrally aroused processes working out new connections and giving correlated meaning to both. But the *how* of perceiving only opens the way for the epistemologist to appreciate the nature of the directed knowledge-claim which, for philosopher and scientist, is the culmination of guided perception. The other animals respond in guided ways and, often, pretty intelligent ones. Man, the conceptualist and linguist, *lifts* perceiving to the level of demonstrative and descriptive terms, in so doing arriving at explicit knowing.

* * * * *

To sum up: Critical realism is a direct realism after the manner of naïve realism. But it explains perceiving as a cognitive achievement by studying its mechanism and its development in the framework of S—C—R. In this context, it can account for sense-data theories and "appearances." After all, it *is* sense-perception. . . . We have referential claims and *not* cognitive relations, and reference is a development of response.

REFERENTIAL TRANSCENDENCE[*]

> "I am going to integrate three paramenters." (p. 4 below)

Recently I had occasion to examine, in some detail, the phenomenological status of transcendence in connection with a review of Dr. Farber's new book, *Naturalism and Subjectivism*. The issue of transcendence as against immanence came up constantly. Dr. Farber himself devotes a section to the topic in Chapter VII. His own aim is to return to the general outlook of common sense and of science and to put the EPOCHE or "suspension" in its proper place as a tool of analysis. With this directive, I heartily agree.

But, as I see it, the question of the import and reach of perceiving must be met, even in this dominant outlook of everyday life. It was to this question that American realism addressed itself after its neglect by idealism and, to a lesser extent, by pragmatism. The job was to clarify the foundation, and the nature, of the claim to refer to, and know, external things, that is, the things around us. Science both extends this world in terms of light-years and examines it microscopically. I think it can be said that logical positivism and Wittgensteinism handled the problem of perception in a crabwise fashion, the former as it moved from positivism to logical empiricism and scientific empiricism, the new christenings which symbolized shifts of outlook. Wittgensteinism seems to have made its impact on the language-game and the status of logic more than on any theory of perceiving. All this, of course, meant a technical enrichment which may have had the tendency to obscure traditional problems.

. . . Naturally, I have had long thoughts on the positions taken and on questions of terminology. I am persuaded that I can introduce an increased measure of clarification and simplification into the subject. And, in so doing, it will be possible to tie together a number of issues which have bothered philosophy, such as the proper statement of the correspondence theory of truth, the nature of transcendence, and the import of "free will"

---

[*] *Philosophy and Phenomenological Research*, vol. XXII, No. 1, 1961, pp. 1-11.

or choice. It is the way in which answers to these traditional problems are integrated, or fit in together, that confirms me in my belief that the right approach is opening up. I begin with a set of "parameters," as a framework, and follow leads. These consist of directives in the analysis of perceiving, the brain-consciousness complex, and the notion of levels. The effort to carry these parameters together, or keep them in mind as mutually involved, goes back to the early days of my philosophizing, for I suppose I was always as much of a scientist in my thinking as a philosopher. I never could draw the line sharply between them.

Now I am going [first of all] to emphasize . . . the *mechanism of perceiving* as throwing light on the fact that sensations have a role, or function . . . which is the basis of cognitive transcendence. That is, I shall try to show that sensations are *not* terminal, as they have been taken to be in traditional empiricism, but integral to a bio-psychological activity of a directed sort, called response. Their first function is that of guidance; and they are under the causal control of determinate, patterned stimuli. Thus guidance is not an arbitrary affair but causally governed. In looking at a thing, or manipulating it, we are acting under its control. It is the location of sensations in this circuit which brings out their function, or role, and makes us understand that they are not terminal, as the purely introspective tradition in psychology and philosophy was led to hold. We look through our visual field—under control—*at* the object. As I see it, this situation is the foundation of referential transcendence.

Now the importance of this approach cannot, I believe, be overestimated. It is here that science and philosophy can make contact. I can, myself, feel the hot breath of science on my neck as I deal with it. Psychology and neurology are at last getting interested in thinking and in cognition as natural operations. But it is not too late for philosophy to make its contribution within its own frame of reference, the nature and import of the cognitive claims involved, the status of *knowledge* as a human achevement, the correct handling of these categories which belong to no special science as yet, nor will unless philosophy defaults. But philosophy's analysis should, I take it, fit into the mechanisms science is unearthing in biology, neurology and modern communications technique.

Of course, human perceiving with its conceptual thought of things, its references and characterizations, its use of sensations as *evidence*, represents a higher level than guided response but it is founded on it and merely develops its possibilities . . . The cortex, concepts and language are inserted to lift response to this higher level.

In my opinion, this approach leads to a critical, referential realism in which science and philosophy can meet understandingly and work out an accord. There are not many champions of philosophical idealism these days. But there is a kind of hesitant stalemate in philosophy between *experientialism, phenomenalism* and *philosophical behaviorism.* It will be my thesis that much of this stalemate is due to the supposed absence of new leads with respect to perceiving. It is these I am going to try to supply. On the whole, phenomenalism expressed the belief that sensations are terminal in perceiving. Philosophical behaviorism did not see the way clear to locate consciousness in the brain without lapsing into subjectivism. Experientialism, of the Dewey variety . . . turned its back on epistemology and moved into the context of solving problems *in experience.* My diagnosis will be that all three are tarred with the same brush, inability to grasp the mechanism of perceiving and to see how it connects up the percipient with his world. I shall argue that the role of sensations as guiding and evidence goes with their location in the brain. The way this is worked out as giving both reference and disclosure is crucial and may well mark a turning point in philosophy.

Let us take Dewey as exemplifying "experientialism." The logic of the Dewey-Bentley gambit is fairly clear. Traditional epistemology is identified with an "under-the-skin" set-up. This is analogous with Lovejoy's "under-the-hat" schematism. I take Geiger's formulation in his book *John Dewey in Perspective* as fairly accurate. The question is formulated thus: How can the contents of the mind, images and ideas, be related to the actual objects for which they stand? "How can we get out of our heads to compare what is in our heads with what is not?" This, as

Geiger sees it, is the *general* problem of knowledge. It is rejected by Dewey because of its guaranteed insolubility and because it makes "experience" suspect. Dewey and Bentley go on to make knowing a *transaction* between different aspects of a natural world of events. It operates within "experience." The schematism, as we all know, is the development of a subject matter which has become problematic. The object known transactionally is the object of inquiry. Terms like "antecedent reality" and "object of knowledge" are symbols used in this transaction.

Now Geiger admits that the notion of identity, or correspondence, has a natural appeal. But it is bound up with the subjective, in-the-mind outlook which is the bane of epistemology. The thing to do is to be firm and give up the whole illusion since it is tied in with the "under-the-skin" kind of dualism. So far as the term "true" has this context it must be given a cool glance and one must pass on to "warranted assertibility" in transactional discourse.

Obviously, the answer I am going to give to this development is to show that the mechanism of perceiving is responsive and referential and that sensations have a role to play in it of a guiding and evidential sort, which conflicts with the traditional, terminal view of them which Dewey takes to be the base of traditional epistemology. My argument will be in terms of a neglected alternative. Of course, the organism is stimulated *but it reacts*. Sensations and images have a role to play in this reaction. Concepts are developed in the interplay and that is why we always think of concepts as concepts *of*, as applicable. We look *through* the visual field at the *things* stimulating us and apply learned concepts *to them* under the guidance of the visual field. In a way, Dewey was a victim of the Cartesian dualism he rejects. He was fighting a ghost.

With all due respect to the ingenuity of Dewey and Bentley, I cannot but feel that their experiential transactionism and experiential situationism were tangential to more precise analyses. If one begins with this gambit one will inevitably be a *contextualist* stressing transactions. There will always be a measure of validity to it and its appeal to problems, thinking and scientific methods. But to the critical referential realist, all this will depend on a jump from subjectivism to objectivism rather than on a mastery of subjectivism. Dewey's Hegelian training undoubtedly helped. It gave a status to the term *experience*. When pressed, Dewey, I feel, was at times a little uncomfortable. But what was the alternative? The new realism? Santayana's essences? Clearly not.

And so he did a good work of rationalization. Subcutaneous mind, dualism, fixed reality, antecedent reality, the spectator view of knowing, copying. And he was echoed. . . . While all this was going on, I was seeking clues to a better view of perceiving than the traditional empiricists had. Could I escape making sensations terminal and adding to them a mysterious act of inference to get from them to the external world? What if they were not terminal but played a role in perceiving which caught them up in a referential, or directed, act and which made use of their content, which was under causal control, to guide and disclose?

I shall not say much about phenomenalism. For my present purposes, it is enough to point out that it is based on the assumption that sensations are terminal in perceiving. Lewis's conceptual pragmatism makes concepts—*however one comes by them*—ancillary to predicted sensabilia. That is, concepts are not, as they are for me, applicable to the physical things we are perceiving but to a future set of experiences. This gambit will never get Lewis to an explicit physical realism, however much he may yearn for it. As for the logical positivists, they have almost given up trying to translate material-thing statements into sensation-statements. . . . I am offering an alternative.

Philosophical behaviorism took to itself new life with the advent of emphasis upon language. Linguistic idioms were explored and the logic of language valiantly exploited. That was all to the good. But, surely, symbols must be heard, or seen, and communicated. And were concepts picked out of the air? And how about sensations and images? The gambit was nearer to that of Dewey than Ryle and others realized. The subjective was not mastered but pushed aside. As in psychological behaviorism of the extreme sort, the poor old brain was ignored.

Neurology is coming in with new techniques to restore the balance. It will be recalled that I am going to seek to integrate three "parameters": (1) the mechanism of perceiving, (2) the brain-consciousness complex, and (3) the notion of levels. Of course, in language, we have to do with the cultural level of personal interplay and mental activity. Of course, for me, this is, likewise, cerebral activity.

*　*　*　*　*

A good terminology is a resultant of the clarification that goes with the completion of a task. I never, myself, liked the expressions "epistemological monism" and "epistemological dualism," which grew up in connection with the dispute between the new realists and the critical realists. Both were, I take it, advocates of *direct realism* as against the Lockian tradition which made ideas terminal in knowing. But the new realist had, on the whole, a searchlight view of knowing terminating on presentations which were Humian sense-impressions rechristened. Perry saw very clearly that this view involved philosophical behaviorism and the rejection of the location of sensations in the brain. Here, strangely enough, he joined hands with Bergson but tried to be more explicit. This alliance amused me since Perry was a decided intellectualist and did not like the poetic vaguenesses of Bergson.

... I was a direct realist but regarded perceiving as a mediated operation, guided by sensations but concerned with things in the framework of response. Cognizing evolves from a disclosing use of sensations to a stage in which reference and characterization have developed with the growth of concepts and languages. The framework is now that of *aboutness* with a strong sense of physical things, their manipulation, and the application of concepts to them. What I shall try to bring out [as I undertook to do in my article, "Sensations as Guides to Perceiving"] is the functional use of sensations in a directed operation, use which gives them a transcending role. I would illustrate this role by the example of looking *through the visual field* at the things around us. Now, as I see it, this use is not arbitrary but well-founded. The visual field is causally controlled in us by the things we are looking at. It is a circuit of return. After all, our sense organs were not evolved without a function to perform, that of guided adjustment to the environment. The analogy of modern communication technique can be applied here. Input serves output. Pattern is transmitted and applied. We are told that the brain was developed as a result of the need to integrate sensory centers and connect them with response.

* * * * *

Now I do not want to oversimplify the operation. Köhler seems to me quite right in stressing sensory organization as supplementary to the patterned stimulus. The brain is a wonderful organ. It is the job of the epistemologist to clarify human knowing as an achievement with its special categories. But it is well to keep in touch with scientific explorations of processes and functions.

* * * * *

As it is usually put today, the brain is an organ of behavior; but, surely, it is a behavior guided by knowledge. Here is what I call a high level of causality. It is a level of causality which involves decision-making or choice. Such causality is local and enriched. And I suppose it corresponds to what is called free will. That is, it is not a mere function of external compulsions. As a matter of fact, I think that the usual contrast between determinism and indeterminism is sterile and reflects a Newtonian cosmic set-up of a necessitarian type which is being outgrown. I was surprised to find C. D. Broad adhering to it.

We must also keep the brain-consciousness complex before our attention. It was, it will be recalled, one of the parameters. Now, I have argued that sensations and images function in a directive mechanism concerned with response and with voluntary observation at higher levels. As I see it, we must *enlarge our notion of the physical* to include this kind of activity. As humans, we are able to pick out and talk about such factors as *isolates*, and so we have a double knowledge of the functioning brain, one built up by science in terms of external perceiving and one in terms of noting, having, or acquaintance. So far as I can see, these two forms of cognition supplement one another; and the one does not conflict with the other. This is a monist approach.

I suppose one reason why scientists are puzzled, as in extreme behaviorism, is because they assume, through habit, that the external knowing with which they are most familiar reaches the object in an exhaustive fashion. If they were more familiar with epistemology and its complex foundation they would not do so, a point that Bertrand Russell and others have often made. I think we must be empiricists here and accept the brain-consciousness complex and clarify the needed categories. It is interesting to follow the categories of Dr. Warren McCullock and others in this context. In 1916 in my first book, *Critical Realism,* I devoted a chapter to the query, Is Consciousness Alien to the Physical? Shortly thereafter I published an article in the *Journal of Philosophy* with the thesis that consciousness is physical, in the monistic, double-knowledge sense. Pace, Feigl, Wilfrid Sellars and Smart have recently been exploring this outlook.

While I have used distance reception as an illustration of the role of sensations as guiding response and furnishing evidence in a communication way, it is important to emphasize the fact that tactual sensations and muscular ones perform the same function in much the same fashion. In responding to contact, we feel *through* our tactual sensations in a referential manner. The give-and-take of our muscular interplay with the things around us has much the same nervous accompaniment. It has direction and objective import. The point to bear in mind is that the sensations are not terminal in the traditional introspective fashion but functional in the directive mechanism of perceiving. It is in this fashion that animals are aware of their surroundings and adjust to them.

Perceiving develops in human beings to a high level in the context of attitudes, beliefs, expectations, concepts and language with what psychologists and psychiatrists call the body-image as a center. Sensory factors point the way to the growth of concepts continuing the same referential moment in terms of application. I look at this door through my visual field and I apply concepts to it directly in terms of the cues I read off. I "see" that the door is oblong, has a knob and a night-latch, has a pattern, etc. Perhaps I go on to open it and swing it back. I am dealing with a door through my sensations and concepts. Such is the import of direct, physical realism. It is no simple searchlight affair but a referential activity resting on a biological mechanism into which higher levels are inserted. Patterned stimuli causally control and communicate sensory patterns which, embedded in neural media, guide motor response. There is thus a return to the thing stimulating the organism, a return which gives the sensory pattern relevant import for the object. As I have indicated, concepts represent explorations and integrations on this base. The sense of a physical thing confronting us emerges ever more clearly. It is at this level that categories of all sorts arise under control. It is not a case of primitive metaphysics, as Russell in his Humean perspective assumed but a growth of controlled cognitive insight. Such an approach is as definitely opposed to Cartesian intuitionism as to Humeanism. I have long argued that it could hardly have arisen in philosophy before the development of modern biology. Aristotle read off his categories largely from language—not a bad thing to do—but little was known in his day about the nervous system and its mechanisms . . .

Now what is the epistemological upshot of all this? Is it not clear that we are moving away from the universe of discourse of *mind* as a receptacle of sensations and images somehow known terminally and severed from any functional relation to the outside world? As we saw, it was this schematism which led Dewey to declare epistemology, as a general discipline, bankrupt. One must, he argued . . . give up a subcutaneous mind and cast oneself on *experience*—wonderful word—and regard knowing as an experiential transaction. One must turn one's back on identity and correspondence views of truth and press bravely on to reconstruction and prediction and warranted assertibility. As I have already indicated, my analysis of perceiving gives leverage to a new approach to correspondence as founded on the controlled import of sensations. Knowledge is, thus, an achievement with this base . . .

* * * * *

It is well to bear in mind that, at the human level, perceiving operates in the setting of percipient person and thing perceived. There is a conceptual development of both poles. In language, this manifests itself in the use of pronouns, demonstratives and descriptive terms. It is not surprising that such language has its idioms and logic for the framework is realistic and forces categorial explorations. I welcome this linguistic development but seek to give it an epistemological foundation which connects up —as it should—with ontology. We can drop that ambivalent term, metaphysics, for the time being . . .

I have said that a good terminology follows upon a clarification of issues. The expression "epistemological monism" was too tied in with the idea of presentation, acquaintance with and searchlight. Epistemological dualism stressed mediations and mechanisms but it savored of the Lockean double-step procedure. It is, perhaps, better to talk of *direct perceiving* while making it clear that such perceiving involves a guided operation concerned with physical things in the ways I have indicated. . . . When Köhler talks about the realm of "direct experience" he is not concerned with perceiv*ing* but with "percepts" and their ingredients. It is because of this shift of attention that he commits the traditional mistake of making the physical world an inference.

There is another point I should like to make here. Science developed its great concepts of mass, gases, the elements, with which it began to enrich our idea of the physical world, not by concentrating on sensations and logical constructs from them but by using the senses in connection with external perceiving and experimental manipulation. The philosopher should read the history of science and get the feeling of this controlled creation of concepts applicable to the physical world . . .

What, then, about the term, "transcendence"? It is used by Husserl, as Farber points out, as a contrast term to "immanence." Under the control of a combination of motivations, partly technical, partly emotional, he moved from "suspension" of the world to Cartesian idealism, for Descartes got back the world only by way of a scholastic proof of God. Now Farber is rightly critical of the existential modes of jumping to the transcendent as a *transcendental absolute* and the rejection of naturalism. What we both have in mind, I think, is a re-analysis of perceiving which gives sensations a function in perceiving, justified by their being under the causal control of the object perceived. It is in this setting that they have cognitive value and objective import.

Concepts are tools which interplay with sensations in the same cognitive direction. As percipients as well as agents we are *in* the world, not *thrown* into it.

But this, perhaps too exclusively intellectualistic analysis, should be supplemented by the role of drives and needs. As Sir Russell Brain points out, when a child drops a toy at a certain age, he begins to look around for it. What is called infantile omnipotence is brought up short. Perhaps we have here the germ of support for the feeling of a "beyond" of an "other than" which, heaven knows, is driven home to the adult every day. He is one among others in a big and complex world. I have often wondered at the rationalized persistence in philosophy of the tradition of subjectivism. It is there to be seized in an age of *Angst* and blown up like a balloon by its advocates. I suppose one reason is that philosophy has hitherto left gaps in its rationalism and in its interlocking with science. I have tried to show that one could drive a whole carriage and pair through pragmatic scientism and logical phenomenalism. It has been my aim to tighten all this up in what my friend Feigl calls a nomological network. I am persuaded that my analysis of perceiving is strategic for the enterprise. It shows how man comes to see himself in a world of *public objects,* as one of them. Messages from the various sense organs are integrated and ordered in terms of attitudes, expectations, and applicable concepts. It is in this fashion that man becomes world-conscious in a manner impossible to the lower animals. The universe spreads out before him in time and space, its microscopic texture explored by techniques aiding the sense organs and its macroscopic cosmography deciphered in culturally developed ways.

CAUSALITY AND SUBSTANCE[*]

> "[Scientific] facts and theories inexorably involve an ontology for their reference and philosophical meaning." (page 2 below)

It is my wish in the present paper to induce the category of causality to disclose more about itself by putting it in its onto-

---
[*] R. W. Sellars: *Philosophical Review*, vol. 52, 1943, pp. 1-15, 20-27.

logical context. Such a procedure should be suggestive in these days when categories and ontology are somewhat at a discount.

It will be noted that I employ the term ontology rather than metaphysics, since the latter term seems to be easily misleading because of its verbal associations. People have the tradition of thinking of metaphysics as something beyond physics in a theological sort of way; and they have, of course, good Aristotelian and Thomistic and even idealistic precedent for such a perspective. But the naturalist is concerned with being or existence and he considers physics as a basic empirical science about being, chiefly at the inorganic level. It concerns itself with primary constituents, properties and laws. It follows, of course, that, if the physicist were equally concerned with the clear apprehension of categories, he would be an ontologist also.

The dividing line is a matter of degree, for there are capable philosophical physicists. And yet I am persuaded that the interpretation of such categories as matter, space, time, and causality, requires the deepening and supplementation which epistemology and ontology alone can contribute. All of which amounts to saying that the philosophical approach is distinctive and unavoidable.

The reason for this belief will, I hope, become evident in the details of the argument of this paper, which, in the main, will be the nature of an attempt to integrate epistemology and ontology. However, I permit myself at this point the suggestion that the common tendency to take the theory of relativity as an ontological principle illustrates what I have in mind. Equally relevant is the fact that science can be given operational and positivistic translations as well as the more realistic ones which the majority of scientists probably entertain as an extension of common sense. I would hold, then, that science requires a philosophical completion, not as regards facts and theories, but as regards *categorial setting*. Of course, scientists are invited to pass their criticisms upon this attempted philosophical supplementation, for I do not think that there is anything very esoteric about it. It reflects not much more than an intellectual division of labor.

I shall use the term physical realism as an indication of my position. It is, I may point out, a shortened expression for critical realism and evolutionary naturalism taken together. Thus it symbolizes the integration of epistemology and ontology of which I have spoken. Physical realism is a post-Humian position. Much of its effort has had to do with the escape from subjectivism and phenomenalism.

As a physical realist it is my thesis that scientific knowledge, that is, empirical, and not formal or purely mathematical, knowledge, is highly probable knowledge or disclosure about what exists, and that its facts and theories inexorably involve an ontology for their reference and philosophical meaning. This view does not, of course, imply that any particular science need greatly concern itself about this philosophical completion, but that the culture of the time cannot and will not ignore it. Modest as a philosopher must be in this age of science and technology, I would, nevertheless, suggest that the development of science as a whole is affected by its basic assumptions. It is doubtful that science is as completely selfsufficient as it was led in the nineteenth century to regard itself.

The position adopted here signifies that *being* (what exists) has categorial characteristics which are disclosed in the categorial meanings operating in sense-perception, self-awareness, and the sciences, and that it is the job of basic philosophy to apprehend them and to clarify them. It will, perhaps, be remembered that, in my book, *Evolutionary Naturalism,* I argued that categorical meanings have a natural, empirical origin and an ontological reference and significance. While recognizing the value of Kant's stress upon categories as against Hume's scepticism, I criticized his extreme innatism and his phenomenalism. I still regard this contrast as basic and fruitful. In other words, I am not one of those who would throw common-sense categories away in a nonchalant fashion as do those who have the virus of logical apriorism in their veins. I simply regard myself as more adequately empirical than Hume's atomism and sensationalism permitted him to be and far more so than those who hover between sensationalism and conventionalism.

In my opinion, then, knowledge, being, and the categories, are both causally and formally connected. They are reciprocally elucidating. *Being* without categorial characteristics is scarcely thinkable; and in knowledge-claims, being is characterized through categorial meanings. In this fashion all three are tied together. So much in the way of perspective.

I

The category of causality furnishes an excellent illustration of the dangers confronting conceptual apprehension as a result of an inadequate philosophical context. It is well known that Hume rejected its ontological setting and sought to re-conceive it in a subjective and phenomenalistic setting. So taken, causality was reduced to a weak form having something to do with experiential sequences and expectations. Hume was forced to this reduction because he found himself unable to give either it or substance an empirical foundation and so refused to fall back on what rightly seemed to him an obscurantist type of rationalism. The critical realist would suggest that at least one root of the difficulty was the confusion of acts of cognition with the occurrence of sensations and images, *which, after all, but furnish some of the raw material for denotative and depictive acts.** However that may be, both substance and causality were really dismissed together, . . . something weaker which was of the nature of succession in experience was given the name of causation. It was this shift which I have spoken of as taking causality out of its ontological context. I do not deny that a new emphasis, reflecting the newer developments in science, also entered, that temporalism and contingency received overdue recognition. But I do claim that it is really doubtful whether the category of causality remained after this removal of the ontological context.

What, in the main, I shall try to do is to reverse Hume's action and, while retaining temporalism and contingency, give causality once more its ontological setting. By so doing, it will again be linked with physical systems conceived dynamically and relationally; and, through this linkage, it will be tied in with such

---

* Italics added.

categories as substance, activity, time, space, tendency, potentiality, and emergence.

In my opinion it is only in this fashion that scientific knowledge can be given a philosophical completion, that is, can be harmonized with what seem to me basic ontological categories. As I have already indicated, I am quite aware that many contemporary thinkers of distinction do not feel this need. That is the continuing Humian note. But I do, for reasons which I hope to make clearer as I proceed.

The critical realist—for whom empirical knowledge is a mediated affair—recognizes that science is likely to contain some measure of *epistemic translation* in its facts and laws. Thus the past does not exist in nature while it is dated and described in human knowledge. There is something hypothetical in laws in so far as they set up conditions. I suggest that such terms as space-time, change, event, probability, and fact, can only be properly accounted for and understood in the light of an adequate ontology. It is only those who identify empirical knowledge with a direct intuition of reality and do not grasp the manipulations and comparisons involved who are surprised by this descriptive *spreading out* which emphasizes chronologies, predictions, facts, and laws. Let it be remembered that neither the past nor the future exists and it will be realized that the actual cannot be reduced to a mere present *event*. At least, so it seems to me; and that is one reason why I am led to explore such categories as substance and potentiality. These must, however, be so conceived that they harmonize with modern scientific knowledge.

It is not too much to say that many of the paradoxes of philosophy and much of the misunderstanding of the nature of such things as moral decision result from this refusal to correlate scientific knowledge with ontology. Thus causation has been thought of as a push by a non-existent past and moral choice has been conceived, curiously enough, as an *event* succeeding other events and not, more deeply, as an *activity* of the whole organic self. This contrast between event and activity seems to me intriguing. May it not in some measure correspond to the different perspective of scientific knowledge and ontology? Why so many philosophers should ignore such fascinating topics is a marvel to me. But, so long as epistemology and ontology are ignored or kept from their fruitful interaction by positivism and pragmatism, such will be the case.

By linking causality with substance, taken in a dynamic or activistic sense, I shall be led to distinguish between transeunt causality, immanent causality, and emergent causality. These distinctions will be situational in character but also qualitative. I shall attempt to give the notion of emergence a rational ontological ground. It is my thesis that the ontological categories are intrinsically related and that each fades to the extent it is taken from its connection with the others. The ontological situation, as I see it, is analogous to what the logicians call entailment. It is as though substance were a superordinate category which found implication and expression in subordinate ones such as causality, activity, potentiality, space, and time. In other words, these subordinate categories are adjectival in nature and *expose* the dynamic and structural nature of substance. Certainly, one reason for the historical desiccation of the category of substance was its abstraction from these subordinate categories. Only in this fashion did it become "something I know not what" or the reflection of the subject-predicate form. Even the idealist's substitution of self or person for it represents in part this desiccation. We shall, in fact, see that self-awareness is a significant source of the proper apprehension of the category of substance, though it must be taken in the context of emergence or evolutionary naturalism.

Since Hume—and that is one of his recognized glories—no discussion of causality can get intelligently under way without attention being paid to the epistemic side. How do we apprehend this category? And why, and by what right, do we apply it both to ourselves and the things around us? Kant drove these further questions home.

Now I take all categories, from the epistemic side, to be gradually apprehended concepts grasped within experience. And I further suppose such apprehension not to be arbitrary but to be based upon traits of cognitional and conational, or practical, experience. Both of these activities concern themselves, I would hold, with self and things rather than with sensations and feelings. Here is where *denotative realism* makes a profound difference to epistemic analysis. For many reasons, some of which were connected with his views of space and time, Kant turned his back upon physical realism and embraced a phenomenalism for which knowing was a kind of constructing. Hence, though he was even more aware than Hume of categorial meanings, he did not give them realistic significance.

II

The resources of both genetic and analytic psychology would be required for any adequate psychological verification of the categorial meanings with which I am concerned. All I can do here is to indicate the perspective which, it seems to me, any epistemic study of causality and substance must emphasize.

It is not sufficiently recognized that Hume admitted the presence and operation of instincts and beliefs with respect to both things and selves. "It seems also evident that, when men follow this blind and powerful instinct of nature, they always suppose the very images, presented by the senses, to be the external objects, and never entertain any suspicion that the one are nothing but representations of the other." Both here and with respect to the self we find his rational principles at war with his natural beliefs.

But his rational principles turn out upon examination to reflect assumptions which are highly doubtful. These lead him to turn his back upon denotative symbolism and explicit judgment with the use of thinghood as a category and to embrace in a mood of resigned scepticism a radical empiricism of atomic sense-impressions and images, a radical empiricism which has ever since appealed to many as toughminded, though it is really very artificial and tenderminded.

To make a long story short, I would hold that the field of the individual's experience is dominated by denotative reference in both sense-perception and self-awareness, and that these two directions develop together and are of genetic assistance to each other. The individual's attitudes and interests help to give body and objectivity to their objective or *Gegenstand,* and it is for this reason that sensations are caught up into a perceptive form and seem the very surface of the objective not-self which the embodied self is concerned with. All this seems to me genetically and epistemically natural, and I am persuaded that critical realism has shown that it can be epistemologically developed in such a fashion that empirical knowledge turns out to be of the nature of judgmental assertions about denoted, but not intuited, objects in the environment of the organic self.

But into the purely epistemological aspect of the question I do not wish to enter, for I have written about it almost *ad nauseam* and with too little stimulating criticism on the part of fellow philosophers. What I desire to do here is to call attention to the corresponding mechanism and categorial form of self-awareness. In place of the stream-of-consciousness psychology I would put a thing-and-self psychology dominated by directions and categorial meanings. It seems to me, in short, that sense-perception and self-awareness must be taken as co-ordinate and mutually implicated. As I see it, the tension of felt attitudes has a double direction, one outward and the other inward. In its outward direction it gives body to sensations and helps to put them into a perceptive form which is deepened by memories and expectations. But in its inward direction there is a corresponding development of subjectivity, or selfness, also deepened by memories and anticipations. Desires and hopes and fears play about this subjective counter-reference. It is in this fashion, I believe, that the form of self-awareness develops step by step with the form of sense-perception. What deepens the one deepens the other also. But feelings, organic sensations, and desires, constitute the psychical material taken up symbolically and cognitively in this self-reference much as visual and touch sensations are taken up into objective perceptual form. As I shall try to show, in both cases reflection emphasizes reference and denotation and queries intuition of the object. We shall find, indeed, that intuition has more to say for itself in the case of self-knowledge than in the case of external perception. However, ontological questions of the relation of substance to its momentary activation will appear in connection with the equivalence of feeling to the enduring organic self.

Before I go further I should like to point out that explicit categorial meanings like those of thinghood and selfhood are subjects of reflective examination only in philosophic thought. Yet that they are apprehended and verbalized long before cannot be doubted. It is quite evident that such meanings emerge from biologically founded patterns. As factors they are operative in the life of the lower animals. Such meanings are relational and directional in character and are, I suppose, carried by feelings, sensations, and images. I would not take these latter terms atomistically but on a background of attention and action giving continuity and compresence with transition.

What I wish to stress is that categorial meanings emerge and operate in this fashion and that what may be called a *conceptual apprehension* of them presupposes this prior status. Otherwise it would be artificial and without foundation. We perceive things and are aware of the self long before we apprehend with any clarity what things are and what the self is. One aim of the present study is to stimulate such clarified apprehension which, since Hume's dampening scepticism, has not been any too evident. My thesis is that the conceptual apprehension of categories presupposes the empirical presence of categorial meanings in the operative forms of sense-perception and self-awareness. Here is where realistic empiricism differs from Humian empiricism. And yet, as we say, Hume acknowledged these meanings but did not see how they could be given a rational explanation in terms of his psychological and epistemological assumptions. Critical realism breaks with these assumptions in the fashion I have indicated.

III

It is tremendously important that the status of the organism in self-awareness be correctly grasped. I take it to be empirically correct to speak of the embodied self or the organic self. Certainly I have no intuition of the self as distinct from the organism. And it seems to me clear that Cartesian dualism is a theory resting upon assumptions which evolutionary naturalism undercuts. I refer here both to the doctrine of emergence and to the double-knowledge approach to the mind-body problem.

Let us look at our actual experience in self-awareness. Is it not a fact that, guided by organic sensations and feelings, we experience ourselves to be in some sense *in* the body? There is a diffuse localization in the body as against other perceived things set over against it. Psychologists have pointed out this nuclear basis and the attachments and deepening which it acquires in the awareness of desires and aversions and in the localization of eye-movements and muscular activities. But why do more than refer to these well known facts? The self at what one might call the sensuous level is noted through, and by means of, such subjective, intra-bodily localized, data. All this is a matter, not of theory, but of experiential distinctions. It is only later for theory that the mind and the realistically conceived body, or organism, must be integrated anew in answer to dualistically formulated ontological conceptions.

We are concerned here with the awareness of self. And the primary self seems to me to be denoted and symbolized through subjective, psychical material localized within the body. I take it that memory and anticipations play much the same supplementary role here as they do for our perception of thinghood. The self tends to be thought of as indwelling and *more than the passing feelings* which are states or expressions of it. The correspondence with sense-perceptions is fairly complete. In both directions there is the same development of meanings of endurance and capacity. The body may well help to mediate this double development, since the awareness of the body is fairly constant. I am convinced that I could move my body if I would. The self retreats in some measure from the muscular integument and we think of the latter more as an instrument of the self we are aware of. It is in this sense that we seem to ourselves to look out through the eyes and feel with the hands.

But into the subtle details of the conceptualization of the self we cannot here enter. Social intercourse has much to do with this development of desires, actions, and thoughts, which do, quite literally, develop the self upon its biological base.

But the point I wish particularly to make is that, without the primary self-awareness we have discussed above, the concepts of the self could secure no existential reference and attachment. I find that pragmatists like Mead and Dewey have never sufficiently grasped this fact because they were not sufficiently interested in epistemology and ontology. They never clearly distinguished between the concept of the self and the self. And to the physical realist this distinction is basic. . . . [Further and quite fundamentally] the self is never something given alongside of the feelings and desires through which it is disclosed any more than an external thing can be something given alongside of the sense-data. In both cases the denoted object is something apprehended through data and categorial meanings. Hume was on a false search. As I see it, the difference between inorganic things and the self is at least twofold: (1) a difference in capacities, and (2) the self is in some fashion integral to the human organism whose capacities are somehow its capacities. To make a long story short, I see every reason to believe that the organism is the self, not something-I-know-not-what located in liver, heart, or brain. It is the activities and operations of the organism that we apprehend through our feelings and concepts. We may be said to pass from a sensuous to a conceptual apprehension of the self, *apprehension being a directed awareness through concepts.*

IV

It is in this fashion that I argue for a realistic empiricism as against phenomenalistic empiricism. It is evident that such realistic empiricism gives a foundation for ontological categories, for it asserts that categorial meanings develop in both sense-perception and self-awareness and that these meanings are conceptualized and mediate the conceptual apprehension of the categorial characteristics of our world.

Now I take substance to be a category to whose full conception all our knowledge of self and things is necessary. It is to me analysable in the sense that any adequate conceptual apprehension of it involves such meanings as endurance, activities, potentialities, causality, etc. As I see it, such conceptual apprehension is mediated by all relevant knowledge of a generic sort. I doubt that the category of substance excludes even space and time when these are grasped as categorial meanings and not merely equated with scientific measurements. In short, substance is an abstract, but internally complex, concept, and to brush it aside as a mere projection of the subject-predicate linguistic form seems to me the height of absurdity.

In order that we may keep our promised integration of epistemology and ontology let us try to see how this approach to substance through both self and things affects the interpretation of this category.

It is clear that we must distinguish between the generic characteristics of substance and the specific characteristics which distinguish one level of nature from another. I take it that new capacities emerge which are yet compatible with the generic ones of endurance, potentiality, dynamism, and causal capacity. And it is my hypothesis that organization is the clue to such emergence. I shall have more to say of this point later when I study emergent causality.

At present I am primarily interested in clarifying the difference between the knowledge of self and the knowledge of things. I have argued that the categorial meanings apprehended in the concept of substance develop in the situation where we pass back and forth between sense-perception and self-awareness. There is control and countercontrol, action and reaction. It is likewise clear that the body itself helps in this linkage of the two. The body is a thing as well as the embodiment of the self.

For each individual there is an ultimate epistemological difference, which he assumes for other selves, that is, that he is outside of other things and can only get revelatory messages from them while he is participating in the activity of its own body-self. It is the organic self which desires, feels, judges, makes decisions. The data used in knowing the self are expressions of its activity. Nowhere else in nature has the individual the same privileged position. And, of course, it is rationally quite understandable. We should, therefore, expect the inorganic world to be more opaque in the sense that we are limited in its case to the kind of descriptive knowledge disclosed by sensory data. The result is what I called an epistemological translation, or spreading out, especially marked as regards scientific space and time, and a tendency to feel a trifle bewildered by the category of substance itself. It is not surprising, therefore, to find that even causality shares an analogous fate and, with it, the rational basis of induction. It is, I believe, the strategic role of philosophy to emphasize the significance of a naturalistic approach to the organic self. Here we are dominated by the thought of an enduring, highly organized, and active substance which we are and by the conviction that our experiences of feeling, thinking and deciding are one with, and expressions of, such substantial activities. Here is the perspective of empirical realism as against phenomenalism. My break with Hume should now be evident. It is at once epistemological and ontological; and the two are inseparable though distinguishable. It rests on the thesis that empirical knowledge involves a directed claim to disclose a world which is conceptually apprehended as substantial. Because Hume ignored, or rejected, this framework and thought of knowledge as an affair of sensory givenness, his treatment of substance and causality was inevitable.

Let us now turn to the epistemic side of causality. Here, again, I would argue that the categorial concept rests upon a categorial meaning which emerges in experience.

Of late there has been a rise of interest in the subjective source of this category. Ewing, Broad, Stout, Pratt, Swabey, and Parker, have argued for an awareness of causal relatedness in the individual's experience. The epistemic side of the problem is concerned with the experiences in self-awareness and sense-perception which develop into this type of categorial meaning which can then be more and more conceptualized. In large measure it is a genetic question and involves the growth in awareness of the self's doing and suffering. But such awareness is integrated with the perception of things as affecting us and of ourselves as handling and moving things. I take it that our feeling of ourselves as pervading the organism has much to do with the growth of these relational meanings. But as desire, memory, and decision, constitute larger elements in the thought of the self, such experiences as the direction of the attention, trying to remember a name, making a moral choice, seem to me to be regarded as disclosing the self as active. It is not, I suppose, that we intuit a conational element as such, but that we are led to think the self as active and as disclosed in these relational experiences. In short, activity seems to me to be a categorial meaning developing around primary self-awareness. Once this level is reached we are convinced that the self has something to do with the movement of the eyes or the use of the various bodily organs even though we can trace no continuity between volition and action. The important point to bear in mind is that we do not claim to know the self exhaustively and to intuit just how it operates. So far as I can see we have nothing more than the apprehension that the self is operating and expressing itself and that we are consciously on the inside of this operating, consciously participating in it. For instance, to use Dr. Ewing's example, we can note how we react to the thought of the death of a friend; and we are convinced that this reaction gives us knowledge of our character and disposition. We think the self through what we believe to be a set of relevant experiences bearing upon the self.

Now I have not the space to go into the details of this deepening awareness of the self as active, which I take to be the basis of the growth of the categorial meaning of causality. Suffice it to point out that the position I am advocating does not hold to any intuition of force of energy as these terms are used in physical science. We should not expect to intuit how our muscles are innervated nor should we expect to see necessary connections in nature. Rather am I pointing out that we are led to deepen our conception of the self as a substance, that is, an enduring unity having dispositions and capacities, by this additional category of causal activity. Substance, dispositions, capacities, activity, doing and suffering, what are all of these but supplementary concepts? That we have such concepts and use them in our conceptual apprehension of the self there seems to me little doubt. I am simply arguing that these concepts rest upon categorial meanings developed around sense-perception and self-awareness but more dominantly around the latter.

It would scarcely be fair not to mention Whitehead's appeal to the mode of causal efficacy as against the mode of presentational immediacy. I can appreciate his motive and agree with what may be called his subjective emphasis. My divergence lies chiefly in my stress upon the operation of the category of selfhood. It seems to me that the categorial meaning of causal activity develops from experiences of the sort indicated above as they are used to interpret a substantial self which can do things. I can and do attend to things; I have desires and make a choice; I have capacities and dispositions. All this becomes the more explicit the more conceptually selfconscious we are. That is, the more the awareness of the bodily self is deepened and supplemented by the consciousness of what are usually spoken of as mental operations and moral decisions. My argument is that the organism *is* the substantial and active self so known.

It is surely not surprising that a self which feels itself continuous with muscular sensations and able to control their coming through imaged decisions should interpret kinaesthetic sensations symbolically as effort and resistance. We regard our muscular activity as an extension and prolongation of the activity of the self even though we detect no connective bond between decision and the later kinaesthetic sensation. Self-knowledge is not complete physiological knowledge, though it should not conflict with it. And I see no reason to deny that imaged decisions do control muscular movements. In other words, Hume demanded too much. What alone I am arguing for is the growth of the categorial meaning of causality within experience as tied up with the awareness of the self as active and controlling, on the one hand, and as suffering and being controlled, on the other. All this seems to me to emerge in the setting of self and things. . . .

Under these conditions it is not surprising that muscular sensations become, as I said, symbolic of action, passion, and direction, both spatial and temporal. In this fashion causality gets its extra-bodily extension and application. I learn that I can not only move my body but the things around it. And I soon learn instrumental routines outside the organic self which I can set going. Laws of nature are in the offing.

I have suggested that kinaesthetic sensations and even feelings take on *causal symbolism* and give solidity and volume to our thought of causal operations. So far as I can see, they do not do more than this but readily become indicative of the measurements of effort and resistance attached to them by science. It is merely another case of our sensations becoming symbolic through their integration with categorial meanings. Just as I tend to take a colored patch to be the surface of the thing to which I am attending and toward which I am moving, so I take the muscular sensations as expressing my causal effort. In neither case does a critical level of knowing project *sensory qualities into things*. These must find a locus in the self as organism; and that, as we saw, is the mind-body problem.

Now the import of my whole argument is to the effect that the categorial meanings of substance and causality develop together in connection with the awareness of self and things. Such is their setting; and conceptual apprehension of the categories should not violate this mutual involvement. If philosophy violates this setting, substance becomes inert, merely linguistic, and mythological, a parody for positivists to scorn; and causality, abstracted from it, likewise turns into something unempirical and undiscoverable. Both epistemic and epistemological acumen are needed to handle categories.

V

I shall now pass to a study of the categorial setting of science. What I shall be primarily concerned with will be a grounding of scientific concepts in ontological ones under the guidance of the above epistemological and ontological analyses.

The category of substantivity has no similitude to the pictorial eleatic conception of matter of the nineteenth century. We must recognize that our knowledge of physical entities is very abstract; and yet there is nothing in its texture which conflicts with duration and agency and extensity, primary requirements of substantivity. It is in terms of these requirements that scientific concepts of space, time, quantity, and causality, can be rationally understood and what I have called their *descriptive spreading out* comprehended. Duration and agency disclose themselves in our experience in terms of time. And the operations of remembering, anticipating, and dating, spread out our knowledge of *events*, which are cognized facts about activities in nature. We recognize that events are not themselves realities but presuppose the agency, or activity, of that which durationally exists. Many of the paradoxes of time could have been avoided had this ontological basis for time been grasped. The present in contrast to the past and the future is only more actual in the sense that it refers to the actual activities of enduring substances. *It does not then mean a stretch of time but the source and basis of time.* Such is the only meaning I can give to the haunting sense of an absolute now. Does it not express our belief that the universe, as substantial, is a field of coexistential activities? But science develops concepts in relation to techniques of measurement; and so scientific time without a categorial setting has no meaning to assign to absolute simultaneity. The theory of relativity expresses the discovery of this fact. This analysis illustrates what I mean by a philosophic supplementation of science by giving it a categorial setting.

Now much the same sort of operation must be applied to causality, as used in science, to make it ontologically adequate. It is clear that the past cannot push the present, rather that the activity of an agent in its relation or field brings something to pass. Moral decision does not represent a push from a no-longer-existing past. It is an act of self-decision, of moral agency. We must be on our guard, as I have indicated, against a static epistemic spread or else we confuse knowledge with being. What, then, do causal laws mean? *Factually*, a routine in nature; *nomically*, the potency for a determinate kind of activity.

Developments in modern physics are obviously away from eleaticism and from the kind of transcunt causality characteristic of the so-called mechanical view of the world. In field-theory transeunt causality seems to me to be a phase of the immanent causality of the field. And yet physical substances, such as electrons and protons, indicate a center of activity of a dominantly relational sort. It is only as these combine to secure a new wholeness and substantiality that immanent causality begins to emerge as something more localized and specific to be set over against transeunt causality. In a very real sense these become correlatives.

It is at the level of atoms and molecules that the idea of emergence gains its first definite applicability, though there are hints in physics of the emergence of matter from energy. But what is really implied by emergence? Surely, in order to become rational, it must secure an ontological status and be linked with substance and causality. To me it seems most plausible to connect it, as evolutionary naturalism does, not with natural piety but with causality. The fact of emergence must be explained in terms of the synthetic rise of higher-order substances or functionally unified continuants. We must take relations and organization seriously as characteristics of nature. What Professor Savery calls concatenism, which is a kind of effective togetherness, gives a better categorial context than does the atomism of purely external relations, whatever the latter may mean.

Suppose we put it in this fashion: emergence is an expression of an emergent causality which should be conceived as an activity of synthesizing upon the basis of a prior level of transeunt and immanent causality. As a term it points to the transition from transeunt to immanent causality, for it refers to the operations which make possible a higher level of substance and immanent causality. It is concerned with the genesis of what Locke called "real essences" and I would prefer to call complex constitutions. Transeunt causality involves a receiving from outside, immanent causality an activity dominantly internal, emergent, causality the process of integration into a new whole. There is, so far as I can see, nothing mysterious and unfactual about such an interpretation.

What follows? The Aristotelian must relinquish his fixed natural kinds and his eternal forms together with his vitalistic apparatus of potency and act. Activity must be intrinsic to a substance as a whole and not to some postulated factor in it. And it must pass along the lines of relations and organization. It is foolish to create abstracta called universals and then seek to project them into nature. The *ratio essendi* is the reverse. Ross suggests that Aristotle was moving in a more Ionic direction in the later books of his *Metaphysics*. I think he would have moved still further in that direction were it not for his teleological astronomy and his unwillingness to think in evolutionary terms. What we need today is a materialization of Aristotelianism. I shall have something more to say about this when I come to discuss *functional teleology*.

It was along these lines I was thinking in *Evolutionary Naturalism*. With all due respect for those great thinkers, Lloyd Morgan and S. Alexander, it has been my conviction that the first was too phenomenalistic in his epistemology and so was induced to fall back in his ontology on an Activity with a capital A. Substantialism would have avoided this separation. Activity would have been of the material substances themselves. And emergence could not escape a mysterious air in S. Alexander just because he had no substance in which emergent causality could operate. New qualities just emerged as factually as new colors apparently quiver into being in the sky. No; I believe that empirical realism and evolutionary substantialism alone show promise of making the idea of emergence rational.

It is clear that the fact of emergence must be distinguished from the ground of emergence much as the fact of evolution is distinguishable from the method of evolution. And here it seems to me that two basic points must be noted. The first may be stated thus: New properties do not emerge; what emerges are new substances. The second point concerns the kind of unity brought about by emergent causality and finding expression in immanent causality.

Strictly speaking, of course, properties do not emerge; it is the newly constituted substance which does so. Properties are not adjectival entities which float around mysteriously or come from nowhere in a mysterious fashion, nor are they entities stuck on to an inert substratum as Locke at his worst suggested. Properties are laws to the effect that, if certain conditions be fulfilled, certain facts can be noted. Thus water is *such that* it will boil under specified conditions. Science seeks to understand such a property by attention to the energy-structure of the molecule. Properties must express the *constitution* of the substance or complex of substances of which they are properties.

Locke, quite obviously, had something like this in mind when he talked of real essences. His epistemology was not realistic enough and his ontology too obscure.

What, then, shall we mean by the constitution of a substance? It is clearly something which can emerge through that kind of activity we have called emergent causality. In one direction it points toward genetic potentialities; in the other, toward a unified, or concatenated, togetherness. The active economy of a substance expresses its constitution; and its constitution depends upon the unified togetherness of its constituents. Once grant an active, or dynamic, nature to substance and it follows that we must think in terms of equilibria, wholeness, and dominance.

As I see it, immanent causality must be correlated with a type of togetherness in which causality is in some degree under the control of the constitution of a substance. In this situation a part-whole relation is asymmetrical with a whole-part relation. There is, so far as I can see, no *a priori* way of determining the tightness of the unity involved in higher-order substances. The economy here is so definitely temporal as well as spatial. It is interesting to note that what is apparent at the level of organisms has been shown by physics to apply, in terms of included rhythms, to the microscopic world. Such an outlook signifies the inseparability of activity and duration in substance. And we should expect that a higher-order substance would have rhythms of a longer temporal span than the included ones. How could it be otherwise? To deny it would be to deny the existence of the constituted unity of the new whole.

What I am driving at is that a higher-order substance must have both spatial and temporal unity. Without both we would have but atomism. Another point: the temporal unity is inseparable from the spatial constitution, and the spatial constitution, not being inert, depends upon the temporal rhythms. Only as space and time are taken in this fashion are they compatible with the underlying durational activity of a substance. The general economy of a substance demands the essential inseparability of structure and function. It seems that biologists have long realized this fact, which, I think, must be extended downward to simpler substances.

Here, again, I would suggest that ontology throws light upon, and supplements, epistemology. To the extent that science neglects the categorial setting of its facts it is in danger of a thinness in its interpretation. Its theoretical structure is unable to give meaning to its facts. A materialistic substantialist like myself feels that scientific knowledge about substances in their relations gets added meaning when we grasp it as knowledge about the economies of such substances in their spatial and temporal dimensions. In the strict sense physical time is always local and reflects a durational rhythm. And such rhythm is determined by the economy and constitution of the enduring substance. Such is the source and basis of time. Only by such an approach can, it seems to me, the traditional paradoxes be escaped. We get a sense of on-moving durational activity unattainable by mere eventism.

VI

Materialistic substantialism differs from Aristotelian substantialism in its stress upon relations, upon emergence, and upon enduring constitution. It does not look upon form as either artistically imposed or vitalistically presupposed. Hence it is more Ionic and refuses to dichotomize a substance into form and matter, actuality and potency. And yet it is grateful to the Stagirite for the suggestive handling of change and continuity. I take it, also, that only in terms of enduring substances with dynamic constitutions expressible in economies can we understand powers, aptitudes, habits, and dispositions. All this becomes empirical and obvious at the level of human beings. To human nature or the constitution of human beings, belong powers and aptitudes. And so complex is its economy that aptitudes may remain latent or may be developed. Again, the direction of the economy of a human being may activate a disposition or leave it dormant. Only in terms of emergence and complexification can this be understood. The self is no simple thing but involves an involution of organization within organization. Both external and internal knowledge indicate such a complicated pattern of endurance.

For any emergent view consciousness or togetherness-in-experiencing is of critical importance. This primary fact must be approached both genetically and functionally.

The functional interpretation, while tremendously significant, does not seem to me particularly baffling. From this point of view consciousness must be conceived as a qualitative dimension of the activity of the self expressive of, and significant for, the functional togetherness of the brain-mind. It would seem that here—and here alone—do we have *empirical verification of functional wholeness*. At least, this is the case if we take James's introspection as truer than Hume's form of mental atomism. And I take it that psychology has been moving in this direction. Since emergent causality implies both substantial and functional wholeness, we have here a confirmation of the theory. And, as I have so frequently pointed out, here by the very nature of the situation can the individual have some measure of inside information about a high-level substance. There is nothing about external knowledge, which is very abstract and descriptive, which conflicts with this quite obvious fact. I feel that consciousness must be correlated with the activity of a very complicated and enduring substance. It is for this reason that we all tend to think of it as an illumination rather than as a substance. Here we have a basic categorial problem. It is intrinsic to an activity and is isomorphic with it; but the activity is itself an expression of the activated substance. It is the old question of the inseparability of structure and function in the economy of any system. It is my opinion that we must take endurance and accumulation seriously and always regard the mind-brain as that which furnishes the matrix and medium of consciousness. In this fashion I am too much of a substantialist to be a panpsychist.

The genetic, or evolutionary, approach to the fact of consciousness turns for me on the above status of consciousness. Quite clearly, it is to be correlated with rather complicated functions. And it is something which appears and disappears with the passage from latency to activation. By its very nature we have nothing to contrast it with. It stands to me as an indication that *being* always has an intrinsic nature, that it is *not* qualitatively vacuous, to use Whitehead's term. The best our reason can do—it seems to me—is to ground consciousness in this basic qualitativeness of all substance. Here is its emergent potentiality. We cannot inspectively trace it in a genetic way, for the last term alone is open to inspection. But I can see no reason to assume a complete discontinuity. Consciousness, as I see it, is adjectival, expressive, intrinsic to functional activity. If emergent causality signifies the generation of higher-order substances we must expect basic novelties.

I must turn in conclusion to the question of teleology. My logical path is already indicated. An enduring wholeness with an immanent causal economy implies the rejection of eleatic mechanism. Science is already moving away from pictorial notions based on molar happenings. The field, relations, tensions, equilibria, become relevant terms. But evolutionary substantialism would emphasize immanent causality as the locus of anything akin to purpose.

It is important to get rid of dominance by mensurational time and to stress what I have called the source and basis of time. The more there is of immanent causality, the more important in the economy becomes functioning and its expression, order. It will be recalled that I asserted that all agency is durational like substance itself; that is, there are no mathematical instants in nature, no such existential discontinuity as Descartes supposed. It follows that any subsystem has its native durational rhythm. Wholeness must be conceived as temporal as well as spatial. The nature of a high-order substance involves activities so related that one spreads into another. It is this ordered packing of tendencies, habits and dispositions like an organic spring that accounts for ordered and integrated behavior. Purpose can be understood only on the background of durational organization. Events flow out from such an economy much as music takes its origin from a record, only here the connection is brought about externally by means of a needle sliding from one indentation to another.

What I am arguing for is a teleology of self-direction rather than a teleology of finalism, a teleology intrinsic to an economy which is both spatial and temporal. In such immanent causality traditional ideas of pushes from the past or pulls from the future are transcended. A high-order substance makes its own time in terms of its economy. In all this I am not forgetting that such immanent causality must be adjusted to the play of transeunt causality, for the organism must act in relation to its environment. But to the extent there is self-direction there is escape from blindness and chance. As I see it, the brain-mind is an organ for the highest type of self-direction.

Let me now state in conclusion some of the principles which any philosophy of nature should explore:

(1) The category of causality must be put in its ontological context, which is that of substantive being both endurant and spatial.

(2) Properly understood, categories involve one another.

(3) Aristotelianism must be profoundly modified by a shift which replaces a vitalistic form by an immanent organization.

(4) Realistic empiricism with the recognition of categorial meanings represents a more adequate epistemology than phenomenalistic empiricism.

(5) Relativity is epistemic and not ontological.

(6) The basis and source of time is activity within and between enduring substances.

(7) There are three main types of causality, transeunt, emergent, and immanent.

(8) Properties by themselves do not emerge but higher-order substances do.

(9) Consciousness is the only "natural isolate" we can be acquainted with. It shows that *being* has a qualitative dimension.

(10) Immanent causality is self-directional. Mind is the highest level of such functional, self-directional teleology.

PART II

The Development of Referential Physical Realism

INTRODUCTION TO ESSAYS

THE DEVELOPMENTAL NATURE of any tenable philosophy is one of its essential assets. The developmental nature of Professor Sellars' philosophy necessitates a more extended introduction than we are giving to Parts I, III, IV, and V. The stage needs an historical setting for this play of ideas. Twentieth century realisms in America have not been the simple thesis-antithesis types of development that earlier histories of the movement tended to depict.

It is specifically revealing to study the emergence and development of critical realism. Roy Wood Sellars first used the term in two articles in 1908[1]—a full two years before the publication of the "Program and First Platform of Six [Neo]Realists,"[2] and not in reaction to the earlier writings of any of the latter. Sellars had already, in his "A Fourth Progression in the Relation of Mind and Body,"[3] defined himself as a critical, naturalistic philosopher with a basic concern for the methods and findings of science. His criticisms, in that same year, of Dewey, James,

---

[1] "Critical Realism and the Time Problem I" and "Critical Realism and the Time Problem II." *Philosophy, Psychology, and Scientific Methods* (hereinafter referred to as *JP*), V (1908), 1, 542-548; 597-602.

[2] Edwin B. Holt *et al.*: "Program and First Platform of Six Realists," *JP*, VII (1910).

[3] *Psychological Review*, XIV (1907), 315-328.

Bradley, and the Kantians were realistic.[4] But the idealistic components in each of these viewpoints had real grounds.[5] In those earliest days, therefore, Sellars aimed toward a realism which did justice to the elements of fact underlying idealism while also giving full status to the non-mental realities to which human organisms have discriminatingly to adjust, as well as selectively and appropriately to employ. "Only a realism that passes through idealism," he wrote in 1908,[6] "can hold its ground," but this realism must recognize experience as "a characteristic of parts of our present world, *viz.*, the nervous system of men and animals,"[7] and not a feature of existence apart from the neural systems of organisms. "Qualitative changes in reality are quite possible,"[8] and there is strong evidence to support the view that these are functions of the self-organization (and, therefore, contra Aristotle, the self-forming) of quantitative materials; "reality is a self-conserving process in which organization and the qualitative in general are related to the quantitative aspect as the variant to the invariant. . . . Reality, as a complicated process, conserves the result of past activities in itself. These may be [stones, fossils, mountains],[9] star systems, Greek poems, or forms of government."[10] Thus, "the relation of the individual's experiencing to the rest of him which we call his body, as a part of reality, is the *vital metaphysical problem and the key to critical realism.*"[11]

Despite Sellars' wish to distinguish the kernels of truth and

---

[4] "The Nature of Experience," *JP*, IV (1907), 14-18; and "Professor Dewey's View of Agreement," *JP*, IV (1907), 432-435.

[5] Note in the readings Sellars' referrals to the idealistic elements in the philosophies of both James and Dewey.

[6] "Consciousness and Conservation," *JP*, V (1908), 238.

[7] "Critical Realism and the Time Problem I," *JP*, V (1908), 544.

[8] *Ibid.*

[9] *Ibid.*, 546.

[10] *Ibid.*, 547.

[11] "Critical Realism and the Time Problem II," *JP*, V, 598. Sellars adds a footnote at this point. "Since my solution of the mind-body problem emphasizes the reactive unity of the whole individual, just as Professor Dewey's does, a statement of the main difference may be worth while. This can best be brought out in connection with the note (p. 65) in his essay in the James 'Festschrift.' 'It is interesting to note how the metaphysical puzzles regarding "parallelism," "interaction," "automatism," evaporate when one ceases isolating the brain into a peculiar physical substrate of mind at large and treats it simply as one portion

value in philosophic idealism, idealisms and phenomenalisms were, at this stage, prime targets.[12] Pragmatists came into the picture because both Dewey and James swung "between realism and idealism"[13] in lieu of "passing through" idealism. None of the realists as such gets any reference in the 1907 and 1908 articles,* though C. A. Strong, who was later to identify himself with critical realism, is treated for his panpsychism. Sellars was working, quite independently, on a broad base to find and develop "the neglected alternative"[14] which even the later realists were to fail to discriminate. His was both a basic and a con-

---

[12] The idealists with whom he is generally concerned are Bradley, Taylor, Bosanquet and James Ward; the phenomenalists: Karl Pearson and Ernst Mach Lippman. In contrast to the writers of the Eastern Seaboard, Sellars gives Royce rather incidental treatment. Cf. e.g., "An Important Antinomy," PR, XV (1908), 237, where he has two sentences on Royce: "A slightly different form of this antinomy including the traditional Kantian emphasis on man's reason as law-giver to nature is given by Professor Royce: 'But we, of course, all recognize a sense in which man is to be conceived as a part of nature; while, on the other hand, nothing is clearer than that for us, all our beliefs about nature are determined by conditions which belong in one respect to the mind of man.' "

[13] In James' *Principles of Psychology* Schneider points out a swing between psychological introspectionism and biological naturalism with attention rather equally divided between them. Elsewhere also James displays a shifting between subjectivism and realism, though also with a recourse to ill-defined working values to resolve the conflict.

[14] A phrase to which he gives special emphasis later. In "Levels of Causality . . . ," PPR, 1959, he states: "It was this hidden alternative between traditional presentationalism and Lockean representationalism which I early tried to find. I called it critical realism. It is direct referential realism." "It is always the *hidden* alternative which is hard to find." In "Sensations as Guides to Perceiving" (Mind, LXV, No. 269, p. 5) he wrote: "Since I was a contributor to the American series in the thirties, my analyses may have historical interest. At least, it may call attention to a neglected possibility." In "Referential Transcendence" (PPR, XXII, Sept. 1961) he announced: "My argument shall be in terms of a neglected alternative." The failure of all of the philosophical "isms" to do justice to the interrelations of conceptual knowledge required a reanalysis in terms of both practical and scientific knowledge.

* There is a scant one sentence reference to "the new realism" as a logical realism" which has "overcome confusions due to the special viewpoint of psychology" ("Critical Realism and Time Problem I" HPV, 1908, p. 598).

---

of the body, as the instrumentality of adaptive behavior.' This is distinctly the objective, biological, outlook, and might well have been written, say, by Jennings. Instead of passing through and beyond subjectivism to an adequate conception of the individual, Professor Dewey has taken refuge in the impersonal objectivism of science."

flationary approach. He sought the foundations of a realism which not only excluded the extravagances of what Peirce called "happy thoughts" yet included the factors that were the occasions of such thoughts. It was not, however, only idealism, phenomenalism, and pragmatism that were thus to be taken into account but, first and foremost, natural realism—and, ere long, neo-realism, and soon again the "essence" variety of critical realism.[15] Even the "intentionalist" wing of critical realism, with which he had closest affinity, neglected the evolutionary, biological basis of intentionality. It is not surprising, in consequence, that Sellars came to distinguish his critical realism from that of the intentionalist triad: Lovejoy, Pratt, Rogers. "I believe," he asserted in 1963, "that I, alone, explored the biological bases of perceiving."[16]

Let us now attempt to set this historical development in more definitive perspective. America had a notable number of philosophers early in the 1900's writing in variously realistic veins: Woodbridge and Montague of Columbia, Fullerton of Pennsylvania, Perry and Holt of Harvard, Spaulding of Princeton, Pitkin of Rutgers, Pratt of Williams, McGilvary of Wisconsin, Sellars of Michigan, Boodin of California, Macintosh of Yale, Lovejoy of Johns Hopkins, Cohen of C.C.N.Y., to mention a scattering of these.[17] Two relatively coordinated efforts developed among some of these realists in the periods of 1910-1912 and 1915-1920: the neo-realists publishing their "Program and First Platform" in 1910[18] and *The New Realism* in 1912;[19] the critical realists offering their *Essays in Critical Realism* in 1920.[20]

Sellars, whose realism had begun to take form in 1906-1908,

---

[15] Later still, his "Conflation of Philosophical Positions" was to attempt to isolate and demonstrably integrate essential and important features of behaviorism, logical empiricism, existentialism, and philosophical analysis.

[16] "Direct Referential Realism." *Dialogue*, II (1963), 2, 136.

[17] Cf. particularly, Victor E. Harlow, *Bibliography and Genetic Study of American Realism* (hereinafter referred to as BGS), Harlow Publishing Co., 1931. See also Montague, W. P., "The Story of American Realism" *Ways of Things* (New York, Prentice-Hall), 1940.

[18] *JP*, II (1910).

[19] *New Realism: Cooperative Studies in Philosophy*, New York, Macmillan Company, 1912.

[20] Durant Drake, Editor, Macmillan Company, New York, publisher.

was, we have indicated, the initial formulator of a "critical realism." Douglas C. Macintosh, the philosopher of religion the denial of whose citizenship became a *cause celebre*, was reportedly the second user of the term.[21] Macintosh could not accept the essence doctrine propounded by Santayana, Drake, and Strong, and therefore refused an invitation to participate in the *Esseys on Critical Realism*. He was, thereupon, along with others, labelled an "unofficial" realist, though he had published under the label of critical realism in 1913 and had detailed realistic chapters in a tome on *The Problem of Knowledge*—in 1915—five years before the *Essays in Critical Realism*.

How now did it happen that six realists joined with R. W. Sellars in the publication of the *Essays* in 1920? Sellars relates conversationally[22] that Durant Drake visited him in Ann Arbor following the publication of the former's *Critical Realism* in 1916[23] and asked whether it would be acceptable to him if six realists,[24] who were planning a critical volume on realism, were to use the title Sellars had adopted—with the latter sharing in the volume. On Sellars' agreement to this proposal, Drake, as editor, secured the approval of the others.

The outcome was the combining of two quite different "gambits" in non-presentational realism, the second of which divided later into two sub-groups. Sellars summarizes: "there were [thus] three strands in critical realism: (1) the notion of mind—as having the power of self-transcendence [held by the "intentionalists"], (2) the essence doctrine; and (3) the re-analysis of perceiving as a referential operation guided by sensations and founded on a biological mechanism of the sensori-motor type. In all three there was the search for a direct realism as against Lockeanism. All three held that presentationalism [of the Neo-Realists] was not the answer."[25]

---

[21] Cf. BGS, 73n-74n.

[22] In Ann Arbor, June, 1968.

[23] Rand McNally & Company, *Critical Realism* is hereinafter referred to as CR.

[24] Besides Santayana, Drake, and Strong, the group included James B. Pratt, Arthur Rogers, and Arthur O. Lovejoy.

[25] "American Realism: Perspective and Framework," in *Self, Religion and Metaphysics,* Gerald E. Myers, editor (New York, Macmillan, 1961), 174-200.

This was in 1920. In 1908-1916, critical realism was a realism informed by science, in contrast to natural realism, and which had coped basically with the issues which had given rise to idealism. J. E. Boodin's attack on "critical realism"—he held it to be a presumptuous labelling of Neo-Realism as naive—is both chronologically and simplistically in error.[26]

Similarly inaccurate, as I have shown elsewhere,[27] are Montague's claims that none of the critical realists advanced beyond the epistemological dualism of Locke,[28] that realism had become bogged in its own inherent inadequacies,[29] and that, as Schneider writes, Realists had turned to other issues which were "more attractive and more general."[30] However one interprets the critical realism of the other six—and a good claim can be made that each of them went *significantly* beyond Locke— none of these criticisms was applicable to Sellars. Though explicitly dualistic in his early epistemology, he insistently, as he later states, explored the mechanism of perceiving, and over decades developed a scientifically documented theory of the referential component in perception and of the processes by which reference enters into, and is validated in, both perceptual and scientific knowledge. In his *Evolutionary Naturalism*, further, he tied these processes in with a biological realism thereby giving his epistemology a demonstrably ontological basis. This, in turn, he showed to be capable of a far-reaching axiological and social development.

Professor Sellars' philosophy is, accordingly, an excellent instance of the processes of development that all except impossibly one-sided philosophies need to undergo. Whitehead, in paraphrase, has said that every philosophy has two expositors: one states the view adequately but inconsistently; the other carries certain basic features to their explicit conclusions. It

---

[26] "Functional Realism," *Addresses and Proceedings of the American Philosophical Association*, 1933, 147.

[27] "The Mote in the Eye of the Critic of Critical Realism," PPR, XXVI, (1965), 35-50.

[28] In "The Story of American Realism," *Ways of Things* (New York, Prentice Hall), 1940, p. 254ff.

[29] *Ibid.*, 255-259.

[30] Herbert Schneider, *Sources of Contemporary Philosophic Realism in America*, New York, Bobbs Merrill, 1964, 23.

is a fortunate circumstance in which the two expositors are the same man in different stages of intellectual advancement. This is distinctively true of Professor Sellars, though between the two stages we have developments in critical realism involving the essence and intentionalist wings. It is the genius of Sellars to have used these formulations as foils for the clarification and development of his distinctive position.

The fact of *development* applies pre-eminently to Sellars' epistemology. I have mentioned his quest of a critical realism in two of his articles in 1908. He began this quest in two other articles published early that year. We include the relevant excerpts from one of these sources. He had from the first been concerned with the role of concepts and categories in knowing. Witness the epochal course on "Main Concepts of Science" he began offering in 1910,[31] and his publications in 1908, 1909, and subsequently, on "Space," "Time," "Causality," "A Thing and its Properties," and the categories of knowledge in distinction from the categories of things, etc. His critical realism was thus a development collateral with that of the new realism yet extending over five decades.

One can indeed distinguish two motifs in his philosophy: one relatively recessive up to about 1920 yet moving to the fore; the other dominant in this earlier period but becoming ancillary in the twenties; both essential to philosophy. We can characterize the early dominant motif as the analysis of concepts. This relates him both to earlier rationalistic and idealistic systems and also to recent developments in critical analytic philosophy. Sellars' analyses are different from both the antecedent and most of the more recent modes of analysis—and he differs precisely at the point of his dynamic, yet critical, functional realism.

His work on the concepts has striking examples: referential realism and emergent naturalism are two such examples, and the concept of consciousness as a physical category a rather

---

[31] The first statement of this course in the University of Michigan Catalogue (1910-11) reads: "Philosophical implications and fundamental conceptions of science. Place of general concepts in science. Main conceptions employed in the synthesis of physics, chemistry, biology. What they imply. How they subserve the knowledge of nature. Their necessary conditions and limits."

close third. Less dramatic, yet no less functional instances, are his focal concerns between 1908 and 1916: Time, Space, Causality, Thinghood. Substance as thinghood is indispensable. Our typical question when confronted by an obtrusive stimulus is: "What is that?"

His course on "Main Concepts of Science," was the outgrowth of his articles and his thesis. These, in turn, became the basis of his first major publication in philosophy, his *Critical Realism*. In the Preface he wrote:

> "Science offers us measurements of things and statements of their properties, *i.e.*, their effects upon us and upon other things . . . but it unconsciously swings ever more completely away from the assumption that physical things are open to our inspection or that copies of them are open to our inspection.
> . . . [And] I immediately saw how Berkeley's arguments could be outflanked. They are based on a conception of knowledge which did not [now] hold for science. The scientist as such was not aware of the problem nor was he in a position to see the exact bearing of his own results on epistemology. That was the task of the philosopher."[32]

Analysis of concepts becomes indeed analysis of the meaning of ideas in functional relations. His chapter in *Critical Realism*, "Is Consciousness Alien to the Physical?" is a paradigm instance. We shall include Professor Sellars' own summary of this in Part III ("The Mind-Body Test Case"). In 1920, he elaborated the meaning and role of basic conceptions in an article on "The Status of the Categories." There he wrote: "If the individual's field of experience is a growth which reflects—if it does not do more—the active interplay of organism and environment, we need not be surprised that it contains distinctions of significance."[33] He proceeds to elaborate the more basic distinctions: things, spatial interactions, self.

Sellars' resultant summary, comprising pp. 235-239 of his article in vol. 30 of *The Monist* (1920), is included in Part II of the readings. Primary "knowledge is a function of the capacities of the organism under stimulation by its environment. These capacities correspond to different levels, and their opera-

---

[32] *CR*, vi.
[33] *The Monist*, XXX (1920), 226.

tion finally results in cognitive ideas directed toward affirmed existents. *The standard elements and distinctions of this knowledge are the categories.*"[34]

That the nature and role of the basic categories continues to be a fundamental concern is shown in his later articles: "Critical Realism and Substance" (1929),[35] "Verification of Categories: Existence and Substance" (1943),[36] "Causality and Substance" (1943).[37] Yet the categories come to be conceived as derivative components in a complex pattern of directed responses to particular entities relating to the survival of the organism and the service of its interests. The idea of directed response was the recessive element in Sellars' early writings.

In its first stages, Professor Sellars was epistemologically dualistic in his critical realism. He published at least one article as an avowed epistemological dualist.[38] But the beginnings of a direct referential realism were already there. In 1912 he had denied that there was any special cognitive relation. Knowledge, the idealists had maintained, is an internal relation; you cannot separate subject and object. You cannot even conceive of anything existing except in relation to a mind. Reality is thus vacuous apart from a constituting mind. Neo-realists, in turn, urged that knowledge was an external, not a constitutive, relation; knowing as such does not directly produce or directly modify external things or existents.

In his article in 1912 asking the question "Is there a Cognitive Relation?" Sellars denied that there is a special relation that comprises cognition. Cognition is an attitude issuing in a complex of activity and achievement.[39] The precise nature of this activity and the grounds for its claim of access to external things has to await a rather extensive development. In his *Critical Realism* he had used the notion of reference, but its instrumenta-

---

[34] *Ibid.*, 235.
[35] *Mind*, XXXVIII, 473-488.
[36] *JP*, XL, 197-205.
[37] *PR*, LII, 1-27.
[38] "Epistemological Dualism versus Metaphysical Dualism," PR, XXX(1921), 482-493.
[39] *JP*, IX, 226, 231, etc.

tion was social. It involved "the correspondence of my means of organizing objects with yours. . . . Such reference as knowledge demands is worked out within experience" by this social coordination.[40] The biological mechanism is not yet envisaged. This buds quite clearly in the twenties. In the *Principles and Problems of Philosophy* (1926), he wrote that in perception the

> "Organism attends to, turns toward, selects, behaves in relation to, things, and thus makes them its objects. Hence we should not speak of things as though they were *objects* in their own right. They are existents in their own right, but they are objects of the organism's *behavior*[41] and conscious attention. 'Object' is thus a relative term and implies an activity focussed upon a thing. It is for this reason that we speak of a thing as an object. . . .
>
> "The following diagram indicates the double relation between a thing and a percipient organism:

> The lower continuous line represents the causal relation from the thing to the organism, while the upper, discontinuous line represents the cognitive, perceptual relation."[42]

Later, he modifies this diagram to have two continuous arrowed lines which he calls the "from-and-to circuit" (or "circuit of return") and to maintain that perceptual cognition is built around organic response, that sensations are signs not percepts, that feedback elicits the development of conceptions which assist the adjustment and specific adequacies of the response. Perceptual knowledge is thus an achievement of highly developed organisms. There are rudimentary parallels in other animals from pecking chicks to Köhlerian apes. On these levels sensations may also function as guides and signals, but in man they are put to a "more overt cognizing use."[43] Man has evolved to a level in which perceptual reference is capable of elaboration in terms of patterns of relations and functional meanings. These may be extensive spatially, temporally, con-

---

[40] *CR*, 193.
[41] Italics added.
[42] *Principles and Problems of Philosophy* (hereinafter referred to as PPP), New York, Macmillan, 1926, 122.
[43] Paper in symposium in tribute to Marvin Farber, 1968.

ceptually, logically, and imaginatively. This is a level distinctively higher than that of guided animal response.

By 1932, Sellars could, therefore, write: "If the expression, epistemological dualism, stands for anything more than the recognition of the mechanism of knowing, I reject it."[44] And in 1939: "critical realism in my opinion has nothing to do with dualism of any variety."[45] Epistemological dualism was and is the persistent view that what we directly perceive are our own sensations, or complexes of sensations, or our own ideas and experiences.[46] We may infer external objects or instinctively believe in them but what we experience is purely subjective. Yet the functional approach which Sellars found to be a basic ingredient of both common sense and biological science (including psychology) yields a very different result. Sensations are our cues to seeing, and ideas are "the windows" through which we

---

[44] *The Philosophy of Physical Realism* (New York, Macmillan), 1932, vi.

[45] "A Clarification of Critical Realism," *Philosophy of Science*, VI, 1939, 420.

[46] Professor Norman Melchert contends that Sellars never was an epistemological dualist in this sense (Cf. *Realism, Naturalism, and the Mind*, 81-82). It is my contention that Professor Sellars had a recessive anti-dualist referentialism in his earlier writings, but that the object of direct awareness, and the actually existing entity to which we relate our immediate experience are different. Professor Melchert quotes Sellars as stating in "Epistemological Dualism versus Metaphysical Dualism" (1921) that all he means by epistemological dualism is that "one's idea in knowledge is numerically distinct from the object known . . ." Yet in the Preface to *Critical Realism* (1916) he writes that "it is to the triad consisting of subject, idea-object . . . and physical existent that critical realism calls attention," and that science "unconsciously swings ever more completely away from the assumption that physical things are open to our inspection . . ." (vi). In the article referred to by Melchert above, though he offers ameliorating considerations, Sellars does not clearly see his way out of the problem posed by the idea that idea-objects are different from the things they are presumed to characterize. He continued indeed to hold that only the objects of introspection are open to inspection. It seems evident to me that this difficulty begins to be more clearly surmounted with some shift in the focus of his inquiry and with the aid of developments in neurology. He is then able to elaborate a direct, referential realism with the notion of at least a germ of awareness (though not of inspection *per se*), along with the mechanism of response, at its core. 1926 is a turning point in his writings, as his first usage of the "from-and-to circuit" evidences. The conception of ideas as channels of knowledge rather than as objects *per se*—soon follows (in *Contemporary American Philosophy*, II, 1930). The difference between the later and earlier views seems in consequence to involve an elaboration and readjustment of conceptions.

see. Sellars' biological naturalism had enabled him from the beginning to have a referential component in his theory of perceiving. It is this feature that enabled him to develop a direct rather than inferential realism. It is the development of the referential focus of perceptual knowledge and the processes of its refinement and validation that extends into the sixties of this century. His articles on "Referential Transcendence" (1961) and "Direct Referential Realism" (1963) add to a notably informative article on "Sensations as Guides to Perceiving" (1959).

Hypothetically it may seem possible to have a direct yet critical realism without a monistic metaphysics. Indeed, the editor's teacher, Douglas C. Macintosh, who was one of the very earliest, after Professor Sellars, to adopt the caption of "critical realism" and to give it an epistemologically monistic formulation,[47] was a metaphysical dualist.

It is also preliminarily possible, as we have noted in Sellars' development, to have a monistic metaphysics and a dualistic epistemology. It is Sellars' growing contention, however, that an intelligible realism is a referential realism and that the cosmological basis for referential realism is an evolutionary naturalism, and therefore, that a critically referential realism and evolutionary naturalism go together. The referential factor in perceiving, in short, gains importance from his biological naturalism, and this in turn from his emergent evolution.

The element of development in Sellars' *evolutionary naturalism* is not as sharp as in his critical realism. There are, however, discriminable stages: 1) from a rather general naturalism evident in "A Fourth Progression in the Relation of Mind and Body" (1907) to the acknowledgment of points of emergence in nature of distinctively new functions with new levels of material organization. We have already noted that in his *Evoluntionary Naturalism* (1922), Professor Sellars anticipated the emergent evolutionisms of both Lloyd Morgan and Samuel Alexander. Sellars' emergent evolution was not only an earlier statement

---

[47] D. C. Macintosh, *JP*, X (1913), 701; also Macintosh, *The Problem of Knowledge* (New York, Macmillan), 1915, 310ff, pp. 476ff. Cf. Victor E. Harlow, *BGS*, 1913, 73-74.

of the principle of emergence, but a completely naturalistic formulation. Diversity in self-organization, not chance or *nisus*, is the source of novelty. Mind arises as a mode of guidance in nature. It perpetuates itself and evolves through further biological organization that serves the organic species.

2) From a stage of insistence that evolutionary naturalism was not materialism to a reformed materialism. The older materialisms had done a crude job of accounting for the mind and human values and therewith of accounting for themselves. As early as 1907, Sellars found that in the attempt to answer the question, what is an individual?, our conclusion must be in terms of naturalistic dynamisms and process and not in terms of either idealism or materialism,[48] "Why Naturalism and Not Materialism?" he asked as late as 1927. An adequate naturalism must not be reductive. But in 1944 he asks, "Is Naturalism Enough?" And in a review of *Naturalism and the Human Spirit* in 1945, he explains why the tenuous methodological kind of thing that has been treated as naturalism is not enough. Literally, it has no "substance" or foundation. The notion of organization which is fundamental to emergent evolution is the organization of entities and so of substances. The notion of events without substantial content is one of real vacuity. We require a naturalism in which substance is an essential ingredient. If naturalism has been appropriated for an almost purely methodological system, we must reform materialism so that it includes what emergent naturalism has enabled Sellars to understand. "The New Materialism," "Reformed Materialism and Intrinsic Endurance," "Materialism and Human Knowing," "Can a Reformed Materialism do Justice to Values?" are four of his articles at this stage. The second is the most basic ontologically and is our selection for the concluding article of Part II. The concept of matter becomes a far richer concept than in the earlier materialisms. It becomes a concept which accounts operationally and realistically for both the theory of knowledge and the theory of values, and for a theory of responsible, agential causality.

---

[48] "A Fourth Progression in the Relation of Mind and Body" *Psychological Review*, XIV (1907), pp. 303-4. Cf. also "Consciousness and Conservation" (1908) and "Critical Realism and the Time Problem I" and II (1908).

Sellars' critical realism and emergent materialism are integral facets of a single intellectual perspective. Indeed his first major article on "A Fourth Progression in the Relation of Mind and Body" (1907), relates science, epistemology, cosmology and ontology. And in 1918, he states explicitly that "critical realism is a form of physical realism."[49] Referential realism, in turn, is a biopsychological realism and has its grounds therefore in evolved physical organisms in physical, as well as socio-cultural, environments.

The wealth of materials on the development of this emergent realism can only be demonstrated by inviting attention to the Sellars' bibliography at the end of this volume. The need for selection has necessarily meant that there are significant omissions. The student or scholar can, of course, explore these sources without basic difficulty.

IN QUEST OF A FUNCTIONALLY DEFINITIVE REALISM

    1. In "An Important Antinomy" (1908)
    2. In "Critical Realism and Time Problem I" and "Critical Realism and Time Problem II" (1908)

An Important Antinomy*

What, however, is realism, and what is a realistic attitude towards a thing? This we are in a position to define more clearly. Starting, as I believe metaphysics must, from an individual's conscious experience, realism signifies that things are independent for their existence of his experience of them. In short, my experience does not affect the things around my body in any way unless it leads to an overt action on the part of my body. I may think about the book before me in any manner I choose but, until I take it up, an act mediated by my body, it is not changed. This does not mean that the book is as it is experienced as independently of my experience of it. That would be naïve realism, which, like idealism, is a stuff-theory of reality. Realism, as I have defined it, is not concerned, at least at first, with the character of the stuff of reality but with the relationship of the

---

[49] "On the Nature of our Knowledge of the Physical World," PR, XVII, 502.
* Psychological Review, XV (1908), 243-249.

'microcosm' of the individual's experience with the 'macrocosm' of reality and the conclusion we have been forced to arrive at from a study of the dilemma is that nature has two meanings, my nature, a construct in my experience, and nature as *other than* my experience.

Now these 'microcosms,' or minds, seem to be intimately associated with certain peculiarly differentiated and organized nodes of this 'macrocosm.' This primacy of the brain was expressed above in the first thesis, "the proper consequence of (*a*) appears to be that everything else is a state of my brain." Consequently our problem has changed into the brain-mind relation, for, in the brain, microcosm and macrocosm meet. Can any clue be found to rede the riddle? I think so—*consciousness is a variant.*[1] An experience, once gone, is gone forever. The Heracleitean flux is surely true of the stream of consciousness. My approach, then, has led me to a possible solution of the old problem of change and permanence, or change and conservation. Reality is a process but a stereometrical and conserving process and a careful reflection finds no reason why activity should involve destruction of the capacity for action on the part of reality, every reason, however, why activity should imply changes. As a matter of fact, conservation of the capacity of reality (conservation of energy) exists and there is also change, since transformations of energy are as evident as quantitative identity. Now change involves variancy of some sort. But consciousness, as we have seen, is a variant. Does this not lead us to the position that consciousness is the variant of the change-process of that part of reality called the pallium or cortex? The macrocosm thus embraces consciousness, does not reject it as alien. This result is further enforced by the facts of death and sleep. When the brain ceases to function, consciousness disappears. Such a functional identity is hinted at by Höffding though his double-aspect theory prevented his realization of it. "Sensations, thoughts and feelings are mental activities which cannot persist when the definite individual connection in which they occur, has come to an end. *They correspond to the*

---

[1] Cf. *Journal of Philosophy,* etc., Vol. V., No. 9, 'Consciousness and Conservation.'

organic functions (italics mine), but not to the chemical elements. If the organism is resolved into its elements, organic function is impossible."

It is highly probable that a question may arise in some reader's mind with respect to the relation of variant and invariant, so I hasten to make my position clearer on this point. It is, in a certain sense, the application of a double-aspect theory to reality. Reality is a process, everything in modern science cries this aloud, but it is somehow a self-conserving process. Dynamics precedes statics. "From motion we attain the notion of force or energy, by means of which equilibrium becomes intelligible."[1] But dynamics in no wise precludes change nor does it negate permanence and lawfulness. The category of process, then, contains in itself both attributes in peaceful contiguity. The invariant is not a thing somehow related to another thing called the variant in a most paradoxical fashion, it is not an atom or a piece of so-called energy, and any question as to whether the variant or invariant is effective in the process of reality is, therefore, absurd and results from a misunderstanding. Reality, as a process, may be regarded from the side of conservation, and this gives its invariant aspect, for us stated in terms of phenomenal energy; or from the side of change or variancy and here we are fortunately, direct participators, we experience change immediately. We are, in short, dealing with distinctions, not with things, and there is no reason why we should reify these aspects of the reality-process and thereupon bewilder ourselves in the attempt at their relation.

* * * * *

We have gleaned two things at least . . . There are weighty reasons for belief in the efficacy of consciousness and the clue seems to rest in the relation of function and structure and thus to growth and organization. But death and disease or disintegration of any kind show that *organization is also a variant in the process of reality.* What could be more natural than to conclude that these are related directly? What stands in our way? Not

---

[1] Höffding, *The Problems of Philosophy*, p. 91.

conservation of energy, for we have surmounted that, but mechanism. And here is where the doctrine of grades of causal relation comes into use.¹ Reactions are undoubtedly selective in organisms, enzymes² and even in chemical elements. I have not decided yet whether resonance in physics can be brought under the same idea. The type of causal process depends apparently on the organization of the interacting nodes of reality. This is what one would expect, and only the atomism of mechanical theory can have prevented its recognition for so long. Man, of course, with his tremendously delicate and complex functional organization presents the highest type of causal reaction, ordinarily called teleological. If we look at the process temporally and call the antecedent, conceptually delimited in a continuous process,³ the cause, and the consequent, the effect, there is of course in such a system no loss or gain of energy or capacity. But this is true of any such system and represents the aspect of conservation in a process. It, therefore, misses some vital aspect since it has no qualitative differentia for different processes, only differences in time coming to the fore. But if we pay attention to space and to the time during which certain amounts of energy are transformed and to the organization of the interacting 'nodes' of reality in any causal process system, marked differences appear. . . .⁴ Höffding . . . has this view almost in his grasp when he says, "Maxwell himself recognizes that geometrical as well as dynamic concepts are indispensable to the explanation of nature. In contrast to the dynamic, the geometric denotes simultaneity."⁵ This explains in part why I have always called reality a stereometrical process with grades of organization and kinds of differentiation and, hence, degrees in selective reaction and influence. This in no wise conflicts with conservation, which is a temporal idea. Here is, I believe,

---

[1] Cf. 'Consciousness and Conservation,' *Journal of Philosophy*, etc., Vol. V., No. 9.

[2] Cf. *Science*, February 14, 1908, Chittenden.

[3] Cf. Bradley, *Principles of Logic*, p. 488.

[4] V. *Vorlesung über Natur-Philosophie*, p. 325, 'Regelung der Reaktionsgeschwindigkeit durch räumliche Bedingungen.'

[5] *Problems*, p. 93.

a theory which may give articulation to the dissatisfaction with mechanism so widely current in late years among scientists themselves.

To sum up. By means of a study of an antinomy and the mind-body relation, I have sought to prove that we can handle reality as it is about our body even while it is independent for its existence, of our consciousness. This position affirms that the true starting-point for metaphysics is the individual and his experience, not experience-in-general, and that in the mind-body problem nearly all the critical questions can be seen to focus. The realism we obtained is not a stuff-theory and is perfectly compatible with personal idealism, since consciousness is embraced by reality. Just because it is not a stuff-theory, in the old sense, it cannot be called materialism or energism, for these are logical realisms, *i.e.*, result from the reification of concepts. It is not an idealism, in the old sense, also, *because there may be kinds of variants* of which consciousness is but the one concomitant with that peculiarly organized and differentiated part of reality called the nervous system. Furthermore, this position is pluralistic in regard to the acknowledgment of separate centers of the experiencing. The doctrine of functional identity or variancy implies this. I cannot have your experience, *i.e.*, my experience cannot be numerically identical with yours any more than my body can be your body. This position makes *communication on the basis of interpretation* possible. The monads, if one wishes so to call these 'microcosms,' thus get their windows through the body and its dynamic relations to other bodies. This agrees with logic, apperception, language and comparative psychology.

Critical Realism and the Time Problem. I (1908)*

. . . Absolute idealism generally takes refuge in experience-in-general or in a changeless fusion of changing and empirically-unconserved experiences. Mr. Bradley declares, "If time is not unreal, I admit our absolute is a delusion" ("Appearance and Reality," p. 206). Space forbids a critical study of absolute idealism, but this I will say: that disregard of, or lack of explana-

---

* *JP*, V, 1 (1908), 544-547.

tion for, the patent facts of our experience is characteristic of it, and any position that acknowledges and explains these facts is, therefore, preferable. Personal idealism either lapses into panpsychism or, in order to avoid, pluralism, must supplement itself with critical realism. In a recent article, I have sought to show how this last movement can take place. (*Psychological Review*, July, 1908.) Naturally enough, a mystic theism may satisfy those who are not interested mainly in science and who believe in immortality, preexistence and creationalism.

Critical realism,** although it regards experience as a characteristic of parts of our present world, viz., the nervous system of men and animals, is not forced to assume that this was the case in the past. Qualitative changes in reality are quite possible. As I understand it, critical realism believes that the things a man handles are independent of his experience for their existence. The word "thing," like the word "nature," has two meanings, as I have recently indicated, and these must not be confused. A table-experience is a physical-thing experience and is objective, but it is not the same as the thing as an existence in dynamic continuity with my body as an existence. The double use of the word "know," in this connection, has also led to misunderstanding.

*Critical realism*** is compelled to meet the problem of permanence and change. "The central paradox consists in the assertion that only the identical and permanent can change" (Taylor, "Elements of Metaphysics," p. 159). Why is this a paradox? It seems to me that Mr. Taylor has so defined his terms as to make them contradictories. It is no wonder, then, that they conflict. The pressure of change in the world around us and in our lives should have led him to a critical examination of his categories, for it is better to modify concepts than to ignore facts. Can we, by taking process as the fundamental category, make the relations of permanence and change more fluid, so to speak, and overcome this abrupt *Verstandsantithese?*

Process portrays, to my mind, the dynamic character of reality. It signifies that "to be" is "to be active." By working from this category we can avoid the problem of a substratum or substance or identity which somehow possesses change or of

---
** Italics added.

which change is an adjective. This position is in accord with modern science at its best. A chemical reaction is no longer regarded as a mere exchange of partners, but as a complex process of establishing equilibrium in a disturbed system of energies. Rest is, also, explained by motion, not motion by rest. A complete reversal is thus made from the static view of permanence to the dynamic view of process.

But how can the demand for stability and continuance be satisfied in this apparent return to Heracliteanism? In two ways: First, conservation is an experimental fact which, unlike permanence, does not exclude change, but implies it. Second, organization supplies a relatively persistent structure to reality.

Organization is not an entity, but the form, εἶδος—to use an Aristotelian word—and its persistence does not involve an entity or atomic view of reality any more than the relative persistence of about the same meanings in consciousness involves the preservation of the same pulse of consciousness. Organization may be analyzed into structure and function. A clear idea of "form" can be obtained from a critical study of Aristotle. His failure completely to overcome the Platonic dualism between "ideas" and spatial things, the timeless and the temporal, permanence and change, the one and the many, matter and form, is extremely suggestive. These dualisms are really varied expressions of exactly the same dualism, and all have their roots in the embarrassment of permanence and change. Granted the timelessness and the universality of the forms, and potentiality and change must reside in matter alone. Standing upon the results of modern science and epistemology, is it possible for us so to reform his idea of form as to escape these dualisms and, also, to free it from any shadow of a logical realism? I think this result is made possible by an elimination of timelessness from form.

A few words in regard to Aristotle's epistemology may bring out more distinctly the view of "form" which I am seeking to present. According to the usual Greek theory, like could only be known by like. This led inevitably to a logical realism and, thence, to the dualisms referred to above. Now, suppose we believe that reality, as a process, organizes itself in various ways and that we, through experimentation and reflection, involving actual handling and dissection of parts of reality, can comprehend this organization on both the structural and functional sides, this comprehension, on our part, does not imply that the organization is an entity residing in the various things. Such an hypostatization must be avoided at all hazard, for it is responsible for a great many false problems. It is this comprehension of the "form" of things, which, as I shall show, often changes very slowly or is constantly repeated in like things, that lifts knowledge above the psychological relativism of the concrete situation as such.

Accordingly, if we conceive reality as a stereometrical process more complicated in some portions than in others (this being explained by evolution), yet constantly in the moving stress of the reciprocal adaptation and self-achievement of its parts, we can gain the idea of an immanent change in no wise opposed to the conservation of energies or capacities. In Aristotelian language, we must commence with ἐνέργεια, and this requires nothing of the nature of an "unmoved mover" for its explanation, since there is no foil of a passive matter. Furthermore, avoiding the usual philosophical fault of extremes, we must protest against the objection that such a position lapses into the doctrine of flux. Philosophy has been ridden too long by violent contrasts like free-will and determinism, material and spiritual, mechanism and teleology, permanence and change; for it has, in being so ruled, shown a lack of balance and of feeling for fine discriminations. Let us be empirical enough to recognize that all things do not change with equal rapidity. Stones are fairly permanent in structure and function—witness the pyramids and cathedrals—so are fossils, and the mountains have stood in all ages as symbols of unchangingness. Ephemeræ rise and perish in a day, while man is able to maintain an equilibrium of anabolism and katabolism for some threescore years. Change is a comparative term, and to call the universe a process does not imply that the organization or "forms" of its parts vary in monotonous uniformity. A process is capable of differential organization—this is the essential significance of evolution—and these forms may have all degrees of stability from that of the so-called atom to the shifting variancy of the higher cortical areas.

I have sought to prove that real time is identical with change; that reality, as a process, is complicated; and that the more complicated a part is, the greater the complexity and the intensity of change. . . .

Critical Realism and the Time Problem. II[*]

In a previous article, I sought to show that real time is identical with change in a self-conserving process; that the puzzle of permanence or identity and change no longer balks advance when "process" is made the prime category; that a complete reversal of outlook in modern times makes the adoption of a "process view" imperative and forces us to discard an identity based on static permanence and to substitute, in its stead, organization—organization which is maintained immanently and which is neither changeless nor an entity; also that change is greater the more intricate, differentiated, and complex the organization.

I wish now to indicate how such a position can be used to explain the individual's time-experience and time-construction. Before I attempt the explanation of this extremely difficult problem, however, I would like to make as clear as possible the theory of knowledge bound up with, and supporting, critical realism. The connection of the individual with the larger process of which he is a freely-moving part must be realized before the conclusions of the first article can be seen to have definite bearings. Since, then, comprehension of the ensuing discussion of time will depend in large measure upon a grasp of the main principles of critical realism, I state these principles, and as concisely as is compatible with clearness.

First, the individual's experience is a changing "microcosm"; and logic is concerned with the study of processes within this "microcosm," especially with the inferential relations among thing-experiences and with the development and significance of meanings and distinctions, such as, physical and psychical, matter and consciousness, etc. In short, logic is not metaphysics, but clears the way for metaphysics and is not directly interested in

---

[*] R. W. Sellars, *JP*, V, 1 (1908), 597-600.

solipsism or pluralism. Logic "might well be written from the standpoint of solipsism." Elsewhere I have protested that a large share of the new realism is a logical realism which has at last overcome the confusions due to the special view-point of psychology.

Second, the protest of Professors Taylor, Dewey, Bawden, and others, that the mind-body relation is a methodological problem, more or less an artifact, holds against the reification of such contrast-categories as the physical and the psychical, matter or energy, and mind. These dualisms are developed in the impersonal logic of psychology and physics and have a methodological, not an ontological, import. On the other hand, the relation of the individual's experiencing to the rest of him which we call his body, as a part of reality, is *the vital metaphysical problem and the key to critical realism.*[1]

Third, in order to understand critical realism, the individual's experience must be viewed as incarnated in his body looked upon as an existence functioning in relation to other existences. I have designated this view a *functional identity* or *variancy* view; and, by showing that experience is not a "stuff"—since it is not conserved—I have tried to prove that this position does not conflict with the conservation of the capacity for activity on the part of reality (conservation of energy).[2]

Fourth, the condemnation of experience-in-general and the assertion that experience is always an individual's experience and connected with a body, lead to a frank pluralism in regard to experiencing. Individuals have distinct experiences, just as they

---

[1] Since my solution of the mind-body problem emphasizes the reactive unity of the whole individual, just as Professor Dewey's does, a statement of the main difference may be worth while. This can best be brought out in connection with the note (p. 65) in his essay in the James "Festschrift." "It is interesting to note how the metaphysical puzzles regarding 'parallelism,' 'interaction,' 'automatism,' evaporate when one ceases isolating the brain into a peculiar physical substrate of mind at large and treats it simply as one portion of the body, as the instrumentality of adaptive behavior." This is distinctly the objective, biological, outlook, and might well have been written, say, by Jennings. Instead of passing through and beyond subjectivism to an adequate conception of the individual, Professor Dewey has taken refuge in the impersonal objectivism of science.

[2] Cf. *Psychological Review*, July, 1908.

have different bodies. Their bodies are, however, in dynamic continuity with each other and with other existences.

Fifth, the terror of solipsism is absolutely uncalled for and results from idealism reenforced by the "states of consciousness" fallacy and by a false conception of knowledge. Let us frankly recognize, as *e.g.,* Cornelius does and as James used to do, that we can not have another's experience actually, any more than we can *be* a stone or a tree. . . . A genetic study of how our knowledge of others is obtained—showing how it depends on the interpretation by each of the ways of acting of the bodies of other people, including here the vocal organs—would have led to a correct idea of what knowledge means in this case, and would have prevented the puzzledom called transcendence of experience, which critical realism is supposed to require. The discussion of ejects would take on a healthier tone if the genetic attitude were adopted. I sought to do this some time ago and arrived at an interesting result; viz., that another's body becomes an eject, just as his experience does, and that the two always go hand in hand.

Sixth, the transcendence of an individual's experience—obviously I will have nothing to do with such a phrase as transsubjective reference—which has perplexed so many, is a pseudo-problem. In the first place, experience is looked upon semi-spatially when transcendence is talked about. This is the curse of a still-lingering "states of consciousness" outlook. One is supposed—in a dim, groping way—to perform a magic act; a jumping out of one's spiritual skin is hesitatingly invoked. In the second place, *knowing* an existence is regarded as a sort of *being* that existence, or at least, a mental hand is conjectured to touch the existence with a ghostly, yet reassuring, caress. A study of *experiencing* as incarnated in the body, as an expression of the body in its dynamic relations with other existences, would have led to an apprehension of the unreality of the problem. The correct and illuminating questions are: What is the function of experience? What can it be expected to tell us of the existences around the body? I recognize how important this problem is, if critical realism is ever to shake itself loose from the worrying attacks of idealism and to become more than a bewildered protest. I believe that experience tells us the function, structure, and relations of existences, and that, in doing this, it is not compelled to transcend itself. My present purpose forbids me to enter further into this field at this time.

This is my *credo*. I hope it may give the setting of the individual, which is needed.

IS THERE A COGNITIVE RELATION?*

... I wish to rise to a point of order. Have the postulates which lie back of these combinations [of the terms and distinctions of epistemological theory] been sufficiently examined? Is there, indeed, a cognitive relation either external or internal? I am of the opinion that there is no such relation. I shall now seek to justify and explain this opinion which seems, on the face of it, so revolutionary.

Theories of knowledge are, first of all, divisible into two classes, those which hold cognition to be somehow immediate and those which regard it as mediate. Theories of immediate cognition may, again, be divided into two subclasses. One subclass is idealistic and asserts that an internal relation exists between the object and the knower or subject. There are many slightly divergent forms of this position, but, in essentials, the above statement is not misleading. The second subclass is realistic and holds that an external relation exists between the object and the knower. By external is meant a relation which does not affect the object cognized. There are two current forms of this realistic subclass. The difference between them consists in their views of consciousness. The one considers it an *actus purus* externally related to the object; the other identifies it with the external relations supposed somehow to group objects selectively. Before we pass to a consideration of the mediate theories of cognition, let us ask ourselves what knowledge means for these realistic systems. Knowledge is the actual presence of reals. For the first view, consciousness in its relation to a thing accomplishes knowledge. The nature of the object is

---

* *JP*, IX, 9 (1912), pp. 225-232.

supposed to lie open to the mind and become subject to inspection. Things become transparent, as it were. Out of this peculiar relation, they are, for us, enveloped in darkness; in it, they stand in a glare of light. Knowledge is a presenting, an introducing, an intuition. The second position is even more skeptical of the traditional views of mind than the first. The emphasis shifts from mind as a knower to the objects known. Knowledge is a grouping of these objects. The theory may be designated selective objectivism and cognition is the selection.

I wish now to call attention to a common characteristic of all these theories of immediate knowledge. *They assert a real cognitive relation, external or internal, between the knower and the object.* The only partial exception is the theory that tends to do away with the knower and to substitute a pan-objectivism. Even here, however, a real relation determines a grouping although it does not affect the nature of the objects grouped. Such epistemological hypotheses are statements of our actual experience in terms of logic—or, shall I say, in terms of mathematics? They are professed translations of natural realism. I suspect their correctness. What we actually have in cognition is an *attitude* toward objects considered real. Usually the attention is concentrated on the things and the attitude escapes notice. It lies in the background of consciousness. Even when it does attract attention, there is no experience of a cognitive relation between the individual and the thing. Awareness is simply an attitude towards things which is not supposed to affect them. Plans of action may come to mind and then the attitude becomes more complex; but always the objects retain their independence so far as awareness is concerned. It is, I believe, this character of cognition that makes realistic systems thinkable. *The cognitive attitude involves a dualism and suggests no relation, external or internal, to bridge it.* This is a description of natural realism as I see it. Cognition does not imply a cognitive relation.

Mediate theories of cognition are more complex than immediate theories. That fact is not necessarily in their favor. There are three important classes: the representative, the normative, and the pragmatic. Space forbids me to enter into the analysis which I have made of these. Suffice it to say that, in my opinion, they are all one-sided. But they emphasize some aspects of knowledge which must be borne in mind.

Pragmatism stresses the mediate character of the objects known. It points out their history, the reconstructions they have undergone. Knowledge is an achievement and "ideas" are instruments for this end. This doctrine is rightly considered by Moore to be idealistic in the strictest sense of that much-abused term. The mistake made by the pragmatist is to confuse the reflective attitude with the cognitive. He is so interested in the *use* of knowledge, its *criteria*, and the process of its achievement that he has overlooked the important stratifications and distinctions characteristic of the cognitive attitude. We must thank the realist for his counterbalancing emphasis on them. The reflective attitude is, strictly speaking, precognitive.

The normative position brings us back from the *process* to the *act*. Its mistake is to misinterpret this act. It makes the object consciously depend on the "ought" of the subject. Here, again, there is a misreading of our actual experience. I repeat that the knower's attitude is one of acceptance of an object as being of such a character or as qualified in such a way. This attitude is modeled upon that of natural realism. It is dualistic and no cognitive relation is to be found in the experience.

The representative view is more complex. I shall not enter into the criticism which I must pass upon it. It is, however, the means of pointing out and stressing *the peculiar phenomenon of doubling that seems to telescope itself into the apparently simple act of cognition.* The distinction between thought, consciousness, idea, or concept and its object, which the human mind has been forced to postulate in order to account for error and for the mediate and personal character of the content of knowledge, as against the supposedly common and independent object known, is erected into a theory of knowledge. The real explanation of this distinction is entirely different. It results from a duplication of the cognitive object. This duplication is due to the conflict between the cognitive attitude and the facts which emphasize the personal character of the *objectivum*. For instance, the *objectivum* can be considered mental and dependent and, at the same time, physical and independent of mind as the cognitive attitude requires. It is assigned to two spheres of existence. The duplication of the cognitive object enables both motives to secure satisfaction. And they *must* both secure it. Hence even when we acknowledge the idealistic motives present in mediate theories of cognition, the structure of cognition remains dualistic.

It is interesting to hunt for indications of the twofold use of the cognitive object, as idea and as object, in philosophic literature. Unfortunately idealistic motives and outlook so dominated the thinkers who came nearest to its discovery that its significance was not grasped. A critical study of Hume (Treatise, I., III., 7), Kant ("Critique of Pure Reason," p. 483, Max Müller's translation) and James ("Psychology," Vol. II., p. 290) is illuminating from the present point of view. None of them does justice to the structure of cognition. Professor James substitutes a psychological explanation of cognition for the cognitive experience. He comes much nearer to a realization of the duplication in the article, "Does Consciousness Exist?", but makes it an affair merely of context. The tendency to emphasize the influence of feeling and interest in determining the attitude and object of cognition is natural to a psychologist. The very term, belief, selected as descriptive of the cognitive attitude inevitably leads to an analysis of these subjective factors. It is but a short step from this to the consideration of the object as merely an "idea" and the meaning of the existence of the object its relation to the individual's mind. We noted, in the discussion given to the mediate theories of knowledge, a similar mistake on the part of the pragmatist. The latter seeks to neutralize this result by a denial that there are individual minds. The mediation which leads to cognition overshadows the cognitive structure and meanings and causes their neglect or misinterpretation. In the very interesting and suggestive note in his "Psychology"[1] James discusses the existential judgment and decides that the distinction between it and the attributive judgment is superficial. We might suggest that the reason is not that existential judgments are attributive, but that attributive judg-

---

[1] Vol. II., page 290.

ments are implicitly existential. Let us examine his argument: "'The candle exists' is equivalent to, 'The candle is over there.' And this 'over there' means real space, space related to other reals. The proposition amounts to saying, 'The candle is in the same sphere with other reals.' It affirms of the candle a very concrete predicate, namely, this relation to other particular concrete things." (So far we would agree with his analysis.) *"Their* real existence, as we shall later see, resolves itself into their peculiar relation to ourselves. Existence is thus no substantive quality when we predicate it of an object." This emphasis on the subjective is apparent in another place: "Reality means simply relation to our emotional and active life" (p. 295). He apparently agrees with Hume and Kant whom he quotes with approval. We must ask ourselves this question: "Is not James confusing two standpoints?" A thing is considered real *when* it does touch us vitally, but is the meaning of reality or existence that of a *relation* to ourselves? Existence is a meaning, unique in character, which does not affect the content of the object. It is not a determinant in the attributive sense. But it does qualify the whole object and give it a place with other objects of its own class. Things toward which we take this attitude are considered *as real as ourselves.* In this James is right when he says, "The *pons et origo* of all reality, whether from the absolute or the practical point of view is thus subjective, is ourselves" (p. 296). But the relations which we suppose ourselves to establish with such things are not cognitive. Cognition is a means towards the establishment of practical relations, but is not itself thought of as a real relation. We may suppose that cognition is impossible unless we are in causal relation with things by means of our bodies, but cognition itself means a duality of equally real objects in which one takes a peculiar attitude towards the other. The cognitive relation, so-called, is either an intellectual, logical addition assumed because it is scandalous to think of two terms without a relation between them, or else the reading into the cognitive attitude of genetic relations in the precognitive stage, or else the shadow of the causal relation supposed to exist between us and the object. The first of these mistakes is made by the logician, the second by the psychologist, and the third by the scientist. All three are wrong. When we perceive an object or think of it, we do not have as an essential element a relation between the object and ourselves as knowers.

If this interpretation of the structure of cognition is correct, important consequences flow from it. In the first place idealism is robbed of the defense which has sheltered it for so long against the attacks of realism. Who has not felt the exasperating, baffling power of the dictum that we can not think an object except in relation with a subject. This turns out to be merely a false rendition of the analytic proposition: We can not think of an object unless we think of it. Otherwise, the very nature of cognition is to recognize the independence and reality of the object. A peculiar, non-natural relation, such as the supposed cognitive relation, would be the very denial of such independence. It seems, then, that the subject-object relation is a dogma which has been an article of faith in the philosophic world. The nearest approach, hitherto, to heresy has been the doctrine of external relations. But such a doctrine is half-hearted. We need the complete and final heresy; *there is no cognitive relation.*

Were we to accept the view that cognition is immediate and is the presence of an object to a knower, we would be forced to hold some form of naïve realism. Once deny the existence of a cognitive relation, if such is the view of knowledge, and no other course is open. The presence of objects to a knower would make no difference to them. He would be a spectator in which field of vision they would come and go as people in a thronged street pass before the eyes of a stranger who looks out upon them from a hotel window. If cognition is the actual presence of reals to consciousness, idealism is doomed.

But we have been led to acknowledge that cognition is mediate, not immediate. The idealistic motives, which the precognitive stage of reflective consciousness supports, are unaffected by the denial of the cognitive relation. The history of the material, the mediate or constructive character of the object, the fact of error, all induced us to refuse to acknowledge that the object present in cognition exists apart from the individual's mind. These facts, stressed so emphatically by modern psycho-

The Development of Referential Physical Realism 81

logy and by pragmatism of the Dewey type, are the true defense of idealism. To what do they lead? We have claimed that they lead to a realism broadened by the inclusion of these idealistic motives and *with a new conception of knowledge*. Let us examine this more critical and indirect type of realism. There are many questions which it must answer satisfactorily if it is to justify itself.

There is one problem which will occur to the mind of the reader almost immediately. In cognition does the mind transcend itself? Hitherto those who have denied the possibility of such a transcendence of experience have been idealists. How can the mind pass through the gulf of reality and touch things? To those who hold an organic view of mind, such a feat seems self-contradictory. Even revelation must be somehow immanent and adapted to the understanding of the seer. The reply must be that such a transcendence is both thinkable and unthinkable. It is thinkable so long as we give attention to the cognitive attitude and its meanings. It is unthinkable when mind is regarded as a realm of constructs and feelings, when it is regarded as consciousness in the non-cognitive, generic sense of that word. Real existents can not mix with mind, and knowledge is not a possession. Let us examine both aspects which have been so much confused.

Transcendence is thinkable when we pay regard to the cognitive attitude and its meanings, for here the mind is a limited entity opposed to that which is known as regards both content and existence. Of course the objects known could be called a part of experience, but the victory resulting would be merely verbal. It would consist in so stating the problem that it would be meaningless. We must admit, then, that the cognitive attitude makes the transcendence of mind thinkable. So long as the mind can be opposed to that which it knows in cognition the transcendence of mind is conceivable because it is seemingly a fact. We have, however, acknowledged that the cognitive object does not exist apart from mind even though it demands such an existence. This peculiar contradiction led, as we saw, to the phenomenon of the duplication of the cognitive object as idea and as object. As a result of this doubling, mind is enlarged to satisfy the idealistic motives and at the same time is opposed to the object as an independent existent. Cognition continues dualistic and, hence, realistic in its structure and meanings. The transcendence of mind is, however, unthinkable when mind is regarded as a personal system of ideas.

The answer that critical realism must logically make to this first problem is evident. Knowledge does not involve an actual transcendence of the individual's mind, *but it secures a reference beyond the individual's mind*[*] through the structure and meanings of the cognitive attitude.

What, then, is knowledge and what is the relation of the cognitive object in the individual's mind to the real whose existence cognition demands? Knowledge is an achievement of the individual's mind working in collaboration with other minds in a more or less conscious fashion. The methods and tests used are immanent and arise in large measure from the material. When a conclusion is arrived at it is objectified, *i.e.*, considered to exist as a quality, object, or relation in the sphere of existence presupposed by the nature of the domain investigated. When this domain is the physical world, the construction is considered entirely independent of the mind which has elaborated it. There are types of knowledge of the physical world which are functions of our interest and our point of view. The usual type results from a collaboration between things and man. We do not attempt to separate out our contribution. A landscape is beautiful. The *soft tones* and *harmonious outlines* are assigned to nature. Esthetic knowledge welcomes this collaboration. The scientific type is dominated by another ideal, to separate out and remove from things evidently subjective elements. In neither type is knowledge the actual presence of the *real* in the mind. In both, however, the reference is realistic.

We can turn now to the second part of the question under discussion. What is the relation of the cognitive object in the individual's mind to the real whose existence cognition demands? The answer is simple and presents a negative reply to the question propounded in the title of the article. In the case of physical reals there is no relation of a cognitive sort. The

---

[*] Italics added.

dualism of the cognitive attitude corresponds to an actual dualism. But a causal relation of however indirect a sort between the real and a mind is a presupposition of the possibility of knowledge. This fact is expressed by us in the causal relation assumed to connect percept and physical thing. This epistemological dualism is conceived by means of the duplication of the cognitive object into idea and thing between which no relation is supposed to exist. *The preposition, "of," in the phrase "idea of" is not symbolic of any actual relation, but of a distinction between two spheres with different characteristics.* These spheres are considered existentially distinct.

The second comprehensive question which should be asked of critical realism is the following: In what sense does it differ from the idealism of the critical, phenomenalistic sort, from an up-to-date Kantianism, for instance? The difference lies not in the content of knowledge, not necessarily even in the methods and criteria, which must be those of science, but in the reference of cognition and in the existential meanings connected with it. Idealism has entirely misinterpreted the cognitive attitude. *The Kantian phenomenon is the real as we are compelled to think it.* Kant's interest in the process by which knowledge is secured, together with his leaning towards a Leibnitzian metaphysics, obscured for him the realistic import of cognition. The phenomenon is the thing-in-itself as we think it.

The third question concerns the relation of individual minds to each other. Common sense and psychology hold that minds do not intersect. Critical realism agrees with this natural view and makes it comprehensible. Mind are microcosms whose boundaries are of their own making. Relatively to each other they live in a fourth dimension. But, since knowledge does not involve the actual presence of the real, this pluralism is no barrier to mutual knowledge. What is required is actual causal influence and this is obtained through the body. Knowledge of other minds is, for critical realism, not a whit more mysterious than knowledge of physical reals. Were minds disembodied, there would, indeed, be trouble. As it is, our information is interpretative and comes through the channel of organic activities and language. The cognitive reference and its mechanism is the same as for physical things. The knowledge of physical reals is, however, a means as well as an end in itself. This is seen in imitation and in the actual handling of things, or in pointing towards them to gain a common reference and understanding.

. . . I may state, . . . [further] that the import of this position for the categories is uppermost in my mind.

A THING AND ITS PROPERTIES*

The examination of space and time must have convinced the reader that philosophy can set the categories in their true light only when it studies them genetically. To introduce a view which belongs to one level into another level can only work confusion. It will be our purpose to apply this method to the study of the distinction between a thing and its properties. What does common sense mean by a thing and what does it mean by properties? Does science hold to the same meanings or has it changed them fundamentally? Let us investigate these questions in the endeavor to decide what view philosophy must defend.

Empirical substances or things are believed by common sense to be the direct objects of perception. To the unsophisticated mind, they are as they are perceived and are held to be open to the inspection of all men with their five senses. This attitude with its various assumptions has already been studied by us and we have agreed to call it natural realism. The trees which grow in my neighbor's yard are instinctively regarded by me as real things, things which I must reckon with, which have taken many years to attain their present size and have nourished themselves by their roots and leaves during that time. The things which I perceive are independent of the sensations which they cause in me and are also quite oblivious to any concepts I may form with respect to them. A deal of hard experience has gone into the making of this attitude; the independence and indifference of things has been borne in upon man as a result of the labor he has undergone in trying to make the world more adapted to himself. Now these meanings must be accepted and they spell some sort of realism. What we wish to do is to

---

* JP, XII (1915), 318-328.

examine the outlook attached to these meanings in common sense and to show how untenable it is in many respects.

Things, for common sense, are perceived or at least capable of being perceived and are known to be independent of the perceiver so long as he does not operate upon them by means of his body. They are also known to occupy space, to be in relations of a spatial kind with the other things, to be, more or less stable and perdurable, and to possess qualities or properties of various sorts. All this is common knowledge. The classificatory sciences extend our knowledge of things within this framework and thus add greatly to our information concerning the number of things and what obvious properties they have. As a result, these things fall into natural groups such as the inorganic and the organic and these larger groups split up into smaller ones. So far as possible such classifications try to be "real" or to follow the important properties of the things rather than "artificial" and to wait upon our convenience. Philosophy has little if anything to say as regards such empirical investigations and resultant classifications.

Common sense has no definite theory of what it means by the independence and realness of things. If asked to define its attitude and assumptions, it is at first at a loss to conceive what the question can mean; it seems to it foolish even to ask the question. Of course things are out there; they are as real as my body; I must adapt myself to them; they are a part of nature; I see them. Things are certainly not our experiences, they are as real as we are and as independent of us as we are of other persons. The pressure of human experience lies back of this attitude and in our theory of knowledge we have seen reason to accept it as essentially true. The generalizations of science have likewise but confirmed it. Astronomy, geology, physics, evolutionary biology have piled fact upon fact and theory upon theory, all pointing to the reality of nature and to the belief that we are but insignificant and temporary parts of it.

Things, are, then, experienced as in the same world with ourselves; it is they to which we must adapt ourselves and we must use them in various ways in order to maintain ourselves. Through centuries of conscious and unconscious reasoning, certain distinctions have been drawn and certain meanings have developed, and the realness and independence of things is one of these basic distinctions. Their realness is bound up with their empirical independence; they confront us at every move and compel our recognition and our adjustment. In short, they seem to be as immediately given and as real as ourselves. Here, again, we see the truth of the assertion that our categories are, in the main, products of unconscious thinking, of unreflective distinctions forced upon us by experience.

This genetic approach gives us our clue. Perceptual experience and practical thinking precede theory, with the result that the category of thinghood is found ready to hand* when reflection arises. Things are as real as are enemies and food and shelter. The attitude which goes with the perception of things is thus as old as organic life itself. The centuries of evolution but gave it content and a wider setting. Natural realism and the category of thinghood are, in fact, inseparable.

The delimitation of things in the world to which we react was, so far as we can make out, the function of personal interests guided by perception. Man was built on a scale that enabled him to include a wide field in a single survey and to be interested in the outlines of molar bodies like trees and boulders and animals. Since many of these objects moved in a total fashion, they were included as a unity in the span of attention. The background of nature had as a foreground a large number of "things," which stood out from one another for various concrete reasons and which could each awaken a vital interest to give grip to its power of stimulating the sense-organs. When we examine our experience and the interests which run quivering through it, we are unable to think of any other possible development. Perceptual and empirical space are both filled with a manifold of objects which stand out from one another and from ourselves in the most natural way while yet concerned with one another. That which is given to adult reflection is very complex and the burden of proof rests with the skeptic to show that it is not essentially veracious.

---

* Our first question, when we are confronted by a notably obtrusive type of stimulation, says Sellars, is, "What's that?" [Ed.]

But our present task is to trace the development of the idea of thinghood from its perceptual stage to the scientific level. What is naturally meant by things? What changes, if any, does science introduce into our natural view of things? How much a critical philosophy conceive things? These are the questions we are compelled to ask ourselves in our attempt to understand the framework of our knowledge of nature.

Things have qualities or properties, they are in spatial relations with one another and together compose nature, and they interact. To comprehend things we must, therefore, study them critically in regard to these aspects of our experience of them. It is evident that these aspects involve other categories such as relation and causality which must be taken up for detailed consideration later, but which are here seen to be naturally involved in the adequate conception of *that which* is spatial and is capable of change. Thus, even in the naïve view of nature, we glimpse the essential unity or togetherness of the categories. Space, time, thing, property, relation, and causality, make themselves marked as essentially inseparable in our knowledge of the physical world. Science and philosophy are but more systematic extensions of this knowledge and more painstaking and thorough studies of these implicit categories. We shall seek to justify the belief of critical realism that this development and clarification can be carried through in a satisfactory fashion so that the *framework of knowledge* will fit its *content* and involve no self-contradiction. When this work is done, critical realism as a theory of knowledge will find its completion in critical realism as a metaphysics.

While bearing in mind the fact that spatial relations and causal interaction are inseparably bound up with our notion of things, we shall lay our main stress upon the distinction between things and their qualities or properties. The study of this distinction will put us on the track of what I may fairly call the internal categories, such as structure, arrangement, organization, activity, in contrast to the external categories such as relation, motion, causality.

Man experiences things as complex while yet somehow one. An apple, for instance, has a certain size, a certain shape, a certain odor, a definite taste when eaten, a fixed weight, etc. It is *one* apple and this one apple has various qualities which can be sensed at different times according to the sense-organ that is stimulated. In some way, then, we experience the apple as complex; we keep the same subject of reference while we note quality after quality. It is this double fact of oneness and complexity together which has given rise to the philosophical problem of substance and inherent properties. Let us try to analyze the experience a little more closely to see whether it rightly falls into this customary, philosophical framework. It may be that we have here a typical *pseudo*-problem which, if not guarded against, will lead the unwary into a conceptual labyrinth from which there is no escape. It is my own firm conviction that the whole historical movement from Locke to Hume is but a *reductio ad absurdum* of this customary framework. Berkeley and Hume disproved the existence of substance as implied in this contrast, but, nevertheless, did not, for all their ingenuity, disprove the existence of a physical world of which we can gain valid knowledge. As we shall see, they only proved that Locke's realism was untenable. They did not realize that it was Locke's implicit view of knowledge reflecting the prejudices of natural realism that was at fault. Just how we shall interpret the complexity in unity of things is, therefore, a crucial point.

The distinction between a thing and its qualities is made naturally and inevitably. This pencil which I take up and examine is regarded by me as real and independent of my attention; I note its color and say that it is yellow, its length and say that it is quite short, the quality of its lead and say that it is soft. These judgments, in other words, are all made within the context of natural realism. They imply the category of thinghood and work within that outlook. In short, the world which I perceive breaks up into portions which act together and force me to recognize them as somehow one, to be treated as one and thought of as one, in the same general sense that I myself am one. These things are spatial, their parts hang together, they move as one, and so on. It is evident that their unity is for us both spatial and functional and the recognition of this unity is present in the category of thinghood as an essential element.

But these things are complex; I can note various aspects and pass judgments in which the thing is the given and accredited subject, a subject which natural realism regards as present to the mind. The assignment of attributes is thus an analysis of what is given as a sort of implicit whole. We note that this thing is of a certain color, *that* it is so large, etc. There is nothing mysterious in this process of judgment. The manifoldness of our judgments does not in any way militate against the unity of that about which we are judging. Otherwise analysis would involve a contradiction.

Suppose, then, that, working within the framework of natural realism, our analysis has become complete, that we have passed a large number of judgments of which the thing is the subject. If our position is correct, these judgments do not make the thing disappear, but enrich it. The thing is *known as* all these things, as yellow, as of a certain length, etc. And this fact gives us our clue. The tendency to regard the thing as something distinct from its properties is the expression of a false logic which common sense could hardly understand. The thing is neither the sum of its properties nor something apart from them. The trouble with philosophy is that it has not been empirical enough; it has substituted associational psychology for actual experience. The thing is decidedly not given as a cluster of sensations, but as a thing of complex character *about which* we can make various judgments. When this empirical situation is once realized, it becomes obvious that the various judgments do not pretend to give "parts" of the thing out of which the thing can be composed. The thing is yellow and the thing is of a certain length; but the thing is not thereby proclaimed to be the sum of length and a yellow color. I, for one, resolutely deny that we have the right to interpret judgments of an attributive kind in this mechanical fashion, and I believe that any temptation to do so arises from a false sophistication due to the confusion of the standpoint of associational psychology with that of logic.

I can bring out my meaning by using Locke as my horrible example. This procedure will serve a double purpose since it will introduce us to the traditional category of substance in the proper way. From our standpoint, it should be noted that Locke does not realize the artificiality of his point of view; he does not see that analytic judgment works within a preceding organization of experience and meanings. To understand natural realism does not involve its acceptance, but philosophy, if it is to state our problems correctly, must commence with descriptive empiricism. Just because Locke does not do this, he is at a loss to account for the unity that so evidently accompanies the qualities reduced by him to ideas. "The mind takes notice that a certain number of these simple ideas go constantly together; which *being presumed to belong to one thing* and words being suited to common apprehensions, and made use of for quick dispatch, are called, so united in one subject, by one name; which, by inadvertency we are apt afterward to talk of and consider as one simple idea. . . ." Thus Locke reads the result of a conditioned analysis as a *real division* into parts, in this way mistaking the nature of logical analysis. When he is haunted by a residue, something left out, after he has sought to measure the sum of the "ideas" to the thing, he calls this residue a substratum "because not imagining how these simple ideas can subsist by themselves, we accustom ourselves to suppose some substratum wherein they do subsist and from which they result; which, therefore, we call substance." When Locke is occupying the standpoint of the scientific realism of his day, he names his ideas, qualities, or accidents, and supposes them to exist outside the mind and to be supported in some mysterious fashion by a substance. The theory-of-knowledge difficulty he tries to meet by doubling his ideas which are his data into primary qualities in the mind and their archetypes in the substance.

Now, in opposition to Locke's psychological atomism, the standpoint of descriptive empiricism simply points out that these various judgments about a thing enrich our *knowledge of the thing* or, to put it as common sense experiences it, our *apprehension of the nature of the thing is* deepened by noting that the thing is yellow, of a certain length, hard in texture, etc. The distinction between a substance and its attributes does not exist for natural realism; it is the thing which is yellow and so on. Here, as elsewhere, philosophy has often distorted experience; it has been metaphysical in the bad sense; it has substituted a conceptual construction for the actual experience.

What must be our own position in regard to the sphere of existence of these empirical things which we regard ourselves as apprehending when we occupy the standpoint of natural realism? When we bring our own theory of knowledge to bear, we realize at once that these things are thing-experiences and exist only within experience. They are objects of apprehension within experience, objects which are enriched by analytic and synthetic judgments. There is in them no substratum; they are as they are experienced as. As regards things, we are at the perceptual level. Berkeley was perfectly right in his attack upon Locke's position and in his declaration that sensible things, things immediately perceived, exist only within experience. As a matter of fact, they exist only within each individual's experience and there are as many sensible things as there are percipients.

In order to drive this position home, let us glance at some of the *pseudo*-problems which have arisen from an ungenetic treatment. Common sense does not reflect enough to have theories; it has only attitudes and meanings. Therefore, we shall glance at some of the traditional theories built up around what I have called the conceptual construction substituted for actual experience.

Suppose the concrete thing of experience to be broken up into a substance and its attributes; what is the substance and how does it possess its attributes? It is with this *pseudo*-problem that Berkeley made merry to the bewilderment of all future philosophers and the apparent establishment of idealism. Now Berkeley had little difficult in proving that the Lockean type of substance is unthinkable. How can qualities inhere in something which is unknown and unknowable? Are not inherence and support mere metaphors taken from concrete experience which have no relevance since they can not be taken literally? So soon as we make qualities *entities* we are unable to understand how a substance can possess them. Surely substance has no legal property rights in qualities! So much for substance and for matter as such a substance. Berkeley is right in what he disproved, not in what he thought that he proved.

But many thinkers have fallen back upon the distinction between primary and secondary qualities as somehow an answer to the above problem. There is in this attempt, however, a misunderstanding which perverts a distinction which is significant when properly approached. In the first place, as we shall show later, there is a total misunderstanding of science. No matter what the unphilosophical scientist may think, the scientist is not dealing with perceptual aspects of things. He works at a different genetic level, a fact which our study of scientific space and time has made clear. In the second place, so long as we maintain allegiance to the Lockean construction, the insurmountable objections referred to above remain in full force. How does substance possess the primary qualities? If they are qualities, they can not exist alone, since they are metaphysical adjectives, not substantives. And these difficulties, when their implications are understood, are of themselves sufficient to discredit the conceptual construction which we are attacking. There are, however, other objections in line with the suggestion made above that science does not really deal with primary qualities as these were understood by Locke and Berkeley.

The so-called secondary qualities are thought of as sensations produced in our experience by something acting upon our sense-organs. Rightly stated, this position is, I think, beyond attack. Our thing-experiences develop under the control of the physical world; critical realism accepts this unavoidable doctrine and fits it into its theory of knowledge. But, as both Berkeley and Hume showed, and as modern psychology has doubly proved, the aspects of our thing-experiences which are thought of by Locke as somehow primary, are in the same case with the secondary. All the sensational content of our thing-experiences must be regarded as controlled by our sense-organs. Again, perceptual space is, as we have seen, a filled space; we perceive colored surfaces and tactual surfaces, never empty space. In other words, all sensations are in the same situation and on the same genetic level. If the historical distinction between primary and secondary qualities points to a significant truth, Locke and his defenders did not state this truth properly. Science does not assume primary qualities as literal features of physical things. Only natural realism at first or second remove does this. I would call Locke's realism natural realism at second remove.

It is, unfortunately, necessary to eradicate this notion of

substance completely, to destroy it root and branch, in order to prepare the mind for a correct view of our knowledge of things. We have thus far contented ourselves with showing that the construction of substance and attributes results from a misinterpretation of empirical experience. The object of our apprehension and the subject of our perceptual judgments is the concrete thing. Our judgments enlarge the content of that which is apprehended. Such analytic judgments are at the same time synthetic. Hence, the subject is not diminished to a formal entity or abstract point of reference, but enlarged with each judgment. But we must now point out that this Lockean construction not only reflects a poor logic, because it looks at everything from the standpoint of associational psychology, but leads to all sorts of metaphysical absurdities which complete its overthrow.

If it is not enough to indicate the ambiguous position of the qualities which have one foot in the substance and one foot in the mind, let us call attention to the unintelligible status of the relation between the accidents and the substance. Since the substance is distinct from the accidents, these accidents can not be thought of as expressing its nature; otherwise, we would have an infinite regress, for the nature of the substance must itself consist of accidents and these would require a substance and so on indefinitely. Hence, we are confronted by a dilemma: if the substance has a nature it must consist of accidents which are unknowable and we are landed in a complete agnosticism; if the substance has not a nature, it becomes a mere nothing and we have no right even to postulate its existence. There can be no doubt, therefore, that the construction is not only untrue to experience, but also absolutely unintelligible. Any realism which wishes to withstand the attacks of idealism must shun this form; it must learn a lesson from Berkeley's criticism of Locke.

Having run this false type of realism to earth, we can now return with thorough satisfaction to the development of other possibilities. The thing of common sense is, then, a thing-experience dominantly perceptual in character; it exists only in the field of some individual's experience and contains no peculiar core or substratum. But this thing-experience which is apprehended within experience corresponds to a definite portion of the physical world which exists outside of experience. Such is the position of critical realism. In science, then, we try to gain knowledge of that portion of the physical world in all the ways that are open to us. By superposition, we determine its size in terms of some standard unit; in an analogous manner we discover its mass as a ratio with another unit; we seek also to measure its free energy, to decide how it reacts to certain processes like light-waves, to learn its chemical properties, etc. But these judgments are now thought of as referring to the physical thing and not to the perceptual thing. We are, in other words, at a different genetic level, a level reached by the scientist almost unconsciously by the pressure of his facts and his technique. The scientist has passed beyond perception, yet, as a rule, he retains the thing-experience of the perceptual level as a means of reference. It is the necessity of distinguishing precisely between the thing-experience and the physical thing that the thinker must recognize. Let us now examine the result of such a distinction for our problem.

The scientist discovers certain facts *about* things; these facts are stated in the form of propositions which claim to give knowledge of things as existences apart from our experience. In truth, so soon as we leave common sense with its immediate apprehension and commence to analyze the sort of knowledge which science does achieve, we are struck by the peculiar character of that knowledge. All quantitative knowledge is in terms of ratios, for instance; but a ratio can not, obviously, be an inherent property of any one thing. Does it not follow that the knowledge science possesses will not fit into the form of natural realism? For common sense, the thing is apprehended by itself and comparison is not necessary for knowledge; the thing is red, is large, is heavy, etc. These are aspects of the thing as this is presented. But scientific knowledge is not of this character; it involves a judgment founded on a technique of comparison in which the quantity of a thing is determined in terms of some standard unit. And this ratio is not determined by perception, but by superposition. Perception is merely an instrument to confirm the results of the superposition. Now the other properties of things are likewise statements about the thing in terms of what it does to processes like light-waves, to organisms like ourselves, to chemical substances, and so on. The majority of properties are statements of empirical laws in which the particular thing is a constant factor. But such empirical laws can not be the properties of a thing as properties are conceived on the pre-scientific level; they can not be assigned to one thing in isolation from other things. They are not apprehended features of the physical thing, since this can never be apprehended. It also goes without saying that such empirical laws can not inhere in the scholastic sense in any one substance. Locke's conceptual form betrays its origin in the view that knowledge is an apprehension of a thing; it is, therefore, unadapted to the kind of knowledge that science actually gives.

We saw that Locke's construction at the perceptual level could be best undermined by descriptive empiricism and by a study of the actual logic of attributive judgments. A similar method will give us the proper clue at the scientific level of knowledge. Scientific knowledge consists of judgments which are both analytic and synthetic—analytic so far as they concern different data, synthetic so far as these are organized together by the mind as all giving knowledge of the *same* thing. No more here than in the case of the apprehension of thing-experiences is there the slightest reason for the assumption of a substance in which properties inhere.

What, then, are properties? Is it right to retain this term when its correlative, substance, has been so completely discredited? It is certainly a vague term which is apt to be ambiguous because of its origin in the standpoint of natural realism with its presentative or apprehensional view of knowledge and its historical association with the substance-accident contrast. The majority of the properties of things are statements of what the thing does under certain conditions which are supposedly reproducible. The behavior of things, their reactions, are known in empirical laws such as those of physics and chemistry and biology and supposedly known more fully and deeply in explanatory laws and theories. This behavior rests on the nature of the thing as well as on the total conditions and is so far an index of this nature. But this nature must not be thought of as divisible into entities to be called properties which are somehow possessed by the thing. The far greater number of properties are really nothing more than what Locke called "powers" and the word, power, like that of capacity, is but the expression of our belief that a thing will react in a definite way under definite conditions, and that this reaction is the expression of its nature. We should say a thing has *such a nature that* it does so and so under such and such conditions. The very form of this statement declares that we gain knowledge of the nature of the thing, or, to put it more simply, knowledge of the thing. So long, then, as the category of property can be interpreted in accordance with this form, there can be no objections to it. Unfortunately, however, only the critical thinker interprets it in this fashion. Yet science never presents us with literal aspects of the physical world, aspects which can be intuited or somehow copied in ideas. The habits and prejudices due to natural realism have prevented philosophy from understanding scientific knowledge.

But a distinction must be made at this point. There are certain classes of judgments which we can always make about things. A thing always has mass, although it is not always chemically active; it always has size, although it is not always optically active; it always has position, although it may not be moving in relation to its surroundings; it always has some structure, although it may not be doing work. Certain classes of judgments are, then, always applicable to things and these are not thought of as giving knowledge of the "powers" of things. We shall understand this distinction better, however, when we come to study causality. At present all we need to point out is that certain categories are always applicable to things, while others are not. Things are always extended, massive, structural, but not always moving or acting in certain ways. Yet the capacity to react in certain ways under certain conditions rests on the nature of things and thus involves more than a mere possibility.

To summarize: physical things in contradistinction to thing-experiences exist outside of experience. . . . These physical things are known by means of propositions which claim to give knowledge of them. These propositions fall into natural classes differentiated by the fundamental concept characteristic of each, these concepts being called the categories by the philosopher. Thus things are known in terms of certain definite concepts which are regarded as valid of the physical world in the sense that they are the essential framework of the tested knowledge which we build up in experience. Specific propositions give knowledge of physical things, but this knowledge must not be interpreted in terms of the distinction between substance and its accidents which is a false form or category nowhere justified by experience and actually resulting from bad logic, bad psychology, and bad theory of knowledge. This conclusion we have further validated by showing that the only change involved in the passage from natural realism to critical realism is the adoption of the non-presentative view of knowledge for the presentative or intuitional characteristic of natural realism and of the theories of knowledge developed under its influence. The essential realistic attitude of common sense can be retained. We have *knowledge* of physical things, a knowledge consisting of propositions having the same reference, while we have empirical objects, sensible things, thing-experiences present to the attention within the individual's experience.

THE STATUS OF THE CATEGORIES*

. . . [Primary] knowledge is a function of the capacities of the organism under stimulation by its environment. These capacities correspond to different levels, and their operation finally results in cognitive ideas directed toward affirmed existents. *The standard elements and distinctions of this knowledge are the categories.* Thus physical things are conceived as in a spatial order and as measurable. What direction they are from one another, what distance lies between them, what their size is— all these are specific bits of knowledge that come under the spatial form as such. Space as an abstract universal is exemplified by the specific instances. It is the common form or order. Events, or changes in physical things, happen in a peculiar order,

---

* *The Monist*, XXX (1920), 235-239.

the temporal. This order can be abstracted from its instances and studied as a universal. It is the common character of events, and, since physical things change, our knowledge about them contains this order as an internal form. Thus space and time are categories in that they are *characteristic elements* of the content of our knowledge about the physical world. They are not a peculiar logical type of being which somehow underlies the physical world. Once abstracted, however, they can become subsistential contents of awareness; they are, then, thoughts, not thoughts of.

Space and time illustrate very well this empirical doctrine of the categories. They are not physical things; they are not even peculiar elements of the physical world. They are characters of our knowledge about things. *It follows that the validity of the categories is bound up with the validity of knowledge.* They are not forms to be deduced from the self in some peculiar fashion; they are features to be discovered in objective knowledge, abstracted, and analyzed. Thus the objective idealist was right in his practical procedure. Unfortunately, the constitutive notion of the self vitiated his final interpretation. It is true, also, that he did not take some of the categories seriously enough. This depreciation is especially true of space and time. He wished to introduce the idea of value into the categories and to speak of higher categories and lower categories, degrees of reality, etc. Besides, the Kantian tradition that space and time are self-contradictory lingered in philosophy long after proper analyses of these categories had been made.

We have made it a fundamental principle that the validity of the categories is bound up with the validity of critical knowledge about reality. But it would also be true to say that the categories are themselves instances of the most general knowledge about the physical realm. That things are in the spatial order is a knowledge-claim. And knowledge seeks to conform to that about which it is knowledge, to reflect *in its own medium* that which is reproducible about existence. But we have examined knowledge enough already to realize that it plays over existence connecting the past with the present, comparing things which have no very direct continuity, and in general probing nature. Knowledge conforms to reality in an active way much as an investigator conforms to his material. We shall see that the categories follow knowledge in this regard. They give, as it were, the structure of nature as this is projected into consciousness.

The categories appear first in experience as general characters of its pattern. This pattern is a growth which expresses a necessity to which the would-be adaptive organism is exposed. It is not a blind necessity in the mechanical sense; rather it is a necessity which is freely admitted as means to end. The mind of the organism must produce a pattern in consciousness correspondent to physical reality if it is to further the organism's safety. The result is apparent in what I have called the primary categories, viz., space, time, thinghood, and causality.

These primary categories arise at first in an uncritical form. It has taken much reflection on the part of both philosophy and the sciences to separate the objective essentials from the more subjective ingredients and so to achieve categories which are cases of general knowledge about the physical world. The history of causality is, perhaps, the most instructive example of this clarification.

Other categories arise in connection with these primary categories as knowledge is enlarged. Mass and energy as quantities, conservation as a character of these quantities in nature, and evolution as the genetic side of many empirical substances are examples of later categories which develop and amplify the preliminary categories. These new categories are at once the general features and signs of a fuller knowledge of the world. Their history can be completely investigated since they arose in modern times. Their origin in the data of experience can readily be traced. They are discoveries and not deductions, and yet they are discoveries which require reasoning and precise reflection.

Like all universals, the categories are at once discoveries and standards. Our past experience assumed the temporal and spatial pattern and fell into things causally interacting. Whereupon science marked these features for her domain and formulated her laws in terms of such universal characters. Any thing or any event is expected to obey this framework which has been built up from a wide experience. A thing is assumed to have mass and to be in a definite position or in motion from one position to another; an event is assumed to be a function of antecedent conditions. In this sense, the categories are postulated to apply to all possible experience. They are guides for the mastery of new instances, of complex and tangled fields. Particular laws cannot be deduced beforehand, but it can be maintained that these laws will come under the categories. In this sense, they apply to all possible experience.

The question has at times been raised as to what guaranty there is that nature will recognize the categories. Kant, it will be remembered, tried to meet this difficulty by having the categories make nature. But he could give no guaranty that the ego and its forms would not change. The critical realist meets the difficulty in a different way. The categories are cases of general knowledge about nature resting upon the control by nature of the objective data of consciousness, a control actively furthered by the organism. Hence, nature itself would need to change before they would become invalid. And while we must admit that we cannot demonstrate that nature may not abruptly change its objective order, this thought is essentially unmotivated and can hardly be entertained seriously by any one who realizes the massiveness of nature and the fact that particular changes are expressions of that which changes. This hypothetical catastrophe assumes an uncaused change and so conflicts with our actual knowledge of nature. It should be noted that any gradual change in nature would be reflected in the categories.

In conclusion, attention must be called to the two general classes of categories, the epistemological and the metaphysical. Space, time, causality, organization, conservation, energy, etc., are metaphysical categories, that is, fundamental concepts characteristic of our knowledge about nature. In the following articles we shall deal chiefly with this class of categories; but, if we are to secure mastery in philosophy, we must also bear in mind those categories which concern knowledge. We must be able to get the correct interpretation for such terms as subject, object, idea, awareness, datum, phenomenon, consciousness, etc.

We must be able to appreciate the structure of consciousness, its distinctions, claims, and affirmations. It is this that critical realism claims to do. It is a realism which stresses mental process, which regards the mind as an organ of the psychophysical individual, which relinquishes the myth of a mysterious act of apprehension overleaping the boundaries of space and time, which realizes that knowledge is resident in consciousness. In this way, the epistemological categories harmonize with the metaphysical categories. Critical realism of this naturalistic type has no room for a disembodied knower.

EPISTEMOLOGICAL DUALISM VS. METAPHYSICAL DUALISM[1]*

In the present paper I desire to re-open the question of epistemological dualism in the hope of showing new leads in which good philosophical ore can be mined. To continue the figure, it is my belief—and I know the belief of many others—that modern epistemological realism decided too quickly that the shaft driven by dualism ended in the bare rock. Was there not simply a 'fault' here beyond which careful exploration would have found ore again?

Epistemological dualism has suffered in the main from three things: (1) its association with Cartesian metaphysical dualism, (2) the false bias toward subjectivism assigned to it, and (3) the belief that it cannot escape an indefensible copy-view. Against all three indictments the modern epistemological dualist, who calls himself a critical realist, wishes to enter a plea of not-guilty. In what follows I shall try to defend a critical form of epistemological dualism against these traditional counts. And by so doing I shall hope to justify the discipline of epistemology itself, which is being severely attacked these days by the pragmatists. Not that I wonder at their impatience, for which there has been sufficient cause.

In his recent attack upon epistemology as such, in his essay,

---

[1] This paper was read before the meeting of the Eastern Division of the American Philosophical Association, December, 1920.

* R. W. Sellars, PR, XXX (Sept. 1921), 482-493.

"A Recovery of Philosophy," Professor Dewey argues that *all* epistemology is guilty of the above errors. Beginning with an exposition of his own view of empiricism as contrasted with traditional empiricism, he maintains that epistemology has been a product of false assumptions and unveracious descriptions. And he draws up a tremendous indictment of Humianism, Kantainism and idealism. All of them were founded on a non-empirical doctrine of experience. But why? "The traditional account is derived from a conception once universally entertained regarding the subject or bearer of experience. The description of experience has been forced into conformity with this prior conception; it has been primarily a deduction from it, actual empirical facts being poured into the moulds of the deduction."[1] Thus the self, soul, subject or spirit was taken to be non-natural or supernatural. "Even if they had wished to make a complete break, they had nothing to put as knower in the place of the soul." He argues that the bearer of experience was conceived as outside of the world; so that experience consisted in the bearer's being affected through a type of operations not found anywhere in the world, while knowledge consists in surveying the world, looking at it, getting the view of a spectator. In this way, Professor Dewey argues that epistemology has assumed that "the bearer of experience is antithetical to the world instead of being in and of it."

Now the epistemological dualist is just as desirous as is Professor Dewey to eliminate any such metaphysical dualism. He, also, is a naturalist who is convinced that his data are natural events or occurrences. He, also, means by the subjective a "specific mode of objectivity." He does not use it in any disparaging way, any way which assumes a contrast with a peculiarly *real* object and implies that "the organism *ought* not to make any difference when it operates in conjunction with other things." The epistemological dualist of to-day has no thought of a ghost-like knower who watches the world but is not of it. He is certain that this attack upon epistemology has no other than an historical meaning for him. And it is at his own risk that the pragmatist assumes that the epistemological dualist is self-deceived and

---

[1] *Creative Intelligence*, p. 30.

knows not what he believes. It is a mistake to underestimate your opponents, and savors of sectarian passion. The differentia between pragmatism and epistemological dualism does not lie in the naturalism of the one and the supernaturalism of the other.

The modern epistemological dualist begs to differ from those who identify epistemology with metaphysical dualism. He can see no logical connection between his own epistemology and Cartesian dualism and he is, moreover, no dualist. To assert that one's idea in knowledge is numerically distinct from the object known does not imply that they are parts of different worlds. Only those who take knowledge wholesale and disregard its actual setting would at all be inclined to make this inference.

The modern epistemological dualist always concerns himself with an individual knower and his knowledge-claims. He takes knowledge retail and not wholesale. The idea (which is the *content* of knowledge and not the *object*) is bound up with the knower existentially. It is his accepted idea or thought of the object. But may not the knower be in the same world as the object known? I can see no reason why the epistemological dualist cannot be as biological as the pragmatist. To put the argument concretely, I know the tree outside my window in terms of, and by means of, my percept-datum. The tree is existentially external to me while still in the same objective physical nexus. The percept-datum is subjective only in the sense that it is bound up existentially with me as a specific concrete knower. It assuredly is not subjective in the sense that it is non-natural and belongs to a 'mind' as a mysterious realm apart. Just what mind is, is a problem to be determined in the course of the investigation. Surely there is in this approach nothing opposed to objectivism and naturalism. Sense-data are natural events taken as the material of knowledge, and the content of an act of knowledge is an interpretation of the affirmed object. We can accept all occurrences as equally real. It is a question of their use and status. The subjective is an occurrence which can be used as content of an act of knowledge. The reason for this is that it is in the possession of the active brain-mind of an organic knower. The knower is quite apparently one thing among others; what kind of a thing empirical knowledge, and not epistemology, informs us. To return to the case of knowing the tree outside my window, this knowledge-claim is a specific empirical act and must be empirically analyzed in the light of all the relevant facts. This demand for analysis is simply the expression of scientific standards—and the result is epistemology. Epistemology develops out of specific facts and problems.

And yet because the history of philosophy is so constantly present as a part of the apperceptive system of the thinker, very few philosophers are able to examine an analysis with unprejudiced eyes. "Epistemological dualism? Ah, yes; you assume a 'mind' which *knows* its own states, and you postulate an external world to which those states must somehow correspond." Such is the rapid-fire response of the majority of philosophers. "Yes" and "no" must be our reply. It all depends upon what you mean by the terms mind, states, knows, and correspond. These terms must be taken empirically and away from any substantialist setting.

Historically, epistemological dualism was shipwrecked on the puzzle of the status of ideas in knowledge. Attention swung to the ideas, and the query arose, Is it not possible that in all cognition what is known is never the object itself but only an idea *representing* that object? But how representing? And how can you be certain that there is an object to represent? When epistemological dualism once allowed itself to be formulated thus, its fate was settled. Radical empiricism, or epistemological monism, seemed so much more simple. The idea is given: why not call the idea the object of knowledge? Representing an unknown which you only infer does not sound plausible. So thought Berkeley and Hume; and the neo-realists have followed them.

But this radical empiricism was not empirical enough. Anti-epistemologist as he is, Dewey has seen this fact. Mere subjective occurrences, call them sense-data, images, concepts according to their level, are not ideas in the cognitive sense. It is the *cognitive use* of these subjective events which makes them ideas. The fact was that attention had swung from the cognitive use of mental data to their mere givenness. Logic and epistemology were virtually shoved aside in favor of the elements of physiological psychology. The conditions of the *material* of knowledge were studied to the exclusion of the act, content and claim of knowledge. In the second place, this first burst of empiricism was not empirical enough in another regard. It did not realize the significance of the fact that we have such distinctions as that between the subjective and the external world and that we make cognitive claims to know this external world.

The way of ideas did not win without a protest. Thomas Reid attempted to carry through a distinction between sensation and perception. Unfortunately, he was unable to analyze this distinction and fell back upon common sense as a court of appeal— a refuge denied to one who sets out to be philosopher and so reflective and analytic. "We are so constituted," argues Reid, "that, on the occasion of *sensation,* we *perceive* material objects and their qualities existing independently of the percipient mind. . . . Grasping a ball, we perceive it at once to be hard, figured, and extended, moving the hand along the table, the qualities of hardness, smoothness, extension, and motion are at once *suggested* to the mind. . . . The knowledge of the primary qualities thus obtained is inexplicable; all that can be said is, that *by an original principle of our constitution* sensations of touch arouse in our minds the conception of, and belief in, external things. . . . From the natural sign in sensation the mind passes at once to the thing signified, though reason can discern no tie or connection between them."[1]

Can the modern philosopher with the help of psychology explain the distinction between sensation and perception, and indicate the factors of the process by which we build up the category of thinghood? If so, he can explain that which to Reid was inexplicable. Puzzled as he was, Reid yet held obstinately to the fact that in knowledge we claim to know external things and not ideas. But *how* we could know external things he really did not see. The modern epistemological dualist believes that he has found the opening and that it leads to critical realism.

It is interesting to note that Hodgson, who is generally

---

[1] Cf. Laurie, *Scottish Philosophy in its National Development*, p. 139.

acknowledged to be the father of the English realistic movement, makes a demand or postulate very similar to Reid's. He asserts that a thing is what it is known as, a reality independent of the existence of a perceiving consciousness. But neither was he able to carry this postulate through successfully. He set a problem instead of giving a solution.

The critical realist believes that he can give a solution of the problem in terms of two things: (1) a more complete analysis of perception, and (2) a re-interpretation of knowledge.

Why is it wrong to identify perception with the givenness of a sense-datum? Because a sense-datum is only an elementary part of the total experience of perceiving. There are *two* distinguishable elements in the total experience of perceiving, the datum, or content, of perception and the affirmation of an object. With regard to the *content* of perception, the critical realist points out—in this he is in harmony with modern logic and psychology (*pace* Russell)—that there are many meanings and images in the content of perception. We perceive what we take to be things and not sensations. The category of thinghood has been developed and, with its arrival, sense-data are interpreted as qualities of things.

Perception involves a coördinating and interpretative response to a complex of stimuli, and there is attached to it and implied in it the sense of contrast between my bodily self and the things surrounding it to which it is responding or tending to respond. To remove sense-data from this context is to be unempirical. The modern bio-psychologist can understand the level of perception with its distinctions and categories in a way impossible to either Reid or Kant. They were seeking some innate principle by which to lift sensation to perception.

This approach enables us to discover the factors in the total experience of perceiving responsible for the element we called the affirmation of the object. The attitude, or set, of the organism in perception floods consciousness with a sense of something co-real to which it is responding. The motor impulses to reach out to, or move toward, this something carry out this feeling and develop it. And I think that there can be no doubt that additional meanings, such as externality, independence of direct control, and persistence, all add themselves to this nucleus to constitute the affirmation of, or belief in, a co-real object. Professor Strong calls this affirmation instinctive. It seems to be quite empirical and expressive of the nature and situation of the organism. The structure of the field of consciousness reflects the situation of the organism.

These elements combine into the apparent givenness of an object. Such is the psychological derivation of naïve realism and the reason for its strength. Now the epistemological dualist simply argues that, while all this is natural and inevitable, reflection forces him to declare that the actual physical thing, which is the object of the *organic act* of perception, cannot be given in consciousness as the content of perception is given. Into the facts breaking down naïve realism I shall not here enter. They are a part of the stage property of philosophy which only the desperation of the neo-realist led him to challenge.

I would suggest that the flaw in Berkeley's analysis of perception was due to his lack of attention to the psychological factors mediating the affirmation of the object. In common with all radical empiricists he did not do justice to the category of thing-hood. The inadequacies of Lockeian realism furnish him with a partial excuse. But there can be little doubt that he was too anxious to get rid of a physical world distinct from sense-data to be quite scientific in his approach.

Though in a very summary fashion, we have thus far endeavored to show that modern epistemological dualism does not begin with a metaphysical dualism; nor does it assert that we know ideas first and then infer objects. There is no bias toward subjectivism in it. Objects are affirmed rather than inferred, though reasoning supports the affirmation and develops its implications. We believe from the beginning, as much as the naïve realist does, that we know external things; but reflection on the conditions of knowledge forces us to realize that the external thing cannot be inspected or intuited, that only subjective content is given to awareness. *The consequence of this conclusion is that the exact nature of knowledge becomes a problem in a way that it does not for the naïve realist.* Knowledge of a physical thing cannot be an intuition of it in part or in whole. A thing cannot enter consciousness or be in a cognitive relation of compresence with consciousness. It is the content of perception or the content of judgment which occupies this position.

What, then, is knowledge? Let it be noted that the critical realist does not fall back upon blanket contrasts between two stuffs called mind and matter. His analysis remains empirical. Such contrasts are for him epistemologically unreal because they are not found in the knowledge situation as it presents itself. Any ultimates must be worked up to in the course of empirical reflection rather than assumed.

The critical realist differs, then, from neo-realist and pragmatist on two fundamental points. These are, (1) the acceptance of the distinction between the content of knowledge and the object of knowledge, and (2) the frank recognition of the consciousness (psychical or subjective)-and-organism problem. It is evident that these two positive doctrines of critical realism hang together. And it is probably because of the second doctrine that the epistemological dualist is still so frequently thought of as a metaphysical dualist. But surely fairness suggests that the recognition of a problem is no proof that there is only the traditional dualistic solution of it. And is it not better to admit a problem than to act ostrich-like, as pragmatists and behaviorists are doing? Moreover, epistemology comes first logically and is to be settled on its own data. It has no direct connection with the problem of the relation between the subjective and the organism even though it leads to a closer statement of the problem. The mistake with both Descartes and Locke was the constant injection of metaphysics into epistemology. Our modern empiricism has helped to allay that evil.

But we are now confronted with the most difficult of our tasks, the working out of a clear idea of knowledge. At the beginning of the paper we said that critical realism had to meet the indictment that it could not escape an indefensible copy-view. To this question we now turn. I believe that much that is novel in the position lies here and that it has not been grasped.

The critical realist must show that past representative realism committed certain blunders which he can correct, and then he must work out a critical correspondence theory which is proof against the traditional objections.

In regard to the first point, he argues that the blunders of past representative realism were due to two things in the main: (1) the retention of the idea of the physical thing which grows up through the identification of content of perception with the object of perception, the only change being the rejection of secondary qualities so-called; and (2) the tendency to make an idea of a thing an object in the same sense that a physical thing is an object. The first mistake led to the assumption that physical things possess qualities which are copyable, and that these qualities inhere in an unknowable substratum. Now I, at least, reject this substance-quality schema in its entirety and hold that it is a result of the influence of naïve realism. Representative realism of the Lockeian type has often been called representative perceptionism, and this term expresses exactly what its outlook is. It has not sufficiently broken loose from naïve realism. Its ideal is an indirect intuition of a *sensuous object*. The second mistake, that of treating a cognitive idea as an object in the same sense that a physical thing is an object, led to a substitution of the category of resemblance in place of the act of cognition *by means of the idea*. It is easily seen that this second mistake played into the hands of the first.

Now it is no wonder that the two basic arguments customarily employed against epistemological dualism are, (1) that you can never compare object and idea, and (2) that it assumes that the effect is *like* the cause. The way in which critical realism meets these objections will give a clearer idea of how it conceives knowledge.

Critical realism recognizes, from the first, the different status of cognitive content and object. That came out in our analysis of perception. It follows that you cannot literally compare idea and object. Man's situation is such that, while he responds to things, he cannot apprehend them as naïve realism supposes. But, if there is a good reason to suppose that ideas convey something of the nature of the object, we can still have knowledge. We must have faith in this knowledge-conveying capacity of data of all sorts. So much for the first objection.

The critical realist then asks himself what characteristics of the physical world can be copied or reproduced by data and elicited by an intelligent synthesis and interrogation of data. Let it be noted that the characteristics of the physical world are not qualities in the Lockeian sense. It is the physical thing which is the object of knowledge, and we are not assuming that it has qualities stuck on it which we have to copy.

The answer to this first question is *the order, or structure of the external world.* The correspondence of two orders in different material is quite thinkable and does not demand the kind of specific, end-on, qualitative, cause-and-effect likeness which Lockeian realism presupposes. What, alone, is required is a correlation and order in the subjective field corresponding to the structure in the physical realm. And it is precisely this correspondence that the pattern of perception offers. In other words, the structure of nature can be worked out by the mind through a careful study of the pattern of appearance. And, furthermore, since the sensible appearance is a qualified, or differentiated order, and every datum has meaning to the inquiring mind, much knowledge about the world can be achieved. It is these leads that science rightly follows. The conclusion is that data can be used by the mind to attain knowledge of the structure and properties of things, properties being the name for responses of things to one another and to specific conditions. All this is knowledge, but it is different from the sort of knowledge that naïve realism stresses. We have even got beyond the perennial controversy about primary and secondary qualities.

I have examined in detail the knowledge of the external world which science offers, and have found that it all falls into categories which are either categories of order or categories which fit into and develop order, such as spatial and temporal positions, quantity, structure, composition, interdependence, behavior. These categories permit an immense variety of detail; but nowhere in science do you to-day find an attempt to copy qualities which are like specific sense-data. Knowledge has the external world for its archetype or object, but we must shake ourselves loose from the notion that it copies sensuous qualities which specific, isolated objects possess in their own right. Much of our knowledge tells us how things behave, not how they are dressed, as it were. Knowledge enables us to grasp and understand the structure and interactive process of things. And the crude material upon which this knowledge is built is patterned sense-data. Developed ideas are built up by the mind and asserted to be revelatory of objects by which they have been consciously controlled. Is this Lockeian realism? There has at least been an advance.

The fundamental postulate of critical realism is, then, that patterned and correlated sense-data can mediate just the kind of knowledge of the physical world we actually possess according to science. The claim is there and it does not sound absurd. The content of perception contains a *translation* of the gross structure of the external world, and theory pushes this translation farther. But never do we intuit the very stuff of the physical world. Knowledge has its inevitable limitations. It is the form of reality, so to speak, not reality itself which is grasped by the human mind. But I would not reify this *form* in an Aristotelian way. The implications of this view for naturalism are obvious. It undermines the crude type of materialism. I do not think that it is ordinarily realized that perception is a mixture of sense-data and knowledge and that the fusion of data and knowledge encourages the intuitional idea of knowledge and masks the proper view. I think that neo-realism deceived itself at this point and that pragmatism, though more wary as to the difference between sense-data and knowledge, assumed the impossibility of carrying through epistemological dualism and stressed instrumentalism too blindly.

Let me summarize the way in which critical realism meets the traditional objections to representative realism. First, the physical object is not inferred but is affirmed. In this the critical realist is objective from the beginning. Second, the critical realist admits that he cannot compare his knowledge of the thing with the thing; but he never pretends to do so. Instead, he believes on sufficient grounds that his knowledge grasps much of the nature of the external object and that this knowledge is founded upon the communication with the thing which his data offer. This position is more than semeiology. In knowledge we get a grip on reality. In the third place, the outlook of critical realism is far more subtle than the crude notion of the likeness of object and idea as cause and effect respectively. It relegates the relation between data and object to the *causal condition* of knowledge and examines as distinct the claim of knowledge and its content.

Thus critical realism has outflanked Berkeley by developing a more exact conception of the nature of knowledge, while admitting all that is valid in his attack upon Locke. We gain knowledge of the physical thing, itself, and we discard the metaphysics of a substratum in which copyable qualities inhere. Epistemological dualism of this type meets all the traditional problems in a direct and unsophisticated way. I am not afraid to say that neo-realism will find in it all that it has been contending for in the way of a stress upon analysis and order and the knowledge-claim. The pragmatist, also, will find the recognition of his biological setting and his denial that sense-data are, as such, knowledge. But if my defense of epistemological dualism holds, he must retract his criticisms of epistemology. *Both neo-realism and pragmatism built their doctrines upon the assumption that it was impossible to carry thorugh a valid type of epistemological dualism.* That was what they had in common. They have made their contributions but these can be accepted and related by critical realism.

A RE-EXAMINATION OF CRITICAL REALISM*

I

I am writing this paper in the endeavor to clear up the main principles of critical realism. I shall, accordingly, first restate the essentials of the theory and then examine the divergence between those who think of logical ideas as having a mental status and those who champion the doctrine of essences.

The critical realist looks upon perception as an elementary level of knowing which must be carefully studied both as regards its conditions and its nature. He is convinced that it is both relative to the position of the knower and controlled by practical needs. In this view of perception he would agree with much

---

* PR, XXXVIII (1929), 439-448; 451-455.

that Professor Kemp Smith has recently emphasized. Reflection forces us beyond this elementary knowing to critical knowing of the sort we find in science. But there is something which all knowing has in common which we must study. I shall concern myself primarily with the problems connected with knowing the external world.

We may say that the gist of critical realism is an analysis of the nature and mechanism of knowing. Its thesis is that human knowing is a *direct* knowing of objects—this against representative realism as ordinarily interpreted—*and yet that this knowing is mediated by logical ideas.* By direct knowing of objects I mean knowing directed at objects. Much of my effort will be concerned with showing that directness and mediation are not contradictory terms in theory of knowledge. Thus the critical realist maintains, as firmly as does any other realist, that various people can know identically the same external object, say a tree or a particular person. I mean by identically the same, numerically the same. It is, in short, the tree or John Jones that I know and not my idea of the tree or of John Jones. It is true that I can know my idea if I wish later to focus on my complex act of cognition as an object, but then the categories used and the cognitive situation have shifted. I do not think of the idea as such in my first act of cognition of a physical thing. What the critical realist speaks of as the content of knowing is that which can be exhibited in a proposition or a series of propositions. And this content is the knowledge of the object *in* the complex act of knowing. But more of this later.

I should like at this stage to point out that the critical realist much prefers to use the term knowing rather than the term experiencing whenever he has to do with definite acts of cognition. Experiencing seems to cover both what Professor Alexander calls enjoying and what he calls contemplation. Thus such a criticism as that passed on critical realism by Professor Macintosh seems to the critical realist question-begging. Knowing the external world seems to him to depend upon experiencing it, and yet it is clear that, for him, experiencing is a kind of knowing. I quote: "In other words, if we can experience the physical we can test our ideas of it and know it; if we can never experience it, it does not seem that we can have knowledge of it."[1] Here experiencing would appear to be a kind of immediate givenness of the object, what I would call its existential givenness in the field of experience. I do not deny that this is the sort of thing that naïve realism encourages us to believe in. I simply assert that reflection makes us unable to retain the outlook and leads us to develop certain vital distinctions. I shall reaffirm my continued conviction that the level of perception misleads unless it is handled with caution. I hold that perception is a knowing of an elementary sort but that this knowing is easily confused with the existential givenness of the object known. This means that, to the critical realist, cognitional givenness is something peculiar which we must learn to contrast with existential givenness in the field of consciousness. Knowing is never a literal givenness of the object in the private stream of consciousness. An object given *to* the mind is not given *in* the mind. Given to the mind is only another expression for known; and it is the nature and mechanism of knowing which we shall seek to explain.

Now I find myself at this point more in sympathy with English neo-realism than with American neo-realism. I believe in acts of cognition. And yet this sympathy is a moderate one, for I think that the English neo-realist has denuded the act of cognition and made it too empty of content. Thus my difference from him lies in two things: (1) a complication of the act of cognition to include logical contents, and (2) the view that knowing is a kind of mediated interpretation, or mediated revelation, of the object rather than a givenness of the object to such an empty act of cognition. I shall explain later in more detail what I mean by this contrast. But, if I make myself in any way clear, these two criticisms will be seen to go together. If the act of cognition is simplified, the content of knowledge must be shifted to the object side. This result appears in Alexander in the assertion that images and sensations are non-mental. It must be remembered that I am concerned with the knowledge of physical objects like trees and inkwells.

The divergence between critical realism and the two most

---

[1] *Journal of Philosophy*, Vol. XXIV, p. 129.

conspicuous forms of neo-realism is, accordingly, not a divergence with respect to the objectivity and the directness of knowing but with respect to the *precise mechanism of knowing*. The critical realist builds upon the fact of knowing but reflection has taught him that added insight is possible. He does not seek to reduce knowing to something else but to appreciate it more fully.

Perhaps the difference between critical realism and American new realism will throw light upon this point. The American new realists hold that the object known is itself a constituent in the field of consciousness of the knower, so that two consciousnesses can overlap in a literal fashion. It is upon this point that Professor Perry has laid so much stress, and he has accordingly been led to emphasize the doctrine of externality of relations and the neutral nature of data. All this was, of course, a logical development of the fusion of Mr. Russell's logic and James's famous article. The idea is the object. Knowing is the actual presence or givenness of the object. There is no distinction between cognitional givenness and existential givenness. And we all know to what difficulties such a position leads us in our interpretation of memory and history. This view involved a rejection of the traditional view of the field of consciousness as private. Now the critical realist asserts that this whole development arose from the assumption that the cognitive presence of an object (its being known) means its existential presence within the field of consciousness. It is this assumption which he holds to be unwarranted. May not knowing be something unique made possible by mental contents and activities and not demanding this literal givenness of the object? In other words, the critical realist is convinced that a more careful analysis of the mechanism of knowing enables him to accept the transcendence of the object known. It is this transcendence which differentiates cognitional givenness (knowing) from existential givenness (experiencing). The human mind has developed methods and mechanisms by which it can know that which is genuinely external. The very nature of man as a living organism necessitated that feat.

I shall take Professor Alexander as a representative of the other type of neo-realism. He teaches that knowing is a contemplation of the object, and this means that the object is somehow *linked* with a mental act of awareness in a peculiar fashion called compresence. Now I have already pointed out my partial agreement with this thinker. I believe in acts of cognition. The object known is in some sense present *to* mind and not *in* mind. But I have quite a different notion of mind. My mind has area, as it were, and is rich in content. In this regard I am more in sympathy with idealism and non-behavioristic psychology. In short, I would criticize the limitation of consciousness to a largely contentless act (he does admit some vague measure of differentiation in these acts) and, secondly, the classification of sense-data and images as non-mental. Surely it is contrary to the best evidence to take such a position. Only if every attempt to carry through a position which accepts the larger view of mind fails, should it be resorted to. It is the thesis of the critical realist that the relinquishment of an internally rich, functioning mind was too hasty. Thus the critical realist would enlarge the act of cognition to include the presence of logical predicates and still hold that the object known is cognitively present to the mind, not in the mind. Such a term as compresence is to me a metaphor for knowing or else misleading. And yet to Professor Alexander it is connected with a peculiar ontological linkage, for he has not differentiated existential givenness and cognitional givenness.

We could easily be led here into ontology. This difference between neo-realists and critical realists rests upon the antisubstantialism of the former. Berkeley scored here. The defeat of traditional representative realism led to the belief that the category of substance must be relinquished. There has been a pæan in praise of function and events, Mr. Russell helping to swell the chorus. Now the critical realist is a frank substantialist, though he would not accept a parody of this category. Roughly speaking, substance is a term for the self-existence of the object known. It is a physical system known in terms of its characteristics such as size, mass, structure and behavior. Into this I hope to go into detail at some later time. To me, however, transcendence and substantialism go together. There is, even in perception, a sense of thinghood, of an independent object to be interpreted. It has always been my thesis that the influence of Berkeley led to a neglect of the total experience of perception. The *Gestalt* or configuration with its categories was abstracted from. It has always been this total configuration with its meanings and distinctions which the critical realist has had in view. As I understand his writings, Mr. Broad, also, has reached a similar analysis.

We may sum up our conclusions as follows: The neo-realists have been forced to build upon the essentials of the outlook of naive realism because of an inadequate view of mind and knowing. Deterred by the defeat of traditional representative realism, they have not seen how it would be possible to think of the mind as knowing transcendent physical things in terms of, and by means of, *factors intrinsic to a complex act of knowing*. English neo-realists have, accordingly, denuded the act of cognition and held that the object known is literally linked with this act. The object had to appear in person. And they were in a sense right because they did not distinguish between existential givenness and cognitional givenness. The mechanism of knowing had to consist in a literal compresence. They were right in that they held that the object must be cognitionally given *to* the act of cognition, but they were wrong in their view of the nature of such cognitional givenness to the mind.

What I mean will come out by contrast. Critical realism stands for a basic reinterpretation of the nature of our knowing of external things. While still holding that knowing is direct and objective, it maintains that it is a much more peculiar and mediated affair than the neo-realists admit. Knowing is a revelation of the object known in terms of, and by means of, logical contents, *and in no other way is it an apprehension of the object known*. The object known is present to mind only in this fashion. This means that knowing is *sui generis* and has no likeness to the relations between physical things. It is an evolutionary achievement involving a complex mechanism. In my opinion, a completely naturalistic account of it can be achieved which robs it of all mystery but leaves it unique. In short, knowing is a directed interpretation of an object and not a semi-physical linkage between two entities, one of which is called mind and given wonderful and space-defying abilities. The critical realist thinks of the mind as operating literally in the organism and using signals in its interpretative knowing of objects. Such knowing is a function of the mind-brain resting on the whole organism and its actual commerce with things. The transcendence which knowing an external object involves has no spatial analogy. We must take the mind and its methods seriously. It is because I think of knowing as a mediated revelation that I have always denied the validity of a literal cognitive relation between the mental act and the object. When I know the sun either perceptually or conceptually, my mind does not wander through space to the sun nor is the mind above the limitations of space. This means that knowing is a peculiar kind of activity *resting on* mediations of all sorts, sensory and conceptual. Directness and objectivity call attention to the goal and success of this knowing, while the terms, mediation and mechanism, call attention to what sustains this knowing and makes it possible.

II

We are now ready to contrast critical realism with traditional representative realism and to show that the empiricism, which resulted from the breakdown of representative realism, simply gave up the actual claim, which our minds make, to know external things, because it could not understand how it was possible. Such empiricism fell back upon passive contents such as sensations and images, even in this largely falsifying our actual experience. But why should we blame the psychologist when the philosopher was equally bewildered?

In what follows I shall show myself a thorough believer in categories and functions. But I shall not go into this in detail here because I have taken it up sufficiently in my *Evolutionary Naturalism*.

Representative realism has been pretty well identified in controversial literature with the theory that we know ideas first as mental objects and then infer in some mysterious manner that these mental objects are like external and independent things. Let me illustrate. In a recent article in *Mind* devoted to Cook Wilson's view of judgment the following typical criticism of representative realism is made: "The second main kind of error which, according to Cook Wilson, arises when we try to define knowledge or explain it in terms of something other than itself, is representation or the idea-theory. Each act of knowing is really the knowing its own proper object, and not the knowing of some idea which is not its object. This fact is contradicted by idea-theories of knowledge."[2] Still another instance of this accepted view of traditional representative realism is to be found in Mr. Hoernlé's little book on Idealism. He writes: "It (the theory of representation) suffers from substantially the same defects as the causal theory, *viz.*, it confines us to the circle of our ideas and shuts us off from physical things in such a way that the *relation of representation* between idea and thing, supposing it to exist, can never come directly to our knowledge. We can never compare idea and object so as to verify their correspondence."[3]

These interpretations of traditional representative realism can, I believe, be regarded as typical. And there can be no doubt that Locke laid himself open to this charge because he emphasized the causal conditions of perception and tended to follow Descartes in his introspective treatment of knowledge. The very substantialistic theory of mind, which both had, confirmed the difficulty presented by his very subjectivistic definitions of knowledge. Mind seemed confined to the observation of its own states, and any other kind of knowing was reduced to a vague hope that ideas were in some conformity to external things. And, of course, Descartes's criterion of natural light and God's unwillingness to deceive had retreated into the background.

My own belief is that the problem was too difficult for Locke to solve, that it is only in these days, after all the analyses of the intervening time and with the fuller conception of the mind and its place in the world, that it can be solved. Subjective idealism and the old empiricism were simply denials of our active knowing of external things. They could not see how it could be done.

Let me begin, then, by declaring that critical realism is *not* representative realism of the above kind because it accepts the claim of the human mind to know *directly* the external object. This direct knowing rests on mechanism and mediation but it

---
[2] *Mind*, July, 1928.
[3] Hoernlé: *Idealism*, p. 38.

is direct knowing nevertheless. It is concerned with the object and not with ideas as objects. Knowing is ultimate and not reducible to something else, even though it is the resultant of complex processes such as the use of distinguishable predicates within consciousness. It is to the supposed simplicity and immediate character of knowing rather than to its directness and ultimacy that the critical realist objects. In other words, the critical realist holds that we know physical things by means of, and in terms of, logical ideas, but that it is the external object which we know and to which this complex act of cognition is directed. When the configuration and categorical structure of knowing is made explicit, the presence of such logical ideas in the act of cognition is discernible. It is the object which is cognitionally given—in the way I have explained—*to* the mind, that is, to the act of cognition. Clearly, the cognitive act must be dissociated from the old substantialistic notion of mind. Knowing is a function, a peculiar activity of the conscious organism. The mind is built up around functions. In other words, the enumeration of mental contents neglects what the mind does with these contents. It gives the mind at rest, as it were, or as it has been described by a foolish introspective psychology which neglected the really significant thing, what mind is doing. And is this not like enumerating tools without telling what they are used for? There can be little doubt that the causal, or transmission, approach to mind, which neglected the response completion without which knowing does not exist, encouraged this tearing of ideas from their place in the act of cognition and transformed them into internal objects to which the mind was supposedly limited.

Thus critical realism holds that the mind is active and performs certain functions, and that knowing is one of these. It further asserts that such knowing is directed to physical things external to the mind and that this knowing is mediated by ideas intrinsic to the act of cognition.

III

But such a re-orientation is only a beginning of our task. We have challenged the simpler view of the nature and mechanism of knowing built up around natural realism after the defeat of the 'way of ideas' and the rising dissatisfaction with idealism; and we have shown that critical realism is intentionally different from traditional representative realism. But we must now attempt to clear up questions in regard to the status of these ideas which have been directed against the 'cognitive value' of ideas.

The empirical fact seems to be that the human mind claims to know external things and yet that reflection forces it to admit that these things cannot be given in the same way that sense-data and universals are. I do not like Mr. Santayana's "animal faith" as an expression for this claim of the human mind. What this expression rightly points to is the automatic and natural growth of perceiving and the higher level of knowing. There is interpretative response which flows from conscious living. But only a poet would speak of this as animal faith.

The mind, then, is internally rich. It builds up ideas and uses them in cognition. But upon what quality of an idea does its cognitive value, its value in the act of cognition, rest? It is my thesis that it rests upon the correspondence, or conformity, of the logical content of these ideas and the object known through them. This way of putting it is, I think, technically accurate. I do not think of this logical content as in any way analogous to a physical thing, nor is it a kind of mental atom. It is what is discriminated in thinking and used in the act of cognition. *In our actual knowing these logical contents are molded into the form demanded by our categories.* Thus color becomes a color quality assigned to a thing. Taken from this setting, a color falls back into a sense-datum. Thus our logical ideas in the act of cognition are predicates used in interpreting the object known. What we may call data at the service of the mind are caught up into the categories and demands of the act of cognition. It is in this fashion that we grasp the characteristics of objects. It is a mediated cognitional grasping but a cognitional grasping nevertheless. It is thus that objects are present to the mind (known) while yet not in the mind.

We may say, then, that critical realism is a careful analysis of human knowing freed from the suggestions of Cartesian introspectionism and dualism. It is a representative theory of the mechanism of knowing and not a representative theory of knowing itself. Moreover, it has learned much from idealism in regard to the activity of the mind. Ideas are categorized distinctions, developed thoughts, and not a mosaic of sensations and images. We must do justice to human thinking.

IV

Let us conclude this brief survey of the perspective of critical realism, as I have always championed it, by means of a reference to the causal theory of perception. In the strict sense, theory of knowledge must begin with a study of knowing from its elementary level to its more critical levels. It cannot begin with a causal theory of perception which already implies knowing. The idealist has been right in his insistence on this point and I have never denied it. But, once we are convinced that knowing is mediated, we must try to understand this mediation. To this problem the causal theory of perception, which is surely substantiated by our detailed knowledge, is clearly relevant. And it fits in with the theory of knowledge of critical realism.

But it should be pointed out that the causal theory of perception—if perception be taken as an act of cognition—is, rightly, only a causal theory of the *conditions* of perceptual acts of cognition. And, even then, it is a causal theory of only some of the conditions and antecedents of perception as an elementary act of cognition. The elder tradition thought of perception too much a passive state and identified it with the rise of sensations and images as states of mind. But, surely, perception is more than this. It is an interpretative response to an object. The stimulus aspect is just the beginning of true perception. The empiricist tradition never did justice to the act of cognition because it could not understand it. It broke down the function into mental elements. I must frankly confess that the psychology of many neo-realists—including Mr. Russell—has appeared to me very faulty. . . .

V

I come finally to the problem of the nature and status of the logical ideas which mediate direct knowledge of physical objects. In what sense are these mental? It is on this point that critical realism divides into two schools. Is this divergence a mere matter of terminology? Or is there something deeper underlying the division?

It seems to me that we have here a specific problem on the boundary between epistemology and ontology. My own position should be clear by now. In knowing we have a function of the mind revealing itself in, and guided by, the distinctions and categories of consciousness. Logical ideas must be grasped in this context. And this means a rejection of the old empirical notion of passive mental states. Cognition is a mental act which expresses itself in a configuration in consciousness involving belief and the use of such categories as thing and qualities. It is this whole complex that I regard as mental, in the sense of intrinsic to the activity of the brain-mind and experienced. And it should be noted that I am an emergent naturalist with regard to the brain-mind.

I shall take Professor Drake as the proponent of the 'doctrine of essence.' I do so partly because he has recently gone into controversial detail on the subject and, in so doing, has asked me specific questions, and partly because I can understand his position better than I can Mr. Santayana's odd mixture of Platonism and materialism.

In a recent article in *The Philosophical Review*, Professor Drake begins with a definition of essence. "Anything that could conceivably exist, or could conceivably be mentioned, or imagined, is an essence."[4] As it stands, this definition strikes me as a bit of dogmatic entology. Surely the word anything is ambiguous. Does it mean object or the characteristics of an object? If object, then a physical thing is, by definition, an essence.

I prefer in this matter to move within the context of cognition. The mind deals in cognition with various kinds of objects, some of which are regarded as having physical existence. It is with physical objects and our knowledge of them that I shall deal here.

Professor Drake believes that our precise differences will be made evident by my answer to the following question: "Do these

---
[4] *The Philosophical Review*, Jan. 1928, p. 54.

characters (which we ascribe to an object) have existential embodiment in the psycho-physical organism?" He writes: "The character that I intuit, that I ascribe to an external existent, may be, let us say, the character of being-a-tree-ten-feet-away. Surely *that* character, what we ascribe to the external reality, is not resident in the psycho-physical organism! But it is precisely the characters that we ascribe, essences of that sort, that are our data of perception."

Now what does Professor Drake mean by a character being *resident in* the psycho-physical organism? I cannot answer that question, but I can tell the only meaning such an expression would have for me; and it would be this, intuited by me *within* the complex act of cognition which is interpreting the object. This does not mean that the act of cognition is ten-feet-away but that I can discriminate the predicate and can use it in interpreting the object known. The situation is *sui generis*. We must take consciousness seriously. Without it and its contents we could not know an external world. It is molded on the function of cognition. It is that *through which* we know, and it is not the same kind of thing as that which is known. This means that an intuited character within the act of cognition has a status different from a character as a *quality of* an object. It is resident in the act of cognition in the empirical way already emphasized. Professor Drake has asked me this further question: "Would Professor Sellars then agree to *this* way of putting it: the fact of being aware of that character and of ascribing it to an external existent is a mental fact?" Yes; this whole fact is mental. But what does Professor Drake mean by *ascribing it* to an object? We come to the nature and mechanism of knowing.

For the 'doctrine of essence,' the essence before the attention in the act of cognition *is* the essence of the object. Now this seems to me *a sort of short-cut* which gets us into all sorts of unnecessary difficulties. It suggests an entity which may not exist but which in veridical knowing does exist in the sense that it is embodied in the object known. Why not speak of the characteristics of the object and simply say that objects exist and have their characteristics apart from our acts of cognition? The truth of the matter seems to me to be that the predicates discriminated in the act of cognition have the kind of existence that the whole act of cognition has, but that *within* the act of cognition their status is simply logical, and that they are a *what* with a definite function within that act.

What kind of identity is there, then, between the predicate within the act of cognition and the characteristics of the object? I have come to call it a cognitional identity. I mean that in cognition the mind grasps the characteristics of the object in terms of the predicate within the act of cognition. In this sense the characteristics of the object are cognitively given though never existentially given. And it is this conviction which expresses itself in our language as ascribing a predicate to an object.

VI

I shall sum up. . . . Critical realism is a direct realism which examines very carefully the nature and mechanism of knowing and shows that it harmonizes with all the facts of the causal theory of the conditions of the perceptual act. It asserts that the act of cognition is complex and that knowing is *sui generis*. Cognitional grasping is a unique grasping which turns out to be a revelation of the characteristics of the object known in terms of, and by means of, predicates held before the attention in the act of cognition. We may speak of these predicates as being intuited or given (though given in no passive way) and of the object as known. And, in order to do justice to the reality of knowing, we may speak of the object as being cognitionally given but not literally given within the mind. In other words, this analysis enables us to understand the distinction between given to the mind and given in the mind. . . .

It is the claim of the critical realist that all the valid insights of realist, idealist, and pragmatist, will be found in this position.

A CLARIFICATION OF CRITICAL REALISM*

I

The guiding principle of critical realism is to keep as near to natural realism as the relevant facts permit. This principle

---
* *Philosophy of Science*, VI (1939), 415-421, © Williams & Wilkins.

guards it against the purely causal theory of perception as exhibited in Locke and Berkeley. The preliminary is to find out what perceiving seems to be and to take such an inventory as descriptive or phenomenological. Analysis and interpretation must come later. Now is it not a fact that we denote and characterize what we regard as material things external to the embodied self? In looking out of the window I note, and without hesitation, characterize trees and building and persons walking. Perceiving, then, seems to be some kind of direct awareness of things. I note no peculiar act of inference in the perceptual experience though reflection tells me that there has been much interpretation and funding of experience. The recognition of this non-inferential, denotative awareness of things as a feature of the perceptual experience is becoming wide-spread. It is common to the new realists and the critical realists in America, to positivists like Carnap and Feigl, to Dewey, to Stebbing and Ewing in England, etc. Take Dewey, for instance. "The necessary presence of definite objects repeatedly and familiarly employed as means to further knowledge gives the realistic theory its plausibility; a plausibility so great that any other theory seems like a departure from common sense made only to meet the exigencies of some preconceived theory. That stones, stars, trees, cats and dogs, etc., exist independently of the particular processes of a knower at a given time is as groundedly established a fact of knowledge as anything can be."[1] When there is so much agreement where's the difference? The difference arises in interpretation and explanation when some relevant facts are reflected upon.

It is admitted then, quite generally, that we seem to ourselves to be *in some sense aware* of independent, material things in perception. It is quite evidently the job of epistemology to analyze the perceptual experience in such a way as to bring out the beliefs, attitudes and categories operating in sense-perception. The first thesis of critical realism is, then, that perceiving involves more than sensing or, as the modern psychologist might put it, a percept is a complex organization not reducible to sensations as such. There is motor attitude, quasi-belief, funded facts,

---

[1] Dewey, *Logic*, p. 521.

meanings, expectations. We are far from the atomistic sensationalism of the past.

But, while we seem to ourselves to be in some sense aware of external things and are in our actions clearly concerned with them, notorious facts make the epistemologist introduce distinctions. Must not the sensory appearance be upon reflection assigned to the percipient, not as a naked psychical entity, but in some fashion to be determined by a theory of the status of consciousness in the organism? May not, however, the perceptual claim and denotative reference to external things be valid, and be kept, even though we must give up the natural, yet naive, identification of the sensory appearance with the thing meant and adjusted to? If this distinction is accepted, it leads to an analytic opening up of the perceptual experience with more adequate terminology. We can then speak of the intuition of the sensory appearance and the denotative reference to, and the characterization of, the thing-object. What is at first merged and telescoped together is distinguished by reflection. Is it not because the sensory appearance is intuited that the denoted and characterized object is regarded as in some sense given? Is not the basis of our apparent direct awareness of external things, this guiding function of the intuited sensory appearance? In the same fashion sensory data become *signs* of thing-objects of which we do not regard ourselves as at the time directly aware. It is because of the *function* of the sensory appearance *in* the complex act of perceiving that, in visual perception, we seem to ourselves to be aware of the very surface of the external thing. Let the pragmatist note that I do not assign to the sensory datum any intrinsic representative power. It plays a part in the complex operation of perception as a guide and sign. And any characterization of the denoted thing-object must take its point of departure from it. That, I take it, is factual. We discriminate, verbalize, conceptualize.

Once embarked on the task of reflective distinction—which, after all, is all that the dreaded enterprise called epistemology is—we are forced to distinguish between intuition, on the one side, and denotative selection or reference on the other. Now this is all that the critical realist means by that dreaded term transcendence. It is a term which expresses the difference between the intuited and the denoted. It signifies that what is intuited is bound up with the percipient, constitutes a factor in his consciousness, while what is denoted is transcendent, external, something which we can be concerned with and mean and act towards, *something on a par with the embodied self*. The transcendent can be denoted by the embodied self, can be pointed to, can be characterized—but it cannot be intuited as the sensory appearance is. At the level of common-sense realism, then, we seem to ourselves to be directly aware of thing-objects on a par with ourselves because we have merged intuition and denotation or—to speak more correctly—we have not yet distinguished them. Private and public, immanent and transcendent are distinctions of an essentially correlative sort. They are developments of reflection but, in my opinion, unavoidable. I mention this for the sake of C. I. Lewis who seems to think that transcendence involves something mystical and incomprehensible which should be mentioned only in a footnote. To repeat, transcendence is a meaning which goes with denotation, with that which is to be characterized, with thinghood, with that which is on a par with the embodied and percipient self, with independence, while immanence is a meaning which goes with that which is intuited or experienced, with consciousness, the subjective, the self. These are distinctions of reflection but well-based and necessary. We denote public, transcendent, material things like Dewey's dogs and cats and stars. At the same time we think them through qualities founded on sensory appearances and on funded facts. Critical realism should, accordingly, be thought of as a reconstruction of naïve realism resulting from the reflective distinction between intuition and denotative characterization. It asserts that the directed awareness of common sense expresses a natural growth in which a sensory appearance is taken to be the thing-object to which the percipient is responding and with which he is concerned. Gradually it is intellectually loosened from this identification and functions as an appearance *of*, a sign *of*, a symbol *of*, the denoted thing-object. It is in accordance with this structure of thought that we arrive at ideas *of*, or concepts *of*, the denoted objects. The point I wish to make again, as against Dewey, is that the critical realist does not assign to sensations and images an inherent representative function. The function is developed in connection with the increasing awareness of the difference between intuition and denotation. I take it that what Morris and others are now calling *semantic meaning* involves what I call denotation.

II

And now, in conclusion, a few additional clarifications.

First of all, the view of perception advanced should not be spoken of as the causal theory of perception. And for this reason: it stresses the total perceptual experience which contains such elements as the denotative selection of thing-objects on a par with the percipient organism, interpretations, expectations, funded facts. We *seem* to ourselves to be aware of material existences on a par with our organic selves. Dewey, Gestaltists, critical realists, all agree here. Nevertheless, analysis justifies the view that the element of sensory appearance is caused in us by the stimulation of our sense-organs. Such is the external condition of its generation in the brain-mind. But such a causal theory of the generation of sensory appearances should not be taken to mean the reduction, *à la Locke,* of perception to the awareness of atomic sensations or ideas. Hence I distinguish between the causal theory of sensations and the traditional causal theory of perceiving. Perceiving is more than sensing.

In the second place, explicit perceptual cognition means the denotative characterization of material things, on a par with the percipient organism, in terms of more or less verbalized predicates founded on sensory particulars. Two points should be noted here. First, I stress sensory particulars as furnishing the material for the characterization of thing-objects. It is obvious that my logical analysis is more like Dewey's than like Santayana's. I am skeptical of essences if more is meant than concepts. Second, the cognitive mechanism of sense-perception has nothing in common with traditional representative perceptionism which meant that sensations are asserted to be like a shadowy double. No wonder that Hume rejected this latter formulation! No, explicit perceptual cognition *uses* sense-material but is itself a denotative characterization of the sole primary object of perception. In this sense, critical realism is a form of directed perception and not of representationalism. It is a directed denotation and an accompanying characterization.

In the third place, it was not until the responsive, interpretative, organizing aspect of perception was recognized that atomic sensationalism was doomed. Those who have despaired of epistemology should take this fact into account. Had Dewey recognized that this development made possible a new deal in epistemology he might well have done the sort of pioneering I undertook. But he and the pragmatists felt the realistic impulse too late in their development. I hold out the olive branch to the younger men. Perhaps critical realism may fuse with empirical realism but *only if* its representatives develop a capacity for epistemological analysis. The manipulation of sentences will get them nowhere.

Finally, critical realism in my opinion has nothing to do with *dualism* of any variety. It rejects Cartesian dualism as I have pointed out for some thirty years. Consciousness is a qualitative factor intrinsic to the organized activity of the mind-brain. In the second place, epistemological dualism was at one time adopted merely as a contrast term to the epistemological monism of the new realists. As I see it, the new realists never distinguished sufficiently between intuition and denotation. They followed Berkeley and Hume instead of re-analyzing perception. When Montague asserts that the critical realist is a Lockian it merely signifies that he has not waked up yet to this novel analysis of perception. Now *from the standpoint of denotation* the critical realist is an epistemological monist. We denote and mean material things and characterize them in terms of predicates founded on intuited sensory material. I hope that this clarification will still the old rumor that the critical realist is a Kantian. Quite the contrary, I do not like the distinction between phenomenal objects and noumenal objects. From the first we are concerned with material objects on a par with the organic self. The act of cognition is very complex but concerned with independent, material things. The world is not constructed or inferred but actively denoted within the matrix of our doing and suffering and ever more explicitly characterized. It is within the matrix of our doing and suffering that categories arise, categories like space, time and thinghood. Epistemological categories demand ontological categories. . . .

WHY NATURALISM AND NOT MATERIALISM*

Questions of terminology are less superficial than is often supposed. Precision in terminology usually accompanies clear thinking, and is at once its condition and effect. In other words, the relation between them is reciprocal. The point in terminology which has increasingly attracted my attention and which I wish to examine in the public way of an article is the exact difference between materialism and naturalism. It seems to me that a discussion of these terms is very much in order. Thus a thinker may call himself a naturalist and be called a materialist by a critic. How shall we differentiate these terms?

We must first of all note that terms change their meaning insensibly as the centuries pass. Realism, materialism, hedonism and idealism are positions which have been reformulated again and again. The realism of to-day differs in many respects from that of yesterday; and the same is true of idealism. The outsider who sees eternal recurrence in philosophy is governed too much by words. Because the words are the same, he tends to believe that the ideas indicated by them are exactly the same. I suppose that the adjectives, like 'new' and 'critical,' which are so frequently attached to these old recurrent terms, represent the effort to guard against this lazy, but natural, assumption of sameness.

What underlies this slow transformation of basic positions? Surely the advance in human thought itself, an advance in methods and knowledge. More information, better analysis, wider generalizations, improved methods, all these play their part and bring it to pass that there is difference and novelty along with an underlying constancy of outlook. This is why the kinds of realism which are to-day struggling for mastery are not identical with any form of medieval realism and why the

---

* R. W. Sellars, PR, XXXVI (1927), 216-225.

materialism of the twentieth century shows signs of differing profoundly from the materialism of Democritus, Hobbes and Moleschott. There is, I grant, a certain identity of perspective and of exclusion but there are also marked differences.

Let us concentrate now upon the differences between naturalism and materialism. It may be that we can find a clue in the distinction between cosmology and ontology. I would say that ontology is the more specialized of these two divisions of theory of reality or metaphysics. Materialism is distinctly an ontological theory, a theory of the *stuff* of reality. Its polar opposite is usually taken to be mentalism of some kind. Naturalism, on the other hand, is a cosmological position; its opposite is supernaturalism in the larger meaning of that term. I mean that naturalism takes nature in a definite way as identical with reality, as self-sufficient and as the whole of reality. And by nature is meant the space-time-causal system which is studied by science and in which our lives are passed. The whole nature of nature may not be exhaustively known, but its location and general characteristics come under the above categories. Supernaturalism essentially affirms that nature is only a part of reality. This supernaturalism may be of the myth-believing, popular type bound up with traditional religion or it may be quite opposed to the miraculous. For instance, nature is for Bradley only a part of reality and in that sense it is appearance. The status of matter for Plato is another instance of supernaturalism in this large sense.

When naturalism is taken in this cosmological setting, we can readily understand why naturalism is the inevitable philosophy of science and why it stands in opposition to those movements which are called absolute idealism, transcendentalism, theism, in short, . . . supernaturalism in the large sense. But, of course, it is philosophy and not science which must examine this contrast and defend one side or the other. What is nature? What shall we include under this term? These are, indeed, big questions and they cannot be handled apart from epistemology and a painstaking analysis of all the categories. The present article is no attempt at a short-cut or a quick-and-easy way of dealing with the technical problems of philosophy. These questions I have examined in the leisurely way a book makes possible in my various publications. At present, I am concerned with classification and the indication of relations.

Back of the great struggle between idealism and realism during the nineteenth century lay, in part, the still greater struggle between naturalism and supernaturalism. Only physical realism could justify the claims of naturalism as science understands nature. Idealism by its very logic cast a fog over this term. What is nature for any form of idealism? A very vague term.

It will be noted that I said physical realism and not merely realism. The characteristic of critical realism, as I have always conceived it, is that it is a realistic theory of knowledge which justifies the distinction between the content of knowledge and its object and permits us to conceive these objects as material when they exist. In other words, physical realism accepts physical objects and justifies nature as science conceives it. Critical realism as an epistemology is the gate of entrance to a naturalistic cosmology. But it is only a gate of entrance. The thinker must deal with space, time, causality, matter, energy, life, mind,— in fact, with all the basic categories—before he has his naturalism as a philosophy.

Now because my own thinking has been along the lines sketched above I have employed the term naturalism as the logical term for my position. In that I have stressed novelty and gradients in nature I have called it evolutionary naturalism.

Undeniably there are other species of naturalism resting upon a different epistemology. Thus there is the pragmatic kind of naturalism with its beloved word *experience*. I am quite ready to acknowledge that there is much in the drift and tendency of pragmatism with which I have sympathy; and yet the neglect of epistemology and the almost complete lack of cosmology debar me from anything but a very general feeling of kinship. It still strikes me as a *pseudo*-naturalism, an outlook which is too much of a holdover from idealism to represent the nature of common sense and science. Panpsychism is another species of naturalism which cannot be ignored. At one time, it was the expression of Kantian phenomenalism and was well under the control of idealistic motives—as witness James Ward's and Mr. Carr's revival of monadism—but in the hands of Professors Strong and Drake the naturalistic perspective has come to the front. For this reason, panpsychism must be considered a species of naturalism.

Taken in the large, then, there would seem to be three species of naturalism to-day competing for favor in philosophy; evolutionary, or emergent, naturalism, pragmatic naturalism and panpsychistic naturalism. I have already pointed out the chief technical difference between evolutionary naturalism and pragmatic naturalism. The divergence between it and panpsychism is subtle, and I shall have occasion to say more about it when I come to the ontological side of naturalism. In a summary fashion, the points of contention concern the degree of novelty admitted for evolution and the correctness of taking the psychical as a self-sufficient stuff. On the whole, the panpsychist takes the principle of continuity very literally and, since the psychical is for him a stuff, he regards emergence as a semi-miracle to be disputed. His tradition is the introspective, analogical tradition. The evolutionary naturalist, on the other hand, takes the organism as the unit for the study of the mind-body problem, does not conceive the psychical as a stuff but rather as a patterned event, or qualitative dimension, of a more inclusive system, and takes novelty of organization and properties as an empirical fact. We may say that he takes the categories of physical science a little more seriously and has a flavor of behaviorism in his psychology.

The general situation of naturalism having thus been studied we must pass to ontology. It will be remembered that we said that naturalism has been, traditionally, a cosmological term championing the self-sufficiency of nature and rejecting even the subtler forms of supernaturalism such as transcendentalism and objective idealism.

From the time of the Greek physicists the prime question in ontology has been, What is the stuff of reality? Answers to this question lost their simplicity because philosophy soon became like a three-ringed circus with controversies in cosmology, ontology, and epistemology going on simultaneously. The approach to the prime question became increasingly complicated. I am inclined to think that the human mind is at last getting ready to get back to ontology and to answer the question, What is the stuff of reality?

What possibilities seem open to a naturalistic cosmology on the ontological side? At first glance, certainly, the choice seems to lie between panpsychism, neutralism, experientialism and materialism. Is there any other possibility? Must the evolutionary naturalist find his ontology in a development of materialism? It is this question which I shall have chiefly in mind in the remainder of the article.

It is needless to point out that physical realism opposes experientialism. As for neutralism, this term has been the expression of the epistemological monism of the Mach-James-Russell movement. The critical realism which underlies evolutionary naturalism precludes the appeal to a neutral, semi-experiential stuff which can be taken alternately as mental and physical according to context. The distinction between the content and the object of knowledge and the frank acceptance of consciousness as an existentially—though not a cognitionally—private domain prevents this hypothesis and makes it irrelevant. No; neutralism is a *tour de force* which has no significance for evolutionary naturalism. By rejecting panpsychism must evolutionary naturalism fall back upon materialism? . . .

I shall largely disregard the extrinsic weaknesses of materialism and stress its intrinsic weaknesses as conceived in the past. I mean by extrinsic weaknesses those which flow from the contradiction of cherished beliefs; and by intrinsic weaknesses those which are due to the logical inadequacy of a doctrine to the facts it must cover. These have, of course, been connected. Some of the opprobrium under which materialism has suffered has been due to its logical inadequacy.

There is small doubt in my mind that the extrinsic weaknesses of materialism have had their influence upon even the philosophic standing of materialism. The philosopher has usually been an academic man, and the academic man has been under pressure of various sorts to maintain a genteel tradition. Besides, to be called a materialist has been like being fired at by a blunderbuss. It has come to mean for many irreligion in the sense almost of immorality, lowness of ideas, etc. The extrinsic weaknesses of naturalism have not been as great, although many philosophers have attempted to identify it with complete control by instincts, with psychological hedonism, etc. The truth is that naturalism was never quite so specific an ontological theory as materialism. It was, as I have pointed out, more markedly cosmological. . . .

Let us, then, pass to a consideration of the intrinsic weaknesses of past materialism. If materialism can be redeemed from these, I shall have no objection to evolutionary naturalism's ontology being called materialism. It might then be called the new materialism, or emergent materialism, or critical materialism as I have often called it. Let the reader recall what I said in regard to recurrence in philosophy; it is always recurrence with a difference.

The following doctrines are those which materialism has been identified with in the past and which have been held up as folly: (1) physical realism, (2) mechanism, (3) epiphenomenalism, (4) denial of the significance of values and ideals, and (5) stress on stuff rather than on organization. Now I do think that some of these doctrines are erroneous and that, if materialism inevitably implies them, evolutionary naturalism will refuse to be called materialism. I am frank to confess that some of the extrinsic weaknesses of materialism have followed from intrinsic weaknesses. . . .

The evolutionary naturalist has physical realism in common with the materialist. He would not separate himself on this count. . . . Development and supplementation would here be all that would be necessary.

Another weakness of materialism was its whole-hearted identification of itself with the principles of an elementary mechanics. It was too naively scientific. We may call this species of materialism *reductive materialism.*

By its very principles, evolutionary naturalism is opposed to reductive materialism. It is not finalistic, or teleological, in the old sense whether Aristotelian or theological, but it does not hold that relations in nature are external and that things are machines of atomic complexity. Organization and wholes are genuinely significant. It is on this point that evolutionary naturalism parts company with traditional materialism. But I see no reason to believe that materialism will not adapt itself to this change in the outlook of science itself, for it has no will of its own in the matter, being, by its very motivation, a philosophical reflection of the generalizations of science.

But epiphenomenalism is a more serious matter. I doubt that materialism could overcome this obstacle without a philosophic acuity greater than it has shown. Even Santayana seems to me to have fallen short at this point. The cause of this dogma is the neglect to realize the limitations of the knowledge of things gained through external observation alone. The concept of the physical was thus one-sided and external. When we remember that there was added to this abstractness of the idea of the physical the acceptance of extreme mechanicalism, we do not wonder at epiphenomenalism.

Evolutionary naturalism has brought in this double correction. On the one hand with behaviorism it takes mind to be a category of the physical sciences for a kind of functioning and response and, on the other hand, it deepens its knowledge of a highly integrated physical system, the organism, by supplementary self-acquaintance. Into the subtleties of this double-knowledge view this is not the place to enter. Suffice it to point out that it modifies traditional materialism considerably. The brickbat conception of matter has vanished.

With the admission of levels in nature and the efficacy of mind as a living kind of organization, the rejection of the significance of values and ideals as effective elements in the functioning of a human organism is undermined. Ethics and sociology become natural sciences resting on psychology, just as psychology becomes continuous with biology. The day of the complete supremacy of physics and chemistry has passed with reductive assumptions.

To me the inadequacy of traditional materialism stands out startlingly when it is confronted with political and social problems. What relevance has the movement of atoms in a mechanical way to the growth of institutions and the establishment of associations with their purposes and objectives. The theory does not connect up with the data which are to be interpreted and explained. . . .

These intrinsic weaknesses of materialism make it hard to reform. And yet it stands for the self-sufficiency of the physical world, of nature, for a certain unity of process and material. All events are in the one world, and there are currents passing back and forth with nothing alien and imported from outside. Evolution and devolution, the higher and the lower, the simple and the complex, are components of the one great physical theatre. But it is this that naturalism likewise stresses.

The last doctrine which I identified with traditional materialism was the emphasis upon stuff rather than upon organization. Clearly this emphasis was an expression of the mechanical ideal itself in its atomic form. If relations are external and integration not recognized as intrinsic and strategic, the stuff of nature simmers down to the bare elements which are tossed hither and thither like flotsam and jetsam. Pattern and fibres of connection are ignored; the whole is but the parts or, to put it more exactly, there is no whole. But, as I understand the drift of science and the logic of the facts, integration and organized response are intrinsic to physical things and find expression in behavior and in the energies which are accumulated and discharged. In the strict sense, in short, matter is only a part of a *material system*. There is energy; there is the fact of pattern; there are all sorts of intimate relations. There has been, in other words, something of the abstract and reductive about our thought of matter and of material systems. There is heterogeneity, qualitative diversity in the material world. *The truth of materialism was in its naturalism more than in its oversimplified ontology.* It expressed the faith that everything real must have a locus in nature and have a function to perform in its economy.

* * * * *

. . . What comes home to my mind is the greater need of categories in our ontology. Matter, or stuff, needs to be supplemented by terms like integration, pattern, function. Picture-thinking must be replaced by genuine thought. Matter is a material system, and there are levels of material systems.

Let me in conclusion refer to a criticism of my position by Professor Thilly in a recent article in the REVIEW.[1] Before he begins his summary and criticism of my outlook, he makes this

---
[1] Vol. XXXV, No. 6.

statement: "To regard the living human organism as the locus of consciousness is not materialism *unless the organism is in turn reduced to a mere physical mechanical system.*"[2] But that is precisely what the evolutionary naturalist refuses to do. He stresses levels in nature with new properties and different patterns. There are qualitatively different systems in nature with different modes of causality. Thus teleology is a characteristic feature of human organisms. I am sure that my critic will admit that he did injustice to my position by not emphasizing this essential feature which differentiates it from traditional materialism. . . . In the second place, I do not believe that Professor Thilly has grasped the full significance of what I have called the double-knowledge approach to the organism. Systems of philosophy are fairly subtle things and can be judged adequately only if the whole is analyzed. I may make my position clearer, perhaps, by pointing out that my view of the mind-body situation is a development of the double-aspect theory in the light of evolutionary levels in nature and critical realism. For me, consciousness is intrinsic to the functioning organism but cannot be perceived from the outside.

. . . To have a consciousness intrinsic to the cortex, a factor in its responses, does not seem to me a "full-fledged interactionist dualism." It is only to admit the efficacy of consciousness after its own nature and in its own locus. . . . My point was that neural activity could be known from the outside only in terms of the physical sciences including behaviorism, *while the same neural activity could be known from the inside also in some degree by means of the individual's consciousness which was intrinsic to it.*

Why, then, have I spoken of consciousness as a variant? Because I do not think of it as a stuff so much as an ever-changing qualitative component of the functioning of the brain. It is here that I differ from panpsychism. But it is a variant which has for us a unique status, for in it alone are we conscious, in it alone are we on the inside of nature as conscious beings. It is for this reason that it is a variant in a somewhat different

---

[2] *Op. cit.*, p. 535.

way from that in which "the ether-wave is a variant from the air-wave."

I am convinced that I am right in refusing to call myself a materialist and in rebelling when others call me one until these points of difference from traditional materialism are fully grasped and reckoned with.

IS NATURALISM ENOUGH?[*]

I take it that general usage favors the proposition that all materialists are naturalists but that not all naturalists are materialists. If such is the case it is important to determine the precise points of difference between naturalism and materialism. In what ways does materialism go beyond naturalism in its assertions?

In an article of an expository sort Professor Hook has undertaken to show that much of the controversy between materialism and idealism was motivated by the recognized conflict between naturalism and supernaturalism.[1] And here, he argues, the key concepts are teleology and probability. Now I would agree, in the main, with his excellent analysis of backgrounds and motivations. Where I differ from him is in what seems to me his rather cavalier treatment of materialism as distinguished from a rather generic sort of naturalism applicable to pragmatism, positivism, panpsychism, and other varieties of a naturalistic outlook. It is as though materialism was to be robbed of its name, pushed to one side with scarcely concealed scorn, and witness that name appropriated by naturalism. In short, the thesis seems to be that the only defensible meaning assignable to materialism is that of naturalism.

I am the more confirmed in this impression because of his attack upon materialism in his book, *From Hegel to Marx*, where he overtly rejects materialism in its traditional ontological associations on the ground that it involves an impossible correspondence theory of truth and the assumption that effects are like their causes.[2]

---

[*] R. W. Sellars, *JP*, XLI (1944), 533-544.

[1] *JP*, Vol. XXXI (1934), pp. 235 ff.

[2] Pp. 283 f. Is this not too general? Does not the organism have specialized methods of reproducing patterns and relations?

Now I am not surprised at this position. It is precisely what I should expect from a thinker with Professor Hook's perspective and philosophical affiliations. Yet because I differ from him on important technical points and am more ready that he to believe that materialism is reclaimable and that naturalism is not enough, I take this occasion to invite him to an exploration of the issues involved. Since we have a naturalistic outlook in common and since both of us admire science and its methods, there should be little, if any, emotional tension. I am even ready to grant that Dewey's position *almost* clicks. But, in drawing the philosophical threads of my thought together, I find that pragmatic naturalism has apparently waved aside many issues, largely from an almost morbid fear of the "subjective." If I am mistaken, I hope that Professor Hook can set me right. In these days it would be a pity to have empirically-minded naturalists work at cross-purposes. In what follows, then, let me say in advance that I am not expounding a simple-minded and clearly outmoded form of materialism involving reductionism, denial of connections and organization, and the treatment of consciousness as an epiphenomenon. It is a critical and philosophical form of materialism with, I believe, maturity in its theses.

Since the primary purpose is that of exploration and the determination of differences—if there are such—the best method would seem to be the presentation of a number of theses which seem to me essential to materialism and also defensible. Having stated these, I shall indicate how they seem to me to differ from those characteristic of pragmatic naturalism and then invite comment. An oldish thinker may be excused if he has systematized his principles and interrelated them. And may I say that I believe in systematic exploration as against merely piecemeal analysis? In the long run it gets one further. At any rate, the theses which I regard as alone sufficient to characterize a philosophical form of materialism fall under four headings: (a) epistemological, (b) psychophysical, (c) ontological, and (d) axiological. . . .

I

1. Perception is the basic act of cognition and, upon analysis, is discerned to involve a denotative reference to an *objective*

and a sensory symbolization of that objective, plus additional conceptual meanings characterizing it and its relations.[3]

2. Perception is an elementary level of knowing and too much should not be expected of it. Even the concepts used are largely practical in import.

3. Sensations are neither acts of cognition nor, outside of introspective and inspective attention, objectives of cognition. They are taken up into the perceptual response and used therein as symbols, guides, and points of departure for conceptual characterization of external objectives.

4. Since perception expresses a response of the organic self to stimuli, it is not surprising that it is felt to be an act of the percipient. The awareness of the percipient in perception has been too much neglected in studies of perception. The objective of the directed response, the referent, is correlative to the percipient and is assumed to have a similar existential status. *This is the basis of realism.*

5. The Lockian theory of perception should be rechristened the causal theory of the generation of sensations. It is not a theory of perception at all, since it disregards the directed response of the organic self, reference, and symbolic characterization. This mistake, combined with Cartesian dualism and a false formulation of the correspondence theory of truth, led to all the difficulties which have puzzled epistemologists and to Berkeleian idealism and Humian phenomenalism.

6. We do not first know subjective states of mind and then infer external things but, from the first, in perception are concerned with objectives of organic response. Coghill has shown that motor responses even precede the development of sensory factors.[4]

7. There is no "cognitive relation" between the cognitive act of the percipient and its referent but only a guided pointing.

---

[3] Besides perception we can have the more delicate knowledge-by-acquaintance of physical factors. I am inclined to think that all cognition involves symbolization and concepts. But here what is known is also given, while in perception it is not.

[4] I have talked over this point with Professor C. Judson Herrick who is editing Coghill's papers.

Demonstratives like "this" and "that" are correlated with such pointing.[5]

8. Cognition never involves a literal apprehension of its objective—as naïve realism suggests. It is *as though* this were the case in perception because sensations are caught up in the directed symbolization and *function* as surfaces, appearances, and manifestations.[6]

9. Physical things—including the organic self—are objectives of scientific knowledge, just as they are of perception. There are not two tables *à la* Eddington. We simply know more about the table in science.

10. With this approach it is meaningless to talk about things-in-themselves or about mental space versus physical space.

11. While sustained by a complex mechanism, cognition is simply a directed disclosure of denotables through symbols, an *achievement* which is *sui generis*. It is mythical to talk about spectator theories of cognition.

12. True, as an adjective attached to propositions, means "gives knowledge of the referent," "expresses a fact," which are equivalent. The criteria of trueness are empirical and logical of the sort usually discussed. The correspondence theory of truth should be completely reformulated as the correspondence theory of the *conditions* of knowledge. Such correspondence is a justified inference from the fact of knowledge and a study of its underlying mechanisms.

13. The pragmatic test of *praxis* is like a final examination justifying the human claim to achieve knowledge of the environment. If our validated knowledge-claims left us helpless, we might well be skeptics—if we survived.

I wish now to make a few comments upon the implications of these epistemological theses as related to pragmatism. And here is where the remarks of Professor Hook will be particularly interesting.

---

[5] I notice that Professor Gentry has recently come to the conclusion that symbolic reference involves no literal relation to the referent. He will find this thesis in my *Principles and Problems* (1926).

[6] It is no wonder that Professor Moore is puzzled. Here, again, a more inclusive approach would aid limited-analysis.

With the set-up indicated, it is obvious that I am not defending a merely *passive mirror-theory* of knowledge with an otiose spectator; and yet knowledge is not for me the sort of merely predictive, forward-looking affair within "experience" that it seems to be for the pragmatist. Of course, I recognize empirical predictions, just as I recognize memories and judgments about the past. But it seems to me an undeniable fact that we claim to know things coexistent with ourselves, the "antecedent" reality of Dewey's critics. Now having, from the beginning, studied James's transitive theory of knowing and Dewey's assumption that a representative realism of any sort was embogged in Cartesian dualism and the above-mentioned epistemological difficulties, I can sympathize with the path taken; and yet I hold that the above analysis escapes all these traditional difficulties and enables us to construct a physical realism. *And a physical realism is essential to materialism. So long as Hook adheres to his pragmatic theory of knowledge he can not be a materialist.* Here is a watershed. And I find that pragmatists are seldom willing to go over the ground and ask themselves why realists think that the pragmatists have much in common with idealists. . . .

. . . I turn next to psychophysics.

II

Here, again, I can only be summary and state theses with little enlargement upon them.

1. I take it that the percipient is at least dimly aware of himself as an embodied self over against the things perceived. This awareness is deepened by action, such as walking toward the object, handling it, etc.

2. Again, it is my opinion that self-awareness is quite analogous to external perception and involves reference, symbolization, and characterization. Such self-awareness has a *spread* from awareness of bodily attitudes through kinesthetic sensations, awareness of organic tone through organic sensations, awareness of how the organic self feels through feeling, awareness of desires and purposes through desiderative and purposive experi-

ences. This spread does not conflict with a functional unity, a sense of a reacting embodied self.[7]

3. There is no pure ego nor a disembodied consciousness. These are cultural myths.

4. The chief difference between external perception and self-awareness is that reflection forces us to regard the experiences symbolic of the self as more concerned with intra-bodily activities and adjustments. The sensory data used in external perception are more specialized and peripheral in import. It would seem that they were developed to guide external response. We do, of course, perceive our organic selves in this external fashion also.

5. In self-awareness the experiences we use symbolically are events inseparable from the activities of the organic self. But we regard the organic self as a continuant having capacities which find expression in such activities. This categorial meaning of "being a continuant" develops conjointly in external perception and in self-awareness.

6. The organic self is as complex and differentiated as the organism for it is the organism. The brain seems to be the organ of cognition in that sensory data arise there and are interpreted in the light of organic responses and operations. But it must not be forgotten that the brain is a specialized organ reflecting and developing the sensorimotor arc. It is the whole organism that knows through the brain.

7. Introspection and retrospection are specialized forms of knowing in which attention is directed to the "total experiencing" of the individual involved in both external perception and self-awareness. It is a mistake to regard introspection as self-awareness. That is the error to which idealists, such as Parker and Brightman, are prone.[8]

8. What from the first tends, as Stout pointed out, to be considered an embodied self, can now be identified with the functioning organism. This organic self is thus known by each

---

[7] A large ingredient in our reflective knowledge of the self is knowledge about capacities and tendencies. This knowledge is based on both external observation and self-awareness.

[8] I would ask both of them this question, Do we have knowledge-by-acquaintance of the self?

of us in two supplementary ways, from the outside and from the inside. These are integrated in self-knowledge.

9. But it must be fully realized that the kind of knowledge developed around external perception can never attain "consciousness" and make it an object of acquaintance. But this fact does not make consciousness inaccessible or "subjective" in a mysterious way. A good epistemology enables us to understand the situation.

10. When properly categorized, there is no conflict between external perception, self-awareness, and knowledge-by-acquaintance of consciousness. Consciousness is accessible and can be talked about.

11. Consciousness is as spatial as brain events are for it is intrinsic to them. Cartesianism was a clumsy, dualistic, rationalistic set-up. It was unevolutionary, had a stereotyped conception of matter, and a substantialistic conception of mind. Hobbes had a better approach.

12. Hence, though consciousness, or experiencing, is always personal and organism-centered, it is accessible to knowledge-by-acquaintance and public through reports. It is not "subjective" in some hidden and dualistic way. Nevertheless, it is a fact that, in his consciousness, each one is participating in the functioning of his own organism in a way that he can not participate in the functioning of another's.[9]

13. By means of these theses in psychophysics we can clarify further the points in epistemology. For instance, "transcendence" —a terribly equivocal and mystifying term—can now be seen to signify only the fact that cognitions are guided denotative references. Even at the highest level of knowledge-about, a frame of reference is involved. The objective of such cognition is, intentionally, *a thing made a referent.* Such a reference involves no mysterious, literal cognitive relation; and the referent is considered coexistent with the percipient organism or concrete knower. It is a case of the organic self pointing to, and characterizing, denotables in the same world with itself. It equally points to itself, for all denotables are public in both a behavioral and a

---

[9] Of course, as Dewey points out, we might produce neural Siamese twins by surgery.

linguistic sense. *But this fact signifies that observation is a cognitive term which must be epistemologically analyzed. It is so easy to speak about "observables" without saying what we observe or how we observe.* I claim to be a realistic empiricist and hold that the organic self observes both itself and the things around it. Here is where I break with phenomenalistic empiricism. I reject completely the notion, bound up with dualism, that the "mind" in some transcendental fashion gets literally and existentially over to things and to the past and to the future. I don't believe in such a mind—and I suppose the pragmatist does not either. Knowledge is a tested referential disclosure.

14. Materialism depends upon this identification of the self with the organism.

Again I comment upon these theses with respect to the difference between materialism and pragmatic naturalism.

As I see it, pragmatism has tended to reject a consciousness embodied in the organism. While Dewey admits organism-centered enjoyings in his theory of valuation, he is not clear as to their existential status. And, as I understand it, he never developed an epistemology and a psychophysics along the above lines for fear of Cartesian dualism and epistemological quagmires. By a *volte face* which was encouraged by the traditions of objective idealism, which had the same fears, and by the suggestions contained in James's transitive, or forward-pointing, theory of knowledge, put in the context of a biological radical empiricism, he developed a peculiar kind of *experientialism*, supposedly more naïve than the naïve realism of the new realism, with knowing transformed into a validation of ideas. Am I right in this analysis? . . .

Now it is my ineluctable belief that a pragmatic naturalism which does not have an explicit realistic epistemology and a clear-cut psychophysics is doomed to all sorts of sophistications in the interpretation of scientific results. What are electrons and molecules? How seriously shall we take the patterns worked out by chemists and the molecular-thick coatings verified by Langmuir? Shall we take uncertainty-principles and relativity measurements to be ontological or epistemic? In other words, what kind of an ontology—which is not meta-physics—can one work out?

Thus I have endeavored to make intelligible as two preliminaries to materialism: (a) physical realism, and (b) an analytic way of thinking the insertion of consciousness in the organic self. Somehow pragmatic naturalism does not seem to me to have the sharp contours and reach that a mature materialism can have.

* * * * *

III

I turn now to some ontological theses. It is obvious that a philosopher of any competence will work concurrently downward from the human and upward from the inorganic. There is a floor but no ceiling and only emergent integrations.

1. A positive concept of matter can be constituted in terms of empirically founded categories, such as continuance, existence, causal activity, combined with detailed facts about spatial structure, behavior, and capacities. Such categories are apprehended by intellection working on perception and self-awareness. He who, like the positivists and Hume, reduces perceiving to sensing can have neither things nor selves.

2. A mature materialism is neither reductive nor atomistically mechanical.

3. The universe is eternal and has no linear direction as a whole.[10]

4. Mind is as much a physical category as a psychical one and concerns the operations and capacities of the organic self at the cerebral level.

5. Material substances or continuants are generated and corrupted within the intrinsic endurance of material being.

6. Consciousness is a *qualitative isolate* in which we participate in our functioning. Here alone are we on the inside of nature.

7. As I see it, those who say we have no positive conception of matter are either Berkeleians or else desiderate knowledge-by-acquaintance directly or by analogy. Much turns upon the

---

[10] In the July, 1944, number of the *Philosophical Review* (Vol. LIII, pp. 359-382), I have an article entitled "Reformed Materialism and Intrinsic Endurance" which illustrates in detail what I mean by this thesis.

conception of the self. Is it identifiable with what is *given* in consciousness? Or do we have here merely a base for cognitive insight into the conscious activities of the organic self?

I have offered these ontological principles of a philosophical materialism in order to present to Professor Hook samples of what it means. And so I may put my query at this stage in the hypothetical form: If the epistemological and psychophysical hurdles are surmounted, do the above samples seem plausible? And, if so, in what respects does materialism exceed the limits of pragmatic naturalism? It seems to me to be going further in the same general direction and to suggest improvements upon pragmatic experientialism. It removes a certain cloudiness in technical matters. But it is a reformed, or philosophical, materialism. To me, one amusing thing is the fact that the developments in physics seem to me to have largely helped to make a philosophical materialism possible, while physicists are assuring the public that it liquidates materialism. I suppose it is partly a semantic question. What they should mean is the tautological statement that the new physics liquidates the old physics.

IV

For the present purpose the discussion of axiology can be very brief. I believe that the materialist need differ very little from the pragmatic naturalist in these matters. Personal values and valuation express the developed attitudes and sentiments of the individual in his social setting. These can be repeatedly tested and revalued in the light of experience. Presumably the process is not arbitrary but reflects satisfactions and frustrations of the self in its relations. There is no difference, in principle, when it comes to institutional values and norms. There are, of course, no Platonic, transcendental values, no non-natural values.

As against the positivist, the materialist holds that value-meanings can be developed by the organic self and used in the appraisal of things, events, and possibilities. Such appraisals always have a frame of reference and are not to be regarded as cases of cognition. Valuations and cognitions are not reducible to one another, though knowledge guides valuation. If I am not mistaken, the pragmatic naturalist would also reject the positivist's too simple reductionism of values to emotions and their verbal expression. I wonder, however, whether he has himself done justice to the self as a pretty determinate sort of continuant *and has not been too forward-looking after the pattern set in his transitive theory of knowing*. In other words, has he not overused the application of scientific method in a field where the broad outlines of human insight and integrity express the *quality* of human beings? Such quality is, of course, not static or socially unconditioned. I repeat that there need be no basic conflict between the philosophical materialist and the pragmatic naturalist in the field of values and that all of us owe a great debt to John Dewey. I myself prefer his correlation of values with judgments of valuation as against enjoyings and desirings, as personal experiences. And these judgments can be constantly tested in the light of such enjoyings. But here, again, as shown in his discussion with Professor Rice, it seems to me that Dewey is too afraid of the "subjective." . . . [Personal] consciousness is a basic fact upon which he who has it can make public reports.[11] And he is bound to use his own data in both observational and valuational judgments. It is the reference and the judgment that is communicable. I can not literally transfer my experiencings to another. I can only report upon them verbally and through action.

* * * * *

This approach makes possible an ontological horizon which seems less natural to pragmatism and more congenial to materialism.

REFORMED MATERIALISM AND INTRINSIC ENDURANCE*

There are optional horizons in philosophy. Thus one can ignore ontology or one can commit oneself to the ontological enterprise and grapple, as best one can, with some rather abstract distinctions and their implications. Pragmatism and positivism

---

[11] A really splendid discussion between Dewey and Rice, far above the level of positivistic reductionism of values to commands and interjections, this *Journal*, vol. XL (1943), pp. 5-14; 309-317; 533-543; 543-552; 552-557.

* R. W. Sellars, *PR*, LIII (1944), 359-382.

have, in the main, made the first choice and within that horizon have done, as all acknowledge, admirable analytic work. Realism, on the other hand, has in its various modes accepted an ontological horizon. Even such opposing positions as materialism and neo-Thomism have at least this much in common, that they take ontological categories seriously.

The drift of my own thought has been in the direction of a reformed materialism less dominated by extreme atomism and strict mechanical notions than has usually been the case in materialism. Recognition is given to internal relations, to integration, to immanent causality, to emergence and local wholeness. At the same time, epistemological reflection has convinced me that material systems have far more to them than is grasped by abstract scientific knowledge about their composition and properties. Dualistic traditions have been hurtful here. Likewise injurious has been the Humian denial of causal agency. It is my opinion that we must think more along the lines of a reformed notion of *substantive being* fully capable of doing justice to becoming, events, and process.

Now, as I see the ontological situation, materialism reformed along these lines is confronted by ontologies having a theistic dimension. It is, I take it, the very genius of all forms of materialism to postulate the intrinsic endurance and immanent existence of material systems. Theism, on the other hand, looks upon nature and natural things as pointing beyond themselves for their endurance and existence. Neo-Thomism is very frank about this and conceives *esse*, or existence, as something contributed by God to the vast range of essences or quiddities. And such existence is different in different things, since it is received and not absolute. Non-catholic writers, such as Whitehead and Parker, approach the question from different assumptions; and yet I sense in them the postulate of dependent, or contributed, existence.

It is my desire in the present paper to connect naturalism with the principle of intrinsic endurance and to explore the meanings to be given to such terms as matter, being, and existence, within such a context. It is my intention to use neo-Thomism largely as a foil and to contrast its hylomorphism and its conception of substance and existence with those of reformed materialism. But I shall raise questions which, I feel sure, all anti-naturalists will want to debate. Not only will I give definitions but I will also indicate cosmological principles dealing with such topics as conservation, intrinsic endurance and becoming, being and nothing, existence and non-existence of denotables, eternity, quantity of being and quality, generation and corruption. In short, I shall permit myself something of an ontological debauch.

Now it goes without saying that a philosophically respectable materialism must have some epistemological and ontological subtlety. Atomic materialism united with classical mechanics had neither. The only intrinsic endurance it could think of was Eleatic. But in these energistic and evolutionary days the Eleatic type of intrinsic endurance is out of the question. Intrinsic endurance must be linked with activity, relations, and conservation. It cannot be a static permanence, or, as Whitehead calls it, simple endurance. All this sums up to my conviction that the postulates essential to a non-reductive materialism have as yet scarcely been explored.

It is relevant to recall that, during the first two decades of this century, the most persistent philosophical problem outside the epistemological field was that of the conquest of Cartesian dualism. How could mind and matter be brought together? And it is worthy of note that the dependence of these terms upon a God as a more primary substance was largely disregarded. Cartesian dualism, so conceived, found its focus in the mind-body problem. Radical empiricism and neutralism represented one line of approach which is, perhaps, still reflected in the positivist's double-language formula. The critical realist was, as naturally, led to explore other possibilities such as a double knowledge of the organism and the replacement of reductive mechanism by more evolutionary and integrative principles.

In those days the general drift in American philosophy—far more, I take it, than in English—was towards some sort of naturalism. And I do not say that is not still the case. But, for various cultural reasons, theism cannot now so easily be left out of the picture. Naturalism is being challenged to state and defend its postulates. Theologically inclined physicists have entered the lists; and, in the realm of technical philosophy, we have such distinguished thinkers as Maritain, Gilson, Whitehead, Montague, Parker, Northrop, and Hartshorne, standing for some form or other of theism.

Now any one who has an ontological horizon cannot brush this challenge off as easily as can the pragmatist or the positivist. An existential question is at stake and so a mere redefinition of God as an ideal does not meet the issue.

It is my conviction that this theistic challenge to naturalism is both desirable and stimulating. It should force the naturalistic physical realist to explore his most basic assumptions. In my own thinking, at least, it has led to a study of the existential theory implied by materialism. Of course, the type of materialism must first pass other tests. It must be of a philosophical kind responsive to the niceties of theory of knowledge. The name is of less consequence. It can be called the new materialism, reformed materialism, qualitative materialism—all expressions which I have used.[1] At this philosophical level inert brickbats are left behind and are replaced by categorial analyses. Existence, stuff, activity, relations, space, time, endurance, becoming, all these must be clarified and integrated. All of which means that materialism must be stepped up philosophically.

As I see it, the materialist holds that the cosmos is material in nature *and exists in its own right*. To assert this is to deny the contingency of the world. Another way of putting it is to affirm the *intrinsic endurance* of physical systems in their very becoming.

Now it is this principle that theism denies whether in terms of creation *ex nihilo*, most characteristic of Christian philosophies, or in terms of emanation or Platonic ingredience. The antimaterialist holds either that there is no material world (the idealistic alternative so dear to liberal Protestantism) or that it has a secondary, or derived, sort of existence. There are, of course, all sorts of philosophical complications and combinations.

---

[1] It may be of some slight historical interest to note the fact that I proposed the term, the new materialism, in the preface to *Critical Realism* (1916). Santayana became the only living materialist somewhat later.

Thus Montague and Northrop seem to hold that the physical world needs supplementation to account for order and evolution. But I am, at present, chiefly interested in the question of *aseity* as against contingency.

This question is, of course, a hoary one. Looking up *aseity* in the Oxford Dictionary, I found three interesting quotations: "The natural world for any self stability, aseity, or essential immutability of its own may again cease to be;" "By what mysterious light have you discovered that aseity is entail'd on matter?"; "The obscure and abysmal subject of the divine aseity." To the positivist, no doubt, such quotations reflect obscurantism. To the physical realist they do not. It is important to get clear ideas about the meaning of existence and to connect them up with endurance and becoming. I shall, therefore, be engaged in the present article in looking at such categories from a materialist's point of view. A contrasting position is always of value in such matters; and so I shall employ neo-Thomism . . ., partly because its postulates are so definite and partly because its Aristotelian principles enable me to bring out a contrasting way of handling generation and corruption. For the Thomist there are two modes of existence, the divine and the created; and existence is rather a mysterious *transcendental* along with truth and perfection. I may as well say at once that I shall argue against these transcendentals and change existence into the factual recognition of *existency*, so that to be a denotable entails existence. While I shall not discuss truth as a transcendental, it is obvious that, for the materialist, it cannot be a harmony between essence and the eternal thought of God, while perfection dissolves into properties and triadically founded valuations. All of which indicates that neo-Thomism helps to bring the categories of materialism into relief. Now, while I shall employ Christian Aristotelianism as a contrast, I shall also have in mind Whitehead's union of theism and reformed subjectivism. . . .

Metaphysics has been so much associated with the postulation of a higher reality beyond nature, with a meta-physics, that I have preferred the more neutral term ontology. I note that Marxists have the same preference, as also does Santayana. Materialism, then, is an ontology isomorphic with modern science. Much could be said for the post-Aristotelian division of philosophy into physics, logic, and ethics. But the science of physics, as it increasingly expressed metric knowledge about nature and retreated from natural philosophy (wisely, I think), came to engross the first term of this trinity. But must not the science of physics give us knowledge about physical existence? Materialism holds this belief and is an ontology.

After considerable reflection I have chosen the expression, intrinsic endurance, in place of simple endurance. While intrinsic endurance rejects dependent, derived, or contributed, endurance, it does not entail passivity, Eleatic fixity, or brickbatness. Matter I take to be active, dynamic, relational and self-organizing. It is an endurance which goes with activity for which I am contending. All composite existents which emerge are generated and corrupted, are maintained by activity. My divergence from *eventism* has other roots than a desire to defend outgrown notions of substance. Rather is it the expression of realism, as against sensationalism, and reflects the recognition of structure, ontological causality, *and the generation of composite wholes.* Eventism does not seem to me to do justice to unavoidable categories. Thus those who build upon sensations and feeling, as Russell and Whitehead do, cannot accept substantiveness and force. There is a perpetual perishing of consciousness which, as I pointed out long ago in an article, is not conserved. What, then, can possess intrinsic endurance? Is it creativity? God? the permanent possibility of sensibilia? or material being? *Or can we get along without intrinsic endurance?*

* * * * *

I

Four primary principles of the new materialism may be stated as follows: (1) stuff or material, (2) dynamic connections and organization, (3) intrinsic endurance, and (4) levels of integrative and efficient causality. These principles qualify one another.

Stuff, or material, is a category of a fairly complex sort. It reflects the common notion of thinghood in terms of recoverable constituents. There is danger here since pattern and organization tend to be neglected as they were in traditional mechanical notions. I shall have something to say about this point in the later discussion of quality. Nor is this all. The concept of stuff has a relational moment. Here it ranges from the artist's idea of a medium upon which to work to the scientist's more analytic perspective. The term is realistic, denotative, manipulative, analytic, and synthetic. It does not imply that we need know very much about the intrinsic nature of materials. To the philosopher the concept of stuff, or material, is a challenge to categorial analysis. Plasticity, activity, form-making, recoverableness, intrinsic endurance, all stand out for comprehension.

And this brings us to the consideration of connections and organization. I note that Pepper and many others assume that materialism involves mechanicalism. That, surely, is a prejudice. Why should materialism lag behind science? Classical materialism thought in terms of classical psychics, that is, in terms of Eleatic particles having *simple endurance* of the static variety. But there is nothing about materialism as an ontology which limits it to such outworn postulates. From the very beginning of my thinking I rejected Newtonian absolute space and time and made both space and time, ontologically speaking, adjectival and relational. And I have always argued that s and t as metric qualities presuppose space and time as ontological characteristics of matter. Particles must be conceived in terms of connections, causal activities, fields. And this signifies that ontological time is to be correlated with *change of constitution* but not with a perpetual perishing of matter. I shall, in fact, argue that activity and intrinsic endurance are not contradictory.

From its inception in Greek thought materialism emphasized the positive and independent nature of matter. It did not depend upon the God nor was it under the control of purposes or ends external to itself. Instead, it endured in its own right, was self-sufficient and self-concerned. And it was the possession of these characteristics that made it from the first *the logical correlate of naturalism*. Let us admit at once that intrinsic endurance was conceived too simply and statically in traditional materialism, as it was later in classical physics. Changes were thought of as not involving the atoms themselves and reducible to mere shifts of position. This compromise with Eleaticism satisfied the demands of elementary physics and a philosophy hardly awake to the requirements of biology and psychology.

But I would still hold it true that the genius of materialism, as of naturalism, requires an intrinsic endurance, or self-conservation, on the part of material being. Such endurance must be underived and ultimate. And this, I take it, is a flat rejection of the contingency of nature. We shall have more to say about this as we come to distinguish between the existence of any denotable and the intrinsic endurance of material being. . . .

II

Let it be noted, then, that the overhauling of materialism must needs be a drastic one to make it compatible with evolutionary naturalism. There is no excuse for tying it down to past reductive and mechanical postulates. Simple location must not mean the denial of dynamic connections. At the most it means something of the nature of the law of inverse squares. Even the general relativity-theory admits determinable warpings expressive of the localization of matter. In reading Eddington on *The Philosophy of Physical Science* I find that the only kind of realism he is acquainted with is the Joadian type and I have considerable sympathy with his criticism of it. To make sensations distinct from sensings and thoughts independent of thinking does not appeal to the critical realist. Yet Eddington's conception of mind seems to me unempirical. But I have not the space to consider in detail his epistemology. Jeans, on the other hand, has developed a Kantian kind of agnosticism combined with an ontological Platonism. In any case both have developed a recognition of the difference between the form of scientific knowledge-about and *being*. To the philosopher this points to the need of the clarification of categories. Being, stuff, space, time, causality, as ontological, must be distinguished from their cognitive translation.[2] To use Professor Hall's term, categories are *constants;* and we should not expect ontological statements

---

[2] For this distinction see my article, "Causality and Substance," this *Review*, Jan. 1943.

to be verifiable in quite the fashion of predictive, scientific theories.[3]

It is important to bear in mind that traditional materialism not only had no adequate epistemology back of it but was identified with dualistic assumptions which left material being a washed-out abstraction, such as mere extension, with no positive, intrinsic content. I am led to think of this tradition when I am told that mine is an agnostic kind of materialism. Rather is it a protest against these dualistic caricatures.[4] As I see it, science does not reduce material being to a mere quality but merely deciphers the metric quantities obtainable by its technique. It is such *knowledge about* material systems. It is the very import of ontology to deny that being can be reduced to knowledge. Surely it has been one of the weaknesses of idealism to flirt with such a reduction. Materialism and Aristotelian philosophies have been far healthier in this respect. Matter as *being* must have a positive and determinate content. Its actuality cannot be vacuous. But the materialist takes it to be wise not to jump too hastily to the panpsychistic universalization of feeling as a kind of sample. Have we not expected too much from external knowledge resting on sensory disclosures aided by metrical techniques? Ontology puts scientific knowledge in better perspective. Science does an excellent job. Why should we expect it to make nature transparent? Idealism, sensationalism, and positivism have, as I see it, nourished absurd pretensions which materialism must protest against. Knowledge merely makes certain quantitative, structural, and behavioral facts about nature stand out. So far it is a *disclosure;* but reflection on ontology and its categories should swing us over to the implications of causal agency. Post-Humian philosophy has, in my opinion, been vitiated by the *overstress on prediction.* Predictions

---

[3] I refer to Hall's contribution to the book, *Twentieth Century Philosophy.* I hope the positivists will reply to his critique of their position. Also see Miss Stebbing's criticism of Joad's astonishingly naïve epistemology in the recent *Aristotelian Society symposium.* He is almost as artless as most positivists for whom epistemology is *sinnlos.*

[4] Garnett follows Stout in this tradition and so establishes an immaterial self and God. Not being able to read everything, he limited himself to British theories of emergence. Colonially minded Americans do the same.

and *if-thens* have made philosophers too temporalistic, neglectful of constants and constitution.

* * * * *

Let us grant, again, that materialism has, on the whole, been dominated by its approach in terms of the inorganic sciences. What I have called external, or non-participative, knowledge called the tune. Now the evolutionary materialist recognizes that the organic self is a material system which has the peculiar property of having knowledge directed at itself. This fact is unique for human beings and must have basic significance for reformed materialism. Here we have what I would call *participative knowledge*. Here, and here alone, are the data of knowledge intrinsically integral to functional activities of the brain-mind. What they disclose is a sustained series of processes resting on habits and capacities. In them we have some slight glimpse into organizational complexities, a glimpse which fits in with external knowledge of the brain.

Now, as I see it, the shifting field of private consciousness must be regarded as a "natural isolate" of the functioning brain. As such, it demonstrates that a unified physical system has a qualitative dimension of this sort coterminous with activities. And, surely, that is what we might expect, once we freed ourselves from the negative notions associated with purely external knowledge. Brickbat notions of matter, when united with the Eleatic and Cartesian traditions mentioned above, fostered a reluctance to conceive physical systems as having a qualitative, ontological dimension or insideness. And, as I have argued, phenomenalistic empiricism worked in the same direction by its rejection of ontology. But the critical materialist is forced to postulate a positive content to being, a content responsive to the relations and activities discernible even to external knowledge.

Participative knowing, not realistically enough interpreted, has been, of course, the *raison d'être* of idealism and panpsychism. But because they never did justice to external, or nonparticipative, knowing, they were easily misled even here. It was the question of the epistemology and ontology of the "self" which offered difficulties. Berkeley proclaims only a vague notion of the self. But the self is not the notion. And Kant is agnostic with respect to the noumenal self. How much simpler and franker is the proposal of the materialist that the self is the organism! Here, however, we have a twofold knowledge, the one participative, the other external, or nonparticipative. It is historically interesting to note that, as C. A. Strong and Durant Drake moved from Kantian agnosticism to critical realism, they at the same time became materialists, only materialists of a still mechanistic type who did not see the importance of organization and functional unity. One reason for Drake's theory of essences, which have no existence, was his belief that the brain is merely an aggregate of moving particles and that its functional unity is merely a sort of statistical resultant. It was upon this ground that he rejected my form of the double-knowledge approach to the brain and left to the brain only the vague intrinsic sentiency of material particles. In a conversation I had with Strong at Fiesoli in '37 he admitted that he had not done justice in his thought to organization and a *functional togetherness*. I do not hesitate to say that the dividing line between the old and the new materialism lies here. The wise handling of relational and functional togetherness which avoids the atomism of completely external relations, on the one hand, and the mystical rendition of the phrase that the whole is more than the sum of its parts, on the other, is the desideratum. As I see it, Whitehead's Platonic concretion of events is one alternative to an activistic and pattern-forming materialism. I am also inclined to think that the brain is a very specialized organ for the formation of action-patterns and that what holds of it does not apply to liver or stomach.

While, then, experiencing in the concrete is, I believe, intrinsic to the functioning brain, there is no *intuition* of the ontological context of such experiencing.

Now two conclusions seem to me to follow from these principles: we have (1) no intuition of matter, and (2) no acquaintance with an intrinsic endurant.[5] All of which means that a sample of intrinsic endurance cannot be found in consciousness. And that is precisely what we should deductively expect, since consciousness is correlated with functional activity

---

[5] Hume's discussion of personal identity is illuminating. Memory does not produce the identity but discloses it. But he cannot explain it on his assumptions.

and expresses what I call the qualitative dimension of material systems. *Activity is to me unthinkable without a variable in that which is active.* The antithesis is Eleaticism, inertness. Active intrinsic endurance entails duration, time. But duration applies to existents and their acts. Consciousness is inseparable from cerebral action-patterns. Thoughts are participial events while the organic self is a continuant existent.

It follows that the *mode of being* of consciousness is *participial* rather than substantive. The principle of conservation, or intrinsic endurance, does not apply to it.

The empirical base of the apprehension of the meaning, continuance, is a tantalizing psychological question. And yet the meaning stands out in both external perception and self-awareness and, as I think, by mutual support. That is, I doubt that if we could not develop the apprehension of our numerical selfidentity we could develop the meaning of thinghood. At both poles, as I see it, we have the constant working of interpretative, cognitive activity. As regards the self, continuance and numerical sameness stand out cognitively through continuing felt attitudes and rememberings until we rightly comprehend ourselves as agents. Such experiences, heightened by social relations, operate as natural symbols of the self much as sensations are employed as natural symbols of external things. It is participative knowing since feelings and thoughts are in their mode of being participial to the organic self. By such participation we approach an intuition of the attitudes and activities of the self, for I see no reason to deny that these natural symbols have a disclosure-value with respect to the tides of our being. Certainly, the situation is even more intimate than in the use of sensations in perception as natural symbols having disclosure-value for external things. We must, however, be very careful in our use of the term intuition. I am inclined to think that cognition of the self is mediated, that is, symbolic and referential.

If, then, consciousness has only participial being and does not furnish us with a sample of intrinsic endurance, we must turn to the realm of denotables, that is, to self and things. To these, as we are aware, some measure of continuance is assigned, even though composite denotables are generated and corrupted and, consequently, are commonly characterized as having contingent, or historical, *existence*.

But we must be very careful to distinguish between being and existence. It seems to me clear that all physical denotables are forms of being. To deny this would be to consider them phenomenal or of the nature of illusions. They would be like bubbles which could burst and not leave a wrack behind. As I see it, reformed materialism is here confronted with the perennial question of process or becoming. There must be nothing illusory or transcending being about process and becoming. Matter must by its very nature be active and relational; and, to me, the two expressions imply one another. In short, I shall argue for the aseity of matter and maintain its intrinsic endurance.

And here we come upon basic questions which science alone can in the long run answer. Is the *floor* of physical being particulate even though the particles are never in isolation? Eddington holds strongly that there is a determinate number of both electrons and protons. In some fashion these are integrated to form the nucleus of atoms. They are in the nucleus as the eggs are in the omelette. Some kind of a dynamic organization has taken place which must not be pictorialized in billiard-ball terms. At any rate we must, I take it, postulate primary endurants which form what I called secondary endurants.[6] Thereafter, generation and corruption are on a more macroscopic scale; and we enter the realm of the countable and the describable. It is at this level that the term existence most properly comes into play. Such complex denotables are generated and corrupted so that existence is epistemically balanced by nonexistence. If such a denotable is an existent, in a very real sense *it* can cease to exist. Such is the very nature of history, becoming, and process. It is clear that we must so conceive existence that it permits the significance of nonexistence or ceasing to exist. But *being* must be made of sterner stuff. It is conserved and, as we shall argue, never conceivably becomes nothing. Change of existence is, rather, within being, an affair of constitution and process. In this sense there is no conservation of existence even though there is conservation of being. But we shall have more to say about

---

[6] See *The Philosophy of Physical Realism*, ch. xii.

these distinctions when we come to discuss quality and the kind of substantiality which goes with composite individuality. We humans have only this kind of temporary and contingent existence within the domain of physical being.

III

The ontological alternatives are fairly definite. By its very logic materialism must harmonize the intrinsic endurance of its ultimate stuff with the generation and corruption of composite wholes; and the facts indicate that integrative causality gives rise to the emergence of *novel levels of existence within being*. If wholeness applies, then mechanistic atomism must be rejected with its reductionism and its denial of causal agency to composite existents like human beings. On the other hand, theism moves from the contingency of existents to the contingency of matter, from a contributed kind of existence to an existence of a higher order. In this setting creation is supposed to become logically thinkable if not realizable.

There are many subtle variations of the theistic hypothesis. A brilliant recent development of emanation is Parker's Omega System which makes what I call the floor of being higher in quality than the monads which are sustained by it.

The hylomorphism of materialism, as we have noted, makes the unity and organized wholeness of an existent the expression of integrative causality so that the higher arises from the lower. Such a thesis is contrary to the genius of Christian Aristotelianism just as it was contrary to the unevolutionary outlook of Aristotle. While a composite may have a unity and form, it is, I understand, held that this form must be given an existence commensurate with the potencies of the forms of the parts. The demand is logical and would correspond to the thesis of the evolutionist that the whole is not indifferent to its parts. But where the Thomist says form or quiddity, the materialist says organized wholeness. It is in this fashion that integrative causality makes room for immanent causality.

Lexicographers inform us that the verb "to exist" had a surprisingly late appearance in English and that the primary meaning was "to stand out, to be perceptible." Then came "having being in a specified place, to continue in being, to maintain in existence." Such existence has an epistemic and an ontological pole. The gist of the latter is an acknowledgment of a denotable, that is, of something which can be referred to by pointing and description. Being is not blank and undifferentiated but ordered and cut up into denotables. We do not intuit these denotables but select them through natural symbols and descriptions. But what we are seeking is supposed to have the same sort of reality we have. I take it that appreciation of the brute fact of existence is grounded in self-awareness, in doing and suffering. Those who drop this meaning from perception are unrealistic. Denotables are then reducible to "If-then" predictions. There is no appreciation of expendable energies.

Logicians who have been interested in so-called existential propositions have, very naturally, concerned themselves with the epistemic pole and the applicability of concepts. Russell has never been afraid of paradoxes and so defined existence as a property of concepts. Obviously, it cannot be a property of all concepts but only of those which are exemplified. Hence it must be a relational property. The final test comes in perceptual verification. Is there a denotable describable by the concept? If seems to me clear that it is the denotable which we acknowledge to be an existent, to be out there; and yet the epistemic and relational element in the acknowledgment must not be forgotten. Were we able simply to intuit denotables there would not be this complication. And, as we have noted, the nearest approach to this is in selfawareness.

The Russellian view has something in common with the scholastic tradition with respect to essences or forms. Existence was conceived as a plus except with respect to that essence which necessarily existed or entailed its own existence. It is obvious that the realistic empiricism is skeptical of finding any concept which implies its own exemplification. But even St. Thomas rejected the ontological proof. It is the contingency of the existence of denotables which is emphasized. But what if denotables are but organizations *within being* whose contingency is that of their composite wholeness and unity? Then being is something ultimate which contingent denotables themselves are regarded as being expressions of. Now, as I see it, that has always been the theory of materialism and finds formulation in the concept of recoverable stuff and intrinsic endurance. Contingency and variability are then assigned to relations, organization, to the process side of being. On the other hand, the more theistic and creationalistic theory denies this notion of being.

One of the reasons why the secular realist is accustomed to emphasize the categories of existence and being is his long controversy with idealism and positivism. Idealistic systems, as A. K. Rogers never tired of pointing out, neglected the question of existence and tried to remain within the context of merely logical coherence. The realist, in opposition, asserted that thought, from perception to judgment, always referred to something beyond itself. I have argued that the pragmatist in his rejection of the correspondence-theory of truth[7] still remained with the idealist, though ambiguously and equivocally. But the naturalistic realist is thereupon confronted with the choice between materialism and theism with various forms of panpsychism hovering between.

But must we not have a *sample of being* if the concept is to have empirical meaning? Now I have argued that we have only a sample of participial being as in sensations and feelings; and yet that both external and participative knowing operate in terms of meanings and references involving such categories as endurance, activity, capacity, constitution. All of which signifies that cognition is not the same as sensing and rests upon interpretation and intellection. I once remarked to Russell that perceiving should be distinguished from sensing; but he refused to consider the distinction, and that was that.[8] But without such a distinction eventism follows logically. The whole concept of substantive being arises in cognition. As I see it, then, we should not expect an intuition of substantive being either in selfawareness or in

---

[7] I have reconstructed this traditional theory into a correspondence-theory of the *conditions* of knowledge and truth. I define *true* as a case of knowledge or as expressing a fact. Criteria are empirical and logical. Correspondence is a justified inference.

[8] In my opinion perception has a marked symbolic side. That is why it can be expressed in public terms and has its semantic content.

external perception. And, as a matter of fact, consciousness is to be correlated with becoming and functioning, with patterns and shifts of relations.

IV

We are brought, then, to the question of the proper conception of the relation between being and intrinsic endurance or conservation in activity.

It is fairly evident that composite denotables, such as chemical substances and organisms, are contingent existents, entities which come and go in the tides of being. What I have called qualitative substances, the highest emergent level of which, so far as we know, are human beings, are of this sort. They are generated, live their span, and vanish. They are continuants and have duration. Selfawareness ceases at death but the bodies remain for others to study and science informs us that the stuff of which they are composed is conserved. The kind of self Hume looked for, and could not find, has no existence. There is no inert, and changless, soul-substance. And so we have consciousness, as a natural isolate and a case of experienced participial being, the organic self as a denotable, known externally and participatively and adjudged a continuant, or contingent substance, sustained by processes. Is this all? The materialist says there is more. There must be a stuff, active and relational but selfconserving and having intrinsic endurance.

I take it that fact and reflection push the human mind on to the postulation of intrinsic endurance and the eternal. And the reasoning is not difficult to uncover. For instance, generation and corruption are seen to be supplementary. Already in Heraclitus this note is struck. Empedocles has his recurrent cycles driven by love and hate while the later atomism of Epicurus has much the same *dramatis personae*. Naturalism, in short, has been unable to conceive absolute beginnings and endings. And it should be recognized that orthodox theism has its own eternity of intrinsic endurance. It is to creation that there is assigned a secondary kind of being and endurance.

Now, as I see it, the generation of being from nonbeing is unthinkable for the simple reason that it is meaningless. The nonexistence of a continuant or contingent substance is thinkable since it merely signifies that no denotable is correctly symbolized by A since it has ceased to exist. But being is that which is presupposed by all denotables, for it is that within which they arise and cease to be. That A exists and that A does not exist are contradictories. But *being* cannot in the same logical fashion be set over against *not-being*. So far as I can see, not-being is only a verbalism. Such seems to me the philosophy of the aseity of matter. Out of nothing arises nothing because the term can have no application.

I judge that it was thoughts such as these that led the Greeks to postulate the eternity of the universe and its self-maintenance through change. Aristotle but agreed with the Ionians; and the materialists only emphasized the same postulate. Christian thought merely transferred it to a supernatural realm, while emanation doctrines sought a *via media*.

And so we come to the alternatives: either the intrinsic endurance of materialistic naturalism or the contributed endurance of supernaturalism in all its sophisticated forms. It seems to me evident that physical realism implies the first alternative. Existence signifies an acknowledgment of specified being; and, while we cannot intuit the intrinsic endurance of matter, we equally cannot intuit its dependent endurance. The burden of proof rests, therefore, upon anyone who postulates another kind of being to be granted intrinsic endurance.

Reformed materialism reverses Aristotelianism or, to use Marxism phraseology, stands it on its head. There must be a lowest limit of material texture and an open series of integrative emergence. It is, of course, the task of science to determine the most elementary level of stuff. But, since I do not believe in a linear evolution for the universe, as Lloyd Morgan and Alexander apparently did, I would hold that all levels of material organization are, or can be, contemporaneous. About this I shall have more to say in the next section. It may well be that the universe has always been much as it is at present, that is, has always had a variegated and spatially dispersed cosmography; and this without an eternal recurrence or great year. This would mean that ontological time has no direction since it is always local and is but a name for what is involved in all activity. We must avoid reading the distinctions of our temporal knowledge with its linear implications into nature. Real time is only an actual activity; and activity is local, relational, and spatial.

As I follow the argument of Gilson, it rests upon two bases: (1) the rejection of emergence, and (2) the unempirical, or metaphysical, postulation of an act of existing. And these are closely connected in this form of natural theology.[9]

It is, apparently, Gilson's thesis that philosophers have shut themselves up into essences and have, therefore, never got to existence. A hit, if you will, at Plato, Spinoza, and Santayana. But not a hit at Berkeley or Hume or at the outlook of the more empirical form of critical realism. In ourselves we have participative cognition and, in sensation and feeling, *being* is given participially and denoted both practically and theoretically *through* what is given. Thus being is factual and is both given and acknowledged.

But the materialist, while he does not believe in the metaphysical, recognizes and acknowledges what the pragmatist or the positivist is wont to call the *transexperiential,* but *not,* of course, the undenotable and the unknowable. External being cannot be intuited and internal being can be intuited only participially. The intriguing consequence is that what the neo-Thomist calls *esse* and assigns to God is by the materialist assigned to dynamic and pattern-forming matter. While the former asserts the contingency of the material world and postulates two modes of being, the materialist denies the contingency of the material world and finds no evidence for two modes of being. And with the denial of the contingency of the material world goes the affirmation of its intrinsic endurance.

It would lead us too far to consider Gilson's handling of the principle of emergence. I quite agree with him that it is an ontological principle as well as a scientific one. But he makes it too easy for his argument by assuming that order and organization are not intrinsic to even inorganic systems and that out of simpler forms of order more complex forms cannot emerge through integrative causality. I fear that his scientists are too tempting because of their careless use of categories like chance

---

[9] I refer, of course, to his argument in *God and Philosophy.*

and mechanism. It is a good dialectical display but hardly convincing to the naturalistic philosopher. And, of course, we are brought here to the sharp opposition between finalistic hylomorphism and evolutionary materialism to whose matter activity, relations, and intrinsic order are not alien. A materialism which finds a place for organization reverses Aristotelianism, for its moves in an exploratory way from the lower to the higher and not in a finalistic and hierarchical fashion from the higher to the lower.[10]

V

And so we find ourselves overlooking the perennial problems of becoming with intrinsic endurance, of quantity with quality, of eternity with time. How are composite, individual substances generated, maintained, and corrupted within an ocean of intrinsic endurance? How can there be qualitative gain or loss along with conservation of the amount of stuff or being? How can eternity include time? The logic of reformed materialism points to answers. In this concluding section I can only make suggestions.

As I see it, generation applies to the composite and integrated and presupposes the intrinsic endurance of the stuff which is integrated. Were any part of this to lose its intrinsic endurance that would mean that being had collapsed into not-being, which is unthinkable, meaningless.[11] Generation and becoming, therefore, belong to another ontological dimension than intrinsic endurance. To assert that A is generated and continues to exist for a while and then is corrupted is a statement about the tides of organization within being with its intrinsic endurance. In neither generation nor corruption does one move outside the context of being. All of which means that activity and organization reside in the very substance of being. Here we turn our back on any Eleatic motif in the most drastic manner. Matter implies

---

[10] *Cf.* my article, "Causality and Substance," this *Review*, Jan. 1943.

[11] Perhaps this is too strong. See Parker's comment. I mean that being, unlike an existent, has no contrast term. At most, it would signify the snuffing out of reality by itself, an internal collapse into nothingness. I can see no *why* to this. But the theists assume it; why can't the poor materialist do the same?

process and process implies matter. It is a materialistic *devenir*, not, as with Bergson, a vitalistic and mystical one.

Generable qualities and capacities accompany becoming[12] and it is for this reason that the conservation of the amount of being does not conflict with qualitative gain and loss. We humans are born, live some three score and ten, and then vanish from existence. Is there not quality to our lives, often unique quality? Values are realized; and *lost* because no longer sustained by the persons and groups who found them desirable. Such is the more or less tragic texture of human life.

Now I take it that the whole concept of quality in ontology has been mishandled because stupidly put in the context of projected sensuous qualities, for the naïve realist plastered on the surface of denoted things. Critical realism has turned its back upon such pictorial and external conceptions of quality. No; quality must be internal and intrinsic to being itself and a variable congenital with organization, changing capacities, and abilities. Quality is the changing content of being as causal integration proceeds and recedes. But, alas! our own intuition of it is limited to that "natural isolate," the private stream of our experiencing. But how could it be otherwise? It is important to note the presence of meanings based on operations of denotation and comparison. Consciousness reflects intellection as well as sensing. Empiricism has not always done justice to intellection.

I may remark incidentally that I do not see that, as the Marxists maintain following a clue in Hegel, quantity changes into quality. It is true, however, that the allocation of quantity does affect quality in that it affects wholes and relations. But I intend to examine this question more thoroughly in a paper on dialectical materialism.[13]

It would follow from this ontological analysis that quality, like generation and corruption, is an existential variable in no wise in conflict with the intrinsic endurance of material being. When philosophers, following Leibniz, speak of possible worlds, it seems to me that they should refer to existence rather than to

---

[12] These must rest upon *primordial* qualities and capacities.

[13] This paper will appear in the July issue of *Philosophy and Phenomenological Research*.

being. Being is the context of existence. As I see it, being is beyond fact, for it is the source and foundation of fact. We discover being in its processes and manifestations, of which consciousness is the unique case of qualitative participation.

And here I shall allow myself some cosmological speculations which seem to me reasonable but have no connection with any high *a priori* road. The outlook is existential and pluralistic. Thus it is my feeling that cyclical and linear cosmologies are essentially monistic. By linear cosmologies I mean those that picture the cosmos as moving abreast down a supposed stream of time. Creationalistic analogies are, I think, apt to be operative in such cosmologies. There is a beginning and an end, a cosmic direction and a path; even God has an antecedent and a consequent nature. But, for reformed materialism, ontological time is but the fact of activity and existential process. It is local and covers both emergence and recession. It is tightly tied up with space. Chronology with its past, present, and future stretched out easily leads to ontological illusions. Only, as Eddington saw, if the second law of thermodynamics has cosmic validity is there an ontological arrow intrinsic to being.[14] The process, or existential, capacities of being would thereby be limited. Needless to say, I am skeptical. It seems to me that cyclical notions are really monistic and assume some kind of unified and recurrent cosmic pattern, after the analogy of the great year of the ancients. But pluralism—and I take it that relativity is causally pluralistic—must seek another pattern.

Being a believer in the eternity of the universe and skeptical of linear and cyclical notions, I am naturally led to suppose that the universe has always been much as it is now, a variegated existential domain with a floor, much the same everywhere, above which rise here and there mountain peaks of emergent becoming followed in time by recession. The picture is that of a qualitative rising and subsiding in quite plural and local ways with a cosmic floor woven of particles in their dynamic relations. Biological existents and qualities occur but rarely; and it may well be that mental abilities and symbolic processes are

---

[14] Entropy seems to be statistical and macroscopic and not to apply to the Alpha or "floor" level.

seldom generated. To the traditional religionist this is not a congenial picture and he would like a celestial ceiling or another story. But the naturalistic humanist is ready to accept an austere ontology, austere even though this earth harbors no secret hostility to man. The human drama is local but not without its engrossing qualities of life and death. Cosmic epics must be left to the theist and to all those who, denying the intrinsic endurance of nature, speculate on a metaphysics.

It seems to me logical to hold that the stuff of being neither increases nor decreases. The first possibility suggests minimum beginnings and maximum endings; it is a linear way of approach. The second would be just the reverse of the first. And would not both be based on naïve biological analogies? If the stuff of being is intrinsically active and relational I should expect all generation and corruption to be an affair of integration and disintegration, neither violating the principle of conservation which expresses the intrinsic endurance of being. It is in this fashion that eternity includes existential time or process.

How far the fountain of qualitative, existential life will rise on this planet we do not know. The imagination still has free range. . . . There is relative, cumulative directionism guided by structure but no finalism. It is only in the behavior of individuals —and not in their genesis—that ends-in-view are set up, evaluated, and chosen. I have not the Platonic daring of Whitehead which assigns affective lure to eternal objects. Here, I suppose, is where the materialist has more of an agnostic streak than the panpsychist. What guides integrative causality at levels below the cortex? We have as yet little but words. Least action, equilibrium, dynamic tension? The genius of Whitehead shows in his philosophical daring. . . .

VI

I offer, in conclusion, some summarizing theses:

1. Ontology expresses an horizon entailed by realism.
2. Materialism postulates the intrinsic endurance of material being and is the logical correlate of naturalism.
3. Intrinsic endurance is not Eleatic and is opposed to creation, emanation and, all forms of contributed endurance.

4. The opposite of materialism is meta-physics in its various forms.

5. Reformed materialism rejects the caricatures of reductive materialism associated with Cartesian dualism and classical physics.

6. External, or nonparticipative, knowledge must be supplemented by the fact of the participative knowledge we have of our own organic selves.

7. The intrinsic endurance, or selfconserving, characteristic of being suggests the eternity of the material universe.

8. Linear cosmologies should be replaced by the postulate of a floor from which emergent levels arise quite locally and exceptionally.

9. Existence is best kept as a term for the factual recognition of describable denotables.

10. There may be a denotable corresponding to the symbol A; and there may not be. "A exists" and "A does not exist" are contradictories which bring out the epistemic side of existence.

11. Existents are qualitative and their existence precarious and historical.

12. In contrast to existence, being is a purely ontological term. It is describable only in terms of categorial distinctions.

13. The nonexistence of A has meaning and so has the Leibnizian principle of existential possibility, but I doubt that not-being or nothing is significant. At the most it would signify the denial of intrinsic endurance.

14. Aristotelian hylomorphism must be stood on its head, as the Marxists say of Hegel, by so changing the conception of matter that it includes form and activity. Directionism and emergence would then take the place of finalism and its theistic ceiling.

15. By distinguishing between being and existence and by giving up essences, except as descriptions, existence ceases to be something mysterious added to essences or quiddities.

PART III

The Mind-Body Test Case

INTRODUCTION TO THE ESSAYS

In introducing this group of papers, I cannot do better than quote part of Norman Melchert's introductory paragraph on the import of this problem in R. W. Sellars' philosophy.

> He (Professor Sellars) is convinced that this problem, or tangle of problems, is a touchstone for philosophy. Its solution is critical and will often determine the whole trend and validity of a philosophical system. As he said in 1922, 'It is still—and it has always been—my opinion that the adequate handling of the mind-body problem represents the synthetic stage of my philosophy and is at one and the same time a supreme test and an indication of its power. Epistemology, ontology and science must be marshalled together and all the essential terms must be defined and reintegrated.' Of his long deliberations on this matter, Sellars says, 'I flatter myself that some of my best work has been in connection with this question, the existential relation of consciousness to the minded brain.'[1]

The first of the readings below is from "A Fourth Progression in the Relation of Mind and Body" (1907). This article is indeed a virtual matrix from which his total philosophy unfolds—with its evolutionary naturalism, critical referential realism, double knowledge comprehension of the human mind, and its vista of values. He characterizes his viewpoint in this article as critical and naturalistic. The article discloses a great fund of biological, psychological, and philosophical information and has the ingredients for an extensive development. It depicts the mind-

---

[1] *Realism, Materialism, and the Mind.* Springfield, Ill., Thomas, 1968, 171.

body problem in a functional, genetic context, involving ontology, epistemology, axiology, and all the modes of human thought and action.

We present three other basic articles and the conclusion of an extended chapter of *Critical Realism*. Sellars' "Consciousness and Conservation" (1908) anticipates the issue of the relation of consciousness to a physical system: consciousness is a qualitative ingredient in the discharge of neural energy. It is his thesis in *Critical Realism* (1916) that consciousness is by no means alien to the physical; we offer only the conclusions of this chapter. It is the theme of his *Evolutionary Naturalism* (1922) that consciousness is an emergent function of a certain type of physical organization. We present two major articles which subsume this theme. In the "Double Knowledge Approach to the Mind-Body Problem," (1923) Sellars contends that our knowledge relating to this problem is not *either* introspectionist *or* behavioristic, but *both* behavioristic *and* introspectionist, and, in a special behavioristic sense, likewise neurological. The qualitative ingredients of psychic life are integral functions of brain activities.

In the 1938 "Analytic Approach to the Mind-Body Problem," Sellars brings his study of this problem up to date and puts it into a comprehensive realistic framework. The very beginning of wisdom about the problem is "an adequate physiology built up to cover the facts about organic behavior in relation to an environment." This "kind of physiology is just beginning to appear." (His attention to the fresh findings of physiologists and neurologists has continued to the present.) "The growth of the cortex is noted and its correlation with abilities. . . . The result is that . . . 'minded' . . . becomes a physical category in the context of selective behavior operations." But, again, the fact of man's introspective participation in events—with its full gamut of subjective components and possibilities—must not only be recognized but integrated into the newest physiology. The task of such an integration requires more than psychology; it requires an adequate philosophy. Sellars has aimed at this philosophy in his attempt to solve this crucial problem. His final formulation seems indeed, as Melchert states, "a fitting capstone to his whole systematic effort in philosophy, meshing intricately with his views on perception, knowledge, and emergent naturalism."[2]

* * * * *

Other readings:

"An Approach to the Mind-Body Problem," PR, XXVII (1918), 150-163.
"Evolutionary Naturalism and the Mind-Body Problem," The Monist, XXX (1920), 568-598.
"Is Consciousness Physical?" JP, XIX (1922), 690-694.

A FOURTH PROGRESSION IN THE RELATION OF MIND AND BODY[*]

May I advance a criticism of some recent tendencies by way of orientation? I shall put it in the form of a question. May not function win out at the expense of structure through the erection of a false antithesis between them? Reconstruction, change, experimentation, all these are of great importance and deserve the recognition they are receiving, at last, but organization is just as real. "Our experience is constantly undergoing modification; there are no final truths." Yes, certainly; but our experience is not a flux. We build up vast constructs whose complexity only the scientist (taking science in the sense of Wissenschaft) can realize. Of course, I would protest against the imputation to myself of a radical misunderstanding of pragmatism, such as witnessed to in Joachim's essay on the *Nature of Truth*. Yet, must not the functionalist and, with him, the pragmatist widen the scope of their outlook to history and sociology and behold the slowness of this reconstruction in many important phases of human life? I am inclined to maintain that each individual's experience is a microcosm in the making (at least, this is its transcendental idea, as Kant would phrase it) and that advance is not linear but a complex process of development, working through organization. (Cf. Stout, *Analytic Psychology*, Vol. II.) That this is not contrary to functional views is evident from the following. "Functions, on the other hand,

---

[2] *Ibid.*, 198.
[*] PSYCHOLOGICAL REVIEW, XIV (1907), 315-321.

persist as well in mental as in physical life. We may never have twice exactly the same idea viewed from the side of sensuous structure and composition. But there seems nothing whatever to prevent our having, as often as we will, contents of consciousness which *mean* the same thing." (Angell, this REVIEW, March, 1907.)

Howbeit it is not my intention to engage in general criticisms or commendations, which would be as valueless as uncalled for, but to re-analyze a problem which lies on the border between psychology and metaphysics and which, therefore, is of peculiar interest to both. To attack this Gordian knot may argue to some undue temerity or the breezy rashness of the novice but, perchance, it may keep the World-Mephistophiles engaged while a wiser spirit outflanks him. My earnest conviction is that here is the point where reality is exposed, as it were. Were I to need further defense, a recent utterance of a leading psychologist would suffice. "No courageous psychology of volition is possible which does not squarely face the mind-body problem and in point of fact every important description of mental life contains doctrine of one kind or another upon this matter." (Professor Angell, *ibid.*)

In his brief reference to the problem, Professor Angell makes such a good analysis of the manner of approach adopted by recent writers that I cannot do better than quote. "The position to which I refer regards the mind-body relation as capable of treatment in psychology as a methodological distinction rather than a metaphysically existential one. Certain of its expounders arrive at their view by means of an analysis of the genetic conditions under which the mind-body differentiation first makes itself felt in the experience of the individual (Baldwin). This procedure clearly involves a direct frontal attack on the problem. Others attain the position by flank movement emphasizing, to begin with, the insoluble contradictions with which one is met when the distinction is treated as resting on existential differences in the primordial elements in the Cosmos." Thus, considerable unanimity has been developing of late years in regard to the methodological character of the theories of physiology and psychology in respect to this relation. "Our task in discussing their relation is not to transcend a given dualism, but to get rid of one which we have manufactured for ourselves by the manipulation of experience in the interest of certain special scientific problems. Hence, as Münsterberg well puts it, we have not to find the connection which subsists as an actual fact, between body and soul, but to *invent* a connection in keeping with the general scheme of our artificial physical and psychological hypotheses." (Taylor, *Elements of Metaphysics*, p. 315.) Wundt gives an admirable statement of his own position in his *Ethics* and, since it is to defend himself against misunderstanding, may be regarded as authoritative. "Mechanical causality is thus a subordinate form of psychical causality. But in the case of all empirical relations, where psychical processes may be regarded from an external point of view, these processes may either be assigned to the complex of psychical events by virtue of their immediate characteristics or may be ranked within the causal nexus of mechanical processes by virtue of their external sensible aspect." (Wundt, *Ethics*, Vol. III., pp. 44, note, and 51.) "The psychical and the physical are incompatible only because we have made them so in the development of our scientific description of the universe. The distinction is a functional one, instrumental to the practical ends represented in their methodological demands." (H. Heath Bawden, *Philosophical Review*, 1903, pp. 315-16.) With such agreement, one is, at first, inclined to wonder why the problem still remains. Why do some thinkers hold still to interaction, while others vow allegiance to parallelism? Angell decidedly hankers after some kind of interaction as he must, perforce, since he holds that the mind mediates between the environment and the needs of the organism. As he expresses it: "This is the psychology of the fundamental utilities of consciousness." (Cf. also, his *Psychology*, Ch. III.) On the other hand, Professor Baldwin advocates parallelism, yet insists on a psycho-physical evolution since he, too, holds consciousness to be no negligible factor. (Cf. *Development and Evolution*, Ch. I.) There must be some ghost here which will not down and, since metaphysicians are supposed to prowl about in weird and unseemly realms and delight in unsolvable problems, this must furnish a situation peculiarly inviting. My endeavor will be, then, to consider Baldwin's presentation in the light of recent definitions of the physical and psychical. I hope to give reasons for a fourth progression and to deduce some interesting conclusions therefrom.

According to Baldwin (this journal, 1903), there are three 'progressions': (1) the 'projective progression' which reads projects become personal-pr. and thing-pr.; (2) the 'subjective progression' which reads personal-pr. become subject-self and object-self; and (3) the 'ejective progression' which reads object-self become mind and body—the last alone representing complete dualism of body and mind. "We find that to think of body as presentation is in accordance with progression (3) to think other minds with it as presentation and this involves by progression (2) thinking of one's own mind as presentation. In other words, it is impossible on this hypothesis to take any other than a purely *phenomenalistic* or *presentational* view of both sorts of objects, body and mind. The procedure which involves treating other minds as objective phenomena and, at the same time, maintaining the psychic point of view with reference to one's own mind is illegitimate." (*Ibid.*, p. 230.) "It is only in the one case of the relation of *one mind to one body* and *that its own* that such a point of view is still held. In the theory of interaction the attempt is made to justify this remaining case." (P. 239. Read context.) Here is where Baldwin is untrue to the genetic position he otherwise so well sustains. He does not go far enough. On the other hand, the psychologist when holding to some form of interaction is seeking to adopt a fourth progression which he sees only vaguely. He is really trying to escape from the *physical world considered as a closed universe*, a construction which as Wundt among others has pointed out is untenable. "In consequence, our experience of the constancy of objects has crystallized into the notion of matter as an absolutely permanent substrate of phenomena. It is a concept purely hypothetical in character, but it has proved very useful in the establishment of further principles; and it is, in particular, the foundation of all those laws of constancy referred to above as giving to natural causality its peculiar feature." (*Ethics*, p. 45.) The very nature of the postulates involves, a closed system. But, if the physical and the psychical are merely instrumental distinctions in experience, as modern logic seems to show, this cosmic character of the physical cannot be accepted. To resume: in the third progression, the object-self is looked upon as $M'|B$. This is read back into ourselves "because the theory requires that the view reached should cover the case of the relation of another person's mind to his body and that would mean his *mind presented as object to an onlooker in the same sense that his body is presented as object.*" (*Ibid.*, p. 232.) Baldwin's analysis here is excellent.

Now, what occurs when we move from the psychological point of view, as this undoubtedly is, to the psychic? (Cf. Baldwin's *Dict. of Philos.*, sub verbo.) Do we advance to a higher point of view, genetically speaking, or retrogress? I am strongly inclined to maintain that a new progression is the consequence of such a changed standpoint, and I would designate it the progression of 'duplication.' Each individual is now put on the same basis and regarded as having a unique psychic life. "The only states of consciousness that we naturally deal with are found in personal consciousnesses, minds, selves, concrete particular I's and You's. Each of these minds keeps its own thoughts to itself. There is no giving or bartering between them. No thought even comes into direct *sight* of a thought in another personal consciousness than its own. Absolute insulation, irreducible pluralism, is the law. It seems as if the elementary psychic fact were not *thought* or *this thought* or *that thought* but *my thought,* every thought being *owned.* * * * The breaches between such thoughts are the most absolute breaches in nature." (James, *Principles of Psychology,* Vol. I., p. 226.) I advise careful study of these pages. We hear too much of experience-in-general without mention of the owner. If this be the change that overtakes M' of progression (3) how must B be affected by it *since the terms must be on the same level.* In the third 'progression' B is *my* presentation, a part of my psychic experience, just as M' is. With the advance to this new progression, B must be reinterpreted. If M' becomes unique, must not the other also? To many ears, to advocate the assumption of what corresponds to a psychic point of view with regard to the body, may sound strange, but, before a too hasty decision is reached, let us ask what it implies. Philosophers have so long resided in a world of unincarnated sensations and thoughts, acknowledging, only in their uninspired moments, the facts of death and birth, that the mere suggestion of such an attitude may be looked upon as sub-dignitate. The conventional horror raised by the term 'thing-in-itself' has prevented a thorough reinterpretation of it in the light of recent biological and neurological facts. It is, however, noteworthy, that here, as elsewhere, the heretic is to be found preventing stagnation. Professor Strong has argued at considerable length that other consciousnesses are 'things-in-themselves' and James, in the passage quoted, seems to support similar views; at least, his pluralism has, here, its raison d'etre. "Another man's mind, then, is in the strict sense of the term, a non-empirical existence; something real yet inaccessible to my immediate knowledge; as much so as material or mental substance and differing from them only in the nature of that which is inferred." (Strong, *Why Mind Has a Body*, p. 216.) The criticism one is inclined to pass upon Strong is that he did not approach his subject genetically and logically. Genetic social psychology would have prevented his famous theory of instinctive belief in other minds, and logic, his panpsychism. There has been, as a consequence, an unfortunate neglect of this valuable emphasis on the isolation of minds. To return. Must not B (organism) drop out of my experience in the same way that M' (mind) does? At present, there seems to me no possibility of avoiding this conclusion if our genetic postulate is not to be violated, that *the two terms must be on the same level.* Let us cast about, nevertheless, for corroboration.

It is not difficult to discover. That every individual's experiencing is dependent on what we call his organism is a commonplace of neurology and of pathology today. I could refer to the researches of Kraepelin, Ellis, Flechsig and others, but it would be a work of supererogation. Neurology not only has proved cerebral localization, but has discovered that consciousness arises only in a circuit of at least five neurones involving the Golgi cell type II. (Cf. an article, *Journal of Philosophy, Psychology and Scientific Methods*, where the present argument was given in outline, Vol. IV., No. I.) Now, it would be absurd to assert that another individual's consciousness is dependent on B, *my* presentation; at least, we do not usually credit ourselves with creative power of this kind. From this side, also, we are, accordingly, forced to admit that *B* passes out of my experience, just as *M'* did. Moreover, *B* does not, then, become part of the second individual's experience, else would his experiencing depend on a presentation in his experience. Strongest of all is, I think, an appeal to death. Upon the individual's demise, the body remains. These are trite facts but their full significance has not, it seems to me, been recognized.*

CONSCIOUSNESS AND CONSERVATION[1]

The reasons for the affirmations of things which exist whether we experience them or no, and of the parallel doctrines of the conservation of matter and of energy, need not concern us. Suffice it to point out that idealism recognizes ultimately only the reality of *conscious experience.* If so, must not idealism deny the conservation of reality?

For personal idealism the conclusion is especially interesting, since appeal can not be made to the mysteries of an unknowable absolute whose timelessness precludes all question of change. If reality is composed of finite experiencers and there is no death, reality must increase continually, or at least *may* increase. For either all began at once, and this is nothing other than the assertion that the universe arose spontaneously and the denial of *ex nihilo nihil fit,* or they did not arise together, and this implies that reality is increasing. That all individuals came into existence together, all laws of heredity, Mendelian and Galtonian, deny, unless a most peculiar and static architectonic is permitted, contrary to all evolutionary postulates. If, however, immortality be negated as the present tendency inclines, might not all die and reality cease in the twinkling of an eye? No more than Hume could be certain of the rising of the sun to-morrow, could idealism be assured of the continued existence of the universe. But if it be rejoined that, though experiencers may die, experi-

---

* The remainder of this article treats the questions
   1) "What is the individual?"
   2) "How can two minds know the same thing?"

[1] R. W. Sellars, *JP*, V, 1 (Jan. 2, 1908), 235-238.

ence is always with us, is this not an appeal to a mind-stuff which rearranges itself, and have we any empirical grounds for such a position? As I have indicated, does not psychology deny a resurrection of past experiences as such, frowning upon the myth of a hades where they await disconsolately a return to the sunlit upper world?

Before drawing my moral, I wish to justify the thesis that the mind-body relation is metaphysical, and not merely methodological, by an analysis of an idealist's position. "Now that we have found that at least a part of that order, namely, the bodies of our fellow men, are not mere complexes in our own experience, but have a further existence as themselves experiencing subjects and are so far '*independent*' of their actual presentation in our own experience, we can no longer conclude from the dependence of the physical order for its sensible properties upon presentation to ourselves that it has no further existence of its own."[2] If the physical world is, as Mr. Taylor asserts, *more than* its being perceived, the *body upon the individual's demise* must also be more than its perception in other consciousnesses. Hence a duality is forced to the front; for if immortality is granted, the body is other than the immortal part, since its disintegrates; and the problem is raised for us, How were the individual and the reality represented to us by the body related during life? And if immortality is not granted, a like problem asserts itself, since the body remains in this case also and was, therefore, *more* than the individual's conscious experiences. In short, immortality is dualistic and renders meaningless the complex neuroses which now accompany consciousness.

This relative independence of the organism has direct connection with the problem of conservation, and this was my reason for introducing it. In contrast to the lack of conservation of consciousness is the conservation, not of the organization of the body necessarily, but of its so-called "additive" properties. Elsewhere I have called attention to the importance of organization as supplying the place in modern science of the qualitative. It is like the qualitative and like consciousness in that it is not ultimately conserved, *e.g.*, in organisms at death. To those un-

---

[2] Taylor, "Elements of Metaphysics," p. 207.

acquainted with physical chemistry the term "additive," used above, may require explanation. "In the first class we have those properties which are possessed by the atoms unchanged, no matter in what physical or chemical state these atoms may exist. Such properties are called additive, and the best instance of an additive property is found in weight (or mass). Each atom retains its weight unaltered whether it exists in the free state or whether it is combined with other atoms. When atoms combine the weight of the compound is the sum of the weights of the component atoms."[3] In modern energetics this principle holds without the accompaniment of atomism.

My query is this, May not the quantitative be related to the qualitative and to consciousness and organization as the invariant is to the variant in mathematics, so that we may have conservation of the quantitative and non-conservation of the qualitative? Naturally this involves a reinterpretation of conservation as applied to reality. But is not this reinterpretation shadowed forth in the most general definition of reality, "to be is to be active"? If this were so, the quantitative identity of cause and effect could still remain an ideal not conflicting with the doctrine of *grades of causal relation* depending upon organization, which biology is demanding. Physics has been more mechanical than chemistry because dealing with more general and external relations; it has also been more *a priori* and less empirical. Recent investigations, however, are destroying the barriers and the evolution of the elements and, therewith, the fact of organization is being acknowledged. That there must be grades of causal relation depending on the degree of organization of the interacting terms has not yet been fully recognized although biology, physiology, and chemistry have a suspicion of it. The reaction of an organism as a whole to a stimulus as indicated by Jennings brings out my meaning. In biology, for example, fertility and infertility are seen to be due to surface tension, which varies with the species. Mendelian characters, also, present the effect of evolutionary organization, and natural selection itself can be interpreted as a process of development of grades of causal relation. In fact, this is what adaptation means. The doctrine of specific nerve

---

[3] Walker, "Introduction to Physical Chemistry."

energies and the differentiation of sense-organs and cerebral centers are also best understand by the application of this conception. Scientists and philosophers alike built up their theory of nature on the least complex things, and, lost in the antithesis of mechanism and teleology, did not realize that grades of causal relation due to organization mediate these extremes. "Investigations in physical chemistry are well suited," says Pauli,[4] "to show how all biological methods are of the same value in that they leave no room for strictly mechanistic or vitalistic tendencies." And the death of mechanism makes possible a solution of the mind-brain problem.

IS CONSCIOUSNESS ALIEN TO THE PHYSICAL[*]

Our main purpose has been to prove that consciousness is not alien to the physical. In a general way, this conclusion has been justified. While the physicist does not meet with consciousness either in his facts or in his theories, that circumstance is due to his subject-matter. He attains true knowledge of reality, but this knowledge does not conflict with the presence of consciousness in nature. We have seriously considered the reasons customarily given for the exclusion of consciousness and found them based either on dogmas or on mistakes in logic. Materialism and panpsychism are both extremes which are based on a denial of the validity of part of our actual knowledge; and this denial is due in part to the narrowness of specialism and in part to a false theory of knowledge.

At various times we have hinted that mind cannot be simply identical with consciousness. Consciousness is a flux which comes and goes. It is, moreover, by no means completely self-sufficient. A stimulus which enters consciousness is able to do so only after it has been interpreted by mind in the light of past experience. Thus there are conditions which partly determine what shall be perceived. A recent psychologist has emphasized the part played by types as relatively flexible mental forms which interpret an incoming stimulus. (Pillsbury, *The*

---

[4] "Physical Chemistry in the Service of Medicine."

[*] *Critical Realism* (New York, Rand McNally Co., 1916), 250-253.

Psychology of Reasoning.) In a similar manner, other psychologists stress the importance of the purpose which dominates the mind. This purpose may be only vaguely present in consciousness, yet it is functionally active. We may say, in fact, that consciousness contains only a minor part of the factors which account for the consciousness of the next moment. In the discussion of the self in Chapter IV, we pointed out the evident complexity of the individual's character: his habits, slowly acquired upon the basis of heredity; his ideals; his knowledge, which is largely potential at any one time; and his natural aptitudes along various lines, trained as a result of the experiencing process which works back into the conditions that partly control it. Again, we must not forget that the *structure* of the field of the individual's experience is due to an organization which rests on the past. Consciousness, as we experience it, rests on mental capacities which are apparently the result of evolution.

It appears, then, that consciousness arises within a system which must be studied ontogenetically and phylogenetically. This system is what we call *mind*. In it we have epigenesis and preformation harmonized in a true development. Experiencing leaves its trace in mind and is thus indirectly conserved. We all feel that our minds broaden and gain a wider reach. We achieve more adequate apperceptive systems, and these play into our conscious life in the most intricate fashion.

Although we would not identify mind and consciousness, we would not separate them. Mind somehow flowers into consciousness, and consciousness seems to function as the means to the growth of mind. Mind is conserving and enduring, while consciousness represents the moment of adaptation and change. We may say, then, that consciousness is fundamentally conditioned by mind as well as by the stimulus which comes to the organism from the environment. So far as reality is concerned, its newness is a relative newness which always has a ground. Because this ground carries along with it the past, memory and growth in general are possible; it is in this sense that the self is relatively the same through time. We must remember, however, that this would not help us much did we not feel ourselves to be the same in consciousness. As Locke saw, the sameness of a soul would not make immortality worth while.

Let us glance for a moment at the problem of memory. There are, so far as I can see, only two theoretical possibilities. Either experiences exist in a sort of mental cold-storage and memory is a literal participation in the past experience as it again enters consciousness; or, memory is a new experience qualified by the present, for empirical reasons, as giving us knowledge of the past. The first possibility seems to me to sin against the essential characteristic of consciousness, its temporary nature.... Consciousness does not possess a *durée réelle,* beyond the specious present, but seems to be more like a song which dies away only to be renewed. If, on the other hand, a memory be a new experience based on memory as a function of a conserving organ, this conserving organ must be the mind. That the mind should be capable of producing, under certain conditions, an experience similar to that which it produced once before, seems to me quite within the bounds of naturalness.

But what is the relation of the mind to the brain? Much of our present argument has concerned itself with the relation of consciousness to the brain as a physical reality. We tried to show that consciousness is not alien to the physical when this is rightly conceived. But this result would have no point if we could not establish some sort of identity between the mind and the brain. This identity cannot, however, be that of two substances, since the mind seems to be a developed system of capacities or functions based on evolution and educed and given concrete filling-out by that process which we call "learning by experience." Instead of appealing to psychical dispositions, we are led to suppose that the brain achieves intricate organizations, which grow richer and more flexible as time goes on. The psychologist calls these "apperceptive systems" and holds that they are the ground of meanings and concepts. The mind would thus seem to be the tremendously complex system of sub-systems gradually built up during the lifetime of the individual upon the foundation, and with the assistance, of congenital capacities. It is evident that we look upon the brain as the organ of the mind. When neurology frees itself from bondage to the current mechanical views, I feel sure that it will come to understand the part played by organization in the organic world and will no longer seek to over-simplify. Just as physics is beginning to shake itself loose from the childish idea of matter so long dominant, so biology and neurology will soon come to admit that the brain surpasses the neat system of distinct, neural drainage-paths which has been assigned it. The mind's unity is the unity of the brain as an organ. It is the unity of the mind which gives unity to the stream of consciousness; and the unity of the mind is the unity of the brain as a functioning system.

Such a view could be regarded as the modern interpretatiion of the idea of the soul to be found in Aristotle when he is at his best. The mind is a part of the soul, and the soul of the individual is indissolubly one with the organism. "The soul is the completed realization of the body." For us, of course, nothing is finished, but everything is in process. I presume that I need not warn the reader against taking this comparison with Aristotle's position too literally. His notion of "form" is no longer tenable.

THE DOUBLE-KNOWLEDGE APPROACH TO THE MIND-BODY PROBLEM*

In the present paper my aim is to sketch in broad outline a solution of the traditional mind-body problem and to indicate certain of its more interesting implications. The suggested solution is based upon a theory of knowledge called Critical Realism and a theory of evolution, asserting levels of behaviour and of properties, which I have called Evolutionary Naturalism. I doubt that my argument can be followed with full comprehension unless these two phases are kept in mind. Yet they must be in large measure assumed because of the necessary limitations of a paper.

It has become increasingly evident to those for whom philosophy is more than a dialetic of words or of ready-made concepts that the terms of this traditional puzzle need thorough investigation and re-definition. The suspicion is arising that the conventional metaphysical dualism is a produce of wrong assumptions, that the organism includes in some fashion both mind and consciousness. But to work out the idea underlying this suspicion and to develop its implications is not an easy task. Nothing short

---

* *Aristotelian Society Proceedings*, N.S. 23 (1923), 55-70.

of a system of philosophy is involved. It is my persuasion that the problem is a technical one and cannot be solved—though it may be aided—by the drift of thought. It is with the technicalities as such that I shall concern myself in what follows.

As I try to bring before my mind the dominant positions taken with regard to this problem, they seem to resolve themselves into four classes: (1) idealistic, (2) behaviouristic, (3) dualistic, and (4) naturalistic.

The idealistic group have this in common that they do not take the physical world and its categories seriously. The behaviouristic group tend to ignore, or belittle, consciousness or the subjective. And this either because, for them, science means study by means of external observation (Watson), or because they have turned their back hopelessly on the problems raised by the subjective (Dewey). The dualistic position has been the traditional one of psychology, but we must remember that few psychologists held it as an ultimate philosophical position. It was less a solution than a methodological position. But metaphysical dualism is represented to-day by Bergson, Pratt, Sheldon and others. The naturalistic group are seeking to conceive mind and consciousness as elements and properties of the organism to be correlated with the level of organization and behaviour there attained. It is within this group that I find myself.

I

As I pointed out in my *Evolutionary Naturalism*, there have been at least *four* motives at work leading to the traditional exclusion of mind and consciousness from the organism, the epistemological, the categorical, the methodological, and the theological. Though logically distinct, they have always re-enforced one another. To point out the erroneous character of these motives for dualism and to show that the conclusion usually drawn does not logically follow constituted and essential step in my argument.

The epistemological motive for dualism expresses itself in the assumption that the physical world is *exhaustively* revealed in the knowledge gained by the physical sciences. Basically, the mistake rests on a misinterpretation of the nature and reach of knowledge. Thus Descartes held that extension is the "essence" of matter. In his arguments against a "cerebral soul" Bergson employs much the same tactics, though with the greater subtlety that idealism has made possible. His prime mistake seems to be a misunderstanding of space as a category of knowledge. Even a valid category does not give the "essence" of the object known but only an approximation of its form or order. Many philosophically inclined scientists have begun to express this fact by saying that we know only relations. In various places, I have tried to show that a critical correspondence theory can be framed that avoids all valid objections to Locke's still scholastic formulation.

Now the important point in this connexion is that the assumption that a body is exhaustively apprehended in the categories of physical sciences leads inevitably to dualism because consciousness cannot be found in the object thus supposedly penetratively intuited. It must, therefore, be assigned to a separate realm. And, since mind and consciousness go together, mind must be held distinct from the physical world at whatever level. But is it not clear that a determination of the *reach* and *character* of the knowledge gained by the physical sciences is an essential element in a correct approach to the mind-body problem?

The categorical motive expresses the disparity between the categories which characterize the content of the knowledge gained by the physical sciences, and the categories of introspective psychology. Mass, energy, space, size, shape, behaviour are categories intrinsic to the one; while those of content, fusion, association, recall and attention are distinctive of the other. And allied with this disparity has been the contrast between the mechanical and the teleological. The dominant effort in the past was to draw the whole of nature into the categories of mechanics. To do this for mind seemed impossible. It was, therefore, allowed to rest under the contrasting principle of teleology, seldom analysed. Thus the categorical motive gave further encouragement to the dualism suggested by the epistemological motive.

The methodological motive reflects the methods and interests of the physical sciences in contrast to introspective psychology. It continues the categorical motive. The purpose of the one is knowledge of *bodies* by means of external observation and the technique of measurement. Only certain data are selected as significant, and these are interpreted as means to knowledge about bodies. The different method of introspective psychology separated it from the physical sciences. Clearly the objects of the two types of science are in some sense different. Thus a division of labour and a difference of method supplements and encourages the dualism suggested by the first two motives.

Finally, the theological motive was influential from the beginning of modern philosophy. The soul-concept suggested the notion of a spiritual substance co-equal with matter and having consciousness as its attribute. This motive must be regarded as technically secondary.

How can these motives be met and turned aside? My argument is, that two kinds and directions of knowledge separate for the knower the indissolubly connected. Let me put the situation as I understand it. Suppose consciousness were in the brain as a changing flow of *quales,* and that, in it and by it, the individual had knowledge about the brain, on the one hand, and of it, on the other; would not the situation be exactly that indicated by the above motives? We should expect the categories of the two kinds of knowledge to differ fundamentally and, if the first kind of knowledge were regarded as entirely penetrative, we should be led into dualism.

Now Critical Realism expresses an analysis of the content and nature of scientific knowledge which enforces the distinction between knowledge and its object. An external object can be known by means of the subjective. And the conclusion, in brief, is that such knowledge is necessarily limited to a comprehension of the structure, connexions, composition and behaviour of the bodies studied. Thus the knowledge gained by physical science is inevitably *external to its object* in this sense that it can grasp only those characteristics which are reproducible in another medium (order or form) and that it cannot reach a literal intuition of, or participation in, the life or energies of the thing known. But, on the contrary, within this subjective medium, knowledge of its own content can arise. Here we have the two kinds and directions of knowledge.

If this interpretation of knowledge is correct, the epistemological motive for metaphysical dualism is undermined. Science cannot offer us that inspection of the "filling" of bodies which alone could enable us dogmatically to assert that consciousness is not in the brain. The categorical motive is, likewise, reinterpreted by this approach. Does it not simply indicate that these two kinds of knowledge cannot have *equivalent* objects? This lack of simple equivalence is explicable by the difference in nature and reach of the two kinds of knowledge. The one arises in the "filling" of the brain and inspects *quales* there present; the other deciphers the characteristics of the brain as a body by means of the cognitive value of certain sense-data. It is because consciousness is not a "thing," or "stuff," but a structured complex of *quales* that a relation of partial identity, or inclusion, can be conceived—a relation which harmonizes with the demands of the categorical motive. Thus it is only by doing justice to both sets of categories and to the two kinds of objects of the two kinds of knowledge that a solution of the mind-body problem is made possible.

This solution is not a "philosophical" one in the sense of philosophy so much disliked by science, but one which expresses science itself and is demanded by its content and methods. Physical science deals with the *whole* of reality at any one place, as this can be studied by its methods and through the use of sense-data. It deals with order and quantity as these characterize "space-constituting bodies." But consciousness is a system of *quales* open to inspective examination and clearly internal to one of these bodies, the brain. In my consciousness, I am literally a *participant* in that brain which physical science can know only by a descriptive translation.

Our definite epistemology thus enables us to do justice to an existential situation which was felt, and hinted at, by the so-called double-aspect theory. But what a world of obscurity there was in this term *aspect?* More analysis was needed. The "aspects" had to be related to the two kinds and directions of knowledge in order to be more than a metaphor from common-sense realism; and consciousness—not an "aspect" but an object of knowledge—had to be conceived as existentially included in the brain, the object of physical science. *Epistemologically,* the situation is one of two kinds of knowledge and two kinds of objects corresponding to them; *existentially*, a relation of inclusion between these two kinds of objects. And it is just because consciousness is a complex of *quales* that this existential relation is conceivable. But more of that later.

Another distinction is now in order. Let us speak of "mind" as a term for a class of operations. Ultimately, mind must be enlarged to include a class of operations, that which expresses itself in these operations, and consciousness. Consciousness is included in mind, just as it is included in the brain.

As to the second part of the categorical motive, an asserted difference of *mode of action*, is it so certain that the brain is a mechanical system? "Mind" is for the behaviourist a physical category. It is the organism which, through the nervous system, behaves intelligently, adjusts itself to novel situations, forms habits, etc. Thus there is an identity between the character of the action of the brain and the character of the action of the mind as known by introspection. If we speak of mind as a term for operations, these operaitons are thus known in two ways. The changes in my consciousness are *indices of operations* known about through behaviour also. Since in my consciousness I participate in the brain-mind, this kind of knowledge has even an advantage over the other and certainly supplements it. To sum up, the capacities of the brain-mind are known (1) through the use of sense-data in external observations, (2) through the use of states of consciousness as indices of operations in which they participate. Besides this knowledge, there is also the awareness of the contents of consciousness, the condition of both kinds of knowledge.

The methodological motive, again, indicates that both bodies and consciousness can be objects of study and that different methods are used in the two cases. The danger has been that of identifying the whole of reality with the content of knowledge gained by either of these two kinds of knowledge. In the one case, we have materialism; in the other, panpsychism and idealism. Specialism and an inadequate epistemology have worked hand in hand.

The theological motive is not self-supporting and is logically secondary. I shall disregard it in the present paper.

II

Thus far we have given an exposition of the motives which have mistakenly led to a mind-body dualism and our reasons for regarding them as either erroneous or wrongly interpreted. Let us now try to consolidate our results.

(1) Mind is a term which has been employed rather vaguely and waveringly in the past for (a) consciousness, (b) a class of operations, (c) that which expresses itself in these operations and this consciousness. My argument is that the brain can be regarded as the object of all this knowledge, that is, as inclusive of consciousness, and that which expresses itself in this class of operations. In the larger setting, however, it is best to speak of the brain as the brain-mind. This combination does justice to the two kinds of knowledge. Brain is the natural term for the physical sciences, while mind has more affiliations with consciousness and introspection. The union of the two terms indicates that there is no dualism of existence corresponding to the doubleness of knowledge, and that it is one body that is known in this supplementary fashion. Thus against Bergson I would defend the cerebral-soul.*

It is very important to realize this doubleness of our knowledge of the brain-mind, for certain philosophers have argued to dualism by affirming positively what the physical world cannot do.† It is said that one physical thing cannot know another, or have memory of the past. But are not those who stress these supposed limitations of the physical world but limiting the physical world to the kind of knowledge gained by the sciences of external observation? Change of behaviour as a result of past stimuli and responses is all that observation can give as regards memory; and an attitude of attention is the external correlate of knowledge. The point is that, valid and significant as the one kind of knowledge is, it is not exhaustive of its object. In Sheldon's argument there is, likewise, the epistemological postulate that knowledge involves the literal presence of the object known—a postulate the critical realist denies—and so an existence in two places at once, that of the knower and that of the

---

* See *Evolutionary Naturalism*, pp. 305-6, and Bergson's *Mind-Energy*, p. 244 f.

† I refer particularly to Sheldon. See *The Philosophical Review*, March, 1922.

object, a property impossible to a physical body. This argument of Sheldon's is no stronger than his epistemology. Does knowledge involve this literal doubleness of position, this straddling of space? Once we distinguish between the content and the object of knowledge, this *pseudo*-problem vanishes.

Our conclusion is as follows: the opposition, made popular by Bergson, between the brain as merely a system of habits and the mind as memory is not justified. Leaving aside the question of external observation? Change of behaviour as a result of past stimuli and responses is all that observation can give as regards memory; and an attitude of attention is the external correlate of knowledge. The point is that, valid and significant as the one kind of knowledge is, it is not exhaustive of its object. In Sheldon's argument there is, likewise, the epistemological postulate that knowledge involves the literal presence of the object known—a postulate the critical realist denies—and so an existence in two places at once, that of the knower and that of the of novel cerebral response, the Bergsonian opposition can be interpreted just as easily and more naturally by the double-knowledge theory. Memory in the psychological sense is a participative act which we know from the inside *because we are consciousness*. Far less of this capacity of the brain is revealed to a knowledge mediated by sense-data. The moral is, Let us not underestimate the brain and the physical world in general. Valuable as is the knowledge gained through the cognitive use of sense-data, it is undeniable that in consciousness the individual is on the inside of his brain and a participant. Consciousness, as an index of operations, reveals in some measure the formation of habit, the growth of expertness, the degree and facility of attention, the formation of a novel synthesis, etc.

(2) Mind must be conceived more substantialistically than has been the custom in empirical psychology. It is more than consciousness and inclusive of it. It is that which functions in memory, reasoning, inclination, etc. It is a system, a reality of a tremendously complex sort, a product of evolution and of individual development. Its growth is one of cumulative change. As a system it is only intermittently conscious in the strict, empirical sense. Such is my conception of the brain-mind or cerebral soul.

(3) One of my critics[*] has contended that I have made no advance upon materialism because, for me, mind is subjected to physical laws. Such a criticism shows a refusal to see that, for me, the physical world evolves to the mental level in the content and action of the brain. And laws are but descriptions of how systems operate; they are not controlling forces. I affirm an agreement, and not a contradiction, between the two kinds of knowledge of the brain-mind. If this position is true, it rings the death-knell of strict mechanical atomism, for it shows that, at a high level, syntheses of a most intimate sort do arise and function effectively in nature. The unity and complexity of consciousness is an index of the synthetic unity and interpenetration of the brain-mind. As participants in this brain-mind through consciousness, we come to know this. Thus psychology can throw light upon the physical world. Only the dualistic tradition has prevented scientists themselves from grasping this implication. If this equal recognition of the information given us by the physical and the mental sciences be materialism, it is not of the familiar kind. The essence of materialism seems to me to be the interpretation of nature in terms of the knowledge gained by external observation alone. Consciousness and mind are, then, adjuncts which must, and yet which cannot be fitted in afterwards. A division of labour among the sciences has been interpreted metaphysically.

(4) Consciousness is a structural complex of *quales* compresent in a way that reflects the operation of the brain-mind. Awareness is an experience expressive of the internal relations of such a consciousness. In consciousness, the conscious self arises. It is, also, the seat and medium of overt knowledge. But this very pre-eminence of consciousness for us, as our sole participation in reality as conscious beings, forces it into relief and necessarily isolates it for us from its existential setting. Of its setting we can have only knowledge of structure and behaviour.

III

Our most difficult categorical problems arise when we try to comprehend the connexion of consciousness with the brain-

---

[*] Pratt, *Journal of Philosophy*, June, 1922.

mind. And it is clear that the question of the efficacy of consciousness is intimately bound up with the question of the nature and existential setting of consciousness. The traditional dualism denies the sort of existential unity for which I have been arguing. Hence efficacy meant interaction between distinct bodies. As to the laws of this interaction between disparate entities nothing was known nor could be surmised. On the contrary, we shall seek the *function* which consciousness can perform in accordance with its nature. We must begin with a few distinctions:—

(1) Consciousness must be distinguished from its elements. Let us call the elements of consciousness the psychical.

(2) Two questions now arise. How far is it true that a psychical element exists only in consciousness? If the psychical can exist in some measure apart from the complex whole which is consciousness, to what degree is it modified in its entrance into consciousness? It is obvious that we can make only suggestions here. I am inclined to maintain the relative independence of the psychical. At least something like a psychical element can exist as a *quale* apart from consciousness. It is developed, interpreted and *inspected* in consciousness.

(3) The simplest form of the brain-mind-consciousness problem is that of the setting of a psychical element, like an image or a sensation, in the brain-mind. Such an element must be thought of as a *quale* being its own intrinsic nature.

(4) From such a *quale*, we must remove all features or attitudes which come from consciousness as a whole. A psychical element contains no self-awareness. Our problem, reduced to its simplest terms, becomes this: How shall we conceive the relation of an *intrinsic quale*, like a colour or a pain, to the brain-mind?

(5) We must distinguish between a *quale* and a quality. A quality of a thing implies the operation of perception. It involves the assignment of a *quale* to an affirmed object and implies the operation of the whole mechanism of sense-perception. But a *quale* is what makes the thought of a quality possible. To assert that the *quale* red is a character intrinsic existentially to the brain does not mean that the brain as an object of perception is red. This is still more evident in the case of those *quales*, like

pain, that are not used as qualities. Critical realism comes to our help here.

(6) A *quale* is not an entity in the same sense that a body is. Everything points to the hypothesis that a *quale* is not self-sufficient but is a trait of something more substantial. Its apparent independence and isolation comes from the cognitive situation. It is, as we have pointed out, the only phase of the brain which we as conscious beings *are*. It is our participation in reality. And this situation isolates what is existentially inseparable. It gives an apparent substantiality and independence to what is not substantial and independent. It lures us to make consciousness a substance and we succeed only in making it a will o' the wisp. We must set our face sternly against this natural illusion. We must bring knowledge of the whole situation to our assistance.

Having made these distinctions, we are now in a position to conceive the connexion of the psychical and of consciousness with the brain-mind.

The relation of inclusion for which we are searching is obviously a more subtle one than that of whole and part in the ordinary categories of scientific knowledge, and yet analogous. We have to relate the object of one kind of knowledge to the object of another kind, or, rather, conceive how they are actually related. The psychical is not stuff and is not space-constituting. But it is just because of this that it can exist in a body. Just because it is not space-constituting, it can be space-permeating. Hitherto, to exist in space has always meant to occupy a place exclusively and therefore to be a measurable and ponderable body. We must enlarge our notion of existence in space. Let it be remembered that space, as such, is an abstraction. If, then, bodies constitute space, whatever is internal to bodies and constitutes their nature must be spatial in a very real sense.

But to make my view clear there is need of another category which I shall call the *content of being*. We are too prone to think of the physical world abstractly in terms of our external knowledge of it, and to forget that there must be a content or stuff which has this order and which does so behave. Let us remember that scientific knowledge can never offer us a literal glimpse of the content of being. That remains a dimension, so to speak, which knowledge mediated by sense-data cannot enter. The very character of our valid knowledge of the physical world —the slow deciphering of its structure and behaviour through the cues given in sense-perception—implies its limitations. Such knowledge, valid as it is for the *characteristics* of physical things, must be external. It is always other than an intuition of, or participation in, its object. Does it not seem plausible to hold that the *quales* which we call psychical are traits of the "content of being" as intrinsic and inalienable as those characteristics which we know as structure and organization. This means that the physical world is not qualitatively empty. But quality in this sense is not a surface feature which can be inspected from outside as naïve realism supposes, misled by the mechanism of sense-perception, but an internal *quale* which is a dimension of what is structured, something which can be given only by participation. It seems to me evident that something of this sort is implied by the facts and by the double-knowledge approach suggested by Critical Realism. A deepening of our metaphysical categories is demanded by the situation. One must realize the nature and the limitations of both kinds of knowledge before a synthesis is possible.

If, then, the psychical belongs to the qualitative dimension of being, grasped only by participation or by analogy, it must not be given a separate existence as a sort of substance which buds off from the brain or which the brain produces. The traditional contrast between the physical and the psychical encouraged such a conception. We must have a deeper conception of these *quales,* or contents, and must think of them as inseparable characters of the brain-mind, whose isolation and abstraction, from their existential matrix, comes from the fact that our consciousness consists of them and cannot include that of which they are a qualitative part. The part cannot include the whole. Hence the part appears to itself to be distinct from the whole. Such is the situation of consciousness in the brain.

The qualitative dimension of the physical world rises to the level of the psychical with increase of organization. A stimulus is received by a sympathetic medium which responds at one and the same time both quantitatively and qualitatively. The creative novelty of the response contains and involves the *quale* in which the consciousness of the individual participates. As I understand him, Bergson has attempted to pass from the quantitative to the qualitative by the condensation which memory exercises. For me, there is no such opposition. The qualitative is also quantitative. The qualitative is known by participation and the quantitative characteristics of the same cerebral system by external knowledge. Moreover, the condensation of which Bergson speaks is more of the nature of a *response* of the stimulated medium than a mere knitting together of light waves. The correlation I would stress is that between the creative novelty of response and the qualitative dimension of the responding cerebral system. We do not pass from space to time, for these are abstractions if set in opposition to that which is at the same time spatial and temporal.

But it may be well to point out why time seems to be the category expressive of consciousness. The qualitative dimension of the brain-mind changes as the brain-mind functions. Here we are in the literal presence of change, but a change inseparably connected with, and expressive of, the changing brain-mind. If, then, I speak of these *quales* as variants, it is not to deny that the system in which they arise varies. The structure and pattern of the brain-mind must vary coincidently with consciousness. But the spatial characteristics of the brain-mind are expressed only very dimly in consciousness. Space, as experienced in the content of perception, is a *qualitative order* built up to correspond to the object of perception. It has no significance for the cerebral system of which it is the qualitative expression. One other point, these *quales* come and go much as nervous currents come and go. That which is relatively permanent is the pattern of the brain-mind. Consciousness is evanescent, and yet that of which it is the qualitative dimension is not evanescent. It is for this reason that nearly the same *quales* can arise again and again—not numerically the same, but qualitatively the same. May I refer in this connexion to the thesis of Professor Montague. He would identify consciousness with potential energy. Rather must consciousness, it seems to me, be correlated with activity, with what physical science measures as energy.

We come finally to the question of the efficacy of consciousness. What *rôle* in the economy of the brain-mind do these *quales* play? Here, again, it can be only a question of principles and way of approach.

The brain-mind is an organization of tendencies and memories whose complexity it is difficult for us to conceive. It is certain that the brain-mind is a growth in which central and peripheral processes are united. This means that cortical processes have their motor continuations. My thesis is that mental operations are operations of the brain. And these operations must have their mechanism and medium, so to speak. Association, inhibition, selection, combination are processes which take place in the brain-mind and which fashion its content, set, and functioning. I doubt that nervous anatomy and physiology can throw much light upon these delicate internal processes. I would say that it was more a matter of bio-chemistry. And while I affirm a correspondence between the change of internal cerebral patterns and the mental operation, I doubt that our knowledge will ever be penetrative enough to trace it out. Psychology must work out its own information with confidence. Cerebral laws must harmonize with mental laws. If the response of the mind to a situation is intelligent and creative, so, likewise, must be the response of the brain. Thus there exists in nature a level of causality, of self-determination, which does not easily fit into the traditional interpretation of nature.

The aim of science is to discover *laws*. By the very nature of its type of knowledge it is external and descriptive. The actual process of self-determination must in some measure escape it. But, if my theory is correct, we are, in consciousness, in some measure participants in the actual process of the brain-mind. Valid as scientific knowledge is, it can never be identical with participation. There is this degree of truth in voluntaristic metaphysics. What I have called the "content of being" eludes physical science, for its knowledge is not an intuition.

In consciousness there is a partial coalescence of the psychical. How complete this coalescence is, it is impossible to say. The controlling centre can inspect, and guide itself by, the cues which the psychical presents. Thus my purpose to walk down a road full of obstructions is rendered possible by the sense-data which my organs of sense mediate.

No psychical element is efficacious by itself. In the first

place, it is but the qualitative focus of the brain-mind state; in the second place, it is part of a larger system which selects. In the last analysis, it is the organism as a whole which acts. A psychical content is used by the apperceptive and controlling cerebral system as a warning and as a guiding sign. And this is possible because these *quales* can be brought within the purview of the active system. The synthesis which is consciousness is at once the sign, the expression, and the focal element of the cerebral system. In brief, the guidance which we are aware of in consciousness is at the same time the guidance of the cerebral system of which consciousness is the qualitative dimension. Here, and here alone, we participate in the process of real causality. And yet, because the cerebral background is hidden, this participation is but partial. We know that we desire certain things. In consciousness, the desire consists of images, feelings and motor sensations. But beneath this, and including it, is the bodily system with its organic drive. We must neither exalt nor belittle consciousness, but try to understand its nature and function in the economy of the organism which each of us is.

AN ANALYTIC APPROACH TO THE MIND-BODY PROBLEM*

The mind-body problem attracted my attention very early. Almost my first articles were devoted to it, so convinced was I of its crucial significance for philosophy. I felt strongly drawn to naturalism in a period when it was in disfavor. It goes without saying that idealists were vociferous in their rejection of naturalism, and this, in the main, on two counts: its epistemological vagueness and its inability to do justice to the categories of psychology, ethics and religion. James Ward was not a typical idealist, and yet his book, *Naturalism and Agnosticism*, brought home to me the task confronting any adequate development of naturalism. It was clear that it must have a realistic epistemology and it must take the fact of evolution more seriously to see what its implications were. To me, critical realism was the answer to the first demand, and evolutionary naturalism with its stress upon organization as a physical category and its assertion that novel

---

* PR, XLVII, 5 (1938), 461-487.

organization *involves* novel properties, was the reply to the second. Evolution signified the local rise of new systems with new properties. The terms 'holism' and 'emergence' have since become familiar as labels for similar ideas. Being a naturalist, I stressed space as well as time and took a more pluralistic and localistic view of processes of evolution. Since I held nature to be eternal, I was less inclined to apply what has happened on the surface of this little planet to the cosmic scene, or to bring in the conception of deity. After I had adopted the term 'emergence' as an effective label, I still wished to keep from it any mystical connotation. To me it meant simply the fact that novel organization *involved* novel properties. Such properties must not be considered to be stuck on externally and miraculously, but to be functions of the organization. It was, after all, just the conviction that structure and function are internally related.

When I was first beginning to think along these lines, physics was still almost wholly atomistic or merely aggregative in its conceptions.[1] What I sought to do was to work downward from the human individual, taken in a molar fashion as Koffka would now say, through the biological to the inorganic. This is, of course, what the convinced naturalist would logically do. Organization, system, interdependence were categories which stood out when nature was thus macroscopically approached. It was yet the faith of classic physics that a microscopic approach would destroy these categories and reveal them to be illusions. As we all know, the new physics with its exploratory tools has done quite the reverse. It has shown that atoms and molecules are very complicated systems having properties expressive of their pattern and composition.

It may be of historical interest to mention that I used to suggest to colleagues in the physics department that they must take relations between atoms more seriously; but those were the days of the billiard-ball atom and the imagery of the time favored the idea of merely changing positions. Chemistry spoke of valences and bonds, but had not the ghost of an idea of the physical basis of such factors. The facts were not yet available,

---

[1] See the *Psychological Review*, 1907, in which, in treating the mind-body problem, my stress upon organization first appeared. The essential ideas were already there.

as they are today; and I could but speculate upon the validity and ontological significance of organization for a philosophy of nature. The postulate that the physical world is intrinsically a domain of system seemed to me the primary axiom of any evolutionary naturalism. Once that was granted, all that time has brought forth upon this planet was rationally explicable.

These introductory remarks are, I believe, sufficient to indicate the general character of my approach to the mind body problem. I had to think of the body as *minded*. I was working along the line which is usually called monistic. But, as I pointed out in the beginning, these type-terms do not get one very far. It does not really throw light upon the position taken to hunt around for some synonymous terms such as identity or unity. In the last resort there is no substitute to be had for the analysis of the terms involved; and this achievement, as I have already suggested, must rest upon deeper insights in science and upon accompanying clarifications in epistemology and ontology. The perspective which was opening up for me was, I thought, best indicated by the rather cumbersome description: *the double-knowledge and emergence solution of the mind-body problem.* I felt that this description would at least guide any who desired to grasp my position. It would make them aware that it was bound up with epistemology and with an emergent type of ontology. They would then expect some measure of novelty in the analysis. The family line was, of course, the double-aspect and identity tradition as against dualistic parallelism and interactionism. The task was to redefine the terms in the light of critical realism and evolutionary naturalism.

The best point of departure is to begin with the outlook of the natural sciences in which external objects are being studied and categorized in the light of disclosure mediated by sense-data and the concepts founded on them. *From this standpoint consciousness has only an epistemic function and does not enter into the objective picture.* All the physical sciences from physics to physiology are in the same position in this regard. If I speak of behaviorism here I have this external approach in mind and do not imply any particular theory of nervous and muscular integration. What I would stress is a physiology which studies the processes involved in the activity of an organism as a whole in relation to its environment. It is scarcely necessary to add that I would take the categories of wholeness and integration pretty seriously, much as the Gestaltists do. I recall that when I first met Köhler soon after the war I asked him whether there was not a similarity between *Gestalt* and the emergent theories of Lloyd Morgan and Alexander. He replied that there was and that these two developments seemed to have occurred independently of each other during the war while Germany was isolated. I also asked him whether he did not think that 'organization' more nearly corresponded to his meaning than the term 'pattern' which was used to translate *Gestalt*. He again replied very decidedly in the affirmative. And I note that Koffka criticizes the term 'pattern' and employs that of 'order' instead in his recent *Principles of Gestalt Psychology*.

The first step in the proper handling of the mind-body problem is, then, an adequate physiology built up to cover the facts about organic behavior in relation to an environment. I take it that this kind of physiology is just beginning to appear. Let us admit that little is yet known about the functioning of the brain; there is, nevertheless, a fading away of too simple mechanical notions. The postulate of naturalism—and science is naturalistic—is that the brain must be adequate to perform the operations involved in human behavior. From the point of view of behaviorism in this large sense, the brain is *minded,* that is, it has the capacity to perform in ways that involve learning by experience, discrimination and reasoning, all of these terms being given behavioristic tests and meanings. Any good text in animal psychology, for example Maier and Schneirla's *Principles of Animal Psychology,* reflects this approach. As I have frequently phrased it, mind becomes a physical category. It is, however, redefined in this context. The usual elements of consciousness and awareness are not ingredients. Mind is what mind does; it is a term for abilities and operations *known about* in much the same fashion as the chemical properties of a chemical substance are known about.

It is clear that epistemology is in the offing. What do we know about physical systems? Is scientific knowing, based as it is upon the disclosure-capacity of sense-data and concepts for objects transcending the cognitive act, able to do more than decipher facts and categories descriptive of the structure and functioning of physical systems? Can such knowledge ever penetrate to what I may call the *content of being* to sample it by a kind of intuition? If the reach of external knowing is objective and realistic, while its *grasp* is only of what I may call the *form* of things, this epistemological conclusion is of particular significance for the mind-body problem. Were consciousness in the brain of the animal studied, it could not be a fact for physiology as such; that is, for physiology based upon external sense-perception.

To the philosopher it is quite clear that such physiology no more needs epistemology than does physics. Or, to put it from another angle, needs it just as much as, but no more than, physics. I am inclined to believe that an adequate epistemology will be of value to all the sciences in the way of clarification and elimination of false problems. But all of them can gather facts and build up categories and theories without analyzing the nature of human knowing. For them, consciousness is a mysterious medium somehow essential to the awareness of the facts and theories. But, since it plays the same rôle for every one of the sciences, it does not differentiate them. Hence, it can be left to philosophy in the main. This division of labor, of course, does not prevent the scientist from favoring positivism, operationalism, or idealism according to his bent, nor from giving vent to his conventional scorn of metaphysics, whatever he may mean by that term.

The bearing of this last paragraph upon our argument is that behavioristic physiology develops its categories in relation to its subject-matter. Stereotyped behavior is distinguished from plastic behavior in which the ability to learn declares itself prominently. The growth of the cortex is noted and its correlation with abilities. It is a long story, but always the organism in all its complexity and specialization is kept in sight. It is the organism which behaves, and the nervous system is pivotal for organisms which have evolved beyond the stage of sponges and sea-anemones. The logical result is that, *if the word 'mind' is retained*, it becomes a physical category in the context of selective behavior-operations. Mental development covers development in learning and intelligence, all of which must have behavioral significance and tests. Now it has always seemed quite the natural procedure to me to retain the word 'mind' and to give it this operational, or functional, meaning and make it designate abilities and the operations in which these abilities manifest themselves. These abilities are emergent and are characteristics of evolved organisms with highly developed nervous systems. In this sense, mind as a physical category is adjectival and not substantival. But these mental abilities must be grounded in the organism, particularly in the brain. It is a *minded* brain.

It is obvious that this approach reflects modern evolutionary science and breaks sharply with what may be called the animistic, dualistic tradition. This latter found its extreme expression in Cartesian dualism which satisfied both religious beliefs and physical science until the growth of biology and animal psychology began to weight the scales against dualism. It did this, not so much in the way of a rational disproof of dualism, or even in an adequate development of a comprehensive monism, as in the fashion of a trend which pointed toward such a monism as the implied goal.

But to return to the main thread of the argument. We have maintained that a purely external approach to organic behavior led to the development of mind as a category covering operations of the organism as a whole, operations assignable in large part to the nervous system, particularly the brain. I spoke, therefore, of a *minded brain*. From the standpoint of evolutionary naturalism, it was logical to hold that these operations and the abilities upon which they rest were functions of the integrative organization of the brain. The principle used was that new organizations *involve* new abilities. The *involvement* here referred to is the *ontological analogy* of logical implication. There is a sense in it of existential entailment. I take this to be a meaning essential to causality when this is given, as it should be, objective significance. A cause *involves* its effect, while one proposition implies another.

Now while we have succeeded in applying to the organism, conceived realistically and naturalistically, such terms as mind and intelligence, it will be felt by all who are sensitive to man's self-knowledge and to the fact of consciousness as something personally experienced and the locus of all epistemic awareness, that there is something shadowy and external about mind and intelligence thus defined. Are not these categories as yet immersed in factual knowledge about organisms? It is a fact that rats and dogs are somewhat plastic, that they learn by experience, that they solve simple problems. Mind and intelligence are covering terms for such complexes of facts with the theories developed around them. There is knowledge about, but no participation in the economy of, the animal. And, just because we cannot communicate with the beasts of the field, we almost feel ready to think of their minds as exhausted by this factual knowledge about them. Whatever an animal mind is, it cannot, we tend to think, escape the validity of the concepts we have gradually woven around them. It is a neural system dominating a behavior economy.

But man, the knower, self-conscious, artist and scientist, is aware that, in his own case, other data must be considered which, while they may well fit into the conception of mind achieved by behaviorism, must enlarge it. It is, as I see it, the task of the philosopher to clarify this adjustment by means of epistemological and ontological analysis. Do we have a double knowledge of ourselves, behavioral, physical, external knowledge in which mind is disclosed in what mind does, disclosure to an external observer, and a self-knowledge in which the knower is internal to himself and for which consciousness in its full range is not merely epistemic but also inseparable from the self, the object known? Few philosophers have doubted this double knowledge. The dispute among them has concerned itself with the question whether there were two objects of knowledge, self and body, or only one object, the organism adequately conceived. The dualist takes the first position, the monist the second. It is the second position which I wish to analyze. Why may not the enduring self about which we know in self-knowledge be the organism in respect to its complex strivings and operations? If so, this self-knowledge should enlarge and supplement the conception of mind gained by external study. There would be essentially the philosophical problem of coalescing the results of two ways of knowing the same reality. Modern psychology of the eclectic sort which seeks to combine behaviorism with introspection is really desirous of achieving this coalescence. We shall see that the Gestaltists are quite conscious of the task. I do not believe, however, that their philosophical equipment is quite adequate. At least, I shall try to carry through the analysis as I see it.

Gradually, as evolution is taken seriously and as biology and psychology are admitted to the rank of science, it is seen that humans constitute a critical point in nature and the thought of nature. Even though reluctantly, the scientist must recognize the novelty of the situation. With respect to the inorganic world, man can be disregarded by science except as a remarkable epistemic center. But when man himself is studied, it is recognized that man has a kind of self-knowledge which is not reducible to external observation, and even the fact of consciousness and general cognition must be faced at this point. Because he has always recognized these points the philosopher has escaped the temptation of a naïve materialism. There are data other than the data of value for external cognition, but these data are of value for the self, be this the organism, or something, as Pratt believes, tied in with it. Can it be denied that all an individual's *experiencings* have a disclosure capacity for himself as a continuing creature? It may not be easy for him to read them always aright for it does not follow that self-knowledge is easy, save in its broad outlines. Yet we know that we are creatures capable of perceiving, desiring, loving, remembering and reflecting. We apprehend these facts through and by means of our specific experiences along these lines.

It is, then, only in the case of humans that external scientific knowledge is confronted by self-knowledge. . . . There is . . . another important point to which much of the remainder of this paper will be devoted. It is this: While a critical view of external knowledge refuses to project any datum of consciousness into the external object in a literal fashion, but only holds that concepts based upon, and using, sensuous data have the capacity to disclose facts about the external object, self-knowledge cannot reject consciousness in this fashion. We not only know our selves through our conscious experiences, but we regard these experiences as somehow intrinsic features of the operations known through them. It is in the self that consciousness must find its home. It is for this reason that self-knowledge is so crucial for philosophy. It marks the last point to which consciousness can retreat. There is nowhere else for it to withdraw. Each person recognizes this fact for himself and knows that others do the same. But if, as I hold, the self is the organism, then this retreat of consciousness, from the external object known, to the self, is but an *existential location* of consciousness. The task of the philosopher is to think it in terms of adequate categories.

We must now study the ontological status of consciousness, meaning by that the field of the individual's experience as against the objects disclosed by it. Thus far, we have largely dealt with the epistemic function of consciousness, the fact that all human knowledge rested on conscious acts of cognition using sense-data and concepts knit up with words. But we can no longer ignore the question of the ontological status of these acts and of much else less purely intellectual, such as willing and feeling. Now I flatter myself that some of my best analytic work has been in connection with this question, the existential relation of consciousness to the minded brain. The first task is to categorize consciousness correctly from the ontological standpoint. In order to do this we must at the same time properly categorize the brain-mind to which it is in some sense adjectival. It is clear, I take it, that consciousness is unique in being the only factor given or experienced. In all else we only have knowledge about, disclosed facts about, with the categories they demand. Our ontology must be guided by our epistemology. Thus, it is obvious that consciousness cannot be a quality of the brain in quite the same sense that mental capacities are properties of the brain. In the first case we participate in the changing content, or being, of the brain-mind, while in the second case we are dealing with disclosed facts about the brain. I hope to make this distinction clearer as I proceed and to develop a terminology expressive of it.

In following out this coöperation of epistemology and ontology we shall deal with the following three inevitable elements of the consciousness-brain problem: (1) The proper terminology for the location of consciousness *in* the brain. What can 'in' mean here? (2) The proper logical language to use in speaking of cerebral processes as conscious. And (3) the sense, if any, in which consciousness may be said to have efficacy, given its status and location. These topics will involve some consideration of such basic categories as space, time, matter, quality, quantity and causality. I shall be brief, but I take it to be undeniable that the consciousness-body problem brings to a head, and tests, the adequacy of one's epistemology and ontology.

Let it be understood, then, that we are working along the lines of monism; the organism is to include logically what can be known about it from the outside, what can be known about it by self-knowledge, and it is so to be thought, and consciousness is so to be thought, that consciousness can be located literally in the brain-mind. The first step is to consider the brain-mind as known from the outside.

Now it has long been my thesis that such knowledge, gained as it is by deciphering the disclosures to be elicited from sense-perception, carried further by measurement, constitutes a complex of facts about patterns and relations. At the level of science it is abstract and quantitative, but I take it to be a genuine disclosure of characteristics. Ours is a quantitative, dynamic universe, and various events proceed in accordance with laws and principles which are expressions of the nature of the physical world. It is so far forth that kind of a world. And in this world there are levels of organization and behavior.

But this disclosure, as I see it, has its intrinsic limitations. However far it is carried by a cumulative and ingenious technique into the microscopic, it remains external knowledge of measured patterns and relations. It is only this feature of nature which it is able by its epistemic foundations and methods to grasp. But, surely, physical systems are not reducible ontologically to these abstract decipherments of pattern. Such knowledge does not exhaust the reality of the physical world. There is no existential equivalence between facts and existence. Rather do facts presuppose existence. Existence is that which they are about. Every physical system has what we may metaphorically call a life of its own. It is a region of content and activity. It is something in itself, a center of *substantial* agency. What external science offers us is a description of the pattern of these substantial agents in their fields. Past materialism has always glimpsed this ontological truth but has been too naïve both in its epistemology and in its ontology. It was dominated by picture-thinking, by atomistic mechanical traditions, and did not see the significance of organization and its emergent involvements.

Our conclusion is that scientific knowledge, while a disclosure of pattern in an abstracted reproductive fashion, never samples physical existence in the sense of *participating* in it. In such knowing, genuine as it is, we are never literally on the inside of external objects intuiting, or experiencing, their particular 'go,' their life and substantial being. This intrinsic limitation of scientific knowledge does not derogate from its splendor as a human achievement resting on all sorts of mechanisms and abilities and requiring cultural evolution. Only the naturalist, I believe, fully comprehends this kind of knowing because he, alone, appreciates its levels, operations and development. This remark is incidental and by the way, for the relevant principle for the mind-body problem is this denial that the objective reach and disclosure of knowledge through concepts can ever involve participation in the content of external things.

The indicated thesis from this epistemological analysis is, of course, that knowledge about the brain's structure and behavior, that is, *facts* of that sort about the brain can never give us a literal vision, or intuition, of a participative sort. It remains a cognitive grasp which deciphers facts about the brain but it can never carry the knower into the brain to feel and experience its processes and activities, *to be one with it*. This contrast seems to me significant and unavoidable.

To the evolutionary naturalist this situation inevitably suggests the hypothesis that, in his own consciousness, each of us is on the inside of his own brain, that his consciousness is a factor intrinsic to cortical processes justifying us in speaking of them as conscious processes. But the philosophical, conceptual job is that of categorizing this factor properly in relation to the brain as ontologically conceived in the light of our external knowledge about it.

The first step is to recognize that consciousness, as a term for the field of personal experience, is something open to inspection or intuition. It is the locus of feeling, knowing and willing as qualitatively given *events*. At the human level we can note a polar contrast within this field having a sense, or direction, from the more subjective to the more objective or discriminated. This directional relation is called awareness or consciousness of. It seems quite obvious that this polar contrast is tied up with, and reflects, functional direction in the activity of the organism. But that is a long story which I cannot take up here. Suffice it to say that the meanings and distinctions which we understand and use in both science and everyday life appear in the field of consciousness. This undeniable epistemological fact seems clearly to suggest that the field of consciousness is immersed in the responsible adjustments of the organism to its environment. But how shall we *think* this immersion? That, as we have already indicated, is the conceptual problem.

We can now turn to an explanation of the phrase, a double-knowledge of the organism. The situation is really more complicated than most people suppose. On the one hand, there are actual and hypothetical facts about the organism of the sort that physiology has been working out. According to critical realism, all such facts are the disclosures mediated by true propositions about objects—in this case primarily the brain—which transcend the act of cognition which uses these true propositions. Supplementing these facts and, I take it, harmonizable with them, is the knowledge about the *self*, that is, the human individual, which appears in both common sense and ethics and traditional psychology. This, also, is knowledge about the organism of the transcendent sort. The particular problem here is to adjust the categories so that mental categories shall not conflict with those of physiology. I mean that choice, preference and reasoning must have analogues in the categories of physiology. Otherwise, dualism must needs appear. It is the naturalist's belief that an adequate empiricism will recognize the validity of such categories to human behavior and will seek to give them a physiological expression. Recent literature seems to have shown a movement in that direction. I take it that there must be a basic categorial parallelism between external knowledge of the organism and self-knowledge.

But self-knowledge, we have seen, is confronted with the inescapable conviction that the experiences used as the basis of knowledge of the abilities and modes of the self are also, in some sense, ingredients of the self. It is not strange, therefore, that we feel ourselves to be at once knowing and participating in the self. Thus self-knowledge is at once transcendent and immanent. We know ourselves as having particular desires and as capable of desire and, at the same time, we feel ourselves to be consciously participating in a specific desire. And it is because of this conscious participation that we seem to be at once knowing about the self and being one with it. It is in this fashion that the question of the existential status of consciousness with respect to the self, which is also the organism, takes its form.

Now it is necessary to study consciousness first for itself and then, afterwards, to categorize it with respect to the self as known through self-cognition, and with respect to the self as organism known externally. The chief historical difficulty has been experienced in relation to the last demand, that is, to locate consciousness in the organism. Dualists who believe that the self as known through self-knowledge is other than the body have usually been satisfied to regard conscious experiences as states of the self. It has always seemed to me that this was too simple, that conscious experiences could for the dualist only be adjectives of states of the self but not the whole of such a state. Surely, the self is transcendent to consciousness while possessing it, is more than consciousness, something more permanently organized and cumulative, something which manifests itself in consciousness. Consciousness seems to be like a half-open doorway to the self or like the surface of a flowing stream.

To the monist the abiding thought is that this substantial, cumulative reality, which transcends consciousness while possessing it, is, after all, the living organism with its emergent abilities. It is the organism which, in man's case, has achieved these subtle ingenuities. But, then, it is the task of the philosopher to conceive by means of the proper categorizing of his complex subject-matter how all this is possible; he must break through the abrupt contrasts of Cartesian dualism which shuts out mind and consciousness from a body exhaustively known as mere extension; he must show how conscious experience can be an intrinsic feature of brain-states, a feature which external knowledge, because formal and not participative, cannot attain.

The primary trait of consciousness, when considered for its own sake and not as disclosing objects transcendent to it, is its givenness. It is aesthesis, feeling, awareness, understanding, experiencing. I take it to have varieties because I take it to be a manifestation of brain-mind activities. Yet all these varieties have in common a compresence, they are elements of a field which is specific and contentual. Here, alone, are we participative and inspectional. We *are*, so far forth, feelings and compresent, inspected *qualia*. The result is what I would call an inevitable *ontological abstraction* made by nature itself. It is almost an analytic statement that consciousness is all of the brain-mind state we can consciously participate in. The more of the substantial system with which it is continuous cannot reduce itself to consciousness and become evanescent. It must remain substantial, and we can only have knowledge about it of a transcendent, formal sort.

Now, because consciousness in its concrete compresence is ontologically abstracted from its existential context by the very fact that it can *be* only itself and therefore cannot draw its context into itself and open it up to inspection, there are facts about consciousness, such as its basis and existential relations, which it cannot answer by inspection of itself. Acts of cognition in which it functions as disclosing and categorizing objects transcending itself can, alone, offer help here. We must try to grasp the nature of consciousness while recognizing that it is adjectival and somehow possesses a substantial setting. It must somehow stem from, and be one with, the brain-mind system from which it is, as we have said, abstracted, not in reality, but by the fact that it is all we can consciously participate in.

Panpsychism must, I take it, be dismissed, because consciousness is not substantival enough to meet the demands of the categories of external knowledge. Nothing corresponding to nervous structure and mass can be discovered in it. It is more like a qualitative dimension of integral activities of an emergent order.

A word or so about the verbal solutions of traditional materialism. It is evident that these were epistemologically naïve. Consciousness does not enter the ken of abstract and formal external knowledge about the organism. This fact undercuts such statements as that consciousness is a form of motion or a kind of energy or an epiphenomenon or that it is a by-product. It should be noted that all these statements are working within the categories of the first kind of knowledge. To assert that a molecule moves is to give a *fact about it* with respect to some other thing as a frame of reference. Such knowledge does not penetrate to the content of being but discloses formal characteristics. Energy as a category of science is in the same status. Neural energy is a valid term for the facts about the dynamic activity of the brain. But while consciousness is undoubtedly tied up with the dynamic activity of the brain, it cannot be known externally and made to fit into the concept of energy. To the critical physical realist, the term epiphenomenon is a monstrosity. The brain is not a phenomenon but an actuality, and what can *epi* really mean? Finally, the term 'by-product' moves in the same epistemological setting. To call consciousness a by-product is to class it with physical things left over as in a chemical factory. But my whole argument has been to the effect that consciousness is not a physical system but a *qualitative dimension of the existential content of a highly evolved physical system.*

In what sense, then, is consciousness *in* the brain? I have repeatedly affirmed that it is *not* in the brain as one physical part of a thing is in the whole thing, as, for example, a pea is in a pod or an electron is in an atom. It is not a physical part. The proper correlation of consciousness is with a brain-state; it is an event. The implication is that consciousness is in the brain after the manner that an event, or *state*, is in that of which it is a state. This relationship is, quite obviously, an intrinsic one like that of a change to that physical system which is changing. I take it that, in any integrated system, the 'inness' of the state is that of penetration and participation, of participative presence. It is this internal relatedness of a necessarily qualitied state to its system which I had in mind when I spoke of consciousness as a qualitative dimension of the brain-state. Because we are limited to it in our consciousness, we can have intuitive knowledge only of it and not of its ontological context. Here we have that ontological abstraction which, with other animistic motives, has encouraged dualism.

The proper approach to the 'inness' of consciousness, in short, is to think of the status of functions and operations with respect to the organism which performs these functions and operations. The activities and changing conditions involved in such operations are internal, intrinsic, present to, and *in,* such operations. It is the 'inness' of the state of a physical system with its integrative unity. All one needs to do is to supplement this conception with the recognition of the identity of our consciousness with this content and its unique property of being experienced. Such is my categorization of the phrase that, in consciousness, we are on the *inside* of the functioning brain. It is one with the content of the brain which, otherwise, we have only descriptive knowledge about in terms of facts which disclose the formal characteristics of the brain but never a sample of its stuff or content. An adequate epistemology is necessary if we are to have an adequate ontology which escapes the extremes of panpsychism and naïve materialism.

I have argued in many places that consciousness, thus conceived, must be categorized as spatial. It is *throughout* the physical system which is functioning and of which it is a qualitative dimension. I would call it an internal feature of a *Gestalt* or neural field. It is for this reason that it is existentially private, as private as any individual system is. This fact conflicts in no fashion with the objective intention and disclosure capacity of conceptual transcendent cognition. After all, cognitive claims are an affair of personal experience whether true or false, that is, whether giving knowledge of something other than themselves or not. But to return to the particular question broached in this paragraph, *consciousness is extended after its kind*. It is, clearly, not a thing to be externally measured by superposition. It is the qualitative dimension of a state and, like all states, has the extension of that of which it is a state. This implication of our analysis enables us to break with the Cartesian contrast between the extended and the unextended. There are, of course, some fascinating points for discussion here; but these need not be taken up since I have examined them in the sixteenth chapter of my *Philosophy of Physical Realism*.

We are now ready to take up the second topic, the proper logical form to be used in speaking of the brain as conscious. And I shall use Professor Pratt's discussion in his recent Presidential Address entitled "The Present Status of the Mind-Body Problem."[2] Commenting on my position, he writes as follows: "Consciousness is thus a *quality* of the brain. It is as completely identical with the cerebrum as are the physical qualities of that organ. We may say that the brain is painful, is joyful, is hesitant, *in the same sense* in which we say that it is of a certain shape, size and chemical constitution."

Now I do not want to be too much of a scholastic in these matters, but I would like to point out that such adjectives as painful, joyful and hesitant need interpretation at a critical level just as the adjective red does. I would say that the feeling of joy, that kind of a feeling, is literally a feature of a brain-state, a factor in its content of being which, however, can not be participated in by external knowledge. But what do we mean ordinarily when we assert that a person is joyful? It has in part, it seems to me, a behavioristic meaning to the effect that he behaves joyfully, and partly a claim to know about another person after the analogy of self-knowledge. Now when, in self-knowledge, I judge myself to be joyful, what do I really judge? According to my argument, that the joyous feeling discloses a state of the self which is that of well-being, prosperous functioning, and is, also, a factor in that state in the fashion I have taken such pains to categorize. Now this self which is prosperously functioning is, for me, the brain in the context of the whole organism. I take it also to be factual knowledge about the

---

[2] This *Review*, March 1936.

self-brain that it has a certain size and chemical constitution. But this knowledge can be gained only through the disclosure-value of data of external observation. It is formal knowledge of the characteristics of the brain, as an extended physical thing, supplementary to self-knowledge. It is a disclosure of quantifiable pattern. Both kinds of knowledge are true, then, after their kind and their data. Self-knowledge of the brain on the basis of complex experiences discloses an *integral functioning* of the brain in which these experiences are embedded as a qualitative feature which can be known only by compresent participation or givenness. Not in such a fashion can the structure of the brain be known, but only through the disclosure-capacity of specialized sense-impressions taken to have completely external significance.

I would apply much the same analysis to the statement that the brain is painful. It does not mean that the brain causes pain in the fashion that a wound does, but does mean that it is in a state from some cause, and pain in a factor of this state as extended as it is. "Let us revert," continues Pratt, "to Professor Sellars' assertion of identity between the brain and the *quality* of painfulness. Plainly this may mean either that the brain is a substance and produces in us a painful sensum; or that a given object called brain produces in us both visual and tactual and also painful sensations. In either case we presuppose a sentient self to have the sensations; or, if we prefer the wording, we presuppose a stream of consciousness which is affected by the brain. In neither case, so far as I can see, have we done anything to avoid, solve, or throw light upon, the mind-body problem. We should, indeed, be attempting to solve the problem should we say that the essence *painfulness* is the essence brain-structure and motion of particles; but Professor Sellars is far too clear-sighted to commit himself to anything so manifestly absurd."

Let us examine these supposed alternatives. Professor Pratt speaks of me as asserting an identity between the brain and the quality of painfulness. I suppose a headache would be an example of what he had in mind. Now my interpretation is that the self is thought of in self-cognition as being headachy and the sentient feeling is an actual factor in the state of the self. But this means also for the double-knowledge theory that the brain, which is the self, is headachy and that its state has the factor, a headachy feeling, extended in it as an event in the fashion I have tried to categorize. The identity is of the brain and the self, and of the headache, as a state cognized by the self through the feeling, and as a state known about from outside as a physiologist might know about it. Pratt's causal formulation rather puzzles me. The stream of consciousness is not affected by the brain but is a feature of the brain-self state which can be known only by participation. If Pratt still wants to use causal language, I would distinguish between transeunt and immanent causation. It seems clear to me that the brain-self state is related to the brain in the way of immanent causation, not of transeunt causation. Now this brain-self state, which is a phase of the functioning of the brain-self substance or physical system, does not produce consciousness as something external to it. Consciousness is a feature of its content of being in which the self participates. It is the traditional dualistic tendency to hold that the brain is exhaustively known by external knowledge that still dominates Professor Pratt. External knowledge is of such a character that it can never participate in being but only decipher pattern. Along with this has gone the tradition of underestimating the organism, a tradition against which the theory of emergent naturalism is a protest.

The more I reflect upon Pratt's objections and seek to get to their hidden assumptions, the more I am convinced that he has not forced himself to carry through the implications of his own epistemology. Of course, we do not mean by a physical system or by any of its characteristics as disclosed by external knowledge what we mean by consciousness. The situation is more delicate than that. But can he deny that I have shown that it is logically possible that my flow of consciousness is my participation in the flow of response and activity states of the brain? If so, a self which is more than a stream of consciousness *á la Hume* and which is known in terms of self-knowledge may well be the brain. There is much to show that consciousness depends upon the brain. Why multiply entities if the brain and the self have analogous abilities and if epistemology indicates simply two kinds of knowledge having, in all likelihood, the same ultimate objective? Just as we ordinarily think of physical systems only in terms of formal knowledge-about, so we ordinarily think of such acts and states as thinking, believing, willing, feeling, and striving in terms of direct experiencing and concepts founded on, and interpretative of, that direct experiencing. What I ask is that these two approaches be seen to *supplement* each other, that both be seen to be valid. This would mean that cerebral processes are as the physiologist describes them in terms of factual knowledge about, and are, likewise, as the introspectionist is aware of them. To assert that a cortical process is conscious is to assert that it *contains* the sort of experience we enjoy and contemplate introspectionally. The implication of my whole argument is that a work of synthesis needs to be done, that it is possible to enlarge our physiological knowledge of the brain, and the categories there relevant, by the acceptance of the additional fact that these cerebral operations have this conscious dimension. Professor Pratt talks about material systems, but will he tell us just what is his conception of the *grasp* of scientific knowledge? Does it, in his opinion, penetrate to the content of being? He talks about qualities, or properties, as *qualifying* physical systems; will he give the ontology of this qualification? I have wrestled with the relation between epistemology and ontology long enough to know that there are profound questions here which are very relevant to the consciousness-brain problem.

It may, perhaps, be recalled that I have argued that physiology may well get cues for comprehension of cerebral differentiations and integrations from a careful study of consciousness if, as I have suggested, the field of consciousness is intrinsic to, and isomorphic with, the physiological field. I am, obviously, sympathetic with the thesis of the Gestaltists that "the concrete order of actual experience is a true representation of the dynamic order of the corresponding physiological processes." What I have tried to do is to work out the proper epistemology and ontology for this correspondence. That is, the correspondence rests upon a basic identity, ontologically conceived in this fashion, namely that consciousness is a feature of the content of being of cerebral activities epistemologically conceived along the lines of the two kinds of knowledge.

Let us turn in conclusion to the very tantalizing question of the causal efficacy of consciousness.

It should be noted, first of all, that I have redefined mind as a term for operations and abilities particularly connected with the nervous system. There can, in my opinion, be no question but that such operations and the abilities upon which they rest are efficacious. They are ways in which the brain-mind functions. If you will, it is a case of immanent causality, of activities connected with, and expressive of, a genetically developed structure. This interpretation of the mind in terms of more or less conscious operations of the brain makes the mind, as I have said, a physical category. It stands for emergent abilities of the organism dominently located in the brain. I take pride in recalling that in an article on causality, published in the *Journal of Philosophy* in 1909, I drew the logical conclusion from the acceptance of physical organization, namely, that there must be *levels of causality*. I had in mind *immanent causality or functioning*. A minded brain accounts for intelligent behavior; and intelligent behavior is physically real. This emergent conception of levels in nature with levels of immanent, or functional, causality is the fundamental note of evolutionary naturalism. I have always opposed it to what I called dead-level naturalism, the nightmare of traditional idealism.

The brain-mind is, then, efficacious. Its abilities and organized operations make the difference which distinguishes human conduct. But is there any special rôle in all this which we can assign to consciousness? Let us consult the ontological situation as we have conceived it. There will be need, again, of some subtlety to comprehend this situation.

Pratt quotes Köhler to this effect: "Direct experience is not a 'force' interfering with the chain of physical causation." And Koffka makes the following statement: "In our *ultimate* explanations we can have but one universe of discourse, and it must be the one about which physics has taught us so much." Let me show how I would interpret these assertions in the light of the analysis I have made.

In the category of causation as developed and used in our scientific knowledge of the physical world, we are thinking the world in terms of the facts about it gained by observation. In other words, we are working entirely within the first kind of knowledge, which is descriptive of a transcendent object and not participative. And it is obvious that consciousness here plays a purely epistemological rôle. It is the locus of the sensory data and concepts of the knower. The intent and belief is that these concepts disclose facts about a physiological system. I take it that all forms of behaviorism are correct on this point. And I do not see how any science working *within the comprehensions* of this kind of knowledge can insert consciousness as an alien force interfering with the chain of causation as conceived in terms of descriptive facts. Remember that scientific knowledge, based on external observation, can never make contact with consciousness in the brain. But we must equally note that it never makes contact with any kind of *literal* causal efficacy. Hume has, surely, not lived in vain. While the modern physical realist does not go to the extreme of Hume's subjectivism, he is aware that knowledge does not penetrate to the *content of being* to *sense* the urges of changing systems. The best that can be done is to decipher formal characteristics and to quantify them as forces and energies. The result is knowledge about dynamic activities with a concept of *causal involvement;* that is, that the consequent condition follows from, and expresses the nature of, the physical system under change. Consciousness would be a ghost for such external knowledge; it could not categorize it or relate it to its facts. I suppose that this is what Koffka has in mind when he asserts that the conscious side of the process does not enter into our causal explanations.

Now I have long maintained that, in consciousness—and there alone—we are on the inside of nature, that is, of that highly organized system, the human brain. The situation is unique, and it is no wonder that it puzzles the psychologist. In this consciousness, each one is a participant to some extent in cortical changes. It is on the inside of a causal process, a feature of a change of the content of being. But, be it noted, that the literal context of consciousness is not given, that here is that ontological abstraction to which I earlier called attention. It is not an existential separation but the selection of consciousness *by itself from its context by reason of its very nature*. Now the best I have been able to do in the way of ontological categorization is to classify consciousness as a qualitative dimension of a cortical state or event. And I use the word 'qualitative' here, for want of a better one, to designate the fact that we are aware of patterned qualia, and that we must regard these as features of brain-states, but features which can not be known from outside.

It is obvious that we can not assign efficacy to consciousness by itself, since it is merely a feature of the cortical event. The causal reality is the conscious physiological process. We are led to reject the dualist's notion that consciousness is something which is forced to insert itself causally from outside into the brain in a transeunt fashion. No; we have here to do with immanent causality, with functioning.

Before I go further, I wish to discuss very briefly the question of the emergence of consciousness. As I see it, cortical organization with the processes and abilities assignable to it emerges in an evolutionary way. We have here only a very high level which comes under the common principle of emergence as recognized by the objective sciences. And I want it borne in mind that I have never taken the term mystically but have made it *rational* by connecting it with the rise of new relationships and organization.

I believe that consciousness emerges *with* nervous organization for the reason that I hold it to be intrinsic to it, that is, internally related in the manner I have indicated. As to what *content of being* physiological events have below this level, we can have no intuitive knowledge because we cannot participate in them. But I see no reason to hold that such events do not contain an internal content of a qualitied sort, perhaps some dimly felt urgency. But our situation is such that we cannot share in it and sense it. This epistemological condition makes itself felt throughout animal psychology and is the chief reason for the negative attitude towards consciousness in that field.

For the objective sciences, then, we should speak only of the emergence of new forms of organization with new properties. Mind, as a physical category, stands for nervous organization and for those abilities connected with it which are observable and verifiable by objective psychology. It is my thesis that knowledge about the continuant self and its abilities gained by self-observation supplements, and is continuous with, this external behavioristic knowledge. In both cases we have transcendent knowledge about a physical system, the organism. In the objective sciences, emergence should have this context; the question of consciousness does not enter. But, if we decide that, in the human organism at least, consciousness is a feature of the content of cerebral events intuited by us because we participate in it, then we are allowed to speak of consciousness as a *unique co-emergent* with nervous organization. Out of what internal *content of being* it flashes we cannot say, for the simple reason that it is our only contact with the content of existence. We have a right to assert that physical systems are not vacuous in content even though we cannot peer into their being but only gain descriptive knowledge of their structure and behavior. Certainly, we should relinquish such naïve notions as Victorian physicists had that the inside of atoms was gray and chalky in texture. Eddington has seen this point, though his epistemology has no internal consistency. It is clear, I hope, that I am not saying, with traditional naïve materialism, that consciousness is a form of motion; I am saying that consciousness is what it is experienced as, and that it must be regarded as a feature of the content of being of cerebral events. Its isomorphism, or correspondence, with these events, as known from the outside, points the same moral.

And now we are prepared to discuss the efficacy of consciousness *pro* and *con*. It will be remembered that I asserted that, in scientific knowledge, we can never pentrate to causal efficacy but only have knowledge about facts of causal involvement. To penetrate to causal efficacy would be to experience it, participate in it. As against Hume, the physical realist holds the category of causation to have objective application, but it has application as a category of knowledge about, that is, as interpreting facts about a physical system as having the relation of involvement, analogous to that of implication. We believe that one state of affairs in a physical system involves another, is internally continuous with another. Yet we cannot intuit this involvement, cannot participate in the internal 'go' of changing systems. It is obvious that I think that *in consciousness alone are we inside immanent, or functional, causality.* If consciousness has efficacy, it must not be thought of as a force operating upon cortical systems from the outside as the interactionists do. The efficacy of consciousness can have no meaning for the external view.

People often ask why consciousness *arose* if it had no efficacy. My notion is that neural systems could not but be conscious if my analysis is correct. We must not think of consciousness as something added to a neural system from the outside. The relation is internal and factually inevitable. It is the very nature of an integrative cortical process to have its conscious *quale*. The relation, as I see it, is internal and existentially necessary. To speak of a pain-quale *as such* as having efficacy is to speak of an abstraction as having efficacy.

The only possibility I see with respect to the efficacy of consciousness is along the line of an exploration of such functions as attention, awareness, discrimination and comparison. We are here concerned with action as a whole conditioned by abilities of discrimination and comparison. At the human level there is the development of symbols which become the center of sentiments and attitudes. Now these abilities involve the discrimination of patterns and relations. There is, of course, a physiological base for these distinctions and the polarities of contemplation and action which go with them. In consciousness, as we have maintained, we are on the inside of these polarities and discriminations. We are *aware* of them, that is, these operations are illuminated by consciousness which reflects their directions and tensions. It is all a high-level process in which the units are action-patterns having functional relations bound up with drives and interests. The togetherness of the field of consciousness reflects this integrative and polarized physiological togetherness.

And now I come to a bit of ontology. I have said that, in consciousness alone, are we compresent with existence, are we a conscious phase of a complex integration of cortical systems. It would seem to be a defensible thesis that this apprehension is ontologically necessary for the carrying on of these discriminations and constructions. That is, certainly, what we internally feel. Remember that these processes are conscious ones and that the field of consciousness is absolutely one with the growing point of physiological adjustments of patterns. *This would seem to mean that the conscious aspect of the points of tension is one with the cues and guidances which are directing reorganization.* The ontological reality is, quite literally, a conscious operation, nature become consciously aware. Here, alone, are we on the inside of a causal process, which happens to be one of tremendous emergent complexity.

This suggestion becomes meaningless as soon as the slightest touch of dualism is allowed to enter the picture. The efficacy of consciousness is not that of an external force, for it is not that kind of a reality. We are dealing with immanent, or functional, causality; and we are asking ourselves whether the function of *awareness* is not essential to mental, cerebral processes and whether, since these are *consciously aware* in situations involving discrimination and synthesis, that is, analysis and integration, this *conscious feature* is not as essential to these operations as it seems to us experientially to be. It is at least factually there and, as I see it, inevitably and not accidentally there, emergent in the content of being, as a feature of active cerebral operations, along with the emergent organization and its functional abilities. It is, of course, the sole case of which we know, and can know, of this emergence within the content of being, just because it can be known only by participation. But I can see no reason why it should not have its *unknown analogues.* Certainly, every physical system and field must have its existential content; it cannot be contentually vacuous. But, as I have repeated so often, in consciousness alone are we human beings, quite literally, on the inside of a physical system with peculiar, emergent abilities. It is this consciousness which is the medium of such abstract disclosures of the *formal characteristics* of physical systems as are achieved in science.

The suggestion I have made with respect to the internal, functional efficacy of consciousness is, quite clearly, speculative and metaphysical. There is, however, nothing about it which conflicts with the scientist's rejection of the causal efficacy of consciousness. At most, to the physiologist, man can but be a conscious automaton. That is because he works in terms of facts about the organism from the outside. Even the use of experiences to decipher the form of cerebral processes does not violate this thesis. Even here the physiologist is concerned with formal characteristics and not with the content of being. Causality, in such knowledge about, can signify only factual involvement; it does not represent a participation in immanent causality or functioning.

My whole argument has been to the effect that the mind-body problem could not be analyzed apart from an adequate epistemology and ontology. It is, I believe, a test of such adequacy. Is it surprising that the mind-brain-consciousness problem has hitherto baffled thought? All I ask is the courtesy of a patient effort at comprehension of a rather complex analysis. I have always been grateful to Professor Pratt because he has made such an effort.[3]

---

[3] In *Personal Realism*, published since I wrote this article, Pratt again suggests that I write as though I assumed a real self in such phrases as "we, as conscious, participate," "we, as conscious beings, are on the inside of reality." Of course, I believe in a real self. It is the organism which we apprehend, as functioning, *in* and *through* desires, deliberations, choices, etc. The dualist substitutes for the functioning organism an X which he must claim to know in like fashion but which he argues cannot be the organism. I might appeal to the principle of parsimony. But it is my belief that Pratt is gradually being pushed by critical realism and emergent evolution in the direction of naturalism.

PART IV

Other Tests of Emergent Realism: The Theory of Truth and The Theory of Value

INTRODUCTION

BOTH TRUTH AND value are derivative conceptions. Truth for example is secondary to knowledge in Sellars' philosophy: a justified claim to knowledge. Its tests are tests of knowledge.

Values, in turn, are functions of objects: the roles of objects in the economy of persons in society. Roles are to be determined through assessments—not just feelings or wishes. The term "economy" itself requires assessment: it is to be construed in the broadest sense, to include the meanings of aesthetic objects and of other objects of sentiment, as well as social, moral, and 'economic' objects.

Value theory is thus derivative from ontology, epistemology, and philosophy of mind: the natures of things and of organisms and their determinable relations to each other. Assessment of the roles of objects rests on assumptions regarding persons and things, and therewith on knowledge.

What constitutes a value assessment for Sellars? Is it the experimental process elaborated by Dewey? In his claim that values proper are discriminated by assessment, Sellars seems to be close to Dewey. Dewey, wrote Sellars, "has a keen sense for critical and experimental evaluations." And these are fruitful procedures for the determination of the roles of objects in men's economies. But Dewey treats values as "features of that 'blanket experience' within which his thinking operates,"[1] and does not afford anything like a sufficiently realistic basis for his value judgments. He is too purely an experimentalist, and Sellars has no disposition to limit himself to this variety of assessment. He gives Toulmin credit for a fruitful advance in the determination of the intellectualization required for disclosure and validation of moral values.

In a 1967 article in *Philosophy and Phenomenological Research,* he contends that "philosophy cannot do the work of science" though it must "keep its eyes on science." Nor can it, in ethics or value theory, be intuitionist à la Moore, Prichard and Ross. "To estimate the role an object (or 'objective') plays in the human economy is an objective endeavor in its own fashion. Yet there is often a great delicacy in working it out." Linguistics is involved, and, of course, concepts, likewise feelings—above all, feelings of approval. The validations of approvals or endorsements of the functions of objects for human interests, purposes, and notably human living together: this is the heart of the issue. Feedback is important here, as in epistemology; likewise reciprocity, and long range consequences. Philosophers such as the emotivists and linguistic analysts have had too simple an approach. But recent British analysts have been getting to the issues.

> With Toulmin's stress on *good reasons* for moral judgment and Hare's careful study of moral language, a pathway between intuitionism and emotivism was being opened up. . . . Taking Toulmin, Urmson and Hare together, I find a recognition of the practical reason and of the interplay of criteria and attitude in evaluation. This emphasis is also taken by Nowell-Smith. All of this seems to me in the right direction.[2]

But value judgments are more basically grounded, and morality, in particular, "comes in, in a supervisory way, to judge objectives in their bearing on welfare as envisaged in an accepted way of life." The specific grounds of such judgments

---

[1] "Can a Reformed Materialism Do Justice to Values," Ethics, LV (1944), 33.

[2] "In What Sense do Value Judgments have Objective Import," *Philosophy and Phenomenological Research* (1967), XXVIII, 12.

and the categories involved are suggested in the readings that follow.[3] It is no provincial task.

"In fitting moral philosophy into natural philosophy, it is well to take one's start from biology, psychology, and the social sciences. . . . The horizon should [in fact] be as broad as cultural anthropology . . . No provincialism should be accepted . . . No one who has worked in social philosophy, as I have done, can escape the sense of exploratory openness. . . ." Philosophy can, in conjunction with the total range of science, and most especially the human sciences, work at "perspective, criteria and goals."[4] The humanities indeed are equally grist for a naturalistic moral philosophy. The synthesis in a philosophy of validatable values is the real goal.

Professor Sellars' value theory overlaps naturally with his social philosophy and philosophy of religion. He is insistent on the value basis of his social philosophy. For example, in his *Next Step in Democracy* (1916), Sellars appraised the value of work for rich and poor, skilled and otherwise:

> "Work should be a healthy expression of the mental and physical energies of the individual. . . . In a democratic society it should possess a cooperative atmosphere and link individuals together in the achievement of common social purposes and the satisfaction of common needs. . . . Each worker could then feel that he was doing something of recognized value and this feeling would suffuse his work. . . ."[5]

The functions of work, of health and fitness, economic service, the implementing of notably worthy objectives, cooperation and sense of significant sharing in important activities: these are values disclosed by assessment of a broad range of effects and relations. In 1916, indeed, Professor Sellars was arguing for a group perspective as against unqualified individualism. All rights, he maintains, are social instruments and not anti-social prerogatives or possessions. Import for the person's economy is import for the individual in his social context. The range of social values is therefore as wide as men's mutualities and interdependence.

---

[3] Cf. esp. *Ibid.*, 15-16.
[4] *Ibid.*, 16.
[5] *The Next Step in Democracy*, New York, Macmillan (1916), 154.

The raison d'etre of religion, as we shall note in Part V, is to support and enhance human values. Levels and dimensions of value are at issue here. Is religion preeminently personal, "what one does with his solitariness," to use Whitehead's phrasing? To what extent is religion the bulwark of specifically social values, as Stephen Pepper and numerous others contend it has been? Is the holiness that religion espouses the holiness of rigorous morals or the holiness of mystery and awe? Are there specifically religious values? What is the place of aesthetic quality in religion?

Assessment, in any case, brings the discovery, with some assistance from existentialist and other perspectives, that life has potential greatness and profundities, that life is more than stuff and pother, even with play, and that the more significant values strengthen rather than weaken life—provided they are given their naturalistic bases and contexts.

Our readings in the theory of value, therefore, need complementation from Sellars' social and religious philosophies, though these are contained in Part V.

Supplemental Readings

1. On Truth
    "A Correspondence Theory of Truth," JP, XXXVIII (1941).
    "The Meaning of True and False," PPR, V (1946), 98-103.
2. On Value
    "Cognition and Valuation," PR, XXXV (1926), 124-144.
    "Human Life and Value," PPP, Macmillan (1926), Part III. (Revised and Republished by Pageant Press, 1970).
    "The Nature and Status of Value," *The Philosophy of Physical Realism*, 444-477.
    "Valuational Naturalism and Moral Discourse," PR, LXVII (1958), 243-251.

THE THEORY OF TRUTH

"True" as Contextually Implying Correspondence

I am going to introduce this discussion of the theory of truth by two quotations. The first is from T. V. Smith in the book, *American Philosophers at Work*. The second is from a recent

---
* JOURNAL OF PHILOSOPHY, LVI, 18 (Aug. 1959.)

article in *Mind*[1] by Bernard Mayo. These two quotations seem to me to sum up pretty well the mood of most philosophers with respect to the topic. After making comments, I shall go on to offer my own perspective, which rests on a direct, referential realism. I shall argue—as I have since my book, *Critical Realism* (1916)—that *knowledge* is the primary category and that the adjective "true" signifies the endorsement of a knowledge-claim. Correspondence is not a test but the contextual implication of knowledge achieved through a statement. As I see it, this is the logistics of the problem.

Professor T. V. Smith writes as follows: "The correspondence theory offers no adequate test of truth. One must know already what is true before he can know what beyond his ideas corresponds to his ideas. Of correspondence, then, I remark simply that it is only when men must say something that they say something which they themselves do not understand."[2] It is to be noted that Smith has similar comments on coherence and prediction theories. The classical trinity is rejected. We have come to a dead end.

Mayo writes as follows: "Not surprisingly, philosophers who have grown tired of backing the classical trinity for the theory of Truth are looking to other stables for winners. So far, however, the new favourites, though promising on form, have proved disappointing in the matter of staying power." He then proceeds to dismiss the "performative horse," that is, the theory of truth which calls attention to the various linguistic uses of the word "true," such as that which is equivalent to a nod of agreement. I suppose that what he has in mind is the neglect of verification demands. The other favorite is the "evaluative horse." Here the function of the word is to appraise whatever it is used of, whether statement or object.

It should be noted that American philosophers, such as Ducasse and Chisholm, have for some time been exploring the value approach to truth. To say that a statement is true is to regard it as acceptable. But acceptable for what purpose or reason?

---

[1] *Mind*, January, 1959.
[2] *American Philosophers at Work*, p. 488.

To me, the acceptability is in the context of a knowledge-claim. And there must be relevant criteria used. This brings us back to verification tests. Valuation is not an arbitrary affair.

Professor Mayo points to the scalar, or grading, feature of ordinary valuation and suggests that true and false are polar terms like right and wrong. To say that a statement is true is more like issuing a verdict. One acts like a jury. Now this is a good point. A current expression is that of endorsement. To say that a statement is true is to endorse it. A statement, it would seem, is like a cheque. It is a claim for money in the bank. In endorsing the cheque, we assert the claim.

But what do we endorse a statement as being? What is the role, or function, of a statement? Surely, it is to give *knowledge about what it is about*. We are in the domain of belief, knowledge-claims, cognition. It follows that to endorse a statement as true is to regard it as a *cognitive achievement*. It is this line of thought I am going to explore. If it smacks of epistemology, that may not be a bad thing. Peace to the shades of John Dewey, epistemology has no necessary tie-in with Cartesian dualism or a passive-spectator view of knowing. From perceiving onward, it is concerned with cognition as an activity having its natural mechanism and goal.

The logicians seem to be putting their bets on the so-called semantic theory of truth. The sentence, "The snow is white," is true if, and only if, the snow is white. I suppose the term "sentence" here could be changed to "statement."

Now this sounds like common sense. If, and only if, the snow is white, do we have a case of success in our endorsement of the sentence. But the epistemologist cannot help asking, How do we *know* that the snow is white? If we fall back on perceiving, we must have some adequate theory of veridical perception. Now it may well be that the logician refuses to concern himself with this problem. And, at a certain level, he is within his rights. He can assume that we do have knowledge of what is. We can then set this up as a standard for sentences and statements.

I would put it this way. I hold that all cognizing involves the assumption that there is a state of affairs to know. At the level of perceiving we regard ourselves as successfully perceiving objects we classify as chairs and trees and people. From this point of departure, we go on to deeper explorations, ending up with electrons and so on. Philosophy got puzzled with respect to perceiving and began to issue vetoes. This is a very old story which goes back at least to Plato. Berkeley and Kant just rang the changes.

Now, since I am a physical realist, I am going to accept the semantic theory of truth as a point of departure and connect it with the verdict, or endorsement, view of the use of the term "true." To regard a statement as true is to regard it as an achievement, expressing the objective state of affairs in terms of descriptive facts about it. One must be careful here. As I see it, knowledge does not correspond to facts but expresses, or conveys, them. A fact is a bit of knowledge about an object. It is thus cognitively penetrative, and, because of this, we easily tend to reify it. Knowledge is the achievement of a sort of job which the human mind, perforce, undertakes. I would certainly not say that a statement *corresponds* to the facts, for that would immediately put us into the traditional *impasse*. How do we know they correspond to these entities? What a statement undertakes to do is to give us revealing knowledge about the object of its concern in terms of facts about it as a determinate state of affairs. One just has to take knowledge as an achievement seriously and see what it *implies*. Let analytic philosophers rally around.

So much for the semantic theory of truth of the logicians. As I see it, it expresses a demand but does not explain it. The philosopher has still to gird up his loins. And I think that logician must also, if he wants to understand the *ontological roots* of the applicability of concepts in the ways of consistency. Surely, our concepts are under control. We use them to characterize things; and this cannot be arbitrary. If logic is normative, this normativeness must have a foundation, even though it be not of the Aristotelian type.

Let us now try to summarize the drift of the argument. Knowledge as an *achievement* of objective import is the primary category. A tested statement upon which the verdict, "true," has been passed is the basis of such knowledge. The mechanism of such testing and achievement, as we shall see illustrated in perceiving, is an affair of referential guidance and responsible control. But, since it is the function of a true statement to give knowledge about its object, it must be *such that* it can do so—that is, it must correspond. In short, because of its contextual linkage with knowledge as an achievement of objective import, truth *implies* correspondence. In brief, correspondence is an implication and not a test. As I see it, this analysis fits in with the semantic theory of truth. The differences is that the philosopher has to explore the epistemology of the situation.

What *sort* of correspondence is it? It is, clearly, the sort of correspondence involved in knowledge. And, while we cannot reduce knowledge to something else, we can use terms to throw light upon it, such as description, facts about, decipherment, disclosure. What we really do, as we shall see, is to characterize things in terms of responsibly developed concepts. And this action is backed up by evidence, coherence, and pragmatic working. The alternative is a kind of general skepticism of the Cartesian order which, as Peirce pointed out, is artificial.

Let me, however, point out again that we should not speak of truth as a correspondence with facts. "True" means the verdict that a statement is a case of knowledge and gives us *facts* about its object. Fact is a cognitive category. But, since cognition has objective import, we think of fact as ontologically penetrative. Facts carry us into states of affairs. It is really, of course, knowing that does this. And, as we shall see, knowing is quite an achievement with a complex, operative mechanism involved. But the point I want to make in this paragraph is that knowledge is the primary category and that truth can be said to correspond with facts only in the sense that it involves the acceptance of the factual content of the knowledge-claim. Thus the verdict, "true," implies the kind of achievement, or correspondence, that knowledge claims. What we humans do in our language is to work back and forth. Since we are physical realists, from common sense onwards, we can talk in that fashion. But, as the logicians have shown, we must be careful when we use terms like *all* and *not*.

I could stop here; but, since I have talked so much about the objective import of knowledge and the mechanisms underlying it, I shall add some epistemological notes.

I am going to condense history, in part, because I lived through some of it. Why are acute thinkers, like Blanshard and T. V. Smith, worried about correspondence as a *test* of truth? The answer is that their thought is dominated by the Lockian *impasse*. Ideas were taken to be the primary objects of knowledge and yet there was the belief in a material world beyond, which some ideas copied. But there was something wrong with this schematism as Berkeley and Hume saw. The confusion was, surely, based on a wrong theory of the mechanism of perceiving. I have recently argued that the unit is not S (causal stimulus) but S-R (stimulus and response). Sensations guide perceiving; and perceiving is referentially direct, just as response is. In humans, guided response is lifted to the level of guided reference and conceptual characterization. But we still have a direct, referential realism.[3]

But, for various reasons (the lag in biology and the fear of mechanical materialism counting for much), philosophy did not take the corrected course I indicated above. Kant bowed to things-in-themselves and undertook to construct a phenomenal world, baptized physical and Newtonian, out of the integration of the sense-manifold and innate forms and categories. And then objective idealism dropped the things-in-themselves and exalted the Self. I do not deny the ingenuity and suggestiveness of much of this development. *But epistemology went by the board.* The idealists settled down to the coherence theory, already adumbrated by Spinoza. And then the pragmatists came with their consequential theory of meaning and of truth. But, as both the new realists and the critical realists felt, something was lacking. We had to get back to perception. The job was to get a *direct realism,* for Lockian correspondence would not do. *Somehow, philosophy had painted itself in.*

The new realism was a *tour-de-force.* It was a presentational realism. What I tried to work out was a referential realism in which sensations guided direct reference and the controlled application of concepts. I am sure that recent linguistic developments fits into this framework. This perspective allows us to work out the *mechanism* of perceiving in terms of modern

---

[3] See my article in *Mind,* January, 1959, "Sensations Guide Perceiving."

psychology and neurology and, also, to do justice to the claims of perceiving as an *achievement*. I like Professor Ryle's use of this term. It is this integration of causal mechanism and achievement which makes the tests of knowledge operative and under objective control. Guiding sensations are under control and so are concepts. We are no longer painted in. Perceiving has objective import. It was because what Mayo calls the classical trinity was tied in with a bad epistemology that it simply would not do. What did we not have! The noëtic apprehension of entities called universals; the translation of material-thing statements into statements about sensations; the prediction of consequences in a conceptual, if-then fashion; the bluff patting of scientific method on the back.

It is my hunch that a direct, referential realism with knowledge as an achievement gives the proper framework. "True," as a verdict, affirms knowledge about and so implies contextually what knowledge involves and rests on. The thesis is, in short, that the mechanism of testing perceiving by sensations is just the reverse of that of guiding referential perceiving by them and that both involve causal transactions as the foundation of correspondence.

It is in this way and by this mechanism that knowledge gets the correspondence base it requires. What logic calls evidence has this operational setting. We can thus tie together "true" as endorsement of a knowledge-claim, knowledge as an achievement, biological mechanisms, logical methods, and correspondence as causally mediated.

["It is important to realize," states Sellars in "A Correspondence Theory of Truth" (J. P. vol. 38, 1941, p. 651), "that the tests of truth are not directly tests of correspondence but tests of knowledge claims." Elsewhere, he says that they are simply *the tests of knowledge.* But continuing J.P. 38: "And how can knowledge-claims be tested? The preliminary answer should be factual: how do we actually test them? As a matter of fact, there is really very little disagreement about that. We recognize basic, or elementary knowledge-claims resting upon observation. These are regarded as expressing elementary facts which must be reckoned with in the case of more complex and general statements. We give a high estimate of probability if propositions are consistent, support one another, and agree with basic data. It is really a complex process of a systematic sort in which falsification operates to eliminate particular propositions of different levels. And, as I see it, there are the accompanying, less merely logical, controls of vital application and prediction, controls which pragmatism has stressed. For would it not be paradoxical if an increase of knowledge did not involve an increase of control of things? We expect truth to work and that gives an *initial probability* that that which works is true. The pragmatic test seems to me something supplementary to the more definitely logical tests. It is, as it were, an accompanying check. It assures us that we have to do with knowledge, that is, with disclosure, since plans of action based on our ideas work."]

It is essential to keep perspective and to avoid confusion. It is my suggestion that the notion of guided perceiving concerned directly with objects breaks the spell of representationalism with ideas as terminal and objects unperceived and introduces a framework which makes possible the above analysis. It is in perceiv*ing* as direct and veridical—not *in having percepts*—that we break into the external world. From this point science carries on by newly devised techniques and instruments. But I cannot see that in passing from sheep to electron, we move into a realm of the "unperceivable." We merely supplement our biological equipment by instruments. Of course, we have to do a great deal of thinking but this is already begun in perceiving and common sense.

THE THEORY OF VALUE

Can a Reformed Materialism do Justice to Values?*

... [If] a revised and mature type of materialism can account for mind, consciousness, and the fact of human knowing, can it also adequately handle human values and all that side of human life connected with feeling, desire, volition, and valuation? It is to this question that I wish now to give consideration. Can a reformed materialism do justice to values?

---

* ETHICS, LV (1944), 28-39; 45.

No great culture, I believe, can have the vigor and the intellectual honesty it needs apart from some dominant decisions on such basic points. While the materialist's answers on first and last questions differ in import and direction from those associated with Christianity and with Platonic-Aristotelian tradition, he desires as large a cosmic canvas. He can be satisfied with nothing short of decision on existential foregrounds and backgrounds, decisions which will certainly help to give clarity to the culturally needed conception of the human situation. Speaking as one interested in social philosophy, I would say that it is more than likely that a candid and explicit materialism in the domain of philosophy might well inaugurate a new era of vigor and forthrightness in our culture. Man would then know his cosmic situation and turn with more decision to the human scene.

But such a focusing upon the human scene would make the clarification of questions as to the nature, status, and function of values a need all the more pressing. It is to questions such as these that I now turn. Always, however, I shall try to keep the ontological background in mind. I shall be concerned less with the terms of the debate between various ethical schools than with the fundamentals of axiology. For this reason I shall attack stereotyped conceptions of naturalism, subjectivism, and teleology. In so doing I shall defend a kind of *value realism* which will differ from that of Professor Urban, which I would classify as *value transcendentalism*. And, in the sequel, I shall seek to answer his objections to naturalistic humanism. It will be noted that he makes much of teleology and is inclined to tie it in with theism. I, on the other hand, believe in the emergence of various levels of immanent teleology founded on structural patterns and their directional activities. All of which means, again, that axiology cannot be separated from ontological issues.

* * * * *

I

The most natural context for values seems to me discoverable at the level of social psychology and the social sciences. And it is to me clear that genesis never precludes meaning and validity. It follows that empiricism and naturalism do not imply reductionism or the denial of discoverable meanings and references. In fact, I admit that I have always been perplexed by discussions of naturalistic ethics which claimed to reduce moral to nonmoral terms. As well reduce mathematical concepts to nonmathematical ones just because images may be involved. It is not the genetic novelty of a concept which is vicious but the acceptance of it apart from application and verification.

It will be my thesis that value judgments—including moral ones—are as genuinely interpretative and referential as cognitional ones and that much of the dispute, inaugurated by G. E. Moore, about a supposed naturalistic fallacy and the reduction of ethical terms to non-ethical ones has been due to the lack of a clear distinction between objectively directed appraisal and objectively directed cognition. In accordance with this approach I shall drop the common use of the term "intrinsic values" and stress the difference between terminal values, on the one hand, and instrumental and contributory values, on the other. What are usually spoken of as "intrinsic values" I shall name "satisfactions." I take this to be more than an affair of terminology, since it is my desire to stress value judgments and to make these, so far as possible, communicable and justifiable. After all, we do have such terms as "pleasures" and "satisfactions" and "enjoyings" for experiences assignable to selves; and it would seem sensible to keep the newer term, "value," for the result of appraisal. Of course, as we shall see, value assignments and appraisals are conditioned by satisfactions; and, since the reference is at the same time both objective and subjective in import, it is difficult, and yet necessary, to distinguish the value assignment from the satisfaction which conditions it.

What I shall be trying to do, in short, will be to develop a *via media* between Platonism, on the one hand, and merely affective subjectivism, on the other. I hold that we humans develop value meanings of objective import after their kind. They are not intuitions of something transcendental called the "good," but they are responsible and justifiable appraisals of things, events, and possibilities in the light of their bearing upon human life. The clue to keep in mind is the difference of motivation and purpose between explicit cognitional endeavors and valuational ones.

Obviously, as a materialist, I am naturalistic in my outlook in these matters. What I protest against is the parody of naturalism that is usually involved in the claim that it involves the reduction of ethical notions to nonethical ones. Surely this is a part of the old reductive tradition. Even so-called "natural goods" are subject to critical appraisal. Does this food injure me or nourish me? Is this scientific method the best in handling this particular problem? I have the impression that a kind of *passive factualism* dominates discussion in this field. It is a fact that I feel approval; it is a fact that I like this drink. Now, I see no reason to deny such facts. The point is that in appraisals we go beyond them to statements about continuing approvals in which we are well aware of objective factors as well as of personal ones.

What I shall aim at, accordingly, is a position which does justice to what is true in subjectivism and in statistical naturalism and yet does justice to objective reference and appraisal. The emphasis will be upon value judgments and their assignments; and yet it will be seen that there is no need to resort to transcendentalism or value reification. The method I shall use will be that of working out the difference between cognitional judgments and value judgments. In this fashion, contrast will assist us in realizing the nature, conditions, and validity of value judgments. In both cases there are, I hold, objective reference and interpretation. But valuation involves a peculiar reflexive story added to the cognitional framework *and having its own kind of objective significance.*

As to the fear some philosophers seem to entertain that ethics will be taken away from them and become a social science, I can only remark that that dread event will happen unless ethics ceases to be a largely formal and puzzled discussion of intuitions and naturalistic fallacies. In America, at least, social psychology and sociology are enlarging the context of ethical discussions. Philosophy cannot stay the growth of the social sciences in technique and range. The job is one of co-operation. The philosopher can contribute by clarifying distinctions and categories. In my opinion, the moral philosopher can today make his best contribution by clearing up the difference between descriptive cognition and valuation.

II

I shall argue, then, that in valuation we go far beyond interjections and the evincing of feelings to a vital estimation of the *bearing* of things, acts, and proposals upon the self and the social group. As the self here is always a socialized self and yet an individual. Needless to say, I shall argue that the shortcomings of the logical positivists in their theory of values parallel their sensationalism in their theory of knowledge. Since they really have only sensations instead of physical continuants, in the one case, we should expect them to have only feelings and not selves aware of feelings and their objective import in the other. What I am seeking to bring out, in short, is a realistic theory of valuation as a dimension additional to strict cognition—a dimension tied up with the fact that human beings are practical agents engaged in the business of living and not merely of knowing.

It is well to remember that the human self is not subjective in some invidious sense, even though its experiences, both cognitional and volitional, belong to it. To the realist, the human organic self, minded and conscious, is a continuant engaged in the business of living in an environment, physical and social, as real as—but no more real than—itself. Does it not sound plausible to argue that value judgments are situational and reflexive appraisals to which are relevant all that bears upon the activity involved? It follows that they cannot have the neutrality and purely factual quality that holds of the aim dominant in cognition. In science we seek to know things as they are apart from ourselves. Let us admit that this ideal is itself a historical achievement. Yet it expresses the nature of knowing.

Were it not for the factual and objective framework which cognition gives us, we would be immersed in feeling of a blind sort. But our actual feelings and emotions have, in the main, directions and objects. We do not merely fear; we fear this or that thing or event. It is because the self is, in its awareness, set over against other things that appraisal passes beyond mere feeling, however evinced, and secures symbolic significance. In this fashion things and events are looked upon *in the light of* present and predictable responses and experiences. Feelings settle down into sentiments and attitudes which become the personal basis of the objective appraisal. All this is verbalized and, in its own fashion, conceptualized. At the same time, operations and methods are worked out for testing value judgments, which, as judgments, make claims which outleap a time and mood. For, as I see it, it is the self as a continuant whose verdict is proclaimed. "I like that." "I *do* like that." "Unless I change more than I now expect to, I shall continue to like that." It is because there is a reference to the self that even expressions of liking are not mere interjections. They reflect the decision of the self with reference to something beyond itself. And that is why it is recognized that they imply the likeableness of the object. Such likeableness is grounded on the nature of the object in its bearing upon the self. As we shall see, it follows from this situation that the predicates assigned in value judgments *are objective after their kind*. They are also justifiable in terms of their relevant bases.

It is, in my opinion, a foolish endeavor to seek to reduce appraisals to facts even though they must have an empirical basis. While there is nothing esoteric and unempirical about them, appraisals are not simply cognitions. They are ways of looking at objects in the light of the self as an effective and conative creature. And it is because the human self has this developed capacity to consider acts with reference to their expected effects upon itself that attitudes toward them arise. In a more complicated way, norms of conduct get socially established. In all this it would be correct to assert that the subjective becomes as objectified as what is external to the self. This point is recognized in the term "attitude." The organic self and its attitude are both admittedly in the same world as things and events. But, by their very nature, the context of attitudes is situational and reflexive. Were these actualities better appreciated, it would be better realized that feelings are regarded as objectively located in attitudes and directed toward objects. It is for this reason that they are not blind and directionless and subjective in some ghostly and isolated way. I fear events; I love this person; I enjoy music. In all these cases the capacity we have to denote and refer to objectivities correlative to the self lifts judgment to objectivity.

The Theory of Truth and the Theory of Value

The point to keep in mind is the fact that, in valuation, we are not simply trying to know. We are objectively and interpretatively trying to appreciate the way in which all sorts of objects and events—actual and possible—would probably link up with our lives in a multitude of varying conditions. The variety of objects is immense and their bearings multiform. And it must not be forgotten that levels and kinds of interest in the self must be touched off. What I am emphasizing is the empirical fact that the self, as a going continuant, is bound to appraise and not merely to know. Factualism is a form of mere intellectualism.

I suppose one of the chief motives for recurrent factualism is the fear of values as mysterious entities having an esoteric status. But, obviously, the materialist would reject Platonism and transcendentalism as sharply as the neo-positivist. He would not seek to make entities out of values. It is better, therefore, to speak of "appraisals" or "value assignments" than of "values." If the term must be used substantively, it would be well to speak of "values" as objects valued. In short, "value" is a relational term because it always involves a reflexive reference to the human center of the situation. A value proposition is incomplete until such centripetal reference is made explicit.

Now my objections to Moore's famous "naturalistic fallacy" have been in part terminological and in part caused by his failure to distinguish sharply enough between cognizing and valuing. He gave the impression of thinking of value as a simple property of a nonphysical kind which should be open to intuition, whereas, as I see it, value predicates reflect not cognitions but appraisals. In other words, value is not the kind of property which cognition concerns itself with. It is not descriptive in nature. Rather is it a justifiable appraisal of the object *in the light of* how it could enter the life of one entering into relations with it. It is that kind of an *interpretation* and not something discoverable about the object upon merely sensory evidence. But it is not arbitrary and without foundation. There must be something about the object which enables it to function situationally and relationally with respect to human interests. And it is important to bear in mind that cognition gives the framework upon which the self embroiders its appraisals. Otherwise, there would be only directionless moods and feelings.

It follows from this general perspective that my outlook is in many ways akin to that exemplified in Dewey, Perry and Parker. . . . All three, I take it, maintain that value judgments are empirically based and testable in terms of data relevant and expressive of contributions and concerns.

In axiology, as in other formal divisions of philosophy, much turns upon some accepted assumption. Now it is obvious that I hold that mistakes in epistemology have played havoc in this field, preventing the proper conception of the framework within which valuation works. Thus Dewey has a keen sense for critical and experimental evaluations but assumes that values are features of that "blanket experience" within which his thinking operates. It is undoubtedly true that cognition and valuation are compresent and interwoven in conscious living. But the overt materialist is one who has pressed through naïve realism, whether epistemic or axiological, and recognized that external things are not open to literal inspection but are denoted and symbolized as over against the organic self in which we feel ourselves to be embodied and of which we become reflexively aware. And I have argued that there is no existential, cognitive, or referential *relation* involved in the self's denoting and describing things. This against both idealism and the new realism.[1] Now, as is well known, Dewey turned his back upon the possibilities discoverable in a reanalysis of representative realism. My quarrel, then, with Dewey is not on the score of his empiricism and his rejection of value transcendentalism but on the absence of a correct framework within which to assess the functional and situational appraisals which human beings make. And, since I am concerned with the thesis that a reformed materialism can do justice to values, this difference of formal perspective is crucial. Since I am a substantialist, too, though not of the old static variety, the pragmatic emphasis upon process and the future seems to me to lack the necessary appreciation of the

---

[1] A typical expression of this rejection of a cognitive relation is to be found in *The Principles and Problems of Philosophy*, New York, Macmillan Co., 1926, p. 114.

generic and cumulative in human nature and to focus too sharply upon an almost complete plasticity. . . .

As regards Perry, the primary divergence stems from epistemology. To define as value "any object of any interest" does call attention, quite properly, to the two bases of valuation which are interwoven situationally, vectorially, and reflexively. But— and this is the point— it makes no proper connection between them, because of the shortcomings of the new realism. He shows no adequate comprehension of the referential selection of the object as that which is both known and appraised, that is, how it is lifted, from being merely thing or event, to the status of being an object of cognition and of interest—a status, of course, to which it may well be indifferent. Other human beings become aware of having that status for another human being, just because they are aware that they make them objects of responsive attention themselves. In other words, "object" is a reflexive term, while "thing" is not. It is this referential play outward from the self in both cognition and valuation, as against the causal impact, actual or possible, from the thing to the self, which the new realism could handle only with the ineptitudes of "external relations" and searchlights, which must be given flexibility. A value is, strictly speaking, a value assignment to that which is made an object. And this value assigment is a complex variable which is a function of many factors brought into awareness with one another *within* the self. . . .

Perhaps because of his metaphysical interests, Parker, on the other hand, has tended to be too subjectivistic in his approach, as in his reversal of Perry's formula into *any interest in any object*. Such a formula makes value factual and psychological in nature. It calls attention to the base in the self which, of course, must be recognized. The materialist does not dispute this fact but has a different conception of the self than has the panpsychist. When questions of the existential basis of value come up for discussion, it must not be forgotten that a mature, philosophical materialism solves the psychophysical problems within the framework of critical realism and emergence. It is clearly a defensible idea that the organized and operative organic self is conscious and that such consciousness is a "natural isolate" from a context of functioning in which it participates. Here, and here alone, is the individual on the inside of nature. It would seem that the cortex is qualitied in this participative fashion, even though abstract, descriptive knowledge using sensory evidence, as a point of departure, cannot attain it from the outside. But why should the cortex not be qualitied in this internal and participative fashion? Nothing but dogma, Cartesian or Newtonian, denies it. As I see it, panpsychism and personal idealism represent the implications of an epistemology unable, or unwilling, to do justice to the denotative and categorial structure of human knowing as regards both external things and the organic self. No objective knowing is knowledge by acquaintance. The self is a continuant which we reflexively denote and categorially know even while, in consciousness, participating in it. The self is not reducible to feeling; and yet feeling is intrinsic to the functioning self. So much the materialist can say of the human level, thereby remaining an empiricist. Any other type of materialism cuts off, by definition, its *pou sto*, its experiential base.

The definition of "value" in terms of desires, satisfactions, and enjoyments as actual experiences, is, of course, permissible; and no one, I suppose, would undertake to deny their factuality. So defined, it is tempting to speak of them as intrinsic values in contrast to instrumental values, which are factors which causally condition them. But value theory would then take the form of psychophysics.

If value is equated with appraisal, or value assignment, it is best to keep one's eye on judgment. Any object which can be selected and which arouses interest can be valued situationally, if in no other respect than as a liking or an approval. The reasons for, or bases of, such liking or approval may well be complex and either reinforcing or opposing. The more explicit the total response becomes, the more it represents an integration of the self. On the whole, one says, I like that person or that kind of action.

The wide varieties of values reflect the bearing of the object upon the self. The aesthetic object connects up with different interests and attitudes than does the object used as a tool. The personal status called "fame" evokes different tendencies than does health or wealth. It is this terrific sweep and range of the self as a living, affective, and conative thing which makes it an ongoing microcosm immersed in the tides of being and aware of their situational impact. It is the self which is the center and which relates objects and objectives in manifold ways, according to their known capacities and relevancies. Language is the instrument of such symbolic ordering and appraisal; and broad groupings, correspondent to recognizable interests, stand out. And these interests are themselves integrated in the self in changing ways according to the pattern of the situation. At times we must eat; and at times nothing is more inconsequential.

Now the import of all this is that the usual mechanical contrast between intrinsic and extrinsic, instrumental and terminal, seems to me not to carry us very far. It is more intellectual than axiological. Of course, I realize that, if I want certain results, I must seek the means for their realization. And this holds in art, economics, health, science, and morality. Likewise, I become aware that achievements, which filled the horizon and were terminal in my interests, turn out to have contributory value for the self. Life is conative and cumulative; and the self, though a continuant, is both cumulative and, within limits, alterative. But the directive center of values is the self in its interests and admirations. There is immersion in a microcosm which is immanently objective, as any living organism is.

It may, to some, appear strange that a materialist should so emphasize the self and call attention to its configurated and balanced interplay of interests and admirations as the decisive source of appraisals. But the philosophical materialist is an empiricist, though a realistic one. He sees no reason not to acknowledge the fact that the human, organic, self is gifted with the capacity of cognitive reference and appraisal and that, in self-consciousness, interests and admirations induce value judgments upon all that can be thought as having bearing upon the economy and aspiration of the self. Expressions, frustrations, interdependence, relative autonomy—all affect the pattern of valuation. Here our categories must be those of life itself, but of a life evolved to the stage of judgment and self-consciousness.

A naturalism which thinks only of facts and has not awakened to the crucial importance of categories may satisfy a positivist but not a philosophical materialist.

Now Parker in his most recent work on value theory has applied to this field the doctrine that there is no referential, or cognitive, *relation*. I anticipate that this application will involve a greater emphasis upon value judgment, as against the subjective data upon which it is based—data which, I have argued, are intrinsic to observable attitudes. Were Dewey to give greater recogntion of the subjective and to admit the framework of physical realism and were Parker to advance from his Berkeleian subjectivism, they would, I anticipate, meet at about the point to which the argument of this paper leads, namely, that value assignments are objective after their kind and express the significance of objects and events to the interests and admirations of the self. Technically, such valuations are *justifiable* because not arbitrary and capricious; but they are not merely intellectual and factual, and so not true in a merely cognitional sense. They do not presuppose some determinate state of affairs to be described in an impersonal fashion. Of course, an act of valuation and its outcome can be known and become a fact for biography and sociology. But such knowledge assumes valuation and its peculiar claims and is in no sense reductive. It strikes me that those pragmatists who, like Lepley, wish to translate judgments of value into equivalent judgments of fact are confusing ultimate genres. Why? I have a suspicion that the motive is the fear of values as esoteric entities.

III

The importance of a correct epistemological framework, if values are to receive their proper interpretation, leads to the brief discussion of values as so-called "tertiary qualities."

The conception of stripping off qualities from things, like layers from an onion, presupposes naïve realism. It is *as though* the very surface of physical things were open to apprehension and that, thereafter, reflection forced one to remove certain of the apprehended qualities as illusory. First, value qualities are removed; and then colors and other sensuous qualities are likewise regarded as really "subjective."

But a more critical kind of epistemology relinquishes the naïve apprehensional conception of knowing, while keeping realistic references and beliefs. . . .

Scientific realism does not, in point of fact, retain any vestige of the direct apprehension of qualities but falls back on conceptual descriptions evidenced by observations as confirmatory of abstract theories. The whole theory of perception, as against sensing, is involved in this view of scientific method. For what we are deciphering is the structure and behavior of things, so far as these are abstractly disclosable. Russell to the contrary, we are thinking ontologically and categorially in the achievement of facts about the physical world. We regard ourselves as measuring not sensations but material things and as gaining facts about them.

. . . Values are no more surface qualities of things than are color and felt hardness. What is more, it is quickly realized that feelings do not have even the degree of *cognitive relevance* that sensations have. Rather do they express the response of the self in a more central and less peripheral way. The function of feeling is not external disclosure—that is left to sensory data—but an indication of the way the self is affected as regards its vital tendencies and desires. It is in this sense that feeling is personal in reference. It has reflexive significance, and its disclosure can be employed in self-awareness.

. . . [Values] are in no sense tertiary and illusory qualities of a cognitional sort. They are the valuation assigned to objects in the light of their recognized bearing upon the self in terms of feeling and experienced attitude. While such values can be verbalized and conceptualized, there usually remains, to give them reality and tang, some degree of actual feeling intrinsic to a directed attitude.

While, then, objects are given value meaning on the basis of the organic self's awareness of its relevant feelings with respect to them and while such value judgments are objective after their own fashion and justifiable, it is misleading to think of such valuations as semicognitive, as somehow intuited in objects through our feelings. Rather must they be conceived, after their specific nature, as appraisals and not as cognitions. My objection to the term "intuition through feeling," as an escape from subjectivism, is not to the assertion of objective reference and significance but to the suggestion of a cognizable, descriptive property somehow apprehended. Values must be well based, but they pertain to objects only in the light of their capacity to bear upon the self. There is nothing esoteric about them, nothing whose foundation escapes empirical awareness and testing.

It is, accordingly, not against the objectivity of value judgments that I protest, but against that kind of value realism which savors of Platonism and transcendentalism. As I see it, values are created by the responsible relations of the life in which they are immersed. They are functional and not supernal edicts. They are immanent in the process of living and not heteronomous and authoritarian. Now I have a suspicion that Urban has more than this in mind when he speaks of "ought-to-be-ness" as a quality of certain possible acts. So far as I can size it up, "ought-to-be-ness" pertains to possibilities in connection with a human situation with its interests, interconnections, affections, and admirations. I omit the question whether "ought" is the right root, since it sounds linguistically more natural to speak of "ought-to-do." I judge that it is the sense of intrinsic authority assigned to values in the transcendental tradition that Urban has in mind. To me, on the contrary, the authority of valuations rests on their justifiability in terms of human life.

IV

... [Tidiness is] necessary.

Now it has been my argument that such formal tidiness in axiology demands clarity in epistemology and ontology. The framework must be there to sustain the further interweaving of valuations. As I see it, the self moves back and forth within the structure deciphered by cognitive activity, working out consequential, reflexive valuations. Thus, ideals are conceived possibilities illuminated by their bearing upon human interests and admirations. The experimental momentum of life is focused upon them.

Perhaps the emphasis upon the immanence, or situational immersion, of value judgments conveys more adequately than the term "relativity" the rejection of transcendental types of absolutism. In its struggle with authoritarianism, relativism usually took on the idea of arbitrariness. The emphasis we have laid upon the justifiability of value judgments excludes this note. It implies objectivity and testability within an immanent situation. Values are not pressed upon man from the outside; they reflect and express relevancies.

Equally important for an adequate perspective is the contrast with the intention of cognition. In cognition the purpose is to achieve facts about a state of affairs. And the adjective "true" signifies the belief that such facts have been achieved through a proposition. There is something absolute and external in the aim—what I call a "disclosure." But, as I see it, the intention in valuation is of a somewhat different sort, and the data and the role of the self are different. There is the effort, as a going concern always approximative, to appraise the bearing of the object upon the interests, loves, and admirations of the self— and of a socialized self at that. There is here internality with responsibility to everything relevant. Sentiments and feelings are clues to the value of objectives under advisement. There is experimentation, deliberation, for the self has to discover what it most enduringly desires and admires: There are gradations, levels, hierarchies—all adjustable to situations and necessities. As I see it, we have in values an understanding of things, acts, and events with respect to their consequences and impacts upon human selves. It is for this reason that they furnish the contours of choice and action. Knowledge as such does not do this, for it is neutral and impersonal.

* * * * *

I take it that this conception of value assignments waits upon an epistemology which, like critical realism, can explain the referential range of the human mind without literal transcendence. And it involves a frank recognition of the different intent native to explicit cognition and valuation. This is why I prefer to keep the adjective "true" for cognitional judgments. Both types of judgments are empirical and testable, but the aim and the data used differ. Moreover, the centrality of the self as a reflexive base brings it about that, in the long run, a merely social table of values remains generic and must permit shadings according to personality and situation. Such shadings in no sense impugn the objectivity and responsibility to relevant data of the value judgment.

The generic character of ideals, norms, and principles reflects their social reference and foundation. They indicate general objectives and workable standards. To that extent they are guides. But ethics and aesthetics have long realized that this generic outline does not entail detailed uniformity. There must be adjustment to the personality and the circumstances of the individual. Tastes vary within a range of positive appreciations. When the objects valued are institutions, a main concern is social working and loyalty. A kind of statistical awareness qualifies many social values. I value actual institutions in the light of what can be expected from the citizenry, given their education and outlook. Were these different, my demands would alter. Social realism looks upon society as a substantive process.

One other point. To what degree is human nature plastic? And by "human nature" I mean, of course, human beings. Were they completely plastic, practically any value assignment could be made justifiable by a transforming pressure upon them. The employment in our day of propaganda has made this question a live one. It should be noted that value judgments are conditioned by factual ones and by circumstances. Othello loved Desdemona even while his complex attitude toward her was being changed by Iago's deceit. My own belief is that human nature is not generically plastic but only specifically so. The demand for happiness, the dislike of frustration, and the capacity for loyalty and admiration are invariables. It is for this reason that the general direction of the ideal of progress can be set. How it is to be worked out depends upon one's philosophy of history.

Suppose, then, that we adopt the terminology suggested and hold value judgments to be objective in import after their kind. There are degrees in their justifiability because of the relevance of individual differences and situations. The self is, likewise, not something specifically determinate in a static way but something growing and finding itself.

Both Dewey and Parker seem to me to be sympathetic with such a perspective. And yet the first has been too afraid of the self and of the "subjective," while the second has emphasized the self and the subjective at the expense of the objective. It is my belief that tidiness in axiology requires the clarification in epistemology and ontology which I have indicated. The referential and existential framework must be deciphered before the added reflexive projections of value can be understood. Then the self can be seen to perform a work of interpretative assignments of values, to whatever comes within the range of its objective reference, in the light of its bearing upon the economy and conative endeavor of its agential drive. Thus do consequential values *pertain*, in their own objective fashion, to objects.

One of the unfortunate features of ethical controversy has been the undefined use of the term "objective." What kind of objectivity is Westermarck attacking? A kind of a priori rationalism? Again, I note a touch of old-fashioned mathematical rationalism in Rashdall. And I may say, in passing, that I wish Dr. Ewing would not so easily content himself with the method of exclusion, by telling us what it is not.[2] I have at least tried to explain in a positive way what I mean by the "objectivity of value judgments."

V

English thinkers—seemingly following the lead of Moore—have given much time to showing that both subjectivism and naturalism are untenable in axiology, especially at the ethical level. And, of course, the *dodges* of the positivists have played their part. . . .

I should now like to summarize my conclusions as follows:

---

[2] I refer particularly to his recent paper, "Subjectivism and Naturalism in Ethics," *Mind*, April, 1944. I recall that Dr. Ewing was convinced that I was a subjectivist because I maintained that value judgments were not true but justifiable. That, however, was long ago—in the summer of 1925.

1. Axiology can be clarified only after ontology and epistemology have given a firm structure to philosophic thought.

2. Values are objectively conditioned and pertain to objects—actual and possible—in the light of their bearing upon individuals and groups.

3. Value judgments are justifiable rather than true in a cognitional sense.

4. The expression "intrinsic values" is misleading. Why not merely speak of "satisfactions"?

5. "Terminal values" can be contrasted with "instrumental values."

6. Value judgments can be communicated but, because of their reflexive base, involve personal shadings.

7. There are levels of emergent teleology, only the highest of which involve ends-in-view.

8. Logical positivism rightly rejects value transcendentalism but does not do justice to cognitional reference or objective appraisal.

9. Though they have one base in moral sentiments, I see no reason to reduce ethical concepts to nonethical ones. Such factual subjectivism ignores objective appraisals. Moral emotions and attitudes are both referential and empirically conditioned.

10. Ontological materialism does not imply "ethical materialism." Reformed materialism, by its recognition of causal levels in nature and its forthright realistic empiricism, can do justice to what is unique in human personality and in the play of human values.

IN WHAT SENSE DO VALUE JUDGMENTS AND MORAL JUDGMENTS HAVE OBJECTIVE IMPORT?*

I think it is generally agreed by the historians of morality and by cultural anthropologists that moral rules arose out of the need to help people to live together. This is the stage of customary morality and we need not idealize it. There was no innate wisdom and groups varied in their emphases. But there was a kind of working consensus. As society became more com-

---

* *PPR*, XXVIII (1967), 6-11; 13-16.

plex, old rules were modified and new ones developed. But I need not go into all this, since it is so well known.

I take it, then, that morality is prescriptive, directional, and concerned with living together. By its very status and function it is public and an affair of convictions. Hume was quite right in emphasizing its distinctive language.

The first move here is to recognize that "right" is a term of endorsement, much as true is. One says that's the way to do it. Those are the rules to keep. Moral education enters here, as does tradition. Aristotle saw this clearly.

But the next move is the question, Why? What is the ground or reason? Reflection cannot avoid this move.

Now I think that intuition is not the answer. I agree with Professor Frankena that it has been undercut by psychology and by postulationism in mathematics. What, then, is its strength? It is a simple explanation of the fact of endorsement; and it has appeal until a more adequate explanation is worked out. It has, for example, a defense of objectivity. Rightness is an intrinsic attribute of rules. Another strength it has is the weakness of supposed alternatives. Paulsen points out that Kant's rigorism was, in part, a reply to a sentimental degeneration of ethical theory in the Germany of his time. The virtues were spoken of as pleasant and charming. For Kant this was a prostitution. And so he worked out his categorical imperative. The "Practical Reason" was given a job it could not accomplish, that is, to disregard the consequences of actions. As I see it, it is the very nature of morality to have these in mind. But in what terms shall we consider them? Here we come up against nonmoral values. And it is to these that I return. One last remark is, however, in order. It is to the effect that deontology reflects linguistically the first move, the emphasis on rightness as an endorsement of *prima facie* duties. This operates constantly along with some awareness of the consequences point of view.

* * * * *

... I grant that commendation, a feeling of approval, a pro-attitude is one element in it. But I take it that there is the second element of a judgmental kind concerning the object or state of affairs. This concerns the role of the object as it connects up with needs and desires. To use C. D. Broad's expression, it is good-making. But, unfortunately, Broad has Moore's idea of good in mind. As I see it, good here stands for a favorable appraisal of the way the object connects up with needs and desires of self or group. It is not a descriptive term but it is meaningful in a referential way. And it supports the attitude. When we are doubtful in detail, we make what are called *evaluations*. Thus we hear of job evaluations, institutional evaluations, etc. All this is conceptual as well as verbal. It means that cognizing alone is insufficient for human living. We must learn to discover how events, objects, plans, patterns, of human living fit into our lives.

* * * * *

. . . F. C. Sharp made a life-study of usages and reactions. For him, the first definitional move was to say that right *means* that the refusal so to act would be blameworthy. The second definitional move was to seek the ground of this in consequences. But here he was more of a hedonist than I. I think of pleasures and pains as guides and indicators for activities rather than primary objectives. But, of course, there are complications here. Ethical hedonism is, certainly, nearer the goal than psychological hedonism. It stresses satisfactions and dissatisfactions as guiding criteria rather than ends. But we come back to the nature of value-judgments. And here I return to the notion of role and interplay. As I understand it, ends, or objectives, stand out and these are estimated in complex ways, taking account of other ends, drives and feelings. It is a kind of balancing affair which issues in choices of goals. And there is always what we call today feed-back. I certainly have no objection to pleasures but would, on the whole, take them in their function as indicators. . . .

But I must return to British ethics. It had, for the time being, culminated in such intuitions as the good and the right. And it held to the kind of objectivity these seemed to imply. Now I have been arguing for external reference and informational input in cognition. But in valuation, as I see it, our concern is with the *bearing* of all sorts of referents—objectives, plans, possibilities, ways of living—upon our needs and desires. Here, also, our outlook is objective enough. As Heidegger would say, these things are *zuhanden*. Our outlook is likely to be that of what I called natural realism, built on perceiving. But we are concerned with the role and import of these things for our lives. This is an objective quest in which the objective interplays with the subjective to work out justifiable appraisals. The context is simply more reflexive and relational. *In this setting, objectivity takes a new shading.* It is a doing justice to what is involved. Moral objectivity, for instance, consists in setting aside private involvements and stressing reciprocity and long-run consequences. . . .

* * * * *

Now it is with the challenge to British, intuitional ethics by logical positivism that I am here concerned. It was an expression of *scientism* at a stage which did not take into account the development of psychology and the social sciences. . . . Its thesis was to the effect that only scientific sentences and logic statements were meaningful. It followed that moral statements must be regarded as commands (Carnap) or the evincing of feelings (Ayer). This did not mean that normative ethics was not important but that it was a non-scientific activity. . . .

While I agreed with the positivists in rejecting intuition and the *truth* of moral judgments, I thought their approach quite inadequate. Man had the job, like other animals but in a higher degree, of sizing up the bearing of objects on his life and prospects. And as pragmatists and existentialists say in common, he is full of projects and lives in the future.

* * * * *

While recognizing the stature of Ayer and Carnap and their motivations, I shall . . . concentrate on Stevenson. . . .

Stevenson presents two models. The first is "This is wrong" means "I disapprove of this; do so as well." Now I cannot accept this model for it combines a factual assertion of personal attitude, with no attempt at justification, with a supplementary command. The second model focuses on the descriptive element within ethical terms and supplements it with an emotive meaning. "This is good" is said to have the meaning of "This has qualities or relations X, Y, Z— and good has as well a laudatory, emotive meaning which permits it to express the speaker's approval, and tends to evoke the approval of the hearer." Here, again, I think that Stevenson's analysis falls short because it does not recognize that moral valuations are objective in import and involve the appraisal of the qualities and relations, X, Y, Z in their bearing on moral demands and convictions. Surely, the moral point of view must be taken into account. And, as we have noted, this outlook is connected with *the very function of morality, namely, to direct and control conduct in the public interest.** At a reflective level, there may well be revision and greater awareness of the consequences of behavior. But the setting remains. What may well happen is the search for justification of the moral judgment which brings together facts and their valuation. This, I hold, is a way of thinking with its own concepts and categories. . . . [logical] positivism rightly rejected intuitionism but was so dominated by the traditions of cognition that it was unable to do justice to what takes place in moral valuation. There is no need to reduce the *ought* to the *is*. What should be done is to bring out the role of duty and oughtness in moral thought. And these terms must have criteria for their application.

In what sense is morality and its categories "in nature?" As I see it, morality and its categories are developments connected with the complexities of human living. Just as cognizing and its achievements are developments whose mode of operation we are learning to understand in an *anagenetic* way, so the supplementation of prudential valuing by moral valuation and its categories stand out as a cultural growth within nature, as enlarged by man's uniqueness.

* * * * *

With Toulmin's stress on *good reasons* for moral judgment and Hare's careful study of moral language, a pathway between intuitionism and emotivism was being opened up. Now I find myself very much in agreement with Toulmin's emphases. He seems, however, to have reached them by way of Wittgenstein's later freeing of language from restraints put on it by intuitionists and emotivists. I, on the other hand, belonged to a different tradition, that of realism and axiological theory. Like most

---

* Italics added.

American thinkers, I had rejected intuitionism. Hence my job was to understand what was involved in valuation and in the framework of morality with its demands or prescriptions.

Taking Toulmin, Urmson and Hare together, I find a recognition of the practical reason and of the interplay of criteria and attitude in evaluation. This emphasis is also taken up by Nowell-Smith. All of this seems to me in the right direction. When Hare defends Moore's criticism of naturalism, he has in mind the difference between factual description and valuation. But, surely, both of these activities are natural though diverse. It still seems to me better to emphasize the human context and to recognize that the aim of knowing is different from that of valuing. These are two types of thinking and each has its logical peculiarities. Valuing concerns itself with a wide range of objective and relates them to situations and needs. Morality comes in in a supervisory way to judge objectives in their bearing on welfare as envisaged in an accepted way of life.*

GUIDED CAUSALITY, USING REASON, AND "FREE-WILL"*

... [One] cannot naturalize the human mind without some adequate conception of how it operates in human agency. And here is where "practical thinking," which displays the mind in action, must come under consideration. Modal terms such as ought, might, can, could have, come into view in a resonating sort of way. We judge, decide, consider alternatives, make up our minds, etc. Now here is where the metaphysics of ethics is unavoidable. While I had long ago arrived at the notion of

---

* In "Valuational Naturalism and Moral Discourse," PR, 67 (1958), p. 248, Sellars states: "Once we give up the idea of intuitable, absolute standards, the path to adequacy in morality is that of the discovery of what meets recognized requirements. ... moral categories emerge to express such recognitions. By their very nature they are normative. 'Right' and 'ought,' the so-called deontological terms, presuppose foundations in the exploratory give-and-take of life." On page 243, he writes that "rules arise to express" the *requirements* of a common life. ... All loyal members of the society will recognize "the import" of these rules. Thus moral categories and concerns grow out of non-moral valuings.

* JP, LIV, 16 (1957), 487-493.

levels of causality, tied in with integrative organization, I had not explored the texture, quality, and economy of human, agential causality. What I am going to try to do in this paper is to bring to a head the characteristics of the causal economy of human agency. I shall seek to show that, at this level, causality rises to the mode of self-guiding and even self-correcting. The biological base is in the mode of operation of the brain-mind of man; and this makes possible the addition of culturally achieved techniques. In this fashion, causality is lifted to a still higher level with consciously employed methods of exploration and guidance. But I shall not, in this paper, be concerned with the causality of social and political planning, contenting myself with pointing out that it depends upon an extension of the kind of causality of which the human brain-mind is capable.

It should not surprise us to find that language both reflects and aids this kind of causal economy. In the thinking of practice where we are confronted with the job of making up our minds this quality of causality manifests itself in modals. The phrase "I could and I would" expresses very well the confrontations antedating choice. The self as symbolized by "I" here is the focal front of attitudes, beliefs, and identifications; it has the crucial function of decision for the living organism, as a going concern, on its hands. The focal self is not a substance but a normative continuant which functionally represents the individual and is subject to challenge, as in remorse. I shall try to show that causality, at this level, cannot avoid being normative in texture. Even at lower levels, habits and patterns of action obviously have a normative dimension. This dimension accrues with directiveness and self-guidance.

It should be noted that this kind of causal process may take a long period before it comes to its critical moment, that of decision. But, surely, this temporal expansion of causality goes with the job set *to* the organism, that of successful action in a changing and complex situation. It goes with the use of *resources* such as learning, intelligence, growth. Both standards and methods of procedure become operative. We learn to use reason because reasonableness has its advantages.

. . . We must enlarge our notion of the category of causality

The Theory of Truth and the Theory of Value 263

in an empirical way, as we pass from the inorganic realm to the organic and thence to the domain of human, agential causality. Even at the inorganic level science has found that the traditional, mechanical model is misleading. Time's arrow has relevance, so that one pattern makes other patterns more possible. Thus causality always has a texture or economy. When living things emerge, this causal economy has two centers, the internal and the adjustmental. The first is symbolized these days by homeostasis, the self-regulating kind of physiological functioning of the nature of dynamic equilibrium. Here we have a kind of regulative ordering whose agencies and cues have been worked out under the control of natural selection through the ages. If you will, the timing and ordering are marvelous; but it is categorially wrong to think in terms of purpose and goals.

It is with the second direction of activity of the organism, tied in with its need of adjustment to the environment for survival, that we shall be primarily concerned in what follows. The stress, here, is upon rapid communication and the means of responding and behaving adequately. The organ of adjustment is the nervous system with its increased facilities for analysis and synthesis. Both learning and intelligence increase with the growth of cortical areas. And these play into basic directional patterns of action set upon in the old brain in the way of guidance.

Now it is my thesis that we should expect the causal economy here operative to be novel in mode and texture. In it, we have the highest level of causal activity of which we know. It represents the other extreme from fixed reflexes. Terms like integrative activity, action as a whole, spontaneity, occur to one as indicative of the line of categorial thought to be taken. So far as I can see, there are assemblages within assemblages, patterned growths interacting with other patterned growths. Let us keep in mind the need to which the mind-brain is subservient. It is the need for adequacy of adjustment. It is this that requires an *exploratory openness* which we call learning by experience. Abilities must secure causal implementation and leverage.

So far as I can see, then, the categorial empiricist must look for the results of the combined efforts of psychology and neurology to give us better ideas of the causal economy involved. But, surely, we can speak here of self-guiding causality. And this self-guiding involves some measure of the improvement involved in self-correction. Trial-error-success is lifted to a level in which insights into relational possibilities are added. Concepts and meanings tied in with orderable symbols increase the power of directive control.

* * * * *

I wish now to introduce the third item of my title, "free-will." In the conclusion, after I shall have given such status to this expression as I feel is justified, I shall turn back to ontology, or the metaphysics of ethics, and discuss the dimensional role of awareness, symbols, and prospective judgment as essential to the responsible function of the "self" as the *focus* of agential decision.

Since the modern context of free-will discussions largely concerns itself with such things as the status of choice and of moral volition, I shall disregard the older settings of fate and predestination. It is generally acknowledged that nature in the large is non-moral and goes its own way, except where man can employ objective techniques to direct its course. In brief, morality is a human quality; and what we want to get clear is *what it involves in a categorial way*.

We have already argued that categorial meanings are empirical affairs in which man is trying to get adequate notions of the constitution and "go" of things. Now the thesis I am exploring is that the texture and mode of operation of causality changes from level to level in nature and that its economy is especially novel when it comes to man with his mind-brain. Here, resources and methods have reached the level of the use of symbols for directional activities. This participation of causality at this locus in the dimensions of intelligence must be comprehended. I really think that philosophy has, here, a topic worthy of its metal.

The program which has seemed to me most promising is to avoid traditional dualisms of the interactionistic or the Kantian type. Nor have I found promise in any appeal to chance or indeterminism. The line of attack is, rather, to enlarge the modality of causality itself. Can we acclimate within it such dimensions as awareness, reference, judgment, valuation? And does not all this involve control and guidance? After all, the brain-mind is an organ with a job to do for the organism in its task of living. I do not see how it could do its job short of these resources. . . .

In the climate of recent philosophy, there has been a shift of interest to man. This is expressed on the Continent in various types of philosophical anthropology. Man has been thrown back upon himself and is seeking to understand himself. From this angle I recognize the power of the literature of *Existenz*. But I do not see any really original metaphysical construction in its support. Nevertheless, I do think that American naturalism has an obligation to explore the texture of agential causality and to cast light upon choice, the status of possibilities, the use of abilities, etc. The recognition of death may well tighten our sense of being. There is nothing about an open-ended materialism to exclude consideration of the existential reality of human creatures and the *quality* of their level. They are inescapably engaged in the adventure of human living. All of which sums up to the point that American naturalism needs a metaphysics of ethics for its completion.

* * * * *

As I see it, the need of the organism for unified behavior continues to dominate; though, at this high and complex level, the job to be done is increasingly difficult. The causal operation needs guidance. Merely to equate causality with determinism is a formal solution. What I am arguing for is an enlargement of the notion of causality, itself, in accordance with the idea of levels.

My thesis is that the "operative self" is a necessary focus through which agential causality works. It is both a resultant of past decisions and a starting-point for new ones. In this sense, it is a functional continuant which carries attitudes, beliefs, methods used, and norms adopted. . . .

To make a possible long story short, I suggest that the exploration of actual possibilities may well be a prelude to choice. Because the self is the locus of control, it is its job to envisage alternatives and to use its powers and resources in weighing them. This signifies that the causal situation of the self is intrinsically problematic. I suppose that this quality is what thinkers have had in mind when they used the term "contingent." Though what will happen will happen and will have an adequate basis, I doubt that deductive prediction can, here, be anything more than an informed guess. The more one knows about a person, the better one can guess what he is going to do in a given situation. The same holds, of course, for oneself. But I doubt that nomically based prediction applies at this level to the degree it applies in the inorganic world under controlled conditions. The operative self is doing a job of meeting the challenge of what it regards—rightly, I think—as open possibilities. And it must work through concepts and norms which are, in some measure, under challenge and must be applied. But there are so many questions to which I cannot here do justice.

When one thinks of the operative self in the context of exploration and weighing, one can, I think, appreciate the naturalness of modal categories and hypothetical statements. "Were I to do this, these consequences would probably ensue." "To be moral in my conduct, I must adopt certain principles." Oughtness and rightness are, so far as I can see, logical characteristics of morality as a human framework. In this sense they are intrinsic to the quality of human existence.

Because science has been largely concerned with cognitive description, its categories were not adjusted to human, agential causality which had to do with participative action. In my opinion, this enlargement of the category of causality, is a first step to an adjustment. In guided causality, *is* and *ought* are inseparably linked. That is, ought is a demand upon agency.

Since this is only meant to be of the nature of an outline of suggestions, I shall conclude with the proposal of a few theses.

1. "Free-will is an agential term which covers both external, permissive conditions and the quality of self-directive decision.

2. The adequacy of a "free-will depends on the use made of learning, intelligence, methods, and other *resources*. These link up with volitional traits such as persistence and "trying."

3. This adequacy can be lifted, or depressed, by cultural traditions and institutional arrangements. At this point, the metaphysics of ethics enters social and political philosophy.

4. Causality must be freed as much as possible from mechanical models. Causal determinism has been too much associated with fixed necessities and deduction. At the brain-mind level, we enter a region of creative adjustment and exploration dominated by needs and a job to do. Our categorial thought must now dwell upon texture, methods, and economy.

5. The operative self is a focal continuant engaged in the *activity* of self-guidance and self-correction. The context is that furnished by guided and directional awareness and the use of concepts and norms. Modalities of *can, could-and-I-would,* and *ought* emerge as native to this setting.

6. Remorse is of the nature of self-condemnation of a responsible continuant and a demand for its improvement. It is a normative activity and involves no causal paradox.

7. An open-ended materialism of the emergent type is, in no sense, reductive in its implications. Metaphysics of ethics in many ways represents its culmination.

PART V

Other Tests of Emergent Realism: Social Philosophy and Philosophy of Religion

SOCIAL PHILOSOPHY

Introduction to Social Philosophy

WHAT KIND OF social philosophy can be developed on the basis of a physical realism? Sellars pinpointed one facet of the answer in *Philosophy for the Future,* 1949.

> It will, I believe, interest my readers to find a materialist recognizing the normative as a guiding factor in the moral order intrinsic to group life . . . surely, group life and with it, the socialized human being lifted to the level of humanity thereby, involves a moral order. The thing to do is to make it explicit. . . . But that does not mean that they [moral principles] are non-natural, for man is, in group life, a moral being.[1]

Sellars' treatment of the mind-body problem in terms of emergent materialism would lead one to expect such a statement. Mind is a function, or set of functions, concerned with man's survival and the adequacy of his life. The principles that guide his relations satisfactorily with other humans, both individuals and groups, are clearly distinguishable. They are not merely customs or simply mores; they are standards which have developed historically through experience and by assessment of practices and policies. They answer to objective conditions,

---

[1] "Social Philosophy and the American Scene," *Philosophy for the Future* (Edited by R. W. Sellars, V. J. McGill, and Marvin Farber), New York, Macmillan, 1949.

affecting an organism's existence, development, and relations with other organisms. The principles must be continually reevaluated by all reflective individuals in the light of changing conditions and problems. Sellars' social philosophy, therefore, presupposes his value theory.

The first factor to be stressed in a social philosophy, however, is the *reality of the social,* contra the purely individual. As an undergraduate, in 1902, Sellars published an article in the *Inlander* in which he asserted that democracy not only must be but is being reinterpreted. A type of democracy that insisted on the equality yet isolation of its citizens, on a negative rather than mutually participative conception of democracy,

> "ended by losing, partially at least, any but the external bond of union. Social forces were curbed by undue emphasis on the non-social and . . . economic interests held almost complete sway . . ." [Yet] "a higher standard . . . than mere dollars . . . began to manifest itself . . . I think [indeed] we can discern through the course of our history a constant reinterpretation of democracy. The extreme . . . of rabid individualism, denying all social bonds and emphasizing the inherent essence of personality, gradually defeated itself under new conditions. . . . Of late years [in consequence] the American people have recognized the social side of life and laid stress on the responsibility of all citizens to all citizens."[2]

That the verve of this statement is not simply a 1902 undergraduate social idealism is more than attested by a 1942 article on "The Quality of Democracy."[3] As this article is included in the readings below, I shall only quote some whetting sentences. The term democracy, during World War II, was becoming

> "a blanket term to be thrown over ourselves and our allies. . . . Now such a use of a golden word does violence to it and may well hurt ourselves even more than those to whom it is politely thrown . . . It becomes a *cliché*. . . . We content ourselves with saying that it is the American way of life, something native to our traditions. . . .
> But is not democracy something also . . . to be striven for? . . . Is it not something we have in part only . . . ? Is it not something whose every stage points beyond itself . . . ?"[4]

---

[2] *Inlander,* University of Michigan, XII (1902), 258-259.
[3] *Michigan Alumnus Quarterly Review,* XLVIII (1942), 98-105.
[4] *Ibid.,* 99.

The filling in of the elements of this article I shall leave to the reader. I cannot, however, omit his concluding paragraph.

> "Being a philosopher, it should not surprise any one to find me closing this sketch of problems and attitudes by dwelling for a moment upon what impresses me as an unavoidable ultimate and background problem of democracy. It is this: it must by effort secure a rational philosophy which will give meaning and ground for its belief in the dignity of the human individual and his worth and perfectibility. Democracy must press its scientific and philosophical leaders to help it interpret itself to itself. In some sense it must secure a moral, and even cosmic, conception upon which it can confidently and intelligently rest its working assumptions."[5]

From this level, we must now return to the ground of Sellars' analyses of factors and facets of a realistic social philosophy. The reality of the social and the moral ingredient in an emergent physical naturalism is the component we have so far distinguished. But how does he get to this?

"From the very start of my thinking," he wrote, "I wanted to cooperate with the sciences. I took a minor for my doctorate in Sociology under Charles Horton Cooley, one of the pioneers in social Psychology.[6] I kept close contact with the Department of Psychology at the University of Michigan. I also spent a summer with J. M. Baldwin and others at the University of Chicago. . . . I was also quite indebted to the functionalism of J. R. Angell, and both positively and negatively, to the instrumental logic of Dewey."[7]

"Drawing from all sciences as well as philosophical insights of others, I proceeded to work out a philosophy encompassing the 'theory of knowledge, metaphysics, and value theory.'[8] I conceived the task of philosophy as the completion of science, and *social philosophy* as:

> "in the nature of an [informed] dialogue on basic social patterns and goals. When combined with political philosophy, all sorts of topics come to the front, such as ways of life, institutions, rights and duties, justifiable procedures, the elucidation of criteria. . . . [Numerous] topics emerge . . . the nature of human nature, the

---
[5] *Ibid.*, 103.
[6] *Social Perspectives and Political Horizons,* hereinafter referred to as *SPPH.*
[7] Conversations, June, 1968.
[8] *SPPH,* 6.

part played by economic institutions, moral values, the conditions of freedom. . . . Nothing seems alien to it: Fascism, Communism, liberalism, democracy, racism, nationalism, war. All intrude themselves. . . . And . . . how about the human condition? Is there any cosmically assigned meaning to human life? Or does it make its own meaning while it goes on? These can be called peripheral . . . questions, but they will not down, for . . . man is a . . . gadget-using, loquacious and metaphysical animal. A Shakespearean drama is in order."[9]

Sellars indeed traces his own development in social thought beginning with the first vague sense of social involvement, to be noted as the initial aspect of ideology:

"My political awareness began, in fact, in a vague way in the eighties of the last century. . . . It happened that a Republican . . . rally was held in a tent on river flats near my home. I was naturally taken to see the 'show.' Of course I did not know what it was all about, but there was singing and snatches of one song remain with me:

> "The ship is coming round the bend,
> It's all loaded with Harrison men.
> Good Bye, Grover, good bye, Oh,
> What makes you cry so?"

"Then," he continues, "I recall the depression years of the nineties, especially tales about those out of work in Chicago. Then came the famous Pullman strike and the World's Fair, which I did not get to see. But the speech of William Jennings Bryan about the Cross of Gold stirred up excitement. Naturally, I read Coin Harvey and talked about free silver. Then came the Spanish-American War. I was now eighteen and becoming skeptical. What was it all about?

I made my entrance to the University of Michigan. It was a brave new world to me. In my second year I took courses in philosophy. It was then dominated by Anglo-American idealism. Later I had a fellowship in philosophy at Wisconsin where I studied under F. C. Sharp. Wisconsin was then the home of progressivism and I suppose I was affected. La Follette was the outstanding figure there. I was called back to Ann Arbor and began my career as teacher and writer.

In those days one sought to box the whole compass. I covered philosophy of religion, where I moved to humanism, philosophy of science, where I worked in the direction of critical realism, evolutionary naturalism, etc. These concerned foundations. I had lots of

---
[9] *Ibid.*, 14.

energy and enthusiasm. Teaching political and social philosophy, I veered toward Fabian socialism. There was a small socialist movement [in America] in those days in protest against a rather tough stage of American capitalism. I was later led to write a book called *The Next Step in Democracy*. It was an exploratory work and I had in mind something akin to Galbraith's and Lippmann's distinction between *the public sector and the private sector.** It was not yet the time of pinkos and reds. Soon everyone was interested in Russia and the Riga Liar. What was really going on?"[10]

The Next Step in Democracy (1916) was one factor that brought about the labelling of Roy Sellars as a radical. His socialism was avowed; its gradualism had little meaning when once the name "socialist" was admitted. But we shall reproduce his three stages of socialism so that the student may gauge how basic, while socially progressive he was. It would have been strange if this native of Canada, descended from a fighting United Empire Loyalist, had not had a sense of enduring social foundations. That his perspective was transnational was equally to be expected.

A second factor in his branding as a radical was his nontheistic humanism. We shall deal with this following his social philosophy, since religion to him is an instrument of sociohuman values. His *Next Step in Religion* (1918) followed his *Next Step in Democracy*. Roy now became "Next Step Sellars."

I am reminded of two other philosophers whose intellectual forthrightness had reverberations. The first is Socrates. The second is a philosopher of similar honesty and courage: T. G. Masaryk, the first President of Czechoslovakia, whose philosophy I had the honor to present in English. (It is pointing directions for Czechs and Slovaks again: Masaryk is still the foremost "Czech Awakener.") Masaryk's attempts to be honestly objective and to get others to be honestly objective led to quite flagrant treatment. His courageous efforts during and after World War I are better known history.[11] We are dealing, in all three of these philosophers, with intellectual openness and honesty, and the actions that express these virtues.

---

[10] *Ibid.*, 473-474.

[11] See especially the Introduction to W. Preston Warren's *Masaryk's Democracy*, University of North Carolina Press (also Allen and Unwin), 1941. Cf. C. J. C. Street, *President Masaryk*, London, Geoffrey Bles, 1930, etc.

* Italics added.

Sellars' work in the social arena has its own distinctions. The contrast between Sellars and Dewey is significant. The sense of the functional, the reality of the social, and the urgencies of reconstruction are common to both, but Sellars is a realist, with an ontology, rather than just an instrumentalist or pragmatic naturalist. The result is a concern for far more than "experience," whether the term be capitalized or not. The difference is literally substantial.

Teaching social philosophy some 34 years and beginning historically with the political thought and textures of the Greek city states—while engaged in a critical examination of socialism as a philosophy—Sellars traced socio-political formulations through Plato, Aristotle, Roman political ideology, Christian medievalism, Machiavelli, Hobbes, Locke, Rousseau, early collectivism, Marx, dialectical and historical materialisms, Russian applications and deviations, ideological democracy, fascism and national socialism, to current issues and trends.

Social philosophy grows out of ideology somewhat as chemistry grew out of alchemy. The word 'ideology' has had of course as loose a set of meanings as any astrologer might want: from vague slogan-type polarizations in social sentiments and unscientific mystical abstractions that may or may not be social, to any intellectualizing of the social life of man. In general, however, ideologies have polarized both the social thought and social emotions of man. Ideologies are "to be regarded as preliminary attempts at social and political philosophy or at least gestures in that direction. [Yet] often they are not more than hasty generalizations."[12]

Sellars early distinguished three approaches which can be made to the problems of social philosophy and the evaluation of ideological systems. He called the first one the "approach from beneath." It is that of a behavioristic objectivism, emphasizing inventions, patterns of action, facts. Secondly, he discriminated an "approach from within." Here behavior deepens into linguistic behavior which has two interacting dimensions, the personal and social, reflection and communication. Here we are brought to cultural history and its great ages.[13] Ideologies are important

---

[12] SPPH, 474.
[13] Ibid., 15.

for this approach. Institutions are expressions of patterns of thought that, in turn, express patterns of value.

The third approach has more psychological balance and philosophical distance. It:

> "sought, in the social sciences and philosophy, to stand back and appraise as validly as possible, criteria and directions . . . a sort of meta-affair. . . . In it one must have balance and breadth of outlook. I have acknowledged that, during the years I have maintained my dialogue on social questions, there have been great advances in the social sciences. Yet there have been certain hesitancies in regard to framework. Is behaviorism adequate? Or must we somehow fit in values? And what, *in hell* are values? [The issue of values and standards of value is indeed fundamental to this approach.]
>
> I shall now break loose and offer what the Germans call a Weltanschauung; and which can be designated, as *per* wish, an ideology, perspective or outlook. As I see it, these approaches converge on some such stance, decision or commitment. And here I speak . . . in my . . . role as a philosopher. . . .
>
> I am *not*, to use A. J. Ayer's term, a pontiff in philosophy nor pontifically inclined. Nor do I quite like his alternative phrase, 'journeyman.' I always thought of myself as facing up to genuine problems upon which, no doubt, science had been working but which were not explicitly on its agenda, such as the nature of perceiving and the reach and status of the knowledge claims which developed within it, the correct formulation of the mind-body problem and the status of mental activity as causally guiding behavior. Here I worked along the line of signals, the role of information, the solving of adjustmental problems and what I called an emergent level of causality. In short, I was not an epiphenomenalist of the Huxley type. I had a high respect for the ingenuity of nature and for its anagenetic resources. All this led me to a double-knowledge approach to the mind-brain situation and, as an empiricist, I was persuaded that in *awareness* we had an operation essential to this level of causal activity.
>
> In short, I had become a critical realist, an emergent evolutionist, and a reformed materialist. These, if you will, are my philosophical *isms.* I think they will have bearing on social philosophy in a not too peripheral way.
>
> I have defined man as not only an historical animal but as a metaphysical one. And here I use this latter term in the setting of an emergent, or reformed, materialism rather than in that of existentialism. I make no play on nothingness and death. Man is recognizedly mortal, yet is able to 'look before and after and sigh for what is not.' He has his frustrations, alienations and estrangements, even in an

affluent society. He is a metaphysical animal in that he wants to know his place in the universe and what meaning he can give to his life. I would put reasoned recognition above religious myths. . . . On what can we build? And what is socially possible and desirable? These questions play back into social philosophy. I think the reader can see why I conceive of it as a responsible dialogue."[14]

It is a dialogue singularly alert to realities. Socio-moral principles may indeed vary from culture to culture and yet be concerned with roles of people and things in the lives of men. Such principles, Sellars has emphasized, are fundamental to the social life of people. They are disclosed by informed discussion of social processes. The function of the physical, together with all basic and higher values, must be envisaged in the principles of good social life.

The role of rationality in Sellars' social philosophy is given special focus in an article in 1943 in the Michigan Alumnus Quarterly Review. The title "Reason and Revolution" indicates its compass. Opposition to World War II had been leading some to call and work for revolution. But is revolution the only alternative? "To be emotionally against an unpleasant event is [surely] not enough. . . . Reason tells us that it is necessary to set forces to work designed to weaken and counteract those factors tending to bring unpleasant and destructive events to pass."[15] The article concludes with a statement based on Aristotle's analysis of kinds of government and their relevance to the causes of revolution. All governments are faulty when tried by an adequate rather than purely relative standard.

> "Is there such an absolute standard which can be applied and rationally defended? If so, educators and churchmen should be on the lookout for it.
> Is it presumptuous of me to suggest that democracy has not yet passed from the stage of ideology and shibboleth to that maturer level of assured principle and commitment at which Aristotle hints? May not a social philosophy of such a kind, if found and adopted, be the best preservative of democracy? If *might* can ever be harnessed to the chariot of *right*, it must be tamed and subdued by a reason

---

[14] *Ibid.*, 20-22.
[15] *Ibid.*, 212.

which has found sponsors in the varied life of mankind. A democracy so informed by reason need have no fear of revolution."[16]

Two comments on key terms of this article: the notion of an "absolute standard" must be thought of in contrast to the quite sheer relativisms that were tending to prevail. Sellars was no Platonic realist. Yet values and principles must answer to objective conditions and to the needs of healthy biologically grounded individuality-in-society. Unqualified relativisms are, in principle, chaotic.

"Reason," secondly, as Sellars envisages it, is based on scientifically factual kinds of evidence—or the closest approximations we can get. It is therefore basically inductive, though it proceeds dialectically in the form of evaluations, debate, and more evaluations.

Above all, it is not *ad hoc* or directed to pleasing—much less to agitation. "I have always," he has said conversationally, "been moderate in my statements. I am a philosopher—concerned to be objective and to have a rationally justified basis for any of my contentions."

We come now to Sellars' conclusions in "Objectives and Priorities." This is a substantial essay written, on the one hand, as his summation of studies in social philosophy and, on the other, as a set of principles for assessing the socio-human situation with a view to determining the most hopeful directions. At this point, we are no longer dealing simply in American democracy or democracy *per se* but in intersystem social space. Gaining a more adequate democracy is still of major moment, but the issues are those of the interplay of social systems through dialogue and interchange between Washington and Moscow, Washington and Hanoi, in the U. N., and in the many ways that could be rather endlessly spelled out.

The essay was rewritten by Professor Sellars in his later eighties. It has all the maturity and mellowness of years of observation and reflection on events. Its sagacity unfolds in its stress on open comparative treatment of systems relative to their social fields of application, in its emphasis on sociological depth, in its theory of value (which goes far beyond the more

---

[16] *Michigan Alumnus Quarterly Review*, XLIX (1943), 215.

standard economic treatments), in depicting the role of moral criteria and determining validity in moral decisions. It argues for the reduction of the cult of the absurd by education in the intelligible bases of life—in terms of a scientifically informed realistic naturalism. The cult of the absurd grows rather naturally out of philosophies which assume non-natural bases.

Our choice of selections attempts to highlight his treatment of sociology in depth, of economics, and of "the cult of the absurd." The essay does not offer solutions except in terms of broadly informed interchanges, growing mutualities, and "gentling," and of course increasing acknowledgment of human individuality, social realities, and comparative value. Yet it is a fitting conclusion to a philosophy which emphasizes science but sees the need of its supplementation and "completion" and which arrives at a frame of reference that is a conflation of sources and viewpoints and yet maintains its scientifically-informed realism. It can in fact be called Critical Realistic Social Humanism.

Sellars' "Orientation in Social Philosophy" is a summation written specifically for this volume.

SOCIALISM AND DEMOCRACY*

Socialism is a democratic movement whose purpose is the securing of an economic organization of society which will give the maximum possible at any one time of justice and liberty. Let us start with this definition and see what it involves.

Socialism would come under the genus, democratic movement. It is democratic in two ways: first, it aims at the good of all instead of the good of the few; second, it is democratic in its location since it finds its leaders among those who have thrown themselves body and soul into the fight for the amelioration of the condition of the masses. Let us consider these two features of the movement.

It is maintained by socialists that the governing class in society has never yet sought the good of all. There has always been a bias in favor of those who were already in control. What was desired at the best was the good of the many so far as this was

---

* *The Next Step in Democracy* (New York, Macmillan), 1916, 9-10.

compatible with the prerogatives of the social group which was dominant. In other words, the socialist maintains that there has never yet been a true democracy. Oligarchies have never succeeded in being anything more than intermittently charitable. Aristocratic societies have inevitably laid stress upon subordination and have regarded the few as the portion which gave meaning to the lives of all. So far as a justification was sought, it was found either in terms of innate differences due to blood or to a necessary divergence in function. Our own plutocracy was founded ostensibly upon a democratic theory, but one which has proven itself to be false because too atomic and with too much stress upon fixed rights. The result has been the shamefaced growth of a vulgar type of aristocracy. It is the inadequacy of the basis adopted by our so-called democracy that socialism attacks. It demands that the good of all become the avowed end of society and that conscious and persistent efforts be made to attain this good in spite of the inertia of institutions. The means to attain his goal should be made the object of reflection and of thorough investigation. Socialism is confident that it is, itself, on the right track in its emphasis on coöperation and its denial of the social value of special privileges.

The location of the movement is democratic as well as its purpose. Modern socialism does not await the benevolent action of those in power nor does it look upon justice and liberty as benefits conferred in an external way upon passive recipients. Liberty and justice have always been achievements bought and paid for by character and effort. Those who would be free must themselves strike the blow. Revolutionary movements must be firmly based on the aspirations and desires of those most interested. Socialism is now and, if it is to win, must always be a popular movement. Its leaders are sometimes manual laborers who have continued to identify themselves with their social group and have fought its fights from a clear and intimate knowledge of its needs and yet with a larger vision of a more happily organized society; sometimes they are men of other social groups who have felt the injustice of present arrangements and have thrown in their lot with those who suffer the most from things as they are. There can be no question that socialism is democratic in both of these ways. It is a continuation of the struggle for political freedom and works for the extension of the conditions of a free life to the people at large.

THREE STAGES OF SOCIALISM*

There are at least three stages in the development of modern socialism and these stages are marked by differing conceptions of the social state to be achieved and of the methods best suited to bring this more ideal condition about. Roughly speaking, the first period lasted until the middle of the nineteenth century and is usually called the Utopian period, a term adopted from the famous romance of Sir Thomas More, that good knight and strange blend of radicalism and conservatism. We may regard the second period as commencing with the Communist Manifesto which was written by Marx and Engels in November of the year 1847. It was in large measure from the peculiar characteristics of this period that political socialism took its rise. This kind of socialism is called by its admirers scientific, by its critics, orthodox socialism. We shall have occasion to point out both its strength and its weakness. The third period represents the modification of the social philosophy of Marx and his contemporaries by influences due to changing political and social conditions and the more adequate knowledge of society consequent upon the growth of the social sciences. Thus the socialist movement is consciously and unconsciously undergoing an alteration of perspective and of doctrine as the result of a better knowledge of the tendencies actually at work in the world at large. This third period is, properly speaking, a time of transition; socialism is losing its orthodoxies while adhering to its purpose and general plan. Such is in summary the history of socialism. Let us now look at this development a little more closely.

Utopian socialism was very fertile in ideas and, with all its faults, contributed far more to the positive content of socialism than the disciples of Marx are usually willing to admit.

---

* *The Next Step in Democracy* (New York, The Macmillan Co.), 1916, 27-30, 33-46.

Fourier, for instance, for all his oddities caught the spirit of socialism in a remarkable degree—its emphasis on coöperation and human welfare, its love of freedom, its sense of justice, its faith in humanity, its dislike of caste. He was one of the first to point out the waste in commercial competition, which does not have excellence but merely profit for its goal, and to challenge the smug optimism of the current economics. For him, socialism had larger aspects than the economic although he recognized the importance of this basic phase of life. Saint Simon, the other French prophet of the regeneration of society, laid his stress upon the possibilities of a kind of scientific organization of society. The fault with society was its lack of order and method, the determination of affairs by chance and custom; the race had just muddled along. This criticism of things as they are, this yearning for a freer, more intelligent, more sanely progressive world was urgently alive in these thinkers. The impulse of creation was abroad at the time sketching in hasty strokes a more rational society, seeking to build it a little nearer to the heart's desire.

But these early socialists had little appreciation of the obstacles which confronted them. They thought out their schemes of a better state with a patience and a thoroughness which command our admiration, but they had little idea of how social changes are actually brought about. In this regard, they were the children of their age. We, to-day, consent to modify our basic institutions only gradually; every change is looked upon as an experiment whose result cannot be predicted and we would shrink back from a reckless unsettling of the whole foundation of society as likely to lead to disaster.

Yet, while these early socialists believed in their ability to reconstruct society in detail and did not realize, as we do to-day, the complexity of social relations and the small part pure reason can play in their better adjustment to human welfare, they were far from advocating violence. Rationalists they were, but rationalists decidedly disillusioned with revolutionary methods. In the early decades of the nineteenth century, men were far less hopeful of the achievements to be brought about by revolution than their fathers had been. The great French Revolution for all its sound and fury seemed to many thinking men to have made little improvement in the general conditions of life. While they were unjust here, it is undoubtedly the case that the improvements made were not commensurate with the means. Reaction had so easily followed upon the heels of political changes and, to make matters worse, the industrial revolution had intervened to make these of far less importance than they had been thought. The world had gone mad over the English parliamentary system, as a kind of beautiful toy, without asking what it was good for. In the meantime, the number of landless workmen living on starvation wages and laboring excessively long hours had increased. For those who realized this fact, the watchwords of the previous century with their exaltation of merely political and legal liberty were beginning to sound stale.

Thus the socialists were this early probing deeper than others of their contemporaries. But they were naïve both in regard to method and end to be aimed at. We who have had a hundred years' experience with political democracy know how slow social change is and how many disappointments the enthusiast must undergo who romantically and sentimentally idealized the mass of men and their capacity to look ahead. We are aware that society is not a mechanism to be remodelled after some clever plan but a slowly developing organism not any too quick to learn by experience.

* * * * *

Toward the middle of the nineteenth century, a marked change in outlook and sentiment made itself felt. New forces were stirring on every hand. The old balance of power was giving way. The city was replacing the country; the proletariat was awaking to a sense of its thralldom; education was spreading among the masses; the ideals of political democracy were giving rise to new sets of values. All this led to the growth of reflection upon social affairs and a resultant knowledge of the way in which changes are effected in society. The consequence was a reaction against the light-hearted optimism and rationalism of the previous century and growth of a semi-pessimistic realism. The idea of social classes came to the fore. In this competitive era, man was looked upon as selfish rather than unselfish and as banding together in accordance with economic interests. This changed outlook immediately affected socialism and caused it to pass into a second stage. This second period is associated with the name of Karl Marx. While he was not the sole creator of this new phase of socialism, he was its most gifted interpreter.

Let us glance at some of the distinctive features of Marxian socialism. We shall see at once that the change in spirit and outlook is very marked.

In the first place, Marx did not pretend to lay down a definite picture of the future organization of society. He did not work out the details of a New Republic or of a Phalanstery. His great work, often called the Socialist Bible, was an analysis of capitalism. He sought to show that the breakdown of capitalism was inevitable, that it was digging its own grave, and that the advent of socialism was assumed. "Marxian socialism, or 'scientific' socialism, as Marx called it," writes Simkhovitch,[1] "differed fundamentally from the various types of socialism which preceded it. Marx ridiculed the invention of an ideal social organization, a perfect state. The fundamental proposition upon which Marx's socialism rested was his economic interpretation of history. This conception implied that the political and legal organization of society is absolutely dependent upon its economic structure, that our future depends entirely upon existing economic tendencies, that no social revolution could socialize scattered and decentralized industry, nor could legions of small property-owners be expropriated." Hence Marx broke sharply with early socialism. He had no faith in isolated experiments and did not believe over much in the power of persuasion. Since the basic assumptions of his outlook were so different from those of the eighteenth century, it was inevitable that he should advocate different tactics. He tried to see society as it actually is and believed that he discerned something of the nature of a class-war, a continuous struggle between two classes whose interests were directly opposed. Hegelian that he was, he believed that he could work out the inner logic of the process and predict its various stages. But he was by nature and training an agitator as well as a speculative thinker and was not satisfied simply to predict.

---

[1] "Marxism Versus Socialism," Introduction, p. 6.

Through his activities and those of his friends, Engels, Liebknecht and others, the socialist movement became a proletarian movement, an organization of the working-people connected with large industries. It has thus brought these people consciously into touch with the ideas of a democracy of a radical kind.

While Marx was, on the whole, a realist of a pretty concrete sort, he was yet tinged with a revolutionary ardor. His imagination was possessed by the series of political revolutions which had convulsed France during the previous half-century and he tended to look upon violent uprisings as the necessary means by which power passed from one class to another. The middle class had in this way shaken off the blighting control of the Feudal Aristocracy and abolished all those privileges which hindered its own development and march to power. Thus Marx believed that a sort of veiled war is always raging in the heart of society and that it comes to a crisis now and then in open revolts with resultant shifts of power and institutional changes. Such was Marx's reading of history in terms of class struggles. Let us see how he applied this interpretation of history to socialism.

The middle class, or bourgeoisie, was slowly but surely gaining the upper hand and replacing absolute monarchies and feudalism by parliaments and by a democratic suffrage. The consequence was a political and economic reorganization of society called democracy and capitalism respectively. These changes were creating a new, or fourth, class, the proletariat, long a relatively unimportant satellite of the middle class but now attaining an unconscious solidarity and a tremendous potential power. Before middle-class democracy and capitalism were completely established, Marx thought, the proletariat would surprise their nominal leaders by rebelling and securing the fruits of the revolution for themselves. "Thus we see," writes Jaurès, "that the proletarian revolution is to be grafted on to a victorious bourgeois revolution. Marx's mind, delicately ironical and even sarcastic in tone, amused itself with these tricks of thought." Class dismounts class from the saddle until the last class is reached, those who bear the chief burden of society. With the sudden ascendency of this basic class, the old privileges cease and class-government ends. By a *coup de surprise*, a relatively weak element of the population takes advantage of a critical situation to overthrow the unjust economic organization of the past. In this way, society will finally be rid of the canker of exploitation and be in a position to develop a healthy and happy life.

What must we say of this revolutionary theory of social change? To the American and to the Englishman, it sounds too romantic and theatrical. England has a capacity for compromise and adjustment which prevents the overt occurrence of revolutions; the same is true of America. For all his long residence in England, it is doubtful that Marx understood the temper and method of its people. His eyes were fixed upon France with its lack of training in government and its Latin sense of the dramatic. Another objection must be raised to his philosophy of history. However it may have been in the past, a minority to-day would be unable to grasp the reins of power and re-organize society in a constructive and permanent fashion. Mere numbers do not constitute social power for the units may be ineffective individually and incapable of constructive efforts; moreover, the proletariat in the Marxian sense of that term do not constitute the majority of any modern state. It would seem to follow that socialism must resign this flirtation with the idea of a spectacular revolution—it is somewhat too childish and superficial to gain credence among those who sense the complexity of society and the part played by ideas, customs and institutions. Society cannot go faster than the social mind and the social mind cannot be taken by storm; it has an inertia which is the despair of rationalists and revolutionaries alike.

At the same time that we reject the philosophy of history of Marx we are forced to abandon much of his economics. Socialism will not come in a political democracy as the result of a spectacular revolution. Society is too plastic to the forces of public opinion for this to occur. We must likewise admit that the belief, encouraged by Marx, that capitalistic society contains within itself the germs of its own bankruptcy has failed to be verified by the facts. If the proletariat waited until the death-throes of capitalism began for their emancipation, they would be forced to wait indefinitely. Neither a sudden economic nor a sudden political cataclysm is probable. Both industry and government has a far broader basis to-day than ever before and consequently have a stabler equilibrium.

But while many of the theories of the second period of socialism are no longer tenable and must be rejected, the situation is quite different with the tendencies set on foot at this time. We say that Utopian socialists appealed to society as a whole and had faith in a vague educative process. Society, they thought, would follow the guidance of reason and this reason was a sort of impersonal reason having little to do with the grim forces which actually control human relations. It was a reason of a transcendental type which ignored selfishness and custom and inertia and privilege. Now the aim dominating the second phase of socialism was the elevation of the mass of the working-people. Leaving in the background, the vision of a beneficent future for all, these reformers fixed their attention upon the actual situation of the laboring classes. Socialism meant for them the emancipation of the proletariat by the proletariat. All their theories revolved around this central motive.

False as many of the prophecies in regard to the future of the working-classes were, the emphasis laid on the necessity of their own initiative was eternally right. This demand that the masses awake and help to control their destiny is in line with the best traditions of liberalism and democracy. Instead of a passive mass controlled from above, Marx and his followers hoped to see the birth of a self-conscious and independent-minded group aware of its condition and of the essential injustice of it. Out of the insistent demands of this hitherto inarticulate part of society, a shifting of the center of gravity of public opinion would take place which would be reflected in all phases of social life. And this shifting of values is what is actually occurring. Socialism has become a movement rather than a vision of an ideal state. It is a ferment within society forcing society to progress toward a fuller democracy.

Thus the second stage of socialism was not so much scientific as realistic. It brought socialism down from the clouds to the earth and led to its entrance as a militant factor in the actual alignment of tendencies and weighted interests which control legislation. We should always remember that theories may be in large measure wrong and yet have a vital correctness in so far as they call attention to conditions which should not be permitted and nourish movements which help to bring about the modification of those socially-hurtful conditions. . . .

The third period into which socialism is now entering represents a time of transition in which the actual movement of events and the growth of new ideas have led to a reconsideration of the rather immature philosophy of the previous era. Naturally enough, the first move was to pour new wine into the old bottles, that is, to broaden out and to qualify the traditional theories. Many of the rather hasty theories of Marx were re-interpreted and robbed of their definiteness. This process was made easier by the vagueness which characterized the formulation of many of these doctrines. In his later years, Marx introduced qualifying phrases and where he had not done this, his friend, Engels, who lived on into the nineties did so. It was not difficult to carry this process further and so formulate such theories as the increasing misery of the working-classes, the labor theory of value, the materialistic interpretation of history, the class-struggle, the over-production theory of crises, and the inherent tendency of capitalism to bankruptcy as to rob them of their old import. Marx was a system-maker, like Hegel and Fichte, and did not realize, as we do to-day, the danger of over-systematization in a changing field. Just because of this, Marxian socialism is exposed to the charge of continually making prophecies which fail to come true.

It is often said that one of the strongest points of Marxian socialism was its determinism. The break-down of capitalism was considered inevitable and so was the triumph of the proletariat. This faith gave a grim optimism to the believer that nothing could shake. But the inevitable criticism of the system weakened the element of necessity and made the foundation of society less mechanically economic. It was more and more realized that human purposes and ideals are of prime importance as driving motives leading to social changes. Dominated as he was by the philosophy and science of the middle of last century, Marx was unable to conceive society except as a process moving forward *en masse* and according to the dialectic method of thesis, antithesis and synthesis. It matters little that he tried to stand German idealism on its head, as Feuerbach had done, and obtain a kind of materialistic realism; the impersonalism and mechanical determinism of the view still remained.

Now this semi-mechanical and almost wholly deterministic outlook has been outgrown by social philosophy and it is the half-conscious recognition of this fact that motivated the movement towards revision. While the older men, naturally enough, desire to make as few changes as possible in the inherited system, others who are younger and therefore more plastic and more in touch with the time are anxious to break pretty definitely with the theories of the previous century. That which is false or inadequate is, they believe, more of a hindrance than a help.

The Marxian phase of socialism brought it into touch with political democracy and worked on the true principle that the people must help to emancipate themselves. We should never forget that those who are opposed have themselves partly to blame. In this realistic and democratic attitude rather than in its economic theories lies the permanent contribution which Marxianism made. Perhaps we should add to this the challenge which it offered to the middle-class tendencies in economics. It helped to give a voice to the masses and drive home to the thinker their point of view in such a way that it would not be ignored. If a group of theories does this, it is thoroughly justified from the historical standpoint. Political economy is always in danger of bowing to the business man's outlook just as American philosophy so easily gives way to a genteel tradition.

But political socialism must immerse itself in the living stream of modern social democracy; it must acquire patience and ingenuity and be content to approach its goal by slow degrees. It must take to heart the sobering lessons that political experience has been teaching even while never losing faith in the ultimate outcome. Such is true realism.

Now a process of experiment and growth takes time, for obvious reasons. In the first place, because a certain smooth working of institutions must be attained before conclusions can be drawn; in the second place, because new habits and customs must be developed in the nation at large; in the third place, because a more social morality must replace the individual morality of the past; in the fourth place, because certain changes must precede others which presuppose them. The economic organization cannot be lightly separated from the whole social organization with its standards and methods and habits. For these reasons, the advance towards socializing industry will be gradual and experimental and cannot outrun political capacity and integrity. The public mind is the ultimate source of change and psychological factors enter into social adjustment to a remarkable degree. So strikingly is this the case that many writers maintain the thesis that the chief obstacle to a systematic reorganization of industry is mental rather than technical. Such thinkers are in line with modern economics and sociology which are awakening to the fact that the industrial system is a psychical creation and only uses the physical world as a tool.

The practical importance of the psychological factor can be illustrated in this way. Those who profit from present conditions usually honestly believe that these conditions are necessary and cannot be improved upon. They do so because they are conventional and have also the will to believe and the will not to investigate other possibilities. On the other hand, those who bear the burden have seldom the capacity to imagine definite remedies. These psychological characteristics account for what I have called the social inertia, the inability to acquire momentum apart from stimuli of a continuously acting and irrepressible sort such as a recognized conflict between the interests of social groups or a new vision of justice which has taken possession of those unselfish minds who form the ethical leaven of society. But I have in mind not only this retarding property of inertia but also the necessary limitation of the field of attention. Just as the individual mind must concentrate on one thing at a time if it is going to master it, so the social mind is unable to cover the whole social order in a satisfactory way unless it takes up one feature thoroughly and only then passes to another. We may call this the principle of mental economy and it is a principle which the revolutionary spirit has never appraised at its true worth.

It is of interest to note that even political socialism is becoming more and more *opportunistic* in its ideals and methods. This unfortunate but much employed word signifies an acquiescence in the method of advance laid down by those features of the social mind and of its instruments, which we have pointed out as necessitating an experimental evolution instead of a fiery revolution. Only those who have a thin and shallow notion of civilization can persuade themselves that a complete change of economic relations and ideals could be carried through at a stroke without rupture of the delicate social tissues which surround industry and the market as the flesh models itself upon the skeleton. For opportunism with its slight association of ethical duplicity, it would probably be better to substitute a term denoting a positive method founded on a clear comprehension of the characteristics of social progress. The ideal of the socialist would then become that of stimulating the social conscience to a desire for better things and of guiding it to a modification of institutions to bring about this end. Such an ideal is one with the function of statesmanship and, in spite of the scorn poured upon it by the orthodox Marxian, demands more knowledge and more concrete reasoning than the concoction of an abstract outline, summed up in a few watchwords such as "an industrial democracy," which, so long as it remains apart from actual life does not create its own criticism. Socialism must possess a principle or it will be possessed by watchwords. And this alternative is a vital one for a principle guides while watchwords blind.

REASON AND REVOLUTION*

To put it mildly, the very idea of revolution is sufficient to arouse a feeling of discomfort in the mind of the average citizen. It has—and I think with much truth—become inseparably associated with violence, revolt, and destruction. Hence it is, so far, something to be condemned and avoided. . . .

But things are not as simple as all that. Large numbers of people are against war—and yet wars occur. In like manner they

---

* MICHIGAN ALUMNUS QUARTERLY REVIEW, XLIX (1943), 212-215.

are against unemployment—and yet unemployment on a large scale is a recurrent phenomenon. To be emotionally against an unpleasant type of event is not enough. If the causes and conditions of it exist the probability is that it will occur. Reason tells us that it is necessary to set forces to work designed to weaken and counteract those factors tending to bring unpleasant and destructive events to pass.

This does not mean mere repression, the appeal to the *strong man* to maintain the *status quo* by the use of force; for that would not be an appeal to reason . . . and would involve something of the nature of a counter-revolution, a revolution preferred by those in power. And counter-revolutions have not shown themselves to be either peaceful or constructive. I take it that the majority of Americans dislike, almost equally, both revolutions and counter-revolutions. Surely, there is some possible other way out.

That other way out is, of course, *reform*, the experimental, rational location and study of social problems, the conscientious endeavor to make adjustments and bring about a larger measure of social justice. And *abstractly* and *in principle*, reform has been generally accepted by English-speaking countries as the proper alternative. In fact, they are rather proud of what they regard as their genius for concession and adjustment. And I think they have a right to be proud.

The English ruling class discovered this technique as the result of experiences over many centuries, under conditions of a favorable kind into which I need not, here, go. It was interesting to hear Churchill in his recent speech refer to Disraeli, the father of so-called Tory-socialism. The ideal is that of gradualism, change within traditional contours whenever possible. But, of course, this tactic presupposes that social forces are not, themselves, extraordinarily novel and, as we are accustomed to say, revolutionary. It is noteworthy that common speech uses the term revolutionary, in this impersonal and objective way, of trends and changes which, by their very nature and mode of impact, are bound to alter institutions profoundly. . . .

I do not think that I am exaggerating when I state that it is becoming quite clear it is these impersonal revolutionary changes with all their repercussions that is making the present a time in which rational reform must, so to speak, gird up its loins and seriously enter the race with those more savage and primitive twins, revolution and counter-revolution. Rebel and reactionary are psychologically bound together in an *emotional dialectic* which, once it is under way, reason finds itself powerless to stay. The universe contracts to the dimensions of passion and rationalization and, as one wit has said, thought becomes little more than a breathing-spell for the rearrangement of prejudices. Hegel has something of this in mind when he analyzed the dialectic of the relation between master and slave.

I take it that the true democrat of to-day would desire, above all, to escape the fate of falling into such a vicious dialectic of hate and counter-hate. But the alternative in a dynamic and changing age, such as ours, is not mere well-wishing but an informed and purposive will for the solution of urgent problems in terms of some genuinely democratic and humanistic table of values. It is not a matter of knowledge only, though that is important. It is also a matter of social vision and creative imagination.

I

In my opinion America is doing reasonably well though not well enough as yet. It is undergoing a process of education in which it is learning to discount many of its preconceptions. It was not so long ago that people honestly believed there were no important social problems. But hard facts have aroused skepticism about automatic progress. The traditional clichés of *natural harmony* and *laissez faire* sound less convincing to American ears. There is an echo of the receding past about them. It is, I think, beginning to be realized that it would be semi-miraculous if, in our complicated and ever-expanding culture, there were no social rapids and treacherous sandbars, dangerous to the good ship of state with its somewhat eighteenth-century equipment.

Preconceptions about human nature and about social classes must also be brought to the surface and scrutinized. Here, we could learn something from re-reading Madison and Webster with their frank recognition of social factions and the divisions caused by property interests. The use of the term *people,* so characteristic of liberalistic democracy in the latter half of the nineteenth century, was in part the reflection of optimism, in part a refusal to see social problems of an economic sort. There was much rationalization in it. It was assumed that everyone belonged to the middle class psychologically if not actually. What are our pressure-groups but the factions of Madison which he hoped to keep in place by the ingenious system of checks and balances of the constitution, a sort of balance of power technique applied internally? But what might be sufficient for an agrarian society may not work in the era of capitalism and technology.

A word about changing conceptions of human nature is also in order. A convinced neo-Calvinist, like Reinhold Niebuhr, is exhorting us to remember that human nature has a strain of evil in its constitution, a demonic element alien to the sweet reasonableness of liberal and intellectualist preconceptions. And Freud has been added to Calvin and Marx. It is well to have such a challenge issued even though one can be skeptical of the theological dialectic used as a base. The sly remark of G. K. Chesterton to the effect that, in his day, many political liberals looked forward to the time when every man would have *two* votes instead of one as the climax of reform, is not without point. Our growing realism enables us to smile at such simplicity.

But is revolution the alternative to constructive reform? There is, of course, the possibility of . . . an uninspired tournament of pressure groups unillumined by principles of equity. As the scholastics rightly say, let us distinguish. In one sense, the solution of critical problems is always revolutionary in its implications; in another sense it need not be so. It is revolutionary in that it will involve fundamental changes in outlook, methods, and values and, perhaps, in institutions. It need not be revolutionary in the popular meaning of that term as including violence and revolt and irrational destruction.

As I have already stated, there is, *abstractly speaking,* no excuse for turmoil. In the last analysis, it all depends upon the social ingredient of tolerance, knowledge, and willingness to experiment. But we must never forget that learning in such matters is not a mere intellectual affair. It involves the emotions, a capacity for objectivity, wide human sympathy. Here is where a genuinely liberal education with—if I may be bold enough to say so—some flavor of philosophy in it might help. I have often been impressed by the closemindedness of both professional and business men. But it is not confined to them. Technical scientists and scholars often lack the capacity to take wide views outside their domain of specialization. And all this is very unfortunate.

True patriotism involves, I take it, concern for the quality and cultural achievement of one's country as well as for its might and prowess, important as these are in a civilization without the international law of peace. It seriously asks, What kind of a country do we want this to be? And such patriotism, if it is to be effective, must be informed and ready to make commitments.

THE QUALITY OF DEMOCRACY*

. . . [If it is to maintain itself in America and commend itself to the world] democracy should have more of mastery and less of drift. It should be more daring and constructive, more fully aware of its implications and goal. As in moral life, so in social life there must be decisions and tables of value.

At this point, logic suggests that we ought to make the distinction between internal national problems and the international ones which will face democracy. If isolation is relinquished then some policy of international integration should be forthcoming. Such a step would clearly entail limitation of national sovereignty to the extent that the center of gravity of political life could no longer be so circumscribed as it has been in the past. This is not the place to enter into a discussion of the comparative merits of leagues, super-states and confederations. We can, however, say that there must be a departure from the too selfish emphases characteristic of economic nationalism. It should not be forgotten that national and international policies are ultimately inseparable. The methods and ideals

---

* *Michigan Alumnus Quarterly Review*, XLVIII (1942), 98-103.

operating within a country are certain to find expression in external relations; and the reverse is also the case. Lines of force do not recognize legal and political boundaries. That is why economic nationalism always exists in unstable equilibrium with economic imperialism.

Prior to such technical problems is, I would hold, the job—too much neglected—of determining just what we mean or, perhaps ought to mean by the term democracy. Here I am concerned with more than verbal and emotional conditioning. Like Whitman I take democracy to be a challenge.

"Did you, too, O friend, suppose democracy was only for elections, for politics, and for a party name? I say democracy is only of use there that it may pass on and come to its flower and fruits in manners, in the highest forms of interaction between men, and their beliefs—in religion, literature, colleges and schools—democracy in all public and private life, and in the army and navy."

How important such a determination is for any intelligent discourse is evident at a glance. If democracy is a completely elastic term which can be stretched to cover any sort of political and social set-up it will have no peculiar and ineluctable demands and implications. Having little intrinsic meaning it could then be used as a merely honorific term of approval to be applied smugly to ourselves and to those countries towards which, for the time being and for reasons of state, we felt friendly. It is well known that something of this sort was done under the instigations and temptations of the last Great War. Democracy then became a blanket term to be thrown over ourselves and our allies. It was not realized that peace has its defeats no less than war.

Now such a use of a golden word does violence to it and may well hurt ourselves even more than those to whom it is politely thrown. For it is probable that they do not take such labeling too seriously any more than we do. Why it may hurt us who should take the term seriously and attach a well-thought-out concept to it is that we then tend to fall back upon a stereotype. It becomes a *cliché*, a song-and- dance to be run off like a record on a phonograph. We content ourselves with saying that it is the American way of life, something native to our traditions, something which we know as we know our friends and parents.

But is not democracy also something to attain, something to strive for, as much as it is an accomplished and realized way of life? Is it not something we have in part only and whose farther reaches and possibilities we see as in a glass darkly? Is it not something whose every stage points beyond itself as "that which is to be surpassed?" And here, almost unconsciously, I used Nietzschean language. Man, he argued, is something to be transcended by the superman. Grant that we have here a romantic form of Darwinian biology; and yet it strikes the note of activism, of forward-looking. I, myself, acknowledge a liking for one American poet's phrase, "that it may pass on and come to its flower."

If such be the proper approach—and I think it is, despite the apparent belief of my conservative friends who seem to hold fast the idea that things have changed in the past but would not be so ill-mannered and demonic as to change now and in the future—then must we suppose that democracy is something in process of being realized. It may well be that America must wrestle with the Spirit of Democracy as Jacob wrestled with his angel.

What I am leading up to is the suggestion that the problems facing democracy are not merely technological ones to be solved by economists and scientists but also ethical ones. And by ethical I mean a matter of values and principles. Does not democracy involve decisions as to ends, as to the quality of life, as to social justice? It seems to me clear that it does. And, if so, institutions of all sorts are primarily instruments for furthering such ends. They should be good instruments intelligently worked out and used. And yet they are primarily an affair of instruments and machinery.

Let me illustrate what I mean. Political democracy has been classically described as government of the people, by the people and for the people. It is self-government but it is also self-government for the attainment of a policy instrumental for the good of the governed. The motions are not enough. Democracy is stultified to the extent that it does not eventuate in a high quality of life including such features as liberty, justice, education, intellectual and artistic activity, and general happiness.

It is not, as we all know, an easy form of government to maintain and to keep free from inertia, self-seeking and corruption because its machinery is complex and demands for its effective working a fairly high level of intelligence and a widespread sense of responsibility. And yet we suppose self-government both a guarantee of liberties and a training in civic insight and responsibility.

But, beyond these values, it should also bring about a positive good by furthering the high quality of life to which I referred. To the extent it is unimaginative and does not help to foster such a quality it falls short of its purpose. In other words, democracy must be judged by its fruit, just as other governments must be. And it must not expect to escape criticism by a sanctimonious claim that it is somehow intrinsically good apart altogether from the way of life it has linked itself with. I myself think the values of self-government are very high and outweigh the efficiency of even good government from above. And yet it is a pity if to self-government intelligent government be not added, that is, a government which knows what should be aimed at and furthered, what quality of life should be kept in mind.

Another illustration can be taken from the economic side of life. Here, again, the danger is to let the machinery of industry and finance get between us and a clear consciousness of the end which, alone, justifies such machinery. The business of business is ultimately not business but the supply of goods to consumers. That is in the last analysis what the economic life is socially for. It may include for many participating in it the personal values of a game or the possession of power, prestige, security. And yet from the larger social point of view its basic function is the supply of consumption goods and services.

If the economic machinery becomes too complex and involuted so that it turns back on itself and gives too large a place to these subsidiary personal values of strategic participants, then we must query its genuine efficiency. It is then not doing as well as it should what is its basic job. There is imbalance, misdirection, involution about it. The goal is in some measure being lost sight of. Many of us have feared that the capitalistic system, for all its driving power, tends to obscure this primary vision of the ultimate goal. It must be willing to submit itself to the application of criteria such as social justice, the distribution of positive freedom for creative living, a minimum of autocratic power, a general standard of living consonant with the power of production. To the extent that these qualities are absent the economic system needs overhauling for its does not harmonize with the purposes of democracy.

But, one may reply, such reasoning reads too much into the term, democracy. Surely it does not imply such criteria and such human values. That would be too idealistic and utopian. And it is true that, in these days of aggression and world war, we are thankful for the American way of life even if it is—let us frankly acknowledge it—not free from blemishes on both the political and the economic side. But here we are concerned with the postwar problems of democracy and so, having expressed my heartfelt thankfulness for the American scene, I can go on to portray the problems of democracy in the light of its inescapable demands.

I

Democracy in America—and the same may be said of other countries—is a way of life and set of beliefs bound up with our history and culture. While there has been continuity with respect to both these factors, there has also been change—and greater changes than we sometimes suppose. As a consequence we must consider democracy to be a developing thing. The social situation has altered as we have passed from a loose-knit society, largely agrarian and commercial, to the interdependent great society of the present. Old institutions have been modified and new ones created. And all the time complexity has been on the increase.

It is important to realize that a distinction must be made between the principles, ideals, or postulates of democracy and the assumed ways of realizing them. At least analysis leads to such a distinction, even though in practice most people are hardly aware of it. We can speak of these principles, ideals or postulates as giving the ethical philosophy of democracy and of the practice as disclosing the actual methodology. Together they constitute what is currently called an ideology.

Being realistically inclined, it is my opinion that we should become conscious of that complex of ideal, theory and practice which, in the main, has characterized American democracy. It can, perhaps, be not too inadequately summed up in a large degree of respect for the dignity and worth of human beings, in legally recognized civil rights, political rights, and property rights, in confident acceptance of free enterprise or the profit system run along supposedly individualistic or laissez-faire lines, in a limited and rather negative state, in comparatively automatic progress.

... Actual practice has not always been tied very closely with theory. The abstract idealism of the Declaration of Independence represented a manifesto of ideals in an emergency and not a description of actual practice. From the latter standpoint the Constitution better expressed the fact that we constituted a Whiggish republic of a dominantly agrarian and commercial middle-class country largely, though not completely, free from the traditions of feudalism.

And so we went to work multiplying and filling the land, building up wealth very much in the way it was being done in other countries, securing national independence and then a large amount of national economic independence by means of the tariff system, permitting human slavery and allowing immigration. The West was settled, suffrage was extended; and we entered the period of Jacksonian democracy and the spoils system. We had become a gigantic, sprawling, democratic republic. Then came the crisis of the Civil War which was at once economic, social and ethical in character.

It was not until after the Civil War that large-scale capitalism definitely triumphed in the American scene. There was the notorious corruption of the Grant period, increased tempo, ruthless exploitation of natural and human resources, immigration artificially stimulated the growth of enormous fortunes, industrialization. All this was a phase of democracy taken as an actual way of life. In it were mingled inextricably idealism and realism; sentimentalism and cynicism, poverty and wealth. The momentum of the development was terrific in this richly endowed land. It was human, all too human, and inevitable.

But were our postulates working as well as a true democrat

could like? How large a degree of respect was there for the worth and dignity of human beings as such, for the average man? Were not property rights considered too absolute and metaphysical rather than subordinate to moral ends? Were not economic institutions considered, as a consequence, as ends-in-themselves rather than as means to consumption and to standards of living? Was not freedom considered too negatively as freedom from social and moral control and not as positive freedom for widespread human self-realization? Was there not a lower quality of life than we could desire, a quality expressive of poverty, poor education, the absence of art and literature in the common life, a quality of life connected with insecurity, sensationalism, and the dominance of monetary values?

Can it be denied that there has been disappointment despite the enormous returns from that alliance of science and invention we called technology? It seemed to the more reflective and enlightened that we were busy at the further development of improved means for unimproved ends—Thoreau's phrase.

Of course, the world at large was doing much the same thing. The first World War awakened reflective people the world over to certain generic features of modern civilization which were exemplified specifically from nation to nation according to the momentum of its traditional way of life and situation. It was found that democracy, taken realistically, represented a political and moral variation within the large outlines of a neo-technical civilization. On the whole, it was less militaristic, more inclined to grant rights to individuals. And yet it was careless, dominated by machinery and routines, rather thoughtless about ends and the quality of human life. The privileged hung on to their privileges, while the masses were engulfed in the job of making both ends meet and so were not any too educated or morally reflective. The wheels of institutions, legal, political, economic and educational turned ceaselessly.

Such is the picture, as I see it, with its good and its evil. . . . Is it not clear that we must gain *morale* not only by means of folklore and symbols but also by gaining a more definite consciousness of our problems and of directions and methods? It is impressive, the growing feeling of the need of symbols and of a continuity with the more heroic aspects of our past. Thus Lincoln has become a deep and moving symbol of democracy at a time of crisis. . . .

That a nation needs human symbols of greatness of soul is as certain as that America has long been reaching out to make Lincoln such a symbol. But a symbol to be dynamically effective must secure application to present situations and tasks and not be merely meditatively grasped in a moment of subjective feeling. The Civil War ceased its battle clangor over two generations ago. It is for us, the living, to dedicate ourselves anew to the tasks of our day.

II

The crisis of democracy concerns its intelligent and moral handling of a social situation marked by extreme and aggressive nationalism, conflicting social philosophies, intricate technologies, mass-production, huge cities, insecure and perplexed individuals, big business, weakened faiths. In such a world many of the old assumptions must be revised if democracy is to find itself again and meet the challenge of the time.

Suppose we give aid by listing what Merriam in his book *The New Democracy and the New Despotism* regards as the five basic assumptions of democracy: (1) the essential dignity of man, (2) faith in man's perfectibility, (3) that commonwealth gains are mass gains and therefore should be diffused throughout the community, (4) the desirability of popular decision on basic questions of social direction and policy, and (5) confidence in the possibility of conscious social change by way of consent rather than by violence.

It will be noted that these assumptions are at one and the same time moral and political. They call attention to essential ends and equally essential means. What do they imply?

They seem to me to imply that democracy must work against aggressive nationalism and must be willing to limit sovereignty in order to further internationalism. It is the task of the statesman to strike the golden mean between isolationism and a world state. The outcome of the present war will decide the temporary policies of America but the permanent direction of democracy seems to me clear. It cannot limit the application of its moral assumptions. It is universalistic and not pathologically and chauvinistically nationalistic.

These assumptions also imply that progress can no longer be regarded as automatic—or regression, either, for that matter. In moral matters there must be effort and decision. First things must be put first; and second things, second. The economic side of life is a thorny problem and I would deduce no dogmatic *ism*. That capitalism must be basically reformed few thinkers now doubt. The thing to keep in mind is the end, a widespread quality of life including security, activity, and acquaintance with the artistic and humane aspects of life. There must be less stress on property rights, as such, and more stress on consumption, services, and type of life. Those economic institutions are to be sought which are not only efficient and efficiently run but also tie up most effectively with that for which they are, after all, primarily means. There must be experimentation and analysis and no mere phobias, or selfishness, must be allowed, in the long run, to stand in the way. How much collectivism and public ownership will be involved cannot be said *a priori*. But it seems evident to me that the age of rugged individualism and laissez-faire is past.

OBJECTIVES AND PRIORITIES

1. Sociology in Depth

There are two analogical metaphors one hears these days, frontiers and depth . . . The term, frontier, suggests new . . . vistas opening up. Depth, on the other hand, points to different levels within society . . . varying centers and controls . . .

History no doubt gives us a sense of depth but only if it has a cumulative dimension. It must be supplemented by sociology . . . in depth—even a biological background is needed to help free us from . . . naïve teleology or purposiveness in things . . .

Among other things, in the world of today, capitalism and communism confront one another As ideologies, they snarl at each other: but philosophy and sociology must look at them in depth and then it is seen that they have much in common. Both are to be justified only by what they accomplish in the way of a satisfying human life. Capitalism emerged within the framework of private property and private enterprise but has long left *laissez-faire* behind. It is now enveloped within the demands of the welfare state. This may be called "civilizing capitalism." Communism arose in Marxist form as a protest against *laissez-faire* capitalism. It postulated a different framework, public ownership. Unexpectedly, it gained an opportunity to embody itself in a huge and backward country which became the U.S.S.R. Here it has had to work itself out politically, socially and economically—no easy task. It had to experiment and it was beset by enemies. I was both a critic and a sympathizer. It had the task of adjustment to demands. Like capitalism, it needed to be civilized. And that would take time.

But let us turn more sharply to depth. Freud is supposed to have done the probing. . . . Schopenhauer with his stress on the 'will' had influenced him. Nevertheless we began to hear of complexes, the unconscious, the erotic, inferiority feelings, rationalizations, sublimation. Behaviorism was soon added (from "states-side") as a check on introspection. Man began to be considered as much a rationalizing animal as a rational one. Stress began to be placed on myths, shibboleths, stereotypes, and pictures in men's minds (images). One cannot help asking one's self what are the pictures in President Johnson's mind? In Wilson's? In Kosygin's? In DeGaulle's?

. . . To get perspective one must add comparative studies to history. And these must be given the backgrounds of political geography and economic geography. Only after all this has been done has one a sense of depth, of dimension.

* * * * *

It is . . . interesting to observe the coexistences within countries of political parties working in what is called a brokerlike way and internationally embedded ideologies. . . . One cannot look at nineteenth century history without noting that statesmen have been prisoners of their social setting and its table of values. That is why they stumble into wars so egregiously . . . one old lady asked me once, Why do statesmen do such foolish things? That is my answer.

How can one counteract such drifts? Only, as I see it, by

public education, discussion and debate. Political and social philosophy may make its contribution. But . . . it must speak out. It must say such-and-such are the dangers . . . Such-and-such are desirable objectives, and among these there are priorities.

2. Economics

In economic matters, the philosopher must play a modest role; often not much more than that of querying. But he must view them both historically and systematically. Situations change. Yet where there is a pattern there will be relations and laws.

Economics was first tied in with capitalism as a going concern. Say's law assumed that savings would be automatically invested. But Keynes has challenged the assumption that savings are necessarily invested.

Marx approached it from another angle, trying to show that capitalism was cannibalistic, leading to aggregation, on the one hand, and to increasing misery among the proletariat. Later Marxists . . . tied in capitalism with imperialist expansion, as an outlet.

Now I do not think that capitalism can depend on a pre-established harmony. It is a very complex system. And demands will be put on it to achieve desirable results. The market and the context of producers and consumers tend to be focussed on [financial] gains and losses. But as Galbraith points out, there must be concern for larger social values, like education and art. This is often called the 'public sector.' Man is not merely an economic animal.

* * * * *

But if one started with the communistic system of public ownership, there would still be problems . . . Planning from above (à la Plato) lacks knowledge of local situations and misses motivations and distribution needs. It would seem that the communists are recognizing these inadequacies and trying to introduce new methods.

[Evidence seems to indicate indeed that] . . . there may come about a kind of meeting of extremes. [We are already in a capitalistic Welfare State], and personally I cannot get too excited about conflicts between these two programs. There is enough of a stalemate to suggest that social experimentation can take the place of militarism.

❊ ❊ ❊ ❊ ❊

I think it . . . important to look at things both *inside* a theory and from *outside* a system [to see its relevances and the possibility of harmonizing its values with those of other systems. Compromises are variously developing]. The welfare state and post-keynesian economics interest me. But so does Liberman reform in the Soviet Union. I admit that Chinese developments also intrigue me. One can look upon all of these as corresponding to biological mutations. There is no preordained set.

What should statesmen then do? They should at least avoid the *hybris* of self-righteousness and they should become adequately oriented in social anthropology, sociology and history. The development of a really sound and reasonably complete theory of value would be of far-reaching help. But here is where the philosopher, together with the sociologist of depth, can be of major help to the statesmen. Value in simple economic terms is very incomplete. The economic side of life spills over into society at large, as we all know, and manifests itself in class conflicts, nationalism, facism, the common market, communism, and so on. . . . It is a question of getting an adequate perspective.

3. The Cult of the Absurd

[To Professor Sellars, interestingly, the cult of the absurd seems more intelligible from the social than from the religious standpoint. Such irrationality in religion is a basic expression of bad philosophy; with reference to society, it may bespeak something more temporary: the sense of puzzlement and of present futility. He disposes of Sartre's *Nausea* and Heidegger's view of man as "thrown into the world" as inadequately grounded.]

A more empirical and realistic approach might have freed him [Heidegger] from these shackles [of perspectival limitations]. Man is born with an inherited gene-pool into a dynamic world of emergent novelties and possibilities. Acceptance and utilization of nature is an alternative the Existentialists are too ready to neglect.

Socially, however, the cult of the absurd bespeaks the sense of puzzlement and futility confronting present youth. They are not satisfied simply to fit into the world. War and discrimination are two gross evils. And does not middlclass life, as Camus portrayed it, move in circles? Sartre, himself, satirized the values of a small French city.* Even 'socialist realism' would seem to be too set in its horizon, too concentrated on external projects. The cult of the absurd would seem [therefore] a good point of departure for (social) reflection and analyses.

But I take a different approach, stressing evolutionary levels. As I see it, freedom is made possible by a high level of causality in the human brain which is able to include in its working the consideration of alternatives and their consequences. I reject *predetermination* in favor of a decision-making operation. I do think *awareness* makes a causal difference. Thus, at this level we have, I take it, a guided kind of freedom, not always guaranteed to be wise. That is, we make up our minds and, in so doing, often make mistakes. Even our valuations may lack justification. Learning by experience is essential. As I see it, the self is a development with risks involved. In this sense, there is contingency in nature. There is, certainly, an openness about man. That is why he is both an historical and a metaphysical animal.

As is well known, German existentialism stresses *Angst* or anxiety. Man is an anxious creature. Here, too, the absurd is the impersonal and the fixed. Mass man is anathematized. One can take this as a protest.

I mentioned Kafka. . . . Kafka uses descriptive detail and yet leaves a sense of futility and indefiniteness. Something is always about to happen but never quite does. There is in this a kind of withdrawal rather than a facing up to reality.

I am inclined to think that there is at present more a mood of trying to do something about it. But it is a complex and puzzled world which has crept up on us. I hope our young Wordsworths do not have to pass through the stages he went through.

Since I am going to allow myself to consider commitments and priorities, I must examine the validity of moral decisions.

---

* In *Nausea*, set in Bouville ("Mudville").

If there are no good reasons for objectives, the cult of the absurd remains in possession. I do not deny that there has been much that has turned out to be absurd and harmful in human life. That is where progress in morals and institutions has its motivation and reason for being . . .

[Distinction must be drawn not merely between goals (and other values) and present circumstances but between present feasibilities and adequate goals. One should never abandon the quest for adequate goals or other values.] "The status quo is never the best." [Toward achievement of the best Sellars proposes to triangulate between Plato, Locke, Jefferson, and Marx with as objective a consideration as possible. Plato offers clearcut principles intrinsic to what Pepper, Morris, and others call a closed society.] Locke and Jefferson present the outlines of a liberal, rather individualistic society. Marx, on the other hand was the learned prophet of revolution.

"I am going to triangulate between Plato . . . Jefferson, and Marx" I can quite understand why those thinkers of today who find no clear guidance in popular naturalistic behaviorism or in statistical methods turn to Plato. What they are seeking is valuational guidance, a sense of goals and purposes . . . I do think that a clarification of values and goals is important for both social and political thought. . . . At the human level, both description and valuation have their rights. It is because man is an agent and not a mere observer and knower that appraisals of goals become essential. Even oughtness comes to the front. Kant was deontological and imperative in his ethics. But I hold that this note can be struck in a more empirical fashion. We should have good reasons for our moral commitments, reasons connected with human happiness and welfare. So I bow Plato and Kant out, while not lapsing into factualism.

I turn next to Locke. He was . . . an empiricist and a paragon, in his day, of common sense. But he is ambivalent in his ethics, swinging between intuition and hedonism, and, in his social philosophy, he was rather conservative, stressing property rights. Jefferson had to modify this emphasis and introduce the pursuit of happiness, while Madison noted other rights. I take it that Locke's contribution was more political than social. I doubt that he had much sympathy for levelers and diggers.

The social textures of societies are interesting to study. England has always been rather hierarchical and class conscious. This has involved deference and a kind of pecking order. Even the mode of speech has been symbolic of status, and yet we feel the stress on fairness and a kind of gentling. . . .

When we come to the American scene, we can note Locke's continuing influence. But feudalism had been left behind. In Federalism there was a measure of deference expected but this passed with Jacksonian democracy and the strife of parties. What then happened was a spreading out of society in certain recurrent patterns, rural and urban. Gradually, the middle class and business gained dominance. There was really no viable alternative. When the shoe pinched too hard there were protests. Populism was a case in point. But, in general, there was conformity and consensus. What was called the American way of life was worked out. At the most, progressivism was accepted, certainly not radicalism. Yet technological innovation proceeded apace.

The time has come when capitalistic democracy must face up to new horizons. These are now conceived in terms of the welfare state and the great society. If the age of scarcity is past, what kind of social texture do we want? Perhaps the stress will be more on planning and cooperation than on competition. If peace comes, the investment surplus will be enormous. How will it be absorbed? Leisure and standard of living must increase. What will be the effect of this on social patterns? Speculation along these lines is already beginning.

And so I turn to the third peak, Marxism and communism. It is [assuredly] not enough to cry 'totalitarianism' for it may aim at another base for democracy, what it calls a classless society. And how different is this in prinicple from Jacksonian Democracy which has been a motif in American society for a century and a third?

Marx was revolutionary in tone and rejected . . . easy harmony in human affairs . . . conflict and struggle had to be recognized. Possessors do not readily relinquish their privileges. . . . It is generally held that there was both a scientific and philosophical element in his thinking and a romantic, prophetic one. It is also generally granted that he underestimated the capacity of capitalism to make adjustments. . . .

But there was another possibility, grasped by Lenin and actualized by Lenin and his followers. Did not a breakdown caused by war make viable the establishment of another economic system? It was a daring step and a big price had to be paid for it. It was a sort of social mutation. . . . I think it will be granted that only the size of the U.S.S.R. enabled the experiment to be carried through. It is now the beneficiary of modern science and technology. What kind of social pattern will arise?

In some respects, Marxism is more akin to the temper of Platonism than to that of Lockeanism. But Marx turned to materialism rather than to idealism to a kind of historical materialism with Hegelian touches. I, myself, have argued for a more realistic and empirical type stressing novelty and levels. . . . The emphasis should be on humanism and on what one Englishman has called *gentling*. And there is this element in both Christianity and Buddhism.

What Marxism has in common with Platonism is the idea of a pattern which should be carried out at all costs. That is why Lenin has been compared to Plato's philosopher-king.

Well, there is the alternative . . . of exploratory progress. But it so often seems the case that the dominant class in society resists change. It is as though it has to be forced on them by such impersonal developments as science and technology.

The principle of triangulation in this social sense brings into relief insistent values and goals. And extrapolation gives us a sense of social forces and of stages in their approximation.

* * * * *

[Sellars insists on the recognition of the social forces at work and the need for discussion and dialogue. And he does recognize that there are distrusts and other social malignancies, and that you can only have dialogue if you have enough recognition of the realities of the present situation, of common goals and of the conditions for the attainment of these.] He concludes:

When I triangulate these days I find the situation very perplexing. There is a tendency in the United States to universalize its steps and to demand that they be repeated in the underdeveloped world. But it is seldom realized how complex this development was and what it involved. Many scholars argue that it would be better to have a mixed economy and a measure of diverse social experimentation. Could we, in this way, move between the extremes? If politics is the art of compromise, something like this could be worked out. Perhaps a reinvigorated United Nations could work out guiding lines.

* * * * *

What I recommend [above all] is a revitalization of education to make it a freer facing of reality. History books should . . . show that they [wars] were expressions of an, as yet, barbarous culture. I have a conviction that recognition in our culture of the actual human condition might produce a saner outlook. And here I believe that the United States and Soviet Russia might well meet, even if somewhat asymptotically. . . .

When I speak of a revitalization of education I have debates of this kind in mind: to take in science, art, and the world scene. This should . . . be . . . a continuing and informed dialogue stressing participation. Only then could we approach the conditions of a participative democracy.

ORIENTATION IN SOCIAL PHILOSOPHY

Looking at the present, I see social paths which, though divergent, may yet converge in this feature or that. I began in a *laissez-faire* age which ended in the Great Depression. We have to-day capitalistic democracy, mixed economies, and the communistic type of society. And all of these seem to be moving in the direction of what is vaguely called the welfare state.

In the United States, there is now a Keynesian, managerial type of economy with big business in the lead, working with the state. The corporations plan their enterprises and build up their capital. The stress is on management. The result is, in part, a consumer's society with stress on affluence. There has been too little concern with the poor and the alienated. Here I would supplement Galbraith with the Swedish Myrdal. Both, however, recognize that the private, or business, sector must be integrated with the public sector. How this can be done is the moot question, especially in the presence of militarism. An international, coordinating body seems very much needed.

The U.S.S.R. and its satellites represents a competing system. The stress here is on government ownership and centralized planning. The social thinker must study both systems as objectively as possible. Some hold that they are converging in stress on technology and on planning. But the social institutions have different patterns and motivations. And, unfortunately, this divergence has been historically mixed up with national and social antagonisms. There is an analogy here with religious wars. I fear the "cold war," as propagated in the United States, has this flavor. The United States is technologically radical but rather conservative socially. And its very economic strength has been a temptation.

I want to bring into the discussion the topic of what C. P. Snow calls the *two cultures,* the scientific and the humanistic. This clash, as I see it, holds for both capitalistic democracy and communism. There is a fear of a computerized future for both with loss of personal identity. Both Galbraith and Myrdal point to the need of *quality* in culture. And the whole history of philosophy gives the same emphasis. What is really satisfying in human life? Having always been somewhat of a socialist, I have kept this in mind.

Impersonality and militarism are the threats to the developed nations. The underdeveloped nations will find it hard to get a start in industrialization, especially with the danger of overpopulation at work.

Looking at all this, the philosopher must conclude that there is no natural harmony, no "unseen hand" of the Adam Smith persuasion. It is a difficult human adventure which may well go wrong. The philosopher can only seek to discern the wiser path. This he has attempted to do from the time of Plato. We must indulge in dialogues. These must be informed ones.

I have thought of myself as a *reflective radical,* looking to the future. In this sense, I have been leftist rather than rightest. That is, I stressed problems and their possible solutions. I had my eye on goals and the quality of society. I wanted to give meaning to human life and overcome any descent into absurdity.

I admit I cannot fully understand the "new left" except as a protest movement.

I turn now to the past. As Professor Warren indicates, I began to formulate my social and political ideas in the progressive era. I was a fellow in philosophy at Madison in the La Follette epoch. I suppose I picked up some ideas and attitudes then. At Michigan, I gave a course on socialist theory, studying the Fabians as well as Marx. My outlook, as Warren points out, was evolutionary and gradualistic. I published my book, *The Next Step in Democracy*, in 1916, a year before the Russian revolution. I was concerned with equities and experimentation. It was still the period of *laiser faire*, of automatic adjustment.

I find myself largely agreeing with Richard Hofstadter's historical analysis of the shift from the agrarian myth and populism to the cities and to the rise of muckraking and reform. The progressives were moralistic and rather formal. But corporations developed apace. Debs had his socialistic following but Wilson and the Great War put a stop to that. Then came the first stirring of the fear of communism. But with prosperity came what Walter Weyl called the "tired radicals." It required the Great Depression to start up social thinking again. And now attention swung to the New Deal, the aim of which was to start business going again. Keynes's ideas got a hearing. The state could no longer be a night-watchman. Naturally, I was vividly interested in all this. I thought there might well be some experiments in nationalization. But that was not to be. The recognition of the unions was, however, a new departure. After the Second World War came the cold war and the crusade against communism.

Its bad feature was the undercutting of constitutional rights. I did not, myself see communism as a possibility in the United States. But I was interested in its development in the U.S.S.R. Being a pluralist, I thought it quite possible that there could be two lines of socio-economic growth. It was militarism and war that I most feared.

And so I come back to the present. As I analyze the present, my interest would be in the welfare state and the public sector. The task here is to give *meaning to our culture*. Important as economic institutions are, they must be intertwined with social life as a whole. Here I would stress social imagination, the beautifying of the environment, learning to live together, city planning, a wiser sense of nature. Like Spinoza, I would stress the positive in life. This direction of endeavor might help to cut the roots of combativeness and militarism. Social philosophy must be at once realistic and idealistic.

I see this little planet spinning in space and marvel at its history. This is not a story-book tale but one of struggle and tragedy and accomplishment. Stubbornness mixed with kindliness will achieve much but intelligence must be added. Out of these ingredients should come wisdom. Thus I triangulate and extrapolate. It is obvious that I am concerned with participative democracy in the masses, and with the growth of international institutions. Patriotism is not enough. There must be resolution of conflicts. And this is made possible by some openness of mind and by some recognition that it is tactically wise to agree to disagree, and wait on time.*

THE PHILOSOPHY OF RELIGION

Introduction to Philosophy of Religion

Professor Sellars has been a student of the history and philosophy of religion since his undergraduate days at the University of Michigan.[1] Those days, we have noted, were followed by a year at Hartford Theological Seminary (1903-1904); then a year at Wisconsin (1904-1905) which brought him more clearly into the humanist tradition. His first publication on religion, *The Next Step in Religion*, came in 1918. This volume was sufficiently epochal to be rated by Hunecker as one of the two most notable books of the year. Ten years later came Sellars' *Religion Coming of Age;* then the *Humanist Manifesto* (1933) which he drafted for a group of humanist thinkers and leaders. This, in turn, was both preceded and

---

* This last paragraph is transposed from "Objectives and Priorities" to the summary on "Orientation in Social Philosophy."

[1] We have indicated in the Preface that he studied Semitics with Professor Craig at the University of Michigan, and Arabic at the Hartford Theological Seminary, and thereby became acquainted with the cultural character of religion.

followed by a grist of articles in clarification of humanism and its naturalistic interpretation of religion.[2] In 1947 he contributed a chapter, "Accept the Universe as a Going Concern," to *Religious Liberals Reply*,[3] and, in 1948, the chapter on "Naturalistic Humanism" for *Religion in the Twentieth Century*.[4] His most significant addition to his three earliest writings comes, I believe, in a volume which is still at press at the time of this editing; *Reflections on American Philosophy from Within*[5] contains as its final chapter a treatment of "Religious Existentialism" and of Hartshorne's Whiteheadeanism. All who are interested in Sellars' philosophy of religion are therefore advised to supplement the readings which follow with Chapter 11 of the *Reflections on American Philosophy from Within*. Chapter 10 on "The Human Situation and Existentialism" might well be read here also.

In the Introduction to Part IV, I posed a series of questions concerning Sellars' conception of religion which I regard it important to repeat with slight modification here: To what extent is religion pre-eminently personal? To what extent is religion the bulwark of specifically social values, as Stephen Pepper and numerous others contend it has been? In the holiness that religion espouses the holiness of moral ideals or of rigorous standards? Or is it the holiness of the numinous, the mysterium tremendum? Are there specifically religious values?

In his earlier writing Sellars appears as a modern, though essentially traditional, humanist. His distinction came, in *The Next Step in Religion*, with the first full American statement of a faith for scientists and scientifically oriented philosophers. The realistic bettering of the human condition is the positive meaning of religion. "The humanist finds his religious emotions expressed in a heightened sense of personal life and in a cooperative effort to promote social well-being."[6] The selection of his *Next Step in Religion* as a book of the year indicates its timeliness

---

[2] In *The New Humanist*, 1930, 1931, 1933, 1934.
[3] Edited by Henry Wieman, Boston, 1947.
[4] Edited by Vergilius Ferm, New York, The Philosophical Library.
[5] University of Notre Dame Press, 1969. (Hereinafter referred to as RAP.)
[6] *Humanist Manifesto*, Pt. No. 9.

and relevance to human interests. But man is an animal with a cosmic awareness and there is development in Sellars' humanism. *The Humanist Manifesto* expresses the vistas involved: religion represents the unchanging need of man to assess his life in the light of the far-flung nature of things.[7] And his treatment of religious existentialism discloses that wonder and awe, in addition to moral ideals, are facets of religious experience. "This universe in which we find ourselves is terrific in complexity and range."[8] But reflective man is concerned with more than feelings and attitudes; he is concerned with "foundations on which to build."[9] Hence, the need of delving into Sellars' treatment of Tillich, Niebuhr, Heidegger, Whitehead and others.

The Existentialist concern with "encounter'" and with "depth" requires clarifying. Depth concerns foundations: "Being-itself" Tillich calls it. But Tillich proceeds by some sort of "ontological Reason" to bypass the world around us to attain an objective logos—"all of which," states Sellars, "savors of romantic idealism." "I would, myself," he continues, "distinguish the practical and theoretical in a less ecstatic manner and would have the theoretical play back into the practical."[10] The sense of dependence, stressed by adherents of Schleiermacher, "I call a sense of realities." An adequate epistemology which relates directly to the world of our vital activities and an ontology which starts from this world and discovers what things it is capable of: these are the foundations of intellectually honest, effective religion.

We conclude with two brief excerpts which I have entitled "Cosmic Perspective": one from a chapter in *Religious Liberals Reply*; the other from the *Philosophy of Physical Realism*.

THE NEXT STEP IN RELIGION (1918)[*]

Introduction

... [A] new view of the universe and of man's place in it is forming. It is forming in the laboratories of scientists, the studies

---

[7] "Naturalistic Humanism" in V. Ferm (ed.), *Religion in the Twentieth Century* (1948), 418.
[8] *RAP*, ch. XI.
[9] *Ibid.*
[10] *Ibid.*
[*] New York, Macmillan, 1918, 1-10.

of thinkers, the congresses of social workers, the assemblies of reformers, the studios of artists and, even more quietly, in the circles of many homes. This new view is growing beneath the old as a bud grows beneath its covering, and is slowly pushing it aside. While the inherited outlook, still apparently so strong, is losing effectiveness and becoming a thing of conventions and phrases, the ideas and purposes which are replacing it possess the vigor and momentum of contact with the living tendencies and needs of the present.

Mankind grows away from its traditional beliefs as inevitably as does the boy or girl from childhood fancies, and often with much the same lack of realization. But the time is certain to come to both when the change is pressed home and there is need for interpretation and serious self-communing. At such a time, kindly—yet uncompromising and veracious—explanation of the nature and implications of the crisis is the course dictated by wisdom. Nothing can be more cruel, disorganizing, and, in a way, insulting than the attempt to harmonize what cannot in the long run be harmonized. The agony is then sure to be long drawn out and the strength of soul, given by fearlessness, is lost. I feel that the first law of personality is *spiritual courage*. Actions and methods founded on a doubt of this primary law lead to a blunting of the fine edge of the self, an injury greater than which can scarcely be conceived.

In this day of testing, when so few have been found lacking in courage and the capacity for self-sacrifice, it seems peculiarly fitting that spiritual values and beliefs be boldly thrown into the arena, there to prove themselves. In the years after the Great War, mankind must build its life afresh and it will be wisest to see that the foundation is a sound one. And, as a matter of social psychology, I doubt that a people which is unwilling to look carefully to the framework of its social and spiritual edifice can build a noble mansion. Mechanical efficiency and cleverness will not be enough for this task of spiritual creation. We must find lasting values around which to build a humane life. And this, also is, a kind of warfare. Some have expressed to me a doubt whether America is prepared for this effort at reconstruction of a basic, yet intangible, sort. I have hopes, although not blind ones. I refuse to take the vulgarities and ignorances of popular evangelists as completely diagnostic of America's soul.

In the following pages, which are devoted to a clear statement of the new view of man and nature which, in its essentials, has come to stay, I shall act according to this law of personality, to wit, spiritual courage. I shall explain the spiritualized naturalism to which we are ascending in the same spirit that the scientist presents his facts—impersonally, calmly, and simply. . . .

The new view of the universe is founded upon, influenced by, and has for its necessary setting, the exact knowledge which the various special sciences, mental as well as physical, have been accumulating. This knowledge is rounding into something of the nature of a whole whose interpretation does not admit of doubt. Incomplete in detail though his knowledge be, man is no longer in the dark as to the main features of the world and his own origin and destiny. He knows that he is an inhabitant of a small planet in one of the many solar systems of the stellar universe, that he is the product of an age-long evolution in which variation and survival have been the chief methods of advance, that his mind as well as his body has its natural ancestry. While it will always remain a wonder, so to speak, that there is a universe in which and to which we awaken, it is equally certain that the only sensible thing to do is to seek to find out its character and laws. Is it not like exploring the chambers and corridors of a house in which one shall live for a stated period?

As a matter of fact, man has always been curious about his world. Yet before he hit upon the proper methods of investigation, he could only guess and dream about it, under the sway of hopes and fears which too easily threw themselves like gigantic shadows before him. The fire of his untrained intelligence was feeble and unpenetrating and, so, distorted the world which it dimly revealed. The result was what must be called the older religious view of the world—a view which saw personal and super-personal agency at the heart of things. This primitive interpretation of the world we shall be led to criticize, but, in so doing, we shall be the servants of truth and of a more adult spirituality.

It is not surprising that the patiently acquired knowledge,

obtained by science, philosophy and a matured human wisdom, has been found to conflict with the first interpretation of the world. The recognition of this conflict dates back now some centuries—the warfare between science and religion also has its history—but each generation has seen the addition made of some new element to the clash which is leading man to a new view of the world.

What is striking about the present situation is the increase of the positive elements in the outlook which is forming in men's minds. In the past, the traditionalist had some justification in speaking of the opposed ideas as largely negative. What positive doctrine there was in the physical science which theology had to meet, to its discomfort, had only an indirect bearing upon life. But the nineteenth century was the witness of a distinct revolution. . . . I do not refer merely to the fact that the idea of evolution was applied to man. That was prophetic and strategic rather than revolutionary. It symbolized the passage of science from the periphery to the center, from the outlying regions of the universe to man's very self. All the time, however, a new perspective had been arising in man's interests and values. The possibilities and needs of this life were replacing the dream of another life in another world. A busy concern with the things of this world was everywhere evident. Man was seeking to master his environment.

During the first stage of this revolution, the industrial and political changes were the most prominent. A change in the instrumentalities of life, physical, economic and political, occupied men's thoughts to a larger degree than ever before. But as the nineteenth century circled to the twentieth, deeper notes became audible. Humanitarianism, constructive reform, social democracy became the watchwords of the day. I do not think that it has yet been clearly realized how completely these new aims and interests fit in with the results of science and yet pass beyond them to the service of human values. The truth seems to be that, by an imperceptible process, new values and hopes have been replacing the traditional ones, and that these values and aims both find themselves in harmony with the new knowledge and rest upon it.

In spite of the conflict between the rising view of man and nature and the traditional religious conception, there is yet, I believe, a profound continuity in the genuinely spiritual achievements of humanity. It is a pity to be so ridden by the new that the noble in the old is forgotten. Tenderness and love, however obscured at times by formalism and bigotry, owe much to their nurture by Christianity. Hence, the deeper and truer interpretation of all past movements regards them as varying expressions of humanity's growth in social and mental stature. There is, in other words, no real discontinuity in human history. The only difference is, that the dynamic of social conditions and intellectual heritage has varied.

But this acknowledged continuity does not preclude that presence of genuine and effective newness which is revolutionary in its effects. *The perspective, intention, and elements of religion are about to alter.* In the following pages, I shall argue that the attachments of past religion were determined by a mythological, and essentially magical, idea of man's environment. Such attitudes and expectations as prayer, ritual, worship, immortality, providence, are expressions of the prescientific view of the world. But as man partly outgrows, partly learns to reject, the primitive thought of the world, this perspective and these elements will drop from religion. That this alteration has, in surprisingly large measure, already taken place can be seen from the following excerpts from the writings of the best known American authority on Church History: "Traditional Christian ideas, in fact, are undergoing extensive transformation as a result of the new social emphasis. The individualism of evangelicalism, with its primary concern for the salvation of the individual soul, is widely discredited. The old ascetic ideal is everywhere giving way to the social. Instead of holding themselves aloof from the world Christians are throwing themselves into it and striving to reform it. Holiness in the traditional sense of abstinence from sin is less highly valued than it was. The test of virtue is more and more coming to be the social test. The virtuous man is he who makes his influence tell for the improvement of society. Personal probity and uprightness, dissociated from the active service of one's fellows, is frequently regarded to-day as 'mere morality' was by the Evangelicals. As virtue had value to them only in union with and subordination to piety, so without the spirit of service personal morality seems to many a modern social reformer a mere empty husk."[1] Obviously, the center of religious gravity has altered tremendously from what it was in the Victorian Age. We are on the brink of a new period, the period of a realistic, and yet spiritual, social democracy.

"But," I will be asked, "do you advocate a religion of humanity? That is an old effort weighed in the balance and found wanting." Comte's reform was, in a way, premature. Society had not developed enough to give his effort a concrete basis. But, more than this, his mistake was that he did not see that the elements of religion, as well as its perspective, must be altered. Humanity is not an object to be worshiped. The very attitude and implications of worship must be relinquished. In their place must be put the spiritually founded virtue of loyalty to those efforts and values which elevate human beings and give a quality of nobility and significance to our human life here and now.

The positive note of the present work can now be given in a few words: *Religion is loyalty to the values of life.* The idea of the spiritual must be broadened and humanized to include all those purposes, experiences and activities which express man's nature. The spiritual must be seen to be the fine flower of living, which requires no other sanctions than its own inherent worth and appeal. We must outgrow the false notion that religion is inseparable from supernatural objects, and that the spiritual is something alien to man which must be forced upon him from the outside. *The spiritual is man at his best, man loving, daring, creating, fighting loyally and courageously for causes dear to him.* Religion must be concrete instead of formal, and catholic in its count of values. Wherever there is loyal endeavor, the presence of the spiritual must freely be acknowledged. It would seem to follow that religion will have objects only in the sense of purposes to fulfill. It will no longer have need of a special view of the world.

---
[1] McGiffert, *The Rise of Modern Religious Ideas*, p. 272.

The religion of the past has had much to say about salvation. Salvation was only too often something which happened to a man from outside. It was something capricious and uncontrollable like sudden fortune. Let us see what the religion of the present with its more realistic conception of life has to say about salvation. I have written in the book as follows: "Only that soul is saved which is worth saving, and the being worth saving is its salvation. Salvation is no magical hocus-pocus external to the reach and timbre of a man; it is the loyal union of a man with those values of life which have come within his ken." Whatever mixture of magic, fear, ritual, and adoration religion may have been in man's early days upon this earth, it is now increasingly, and henceforth must be, that which concerns his contact with the duties and possibilities of life. Such salvation is an achievement which has personal and social conditions. . . .

The personal conditions of spiritual life are sanity, health, and a capacity to be fired by consuming purposes. No one can be greatly saved who has not a soul capable of being touched in some measure by what is sterling and significant. But one of the discoveries of democracy is the wide distribution of this sensitiveness. The spiritual is not something painful, but it is something which concerns the quality of human life.

The social conditions of salvation are just as necessary. They are the presence of institutions and arrangements which give opportunity to the individual to develop himself. The individual must have a certain amount of leisure and a chance for a vital education. He should have some contact with beautiful things and the stimulus of association with great causes. A healthy and sane society makes possible healthy and sane individuals. It is especially desirable that society put its emphasis on the right things. If it is permissible to speak of society's salvation, we would say that it consists in the wise relation of means to ends, the subordination of the economic side of life to the moral, intellectual and artistic activities. A society which does not order itself in this way is called materialistic; and such a society is certain to contain numberless individuals who live at a far lower spiritual level than they should. It is the very nature of religion to condemn this falling short of loyalty to the finer values of life.

We have said that religion must be catholic in its count of values. Moral souls may still be comparatively starved souls. One of the great mistakes religion has made in the past has been this very lack of sympathy for values of all kinds. For this very reason, religion has often displayed a certain narrowness and harshness. Its loyalty has frequently been a one-sided loyalty which prided itself on its asceticism. But the day of an irrational asceticism has passed. Intensity is good, but intensity and breadth are better still. A humane religion will preach loyalty to many values, harmonized together by the work of a concrete reason and a living art. When religion did not consider itself of this world, it was passive and acquiescent toward many features of human life. But a truer idea of the nature of the spiritual, united with a decay of the old supernaturalistic sanctions, will change all that. Religion will become active and militant, intensely concerned with everything human, a loyal enthusiasm for all the significant phases of life. It will cease to be a matter of taboos, of ritual, of rather conventional routine and become a spirit of vigorous search for whatever elevates and ennobles human beings in their day of life. Into the service of such a religion reason and art will gladly enter.

NATURALIZING THE SPIRITUAL (1928)*

The great need of the present is a new perspective. And such a new perspective will not come without hard thought and spiritual sincerity. It is my aim to show what aid philosophy can render in this crisis.

The new perspective which I shall suggest is indicated by the heading of this chapter; it is the naturalizing of the spiritual. This involves a two-fold operation, the redefinition of the spiritual and the enlargement of the conception of the natural.

That the conception of the natural must be enlarged is obvious. I shall be asked by my startled readers how naturalism can cope with the spiritual. Surely, they will say, man has a spiritual life which is real and significant, and how can this be explained and dealt with on the basis of a naturalistic philosophy? We have been told again and again that such an

---
* *Religion Coming of Age* (New York, Macmillan Co., 1928), 237-254.

achievement is impossible. My reply is simple. The new naturalism differs markedly from the old. For it, man is a living soul sensitive to values, and truth, goodness and beauty are expressions of man's aspirations rather than supersensible realities alien to his nature. This means that we must think of the spiritual as rooted in man's nature and not as alien and introduced in some miraculous fashion from above. We must redefine the spiritual.

Enlarging the Conception of the Natural

To philosophy, naturalism is a very old affair. What has happened of late is the rise of a perspective which bids fair to remove the objections previously urged against it. Naturalism is rounding out, becoming more plastic and delicate. A good way to bring this alteration into relief is to show the advance in our ideas of evolution since the days of Darwinism. I have in mind particularly the interpretation of the moral.

The distinctive feature of Darwinism in ethics was the emphasis upon the struggle for existence and the survival-value of certain virtues. That is, the concepts of biology were carried over to the field of ethics with the minimum of alteration. And this is what biologists still tend to do. They seem to have little conception of the distinctive nature of the social sciences and of the factors which enter into human institutions and human culture. They think of man as an animal and not as a human being, whereas man is a human being developed by society on the potentialities of a gifted animal. Let me illustrate. In my own university a very able biologist recently gave a lecture entitled, *The Religion of a Biologist,* in which he declared that the chief end of man is to produce healthy offspring. But, surely, to reduce religion to eugenics shows a sad lack of appreciation of the complexity of human values. Has the individual nothing to aim at but careful reproduction? What makes human life worth while as a going concern? And if it is not significant in itself, why continue it however carefully? The point I wish to make is that philosophy working hand in hand with sociology has grasped what is distinctive about human life. It has realized that personality is in large measure a social product rooted in the social history of a group. We must add social naturalism to biological naturalism before we get the proper perspective.

Perhaps I had better be even more specific in these matters. What biology deals with is organic structure and general capacities. Thus it studies the general inheritance of man as an animal and tries to decipher the laws of this inheritance and what conditions went to the moulding of man. It can deal directly only with what is inherited. And in the early days of evolutionism too much stress was probably laid upon the struggle for existence and too little upon internal variation and its laws

Now morality is an affair of moral sentiments, judgments and intelligent choice. We distinguish between conventional morality and reflective morality. The first is the morality of the group; the second, the modification introduced by reflection and personal insight. But is it possible to explain either conventional morality or reflective morality in terms of biology? Stress as much as you will the fact that conventional morality is *conditioned* by human endowments, you yet cannot explain morality in detail in this fashion. Why, for example, are the conventions of an African tribe different from those of the natives of Thibet? And these, again, different from the mode of life of the New Yorker? No; biology is quite insufficient. Morality is a social, historical phenomenon. To understand it in any measure you must enter the realm of history. The anthropologist, the geographer, the economist, the historian, the sociologist must work hand in hand with the psychologist and the philosopher. Morality is primarily a social product, an historical achievement. Biology, aided by psychology, may tell you much about instincts but it cannot tell you about human sentiments and social standards.

The new naturalism has added a social level to the biological level of the nineteenth century. It recognizes that man's spiritual life is largely an historical achievement. Thus it is a naturalism which apexes in social humanism. The gap between man and the dumb brute is not minimized nor maximized but understood. The modern thinker knows the part played by language and education in raising the new-born child to the level of humanity. Its capacities are played upon and drawn out. What it has taken many centuries for mankind to learn is presented to it in its perfected form. The very environment is moulded to reflect human plans and purposes into the child's mind. The family, the school, the playground, the church, are the instruments of the spiritualization of the child. And all this procedure is just as natural in its way as biological evolution, itself, presupposing it but not reducible to it.

One reason why good biographies are so fascinating is because they show us the growth of a living soul. First of all, they usually try to suggest to us the hereditary capacities of the individual. The stock is possibly adventurous and strong-willed. Or it is imaginative and given to dreaming. There is, at most, some suggestion found for what the hero or the heroine is to do in after life. And then comes the social medium and the traditions of the country. Bit by bit, we follow the child through the events of his infancy. We are told that the mother had a strong influence or that a teacher fired the ambitions of the child. The soul which we are studying grows before our eyes from year to year until we are in the presence of a Napoleon, a Mirabeau, a Shelley, a Lincoln. The babe has become a man with ideas, feelings, aspirations, trained abilities. It is this transformation into which careful biography introduces us.

Thanks to the stimulus given by Freud, Adler and Jung, the dynamics of human souls is better understood now than in the past. We know how the inability of some children to speak plainly handicaps their first adventure into school life and lays the foundation for a marked sensitiveness which only careful handling on the part of parent and teacher can prevent from becoming morbid. The desire for affection, the desire to excel—desires which are so natural to human beings—may lead to actions which bring the individual into conflict with society. Whence maladjustment and tragedy. Clearly, personality is a growth of a most complex sort. There are repressions and expressions, sublimations and distortions. And so after many years our souls are created within us. . . .

Man is an animal but he is . . . an animal moulded to an astonishing degree by what has been done in the past by the social groups into which he is born. Culture and civilization are terms essential to his understanding. I do not for a moment wish to defend the anti-evolutionist, but I do think that the bareness of the biologist's presentation did not soften the blow he dealt to the justifiable pride of man. It is time for the sociologist and philosopher to speak up.

Actually, then, a man is the heir of all the ages. He is the heir of the poets of the past; their songs sing in his heart. He is the heir of the artists; their creative power has beautified the world and enlarged his vision. He is the heir of the inventors; his sense of mastery comes from them. He is the heir of the saints; their nobility and tenderness have quieted his passions and made him sensitive to suffering. He is the heir of the thinkers; his power of looking before and after comes from them. And it is all this inheritance which lifts him immeasurably above the poor, helpless brutes which he is exterminating or reducing to servants. There they are, akin to him in some degree and yet unable to climb the heights to which brain and hand and social evolution have lifted him.

The new naturalism, in short, is a social and spiritual naturalism as well as a biological and inorganic naturalism. It seeks to do justice to all the levels in nature that exist and refuses to grade down actual differences into the blind motions of inert particles. And, fortunately, physical science, itself, has penetrated so deeply into nature at last that it has seen the error of the old, simplified mechanical schema which once fascinated its imagination. Everywhere there is activity and integration. And philosophy, holding to its perennial task of comprehensive vision, sees that man's spiritual life is a product of a complex and delicate social evolution into the details of which the social sciences are only now beginning to gain insight. The new naturalism is enlarged to include society, human souls and the spiritual.

Redefining the Spiritual

We have argued that society is the home of the spiritual. But, without interpretation, this statement might easily be misleading. There is in it no intention to glorify the *status quo* or to flatter individuals or special groups. It does not mean that the spiritual is equally distributed among the members of society. What it does mean is that the spiritual is an expression of human life as it develops in society. Here are its conditions and medium.

Another way, perhaps, of bringing out what I have in mind is to point out that the spiritual is a term for activities concerned with the true, the good and the beautiful in all their manifestations, however humble. It is human activity which alone is spiritual. In this regard we must think of it, as we are beginning to do of mind, as not a thing but a function. Seen in this light, it will be quickly realized that it is absurd to contrast the spiritual with the physical. The proper opposition is with those activities which lie below the level of the spiritual. Thus we hardly feel it meaningful to speak of the activities of the lobster as spiritual. He may be a vigorous lobster active in his pursuit of food and energetic in his powers of reproduction, but we feel that the texture of this activity does not deserve to be called spiritual. The spiritual emerges when there is intelligence of a fairly high order, a sense of right and wrong, an ability to set up standards, a drive for creation in art and in social relations, a wealth of imagination.

Still another source of confusion is due to a judgment of valuation within the spiritual. The higher rejects the lower and declares it to be unspiritual, fleshly, worldly. Within the realm of the spiritual struggle thus goes on. Qualitative oppositions arise in mode of life and human effort. Our desires may clash with our better judgment and with our more permanent valuations. But, surely, it is clear that we have here a phase of the dynamics of the living soul. The self is an achievement which maintains and advances itself by effort. It seeks harmony and happiness. It relates and rejects. It revalues all values and sets itself new objectives; or it may settle down into habits already established.

This redefinition of the spiritual brings us inevitably to the subject of asceticism. In the old days when man was becoming self-conscious and creating a soul of whose moods and decisions he was aware, he thought of himself in terms of the cosmological dualisms which his reflection upon life and death and good and evil has produced. Recall the fact that he was led to divide man into soul and body and to classify the powers around him as good and evil. The good powers were those of a social nature, ready to enter into compacts with man, those who had the same ideals that he had and aimed at justice and holiness. The evil powers were those in opposition to man, malignant, cruel, destructive, at war with the good powers. Such an interpretation of the universe was inevitable for man with his keen sense of personal agency. The world became for him a stage in which gods fought with demons; and, with the growth of political organization, this disorderly warfare was transformed into an epic battle between God and Satan. And gradually man's own ethical struggle as it became self-conscious seized upon the distinction between soul and body and made these the agents in a corresponding struggle. God was to the soul as Satan was to the body; and the body was conceived as a thing of evil. What shall we say of all this? Surely if our argument holds, it must be regarded as magnificent mythology. . . . The whole situation must be reanalyzed. In so far as historical Christianity has reflected in its ethics an asceticism founded on a cosmological dualism between the body and the spirit as two kinds of realities opposite in nature, it must be reformed. Such asceticism must be condemned as a superstition. The only justifiable asceticism is that of intelligent inhibition and control in the service of a wise and temperate life. There is nothing in our nature which is intrinsically unspiritual.

* * * * *

It would be unjust to asceticism not to point out that it had a partial justification as a program in the life of the world in which it arose. It served in a measure as a protest. But, nevertheless, it was unfortunate that the protest did not have a better theoretical foundation and did not build upon something positive and human. To master pleasure by stirring objectives is the better and more intelligent way, as Spinoza well pointed out and as modern psychology has demonstrated.

To redefine the spiritual is to show it as an expression of active human life. That is the spiritual which appeals to man as significant. And in our highly developed social life with its rich spread of interest and activity the spiritual is manifold. All things of good repute are spiritual. And in the less ascetic parts of the New Testament this is recognized. Nevertheless, Christianity as an historical movement has been afraid of the world. Its perspective did not teach it how to direct and guide human life here and now to human achievement and happiness. We must not blame the churches too severely, for they had neither the technique nor the purpose to do this positive work. In truth, no human institution has adopted social advancement as a program. We are still drifting and muddling along. It is only a new religion, which will revalue many of our values, that can help us lift human life to a higher level. . . .

Naturalizing Religion

Having once naturalized the spiritual, it is an easy step to naturalize religion. The life of society absorbs the one as it does the other. Religion is now seen as an expression of the human spirit, always reflecting its cosmic perspective and its objectives. In this, it is like art and literature, with which it is akin. The breath of the time-spirit is always blowing upon it.

The very choice which confronts religious people to-day drives home the fact of the intrinsic relativity of religion. As I see the present situation, then, there are three lines of interpretation struggling for supremacy. The traditional view takes theism seriously and builds upon it along the lines of historical Christianity. The illusion view maintains that such an outlook is inseparable from religion but that it is obvious to the modern thinker that this perspective is essentially illusory. The humanist view, which seeks to dig down to the proper function of religion, sees it as an expression of man's struggle to further his values.

We have already dealt at such length with the cosmic perspective of the traditional view that it would be useless to discuss it again. It has seemed to us that the old outlook is untenable. Those who hold it are, even to-day, divided against themselves. The result is an inner suspicion of insincerity. Moreover, those who can hold this older view are almost inevitably out of touch with the new knowledge and the new morality.

The illusion theory of religion holds that, in religion, people express their day-dreams and all sorts of desires which are struggling for birth in their souls. We want to ignore this world, turn our backs upon it, deny it. We try to lose our reality-feeling or transfer it to an ideal world. Religion is, then, like poetry, of the stuff of dreams; only people can fool themselves because of the social support they receive.

That there is a measure of truth in this theory there can be no doubt. Men are by nature dramatists and artists. And, in traditional religion, the desires of social groups are, as it were, projected on an immense canvas. But religion has always been more than this. It has expressed the theory of the time. The religious person has not always been a day-dreamer. He has often been active and militant. Thus the Christian has fought for the right as he has seen it, encouraged by the feeling that God was on his side. Traditional religion has been a mixture of day-dream and intellectual belief with moral purpose.

It is the contention of the humanist that the heart of religion, as we study it through the ages, is a struggle for the preservation of values. At first, these values were elementary and crude; but they became more complex and refined as civilization advanced. As long as man interpreted the universe in personal terms and as long as man felt essentially dependent on the Powers he felt around him, religion possessed a perspective and a technique of the traditional sort. What is happening now is that this perspective and its technique are vanishing. Dependence upon nature is giving way to a feeling of control. And, where control stops, courage and resignation begin. Religion is self-conscious, human life functioning in the face of its problems. It is the setting up of objectives and courage in their pursuit.

If the humanist is correct, religion is not inseparable from *Aberglaube* or over-belief. We are just entering another culture, and the old culture with its perspective still sings in our minds and hearts. I venture to prophesy that a hundred years from now, if the word religion be still retained as valuable, it is this humanistic outlook that will stand out. Cosmic perspective as it impinges on human life will be its theme and furnish the continuity with the past. A man's religion will be his imaginative realization of life.

My thesis is, that religion is something larger and more

significant than what we have been told it was. Human life demands interpretation and vision if it is to secure unity, reasonableness, and passion; and is not such interpretation of the very essence of religion? If so, religion is as natural as human living itself. It is not something coming in from outside in a supernatural way. To some, it will be a philosophy of life; to others, a moral perspective; to still others, a code and loyalties. May we not say, then, that the very indefiniteness and conflict of objectives which we note around us to-day is a symptom of the inadequacy of religious traditions to the needs of the present? Is not the great lack of our times a religion adequate to our culture and its possibilities? We need, as never before, social and personal vision and a sense of human values. An inadequate religion has done us much harm.

To call traditional Christianity an inadequate religion will startle those who are dominated by mystical, and dramatic, personal loyalties. But we have seen that Christianity was *primarily* a salvation-religion with a supernatural perspective. This is not to deny the tremendous value and significance of an ethical attitude which it contained. The portrait of Jesus has been its ethical strength. Historically true in detail or not, it yet presented under high sanctions, to the imagination of the West, an ideal whose spirit was love and gentleness. And this note has been recurrent in the history of Christianity. In our humanitarian age it has sounded more and more loudly. But, when we look deeply into the situation, we realize that this element in Christianity is quite separable from the supernatural framework which it was given. And, be it said to the honour of human nature, the same note was struck by religio-ethical leaders from China to Greece. We are in touch with what Professor Cooley calls human-nature values. Love is a social bond. As nobly spiritual, it means imaginative sympathy.

The Christian tradition is a spiritual one. It has been creative of much good in the world. But the point is that it is just one of the aspects of man's creative, spiritual life. It needs supplementation. Its supernaturalism has given it too much pride, held it too much aloof from other spiritual movements. Love by itself easily becomes sentimental and ineffective. And the salvation-tradition of Christianity with its emphasis upon an afterlife worked in the direction of selfish concern with the safety of one's own soul. Nor is this all. Man's spiritual life needs breadth if it is to be healthy. Art, science, statesmanship are activities of immense import, and there was in Christianity, as a going concern, too little interest in social creation. It arose among the humble in a pre-scientific age and in a people knowing little of art and thwarted in their national life. The intellectual perspective which it inherited as a religion made it suspicious, if not hostile, to these genuine things of man's abiding, earthly life. All this is a tragedy which we cannot ignore because our life has suffered from it. Christianity will not be adequate as a religion until it conquers its past limitations and is hospitable to all aspects of the human spirit. When it is reborn to the world of art the world of mind, to the world of creative human endeavour, then and then alone will it be adequate. As it is, we cannot but register our opinion as a philosopher that evangelical Christainity has never sufficiently freed itself from this too thin, spiritual perspective. This is what has made its inadequate. An adequate religion must be full-blooded and alive to all domains of the spiritual life of man. It must yea-say human endeavour.

* * * * *

To the humanist, then, with his social naturalism, man's spiritual life is like a mighty stream to which there are many tributaries. It is said that Erasmus put Socrates in the calendar of his saints. *Sancta Socrate, ora pro nobis.* The modern man who is spiritually alive has many saints in his calendar. Human living produces ever new vistas. The artist is born again to see the beauty in Rembrandt and Beethoven. The statesman gets inspiration from Lincoln and Washington. The philosopher draws renewed courage from the work of Aristotle and Plato. And I have no doubt that, in every line of life, the spiritual torch is thus kept burning. All creators enrich man's heritage. . . . To create is to reveal. The things of the spirit are made in the tension of living and can only so be retained. . . .

A HUMANIST MANIFESTO (1933)*

The time has come for widespread recognition of the radical

---
* R. W. Sellars, *et al.,* in *The New Humanist,* VI, 3 (1933), 1-4.

changes in religious beliefs throughout the modern world. The time is past for mere revision of traditional attitudes. Science and economic change have disrupted the old beliefs. Religions the world over are under the necessity of coming to terms with new conditions created by a vastly increased knowledge and experience. In every field of human activity, the vital movement is now in the direction of a candid and explicit humanism. In order that religious humanism may be better understood we, the undersigned, desire to make certain affirmations which we believe the facts of our contemporary life demonstrate.

There is great danger of a final, and we believe fatal, identification of the word *religion* with doctrines and methods which have lost their significance and which are powerless to solve the problem of human living in the Twentieth Century. Religions have always been means for realizing the highest values of life. Their end has been accomplished through the interpretation of the total environing situation (theology or world view), the sense of values resulting therefrom (goal or ideal), and the technique (cult), established for realizing the satisfactory life. A change in any of these factors results in alteration of the outward forms of religion. This fact explains the changefulness of religions through the centuries. But through all changes religion itself remains constant in its quest for abiding values, an inseparable feature of human life.

Today man's larger understanding of the universe, his scientific achievements, and his deeper appreciation of brotherhood, have created a situation which requires a new statement of the means and purposes of religion. Such a vital, fearless, and frank religion capable of furnishing adequate social goals and personal satisfactions may appear to many people as a complete break with the past. While this age does owe a vast debt to the traditional religions, it is none the less obvious that any religion that can hope to be a synthesizing and dynamic force for today must be shaped for the needs of this age. To establish such a religion is a major necessity of the present. It is a responsibility which rests upon this generation. We therefore affirm the following:

First: Religious humanists regard the universe as self-existing and not created.

Second: Humanism believes that man is a part of nature and that he has emerged as the result of a continuous process.

Third: Holding an organic view of life, humanists find that the traditional dualism of mind and body must be rejected.

Fourth: Humanism recognizes that man's religious culture and civilization, as clearly depicted by anthropology and history, are the product of a gradual development due to his interaction with his natural environment and with his social heritage. The individual born into a particular culture is largely molded by that culture.

Fifth: Humanism asserts that the nature of the universe depicted by modern science makes unacceptable any supernatural or cosmic guarantees of human values. Obviously humanism does not deny the possibility of realities as yet undiscovered, but it does insist that the way to determine the existence and value of any and all realities is by means of intelligent inquiry and by the assessment of their relation to human needs. Religion must formulate its hopes and plans in the light of the scientific spirit and method.

Sixth: We are convinced that the time has passed for theism, deism, modernism, and the several varieties of "new thought."

Seventh: Religion consists of those actions, purposes, and experiences which are humanly significant. Nothing human is alien to the religious. It includes labor, art, science, philosophy, love, friendship, recreation—all that is in its degree expressive of intelligently satisfying human living. The distinction between the sacred and the secular can no longer be maintained.

Eighth: Religious humanism considers the complete realization of human personality to be the end of man's life and seeks its development and fulfillment in the here and now. This is the explanation of the humanist's social passion.

Ninth: In place of the old attitudes involved in worship and prayer the humanist finds his religious emotions expressed in a heightened sense of personal life and in a cooperative effort to promote social well-being.

Tenth: It follows that there will be no uniquely religious emotions and attitudes of the kind hitherto associated with belief in the supernatural.

Eleventh: Man will learn to face the crises of life in terms of his knowledge of their naturalness and probability. Reasonable and manly attitudes will be fostered by education and supported by custom. We assume that humanism will take the path of social and mental hygiene and discourage-sentimental and unreal hopes and wishful thinking.

Twelfth: Believing that religion must work increasingly for joy in living, religious humanists aim to foster the creative in man and to encourage achievements that add to the satisfactions of life.

Thirteenth: Religious humanism maintains that all associations and institutions exist for the fulfillment of human life. The intelligent evaluation, transformation, control, and direction of such associations and institutions with a view to the enhancement of human life is the purpose and program of humanism. Certainly religious institutions, their ritualistic forms, ecclesiastical methods, and communal activities must be reconstituted as rapidly as experience allows, in order to function effectively in the modern world.

Fourteenth: The humanists are firmly convinced that existing acquisitive and profit-motivated society has shown itself to be inadequate and that a radical change in methods, controls, and motives must be instituted. A socialized and cooperative economic order must be established to the end that the equitable distribution of the means of life be possible. The goal of humanism is a free and universal society in which people voluntarily and intelligently cooperate for the common good. Humanists demand a shared life in a shared world.

Fifteenth and last: We assert that humanism will: (a) affirm life rather than deny it; (b) seek to elicit the possibilities of life, not flee from it; and (c) endeavor to establish the conditions of a satisfactory life for all, not merely for the few. By this positive *morale* and intention humanism will be guided, and from this perspective and alignment the techniques and efforts of humanism will flow.

So stand the theses of religious humanism. Though we consider the religious forms and ideas of our fathers no longer adequate, the quest for the good life is still the central task for mankind. Man is at last becoming aware that he alone is responsible for the realization of the world of his dreams, that he has within himself the power for its achievement. He must set intelligence and will to the task.

COSMIC PERSPECTIVE

Yes, man is *in* nature. Nature is his home and area of life and of competence. Let the artist and poet speak out here. Even music and language are inseparable from vibrations. And yet man is himself—not a *part,* merely, but an agent, dreamer, chooser and thinker. Let the existentialism of Kierkegaard be enlarged and made realistic. Aesthetics and ethics? Yes. Religion? Yes. But let it be a religion which courageously looks this-ward at man's inescapable task and opportunity. That, I take it, is the next step in religion. A cosmic view and a planetary view, a social view and an intrinsically personal view. These must be woven into a well-evidenced, and constantly tested, perspective.[1]

All the ontological categories apply to man. He is a creature of time, space and substance. And yet within this immense and inescapable framework man has his unique and specialized capacities and endeavors. He is not only a knower but also an agent and an eager desirer of good things. And this means that he is alive and passionate. It is to the poet that the philosopher must turn to gain again after his journeys in the abstract the sense of creative agency and decision. After his long apprenticeship the academic man may well cry out with Faust in the moment of his felt isolation that theory is gray. And yet it is not gray; it is of the very essence of poetry. Who better than he can appreciate the Testament of Beauty or feel the full power and firm control of chiselled lines.[2]

> Man born of desire
> Cometh out of the night,
> A wandering spark of fire,

---

[1] Excerpt from Roy Wood Sellars, "Accept the Universe as a Going Concern," in *Religious Liberals Reply,* Henry N. Wieman, editor (Beacon Press, 1947), pp. 171-172.

[2] *The Philosophy of Physical Realism,* New York, Russell & Russell, pp. 449-50.

A lonely word of eternal thought
Echoing in chance and forgot.
He seeth the sun,
He calleth the stars by name,
He saluteth the flowers—
Wonders of land and sea,
The mountain towers
Of ice and air
He seeth, and calleth them fair:
Then he hideth his face;—
Whence he came to pass away
Where all is forgot,
Unmade—lost for aye
With the things that are not.[3]

---

[3] Bridges, *Ode to Music*.

Bibliography of the Writings of Roy Wood Sellars*

Books

Critical Realism. Chicago, Rand-McNally & Co., 1916. x + 283 pp.
The Next Step in Democracy. New York, Macmillan, 1916. 272 pp.
The Essentials of Logic. Boston, Houghton, Mifflin Co., 1917. 343 pp.
The Essentials of Philosophy. New York, Macmillan, 1917. x + 301 pp.
The Next Step in Religion. New York, Macmillan, 1918. 225 pp.
Essays in Critical Realism (co-author). London, Macmillan, 1920. ix + 244 pp.
Evolutionary Naturalism. Chicago, Open Court Publishing Co., 1922. 343 pp.
The Principles and Problems of Philosophy. New York, Macmillan, 1926. xiv + 517 pp.
Religion Coming of Age. (In the series: Philosophy for the Layman). New York, Macmillan, 1928. xiv + 293 pp.
The Philosophy of Physical Realism. New York, Macmillan, 1932. xiv + 487 pp.
Philosophy for the Future: Quest of Modern Materialism. (Co-author with V. J. McGill and Marvin Farber.) New York, Macmillan, 1949, xiv + 657 pp.

Contributions to Books

Essays in Critical Realism, London, 1920. Contributor of the chapter "Knowledge and its Categories." Pp. 187-219.
Philosophy Today, ed. Edward L. Schaub, Chicago and London, 1928. Contributor of the chapter "Current Realism." Pp. 19-36.
An Anthology of Recent Philosophy, ed. Daniel S. Robinson. New York. 1929. Contributor of the chapter "Current Realism" (re-printed from *Philosophy Today*). Pp. 279-290.
Contemporary American Philosophy, ed. G. P. Adams and W. P. Montague. New York, 1930. Vol. 11. Contributor of the chapter "Realism, Naturalism, and Humanism." Pp. 261-285.

---

* Compilation of this bibliography was greatly facilitated by the aid of Professor R. W. Sellars, Professor R. M. Chisholm, and Miss Margaret Smith, Chief Reference Librarian of The University of Michigan Library. Gerald E. Myers compiler, PPR, XVI (1954).

The Development of American Philosophy, ed. W. G. Muelder and Laurence Sears. Cambridge, Mass., 1940. Contributor of the chapter "Knowledge and its Categories" (re-printed from *Essays in Critical Realism*). Pp. 431-440.
Religious Liberals Reply, ed. Henry Wieman. Boston, 1947. Contributor of the chapter "Accept the Universe as a Going Concern!"
Philosophy for the Future, ed. R. W. Sellars, V. J. McGill, and Marvin Farber. New York, 1949. Contributor of the chapters "Social Philosophy and the American Scene," pp. 61-75, and "Materialism and Human Knowing," pp. 75-106.
Philosophic Thought in France and the United States, ed. Marvin Farber. Buffalo, 1950. Contributor of the chapter "Critical Realism and Modern Materialism." Pp. 463-481.
A History of Philosophical Systems, ed. Vergilius Ferm. New York, 1950. Contributor of the chapter "The New Materialism." Pp. 418-428.
Religion in the Twentieth Century. ed. Vergilius Ferm. New York, 1948. Philosophical Library. Contributor of the chapter "Naturalistic Humanism." Pp. 415-431.
Evolution of Values. Trans. by Helen Sellars. Henry Holt, 1920. New York. Preface by R. W. Sellars.

Articles

"Re-interpretation of Democracy." *Inlander* (Univ. of Michigan Publication), Vol. 12 (1902), pp. 252-261.
"The Nature of Experience." *Journal of Philosophy, Psychology, and Scientific Methods*, Vol. 4 (1907), pp. 14-18.
"A Fourth Progression in the Relation of Body and Mind." *Psychological Review*, Vol. 14 (1907), pp. 315-328.
"Professor Dewey's View of Agreement." *Journal of Philosophy, Psychology, and Scientific Methods*, Vol. 4 (1907), pp. 432-435.
"An Important Antinomy." *Psychological Review*, Vol. 15 (1908), pp. 237-249.
"Consciousness and Conservation." *Journal of Philosophy, Psychology, and Scientific Methods*, Vol. 5 (1908), pp. 235-238.
"Critical Realism and the Time Problem. I." *Journal of Philosophy, Psychology, and Scientific Methods*, Vol. 5 (1908), pp. 542-548.
"Critical Realism and the Time Problem. II." *Journal of Philosophy, Psychology, and Scientific Methods*, Vol. 5 (1908), pp. 597-602.
"Space." *Journal of Philosophy, Psychology, and Scientific Methods*, Vol. 6 (1909), pp. 617-623.
"Causality." *Journal of Philosophy, Psychology, and Scientific Methods*, Vol. 6 (1909), pp. 323-328.
"Is There a Cognitive Relation?" *Journal of Philosophy, Psychology, and Scientific Methods*, Vol. 9 (1912), pp. 225-232.
"A Thing and its Properties." *Journal of Philosophy, Psychology, and Scientific Methods*, Vol. 12 (1915), pp. 318-328.
"On the Nature of Our Knowledge of the External World." *Philosophical Review*, Vol. 27 (1918), pp. 502-512.

"An Approach to the Mind-Body Problem." *Philosophical Review*, Vol. 27 (1918), pp. 150-163.
"The Epistemology of Evolutionary Naturalism." *Mind*, Vol. 28 (1919), pp. 407-426.
"The Status of the Categories." *The Monist*, Vol. 30 (1920), pp. 220-239.
"Space and Time." *The Monist*, Vol. 30 (1920), pp. 321-364.
"Evolutionary Naturalism and the Mind-Body Problem." *The Monist*, Vol. 30 (1920), pp. 568-598.
"Epistemological Dualism versus Metaphysical Dualism." *Philosophical Review*, Vol. 30 (1921), pp. 482-493.
"The Requirements of an Adequate Naturalism." *The Monist*, Vol. 31 (1921), pp. 249-270.
"Is Consciousness Physical?" *Journal of Philosophy*, Vol. 19 (1922), pp. 690-694.
"Concerning 'Transcendence' and 'Bifurcation'." *Mind*, Vol. 31 (1922), pp. 31-39.
"Le Cerveau, L'âme et La Conscience." *Bulletin de la Société Français de Philosophie*. (January 18, 1923), pp. 1-14.
"The Double-Knowledge Approach to the Mind-Body Problem." *Aristotelian Society Proceedings*, n.s., 23 (1923), pp. 55-70.
"The Emergence of Naturalism." *International Journal of Ethics*, Vol. 34 (1924), pp. 309-338.
"Critical Realism and its Critics." *Philosophical Review*, Vol. 33 (1924), pp. 379-397.
"Cognition and Valuation." *Philosophical Review*, Vol. 35 (1926), pp. 124-144.
"Current Realism in Great Britain and the United States." *The Monist*, Vol. 37 (1927), pp. 503-520.
"Realism and Evolutionary Naturalism." *The Monist*, Vol. 37 (1927), pp. 150-155.
"What is the Correct Interpretation of Critical Realism?" *Journal of Philosophy*, Vol. 24 (1927), pp. 238-241.
"Why Naturalism and not Materialism?" *Philosophical Review*, Vol. 36 (1927), pp. 216-225.
"Critical Realism and Substance." *Mind*, Vol. 38 (1929), pp. 473-488.
"A Re-examination of Critical Realism." *Philosophical Review*, Vol. 38 (1929), pp. 439-455.
"A Naturalistic Interpretation of Religion." *The New Humanist*, Vol. 3, No. 4 (1930), pp. 1-4.
"Humanism, Viewed and Reviewed." *The New Humanist*, Vol. 4, No. 15 (1931), pp. 12-16.
"A Reinterpretation of Relativity." *Philosophical Review*, Vol. 41 (1932), pp. 517-518.
"L'Hypothèse de l'Émergence." *Revue de Métaphysique et de Morale*, Vol. 40 (1933), pp. 309-324.
"A Humanist Manifesto" (Drafter and co-signer). *The New Humanist*, Vol. 6, No. 3 (1933).
"Religious Humanism." *The New Humanist*, Vol. 6, No. 3 (1933), pp. 7-12.
"In Defense of the Manifesto." *The New Humanist*, Vol. 6, No. 6 (1933), pp. 6-12.
"Nature and Naturalism." *The New Humanist*, Vol. 7, No. 2 (1934), pp. 1-8.

"George S. Morris." *Dictionary of American Biography*, Vol. 13 (1935), pp. 208-209.
"Henry Philip Tappan." *Dictionary of American Biography*, Vol. 18 (1937), pp. 302-303.
"Critical Realism and the Independence of the Object." *Journal of Philosophy*, Vol. 34 (1937), pp. 541-550.
"An Analytic Approach to the Mind-Body Problem." *Philosophical Review*, Vol. 47 (1938), pp. 461-487.
"Positivism in Contemporary Philosophical Thought." *American Sociological Review* (1939), pp. 26-42.
"A Statement of Critical Realism." *Philosophy of Science*, Vol. 6 (1939), pp. 412-421.
"Humanism as a Religion." *The Humanist*, Vol. 1, No. 1 (1941), pp. 5-8.
"A Correspondence Theory of Truth." *Journal of Philosophy*, Vol. 38 (1941), pp. 645-654.
"Aspects of Democracy II: the Quality of Democracy." *Michigan Alumnus Quarterly Review*, 48 (1942), pp. 98-103.
"Galileo Galilei." *Michigan Alumnus Quarterly Review*, Vol. 48 (1942), pp. 301-307.
"Dewey on Materialism." *Journal of Philosophy and Phenomenological Research*, Vol. 3 (1942-43), pp. 381-392.
"Verification of Categories: Existence and Substance." *Journal of Philosophy*, Vol. 40 (1943), pp. 197-205.
"Causality and Substance." *Philosophical Review*, Vol. 52 (1943), pp. 1-27.
"Reason and Revolution." *Michigan Alumnus Quarterly Review*, Vol. 49 (1943), pp. 212-214.
"Causation and Perception." *Philosophical Review*, Vol. 53 (1944), pp. 534-556.
"Reformed Materialism and Intrinsic Endurance." *Philosophical Review*, Vol. 53 (1944), pp. 359-382.
"Does Naturalism Need Ontology?" *Journal of Philosophy*, Vol. 41 (1944), pp. 686-694.
"Is Naturalism Enough?" *Journal of Philosophy*, Vol. 41 (1944), pp. 533-544.
"Can a Reformed Materialism Do Justice to Values?" *Ethics*, Vol. 55 (1944), pp. 28-45.
"Reflections on Dialectical Materialism." *Philosophy and Phenomenological Research*, Vol. 5 (1944-45), pp. 157-179.
"Knowing and Knowledge." *Journal of Philosophy and Phenomenological Research*, Vol. 5 (1944-45), pp. 341-344.
"Knowing Through Propositions." *Journal of Philosophy and Phenomenological Research*, Vol. 5 (1944-45), pp. 348-349.
"The Meaning of True and False." *Journal of Philosophy and Phenomenological Research*, Vol. 5 (1944-45), pp. 98-103.
"Materialism and Relativity: A Semantic Analysis." *Philosophical Review*, Vol. 55 (1946), pp. 25-51.
"The Philosophy and Physics of Relativity." *Philosophy of Science*, Vol. 13 (1946), pp. 177-195.
"A Note on the Theory of Relativity." *Journal of Philosophy*, Vol. 43 (1946), pp. 309-317.

"Positivism and Materialism." *Journal of Philosophy and Phenomenological Research*, Vol. 7 (1946-47), pp. 12-40.
"Do the Natural Sciences Have Need of the Social Sciences?" *Philosophy of Science*, Vol. 15 (1948), pp. 104-108.
"The Spiritualism of Lavelle and Le Senne." *Journal of Philosophy and Phenomenological Research*, Vol. 11 (1950-51), pp. 386-393.
"Professor Goudge's Queries with Respect to Materialism." *Philisophical Review*, Vol. 60 (1951), pp. 243-248.

Reviews

Epistemology, P. Coffey. *Journal of Philosophy, Psychology, and Scientific Methods*, Vol. 15 (1918), pp. 557-558.
Christian Belief in God, George Wobbermin. *Journal of Philosophy, Psychology, and Scientific Methods*, Vol. 16 (1919), pp. 277-279.
The Field of Philosophy, J. A. Leighton, *Journal of Philosophy, Psychology, and Scientific Methods*, Vol. 17 (1920), pp. 79-81.
Introduction to Philosophy, Durant Drake. *Journal of Philosophy*, Vol. 3 (1933), pp. 667-669.
Primer for Tomorrow, C. F. Gauss. *Michigan Alumnus Quarterly Review*, Vol. 41 (1935), pp. 465-466.
God and Philosophy, E. Gilson. *The Humanist*, Vol. 2, No. 1 (1942), pp. 36-37.
"Science, Philosophy, and Religion." *Third Symposium*. Conference on Science, Philosophy, and Religion in their Relation to the Democratic Way of Life, Inc. *The Humanist*, Vol. 3, No. 2 (1943), pp. 84-85.
Education at the Cross Roads, J. Maritain. *The Humanist*, Vol. 3, No. 4 (1943), pp. 165-170.
Naturalism and the Human Spirit, ed. Yervant Krikorian. *Journal of Philosophy and Phenomenological Research*, Vol. 6 (1945-46), pp. 436-439.
Essays in Science and Philosophy, A. N. Whitehead. *The Humanist*, Vol. 8, No. 2 (1948), pp. 92-93.
The Science of Culture, Leslie A. White. *Journal of Philosophy and Phenomenological Research*, Vol. 10 (1949-50), pp. 586-587.
Good Will and Ill Will, Frank Chapman Sharp. *The Humanist*, Vol. 10, No. 6 (1950), pp. 277-278.
The Science of Culture, Leslie A. White. *Michigan Alumnus Quarterly Review*, Vol. 56 (1950), pp. 175-176.
Beyond Mythology, R. W. Boynton. *Journal of Philosophy and Phenomenological Research*, Vol. 12 (1951-52), pp. 146-148.
Man: Mind or Matter, Charles Mayer. *Journal of Philosophy and Phenomenological Research*, Vol. 12 (1951-52), pp. 436-442.

Miscellaneous

Resume of W. Cook Foundation lectures delivered by Ralph Barton Perry. *Michigan Alumnus Quarterly Review*, Vol. 55 (1949), pp. 185-194.

Bibliographical Supplement
Compiled by W. PRESTON WARREN

"My Philosophical Position: A Rejoinder," *Philosophy and Philosophical Research*, XVI (1955), 72-97.

"Guided Causality, Using Reason and 'Free Will'," *Journal of Philosophy*, LIV (1957), 16, 485-493.

"Valuational Naturalism and Moral Discourse," *Philosophical Review*, LXVII (1958), 243-251.

"Philosophical Orientation and Peace," Introductory Essay in Irving Louis Horowitz, *The Idea of War and Peace in Contemporary Philosophy* (New York, Paine-Whitman), xii-xx, 1957.

" 'True' as Contextually Implying Correspondence," *Journal of Philosophy*, LVI (1959), 18, 717-722.

"Sensations as Guides to Perceiving," *Mind*, LXVIII (1959), 269, 2-15.

"Levels of Causality: The Emergence of Guidance and Reason in Nature," *Philosophy and Phenomenological Research*, XX (1959), 1, 1-16.

"Panpsychism or Evolutionary Naturalism," *Philosophy of Science*, XXVII (1960), 4, 329-350.

"American Realism: Perspective and Framework," in *Self, Religion, and Metaphysics*: Essays in Memory of James Bissett Pratt. Edited by Gerald E. Myers. New York, Macmillan Co., 1961, 174-200.

"Referential Transcendence," *Philosophy and Phenomenological Research*, XXII (1961), 1, 1-14.

"Querying Whitehead's Framework," *Revue Internationale de Philosophie*, No. 56-57, Fasc. 3-4 (1961), 1-32.

"American Critical Realism and British Theories of Sense Perception"—in two parts, *Estratto Rivista Methodos*, XIV, 55-56, 1962, 61-87, 89-108. Reprinted in new edition of *The Philosophy of Physical Realism*, Russell and Russell, 1966, 478-524.

"Direct Referential Realism," *Dialogue*, II (1963), 2, 135-143.

"Existentialism, Realistic Empiricism, and Materialism," *Philosophy and Phenomenological Research*, XXV (1965), 3, 315-332.

"In What Sense do Value Judgments and Moral Judgments Have Objective Import," *Philosophy and Phenomenological Research*, XXVIII (1967), 1, 1-16.

Lending a Hand to Hylas, Ann Arbor, Edwards Bros., 1968, 1-102.

Review of "Farber's *Aims of Phenomenology: The Motives, Methods and Impact of Husserl's Thought*," *Philosophy and Phenomenological Research*, XXIX (1968), 1, 125-129.

"In Defense of 'Metaphysical Veracity'," *The Philosophy of C. I. Lewis*, Paul A. Schilpp, editor (La Salle, Ill., Open Court), 1968, 287-308.

American Philosophy from Within, Notre Dame Press, 1969.

Recent Reprintings

The Philosophy of Physical Realism (1932), augmented by two chapters, New York, Russell and Russell, 1966.

Critical Realism: A Study of the Nature and Conditions of Knowledge (1916), with a new Preface, New York, Russell and Russell, 1969.
Evolutionary Naturalism, with Preface by T. A. Goudge, New York, Russell and Russell, 1969.

A Revision at Press

Principles, Perspectives, and Problems of Philosophy—Pageant Press—1970, a revision of *Principles and Problems of Philosophy* (1926).

Index

A

Absurd, 277, 304-305
Activity, 31, 40, 45
Adler, 324
Aesthetic object, 248
Aesthetics, 254, 322, 326, 335
Agnosticism, 157
Alexander, Samuel, xviii, 45, 62, 113, 114, 115-116, 167, 205
Angell, J. R., 176-177, 178, 270
Animal faith, 121
Aristotle, xxiii, 25, 44, 47, 60-61, 163, 167, 235, 257, 273, 275
Aristoteleanism, 28, 44-45, 50, 111, 136, 158, 167, 169, 173
Aristotelean substantialism, 47
Aseity, 154
Associational psychology, 89
Atomic materialism, 152, 212
Atomic sensationalism, 130
Atomism, 29, 33, 46, 48, 90, 127, 148, 151, 160, 166, 196
Awareness, 36, 75-84, 144, 226, 227
Axiology, 141, 175, 240, 246, 256, 260, 322, *See* Values
Ayer, A. J., 8, 9, 12, 259, 274

B

Baldwin, James Mark, xix, xxiii, xxix, 6, 177, 178-180, 270
Barnes, 8, 9
Bawden, H. Heath, 73, 178
Beauty, *See* Aesthetics

Behaviorism, xvii, xviii, xxiv, 6, 11, 12, 14, 15, 19, 21, 24, 54n, 108, 134, 138, 175, 189, 193, 205, 206, 208, 302
Bentley, 20
Bergson, Henry, xviii, xxiii, 15, 22, 170, 189, 190, 194, 195, 200
Berkeley, 9, 58, 88, 91, 92, 93, 104, 107, 112, 116-117, 126, 130, 159, 168, 235, 237
Berkelian idealism, 142, 250
Berkelians, 148
Bio-psychological realism, 64
Blanshard, Brand, xii, 237
Blau, Joseph, xxv
Boodin, J. E., 54, 56
Bosanquet, 53n
Bradley, 52, 53n, 68, 132
Brightman, 145
Brain-mind, *See* Mind-brain
Brain, Sir Russell, xiv, 27
Bridges, 335-336
Broad, C. D., 6n, 23, 39, 117, 258
Buddhism, 308

C

Calvin, 292
Camus, 305
Capitalism, 301-302, 303, 307, 310
Carlyle, xxii
Carnap, xvi, xxiv, 126, 259
Carr, 133
Cartesian dualism, xii, 5, 6, 11, 16, 20, 35-36, 101, 103, 121, 130, 142,

144, 147, 152, 173, 189ff, 207, 218, 234
Cartesian idealism, 26
Cartesian intuitionism, 25, 121
Cartesianism, 146, 159, 218, 236, 248
Categories, xix, 4, 24, 27-33, 72, 84, 85-88, 97-101, 110, 118, 121-122, 131, 132, 145, 151, 157-159, 174, 189, 190-191, 206, 207, 214, 215, 216, 224-225, 249-250, 264-265, See also specific categories
Causal agency, xi, 3, 151, 201, 261-267, 305, See also Free will
Causality, 32, 42, 97, 100, 222-223
Causality and substance, 27-49, 57, 59, 84-97
Causal laws, 31, 95-96, 201
Causal symbolism, 42
Causal theory of perception, 9, 11, 14, 122, 126, 129, See also Mechanism of perceiving
Chesterton, G. K., 292
Chisholm, 233
Christian Aristotelianism, See Thomas
Christianity, 240, 308, 318-319, 327-331
Churchill, 290
Coghill, 142
Cognition, xi, 30, 59-60, 75-84, 118, 120-122, 123-125, 129, 130-131, 141, 142-144, 149, 165, 215-216, 241, 242
Cognitive relation, 79-80, 142
Comte, 319
Common reference, 84
Common sense, 8, 17, 28, 29, 61, 83, 84-85, 93, 105, 126
Communism, 301-302, 307, 310, 311
Conceptual apprehension, 35-37, 42
Conceptual pragmatism, 21
Consciousness, 5-6, 12, 19, 24, 48-49, 50, 57-58, 65-66, 68, 76, 99, 100-101, 124, 128, 130, 139-140, 146, 148-149, 159-162, 175, 177, 178, 180, 181, 182-185, 185-188, 188-202, 205, 208, 209-211, 213, 214-218, 220-228, 239
Context of perception, 106, 122
Contextualism, 20

Conventionalism, 29
Cooley, Charles Horton, 270, 330
Cornelius, 74
Correspondence as a theory of truth, xiv, xix, 17, 20, 108, 121, 142, 143, 165, 190, 221, 233, 235-239, See also Truth
Cosmology, 132-133, 134, 136, 142, 171
Craig, xxiii, 312n
Critical realism as a school, 5, 22, 51, 53, 54-57, 69; the "Essence" variety of, 5, 54; the "Intentionalist" wing of, xvii, 5, 54

D

Darwinian biology, 295, 322
Debs, 311
Democracy, 269, 270, 273, 276, 277-279, 289, 291, 293-301, 307-309, 310-311, 319
Democratic social realism, xx
Democritus, 132
Denotative realism, 33, 128-129, 129, 130, 141, 147, 161
Descartes, 26, 49, 108, 119, 190, See also Cartesianism
Dewey, John, xii, xix, xx, xxi, 6, 19-21, 25, 37, 51, 52n-53n, 53, 73, 73n, 81, 102-103, 104, 126, 128-129, 129, 130, 141, 144, 146n, 147, 150, 150n, 189, 229-230, 234, 246, 250, 255, 270, 272
Dewey-Bentley gambit, 19
Direct realism, xii, xiv, 5, 11, 15, 16, 22, 25, 55, 125, 237
Directionalism See Emergence
Disraeli, 290
Double-knowledge approach to the brain-mind, xii, xix, 7, 11, 24, 35, 137, 139, 160, 174, 188-202, 204-223
Drake, Durant, 55, 55n, 123-124, 133, 160
Driesch, Hans, xviii, xxiii
Ducasse, C. J., 233
Duration, 42-43

E

Eddington, xv, 143, 157, 162, 171, 225
Eleaticism, 152, 156-157, 159, 161, 169, 172
Ellis, 181
Emanation, See Emergence
Emergence, xxiii-xxiv, 31, 32, 36, 44-47, 51, 63, 148, 163, 168, 172, 173, 204, 215, 247, 332-333
Emergent evolution, 62-63, 207
Emergent materialism, 64
Emergent naturalism, See Evolutionary naturalism
Emerson, xxii
Emotivism, xx, 230, 259-260
Empedocles, 166
Engles, 279, 283, 286
English neo-realism, 5-6, 114
Epicurus, 166
Epiphenomenalism, 136, 137, 141, 274
Epistemological dualism, 22, 26, 59, 61, 61n, 83, 98-99, 101-118; in Sellars early writings, 59, 61, 61n, 101-112
Epistemology, 4, 7, 11, 12, 15, 19, 23, 24, 25, 32, 35, 37, 38, 39, 42, 46, 57, 58, 74, 75, 101-112, 123, 126, 127, 130, 132, 134, 141, 157, 164, 175, 188, 204, 210, 211, 220, 221, 229, 256
Erasmus, 331
Essences, xvii, 5, 112, 123, 164, 173, 190
"Doctrine of essence," 124
Eventism, 115
Evolutionary approach to consciousness, 48-49
Evolutionary materialism, 159
Evolutionary naturalism, xiv, xv, xviii, xxiv, 29, 32, 62, 63, 133, 175, 189, 202-204, 207, 213
Evolutionary substantialism, 45-49
Evolutionism, xii, xiv, xv, xviii-xix, 134, 138, 139, 157, 159, 163, 174, 182, 184, 186, 188, 203, 207
Ewing, 39, 40, 126, 255, 255n
Experience, xii, 19-20, 68, 69, 73-75, 84-85, 87-88, 90-91, 102, 113-114
Experientialism, 147, See also Dewey
Experiential situationalism, 20
Experimentalism, 6, 19-21, 26, 135, 230
Existentialism, xv, xxiv, 54n, 259, 265, 274, 304-305, 314, 335

F

Fabian socialism, xx, 273, See Socialism
Farber, Marvin, xiii, 17, 26, 59n
Federalism, 307
Feigl, Herbert, 24, 26, 126
Feuer, Lewis, xvii-xviii
Feuerbach, 287
Fichte, 286
Finalism, 172, 173
Flechsig, 181
Form, 70-71, 111, 188
Fourier, 280
Frankena, 257
Free-will, xv, 17-18, 239, 261-267, 305, See also Causal agency
Freud, Sigmund, xiv, 292, 302, 324
Fromm, Eric, xiv
Fullerton, 54
Functional realism, xvii, xxiv
Functions, 175, 176-177, See also Process

G

Galbraith, 272, 303, 309, 310
Galileo, xv
Galtonian Law of Heredity, 182
Garnett, 158n
Geiger, 19-20
Gestaltists, 117, 129, 205, 221
Gestalt behaviorists, 6, 12, 205, 209, 218
Gilson, 153, 168-169
Guided causality, 16

H

Hall, 157, 158n
Hampshire, Stuart, 8, 9
Hare, R. M., 230, 260, 261

Harlow, Victor E., xxv, 54n, 62n
Hartshorne, 153, 313
Hedonism, 131, 258
Hegel, 170, 173, 286, 291
Hegelian, 21, 308
Heidegger, Martin, xvi, 258-259, 304, 314
Heracleitean flux, 65, 70
Heracleitus, 166
Herrick, C. Judson, xiii, 6, 14, 142n
Hobbes, 132, 146, 273
Hodgson, 105-106
Hoernle, 119
Höffding, 65-66, 67
Hofstadter, Richard, 311
Holt, E. B., 54
Hook, Sidney, 140-141, 143, 144, 149
Horney, Karen, xiv
Humanism, xxi, 15, 172, 240, 280, 310, 312-314, 317, 319, 323, 328, 329, 331, 331-335
Hume, David, xiii, xvii, 9, 11, 12, 29, 30-31, 32, 33, 35, 37, 39, 41, 48, 78, 79, 88, 92, 104, 129, 130, 148, 151, 160n, 166, 168, 182, 221, 223, 226, 237, 257; Post-Humean, 29, 158
Humeanism, 12, 15, 102, 142
Hunecker, 312
Husserl, 26
Huxley, 274
Hylomorphism, 151, 163, 173

I

Idealism as a school, 17, 53, 54, 59, 64, 80-81, 102, 133, 140, 158, 159, 165, 183, 189, 202, 206, 246; absolute idealism, 68-69; objective idealism, 237; personal idealism, 69, 248
Identity, 204, 219, 220, See also Correspondence and mind-brain
Immanence, 17, 128, 214
Immanent causality, 222, 224, 226-228
Instrumentalism, 112, See Dewey
Intrinsic endurance, 164-169, 173

Introspectionism, 6, 85, 134, 174, 212, 221
Intuition, xiv, 124, 125, 128, 164, 201, 212, 213
Intuitional ethics, 259, 260, See Moore
Intuitionism, 230, 258, 260, 261

J

Jacksonian Democracy, 298, 307
James, William, 5, 48, 51, 52-53n, 73n, 74, 78, 79, 115, 144, 147, 180-181
Jeans, xv, 157
Jefferson, 306
Jennings, 73n, 184
Joachim, 176
Joad, 157, 158n
Jung, 324

K

Kafka, 305
Kant, 29, 32, 33, 78, 79, 83, 100, 102, 106, 159-160, 176, 235, 237, 257, 264, 306; Kantian agnosticism, 157; Kantian perception, 3, 130; Kantian phenomenalism, 133; Kantian space and time, 98; Kantians, 52, 53n, 83
Kemp Smith, Norman, 113
Keynes, 303, 311
Keynesianism, 309
Kierkegaard, 335
Kinaesthetic sensations, 41-42
Koffka, 203, 205, 223
Köhler, 23, 26, 205, 222
Köhlerian Apes, 60
Kraepelin, 181

L

Laissez faire, 291, 298, 301, 302, 309
Langmuir, 147
Leibniz, 170
Leibnitzian metaphysics, 83
Lenin, 308

Lepley, 250
Lewis, C. I., 11, 128
Levels of causality, xiv, 222, 256, 262, 305, See also Emergence
Liberalism, xxiii
Liebknecht, 283
Lincoln, 300
Lippmann, 272
Locke, John, xiii, 5, 22, 26, 44, 45-46, 56, 88, 89-93, 95-96, 108, 112, 119, 126, 129, 186, 190, 237, 273, 306, 307
Lockeanism, 55, 110, 130
Lockean politics, 308
Lockean realism, 109, 110, 111
Lockean representationalism, 53n, 109, 142, 237
Logic, 72-73, 89
Logical empiricism, 17, 54n
Logical positivism, xiii, xv, 8, 14, 17, 21, 243, 256, 259, 260
Logical realism, 70
Love, 330
Lovejoy, A. O., xii, xvii, 19, 54, 55n

M

Mach, Ernst, xv, 53n
Machiavelli, 273
Macintosh, D. C., xviii, 54, 55, 62, 113-114
Madison, 291-292, 306
Maier, 205
Maritain, 153
Marx, 273, 279, 282-287, 292, 303, 306, 308, 311
Marxism, 281-287, 303, 307, 308
Marxists, 154, 170, 173, 189, 303
Masaryk, T. G., 272
Materialism, 63, 111, 131-140, 140, 147, 148, 149, 150, 150-173, 184, 216, 225
Materialistic substantialism, 47
Maxwell, 67
May, Rollo, xiv
Mayo, Bernard, 233, 234, 238
McCullock, Warren, 24

McGiffert, 319n
McGilvary, xvi, xvii, 54
Mead, 37
Mechanism of knowing, 113, 114, 117, 141
Mechanism of perception, 8-10, 12-16, 18-22, 23-27, 33-35, 37-43
Medieval realism, 131
Melchert, Norman, xiii, 61n, 174, 175-176
Memory, 187-188
Mendelian Law of Heredity, 182, 184
Merriam, 300
Metaphysical dualism, 189ff, 220, 333. See Cartesian dualism
Methodology, 188, 190-191, 193
Mind, 186, 190, 193, 194-196, 207-209, 239
Mind-body problem, xii, xix, xxiv, 12, 15, 174-176, 176-229, 267
Mind-brain complex (or brain-mind), 3, 7, 129, 130, 145, 186, 188, 197-198, 198-200, 204, 207, 210-211, 216-217
Moleschott, 132
Monadism, 133
Monism, 12, 13, 16, 124, 204, 209
Montague, W. P., xiii, 5, 54, 54n, 56, 130, 153, 154, 201
Moore, G. E., 7-8, 13, 230, 241, 245-246, 255, 258, 261
More, Sir Thomas, 279
Morgan, Lloyd, xii, xviii-xix, 45, 62, 167, 205
Morris, 129, 306
Münsterberg, 178
Myrdal, 309, 310

N

Naïve materialism, 209, 225
Naïve realism, 64, 80, 107, 109, 110, 114, 117, 128, 143, 147, 170, 246
Natural realism, 92, 93, 111, 125, 137
Naturalism, xiii, xv, xix, xxiv, 26, 54, 55, 56, 59, 62, 76, 88-89, 90, 101, 103, 104, 108, 111, 112, 114, 115-117,

122, 131-140, 140-150, 152-153, 166, 172, 176, 179, 189, 202-204, 205, 212-214, 240, 241, 321-331, 332-343, 345
Naturalistic fallacy, 241, 245-246
Naturalistic humanism, xxi, 172
Neo-realism, 54, 55, 56, 59, 104, 108, 111, 112, 114, 115-117, 122
Neo-Thomism, 151, 154, 168
New realists, xvii, 5-6, 21, 22, 115, 126, 147, 237, 246, 247
Newton, Isaac, xv, 156
Newtonianism, xiv, 23, 237, 248
Niebuhr, Reinhold, 292, 314
Nietzscheanism, 295
Normative theory of knowledge, 76-77
Northrop, F. S. C., 143, 154
Nowell-Smith, 230, 261

O

Objective relativism, xvi
Objectivism, 103
Ontological Platonism, 157
Ontological proof, 164
Ontology, xviii, xxi, 3, 26, 27-28, 30, 31, 32, 34, 36, 37, 38, 49, 53, 54, 56, 116, 131, 134-136, 138, 140, 141, 148, 150-151, 153, 154, 158, 163, 164, 169-171, 172, 175, 204, 208, 210, 211, 227-228, 229, 240, 252, 256, 273
Operationalism, 206
Organization, 60, 63, 68, 70-72, 87, 100, 136, 138, 141, 163, 169, 176, 184, 198, 203, 211, 224, 227-228

P

Pace, 24
Pan-objectivism, 5, 15
Panpsychism, xiv, 53, 69, 133, 134, 135, 139, 140, 158, 159, 165, 185, 216, 248
Parker, DeWitt, xx, xxi, 39, 145, 151, 153, 163, 169n, 246, 247, 250, 255

Parallelism, 178
Pauli, 185
Paulsen, 257
Pearson, Karl, 53n
Peirce, Charles, xxi, 54, 236
Pepper, Stephen C., 156, 232, 306
"Perception in a Complex," xviii
Perry, R. B., xx, 5, 15, 22, 54, 115, 246, 247
Phenomenalism, xiii, 8, 9, 19, 21, 27, 29, 39, 53, 54, 83, 147, 179
Phenomenology, xxiv
Philosophical analysis, 54n
Physical realism, 3
Pillsbury, 185-186
Pitkin, 54
Plato, 132, 168, 235, 273, 303, 306, 308, 310
Platonic-Aristotelean tradition, 239
Platonic dualism, 70
Platonic ingredience, 153
Platonic perception, 13
Platonic realism, 276
Platonic values, 149, 241, 245, 252
Positivism, 32, 140, 148, 149, 150, 152, 153, 154, 158, 168, 206, 250, 255
Pragmatic naturalism, 134, 141, 147, 148, 149, 150, 272, 273
Pragmatic scientism, 27
Pragmatism, 17, 21, 32, 54, 76-77, 81, 111, 133, 140, 143, 150, 176, 236, 246, 259
Pragmatists, xvii, 53, 101, 108, 112, 127, 130, 144, 147, 153, 168, 237, 250
Pratt, J. B., 39, 54, 55n, 189, 196n, 209, 218-221, 222, 228, 228n
Presentationalism, See Presentational realism
Presentational realism, xii, xiii, 5, 15, 55, 179, 237
Pritchard, 230
Primary and secondary qualities, 84-97
Process, 23, 52, 66, 69-75, 77, 138, 155, 162, 169-170, 172, 332-333, See also Organization and function
Psychoanalytic realism, xviii, See also Mechanism of knowing

Psycho-therapists, xiv
Public objects, 27

R

Radical empiricism, 37, 104, 152, See also Pragmatism
Rashdall, 255
Realistic empiricism, 37, 45
Rebec, xxiii
Reck, Andrew, xxi, xxv
Reductionism, 136, 141, 149, 240-241
Referential realism, xiii, 5, 17-27, 57, 64, 237, 238, See also Referential theory of perception
Referential theory of perception, xviii, 3, 6-7, 8, 13, 15-16, 33-35
Reformed materialism, 150-173, 239-256
Reid, Thomas, 105, 106
Relativity, theory of, 43, 50
Representative realism, xiii, 11, 76-78, 108-109, 111, 112, 113, 117, 118-120, 444, See also Locke
Representative theory of knowing, 121-122, 127, 129, See also Representative theory of perception
Revolution, 275, 278, 280-281, 283-285, 289-293
Rice, 150, 150n
Riley, Woodbridge, xxv
Rogers, Arthur K., 54, 55, 175
Roman politic, 272
Ross, 44, 230
Rousseau, 273
Royce, 53n
Russell, Bertrand, xiii, xvii, 6, 8, 12, 13, 14, 24, 106, 115, 116, 122, 164, 165, 251
Ryle, Gilbert, 8, 9, 12-13, 15, 21, 238

S

Saint Simon, 280
Salvation, 320
Santayana, George, xvi, xvii, 5, 21, 55, 55n, 121, 129, 137, 153n, 154, 168

Sartre, J. P., xvi, 304, 305
Savery, Professor, 44
Say's Law, 303
Scepticism, 9, 15, 33, 143
Schleiermacher, 314
Schneider, Herbert, 53n, 56
Schneirla, 205
Self-awareness, 33, 35-37, 39-41, 145n, 146, 148, 164, 165, 166, 197, 251
Self-determination, See Causal agency
Self-knowledge, 208-210, 214, 219
Sellars, Wilfrid, xiii, 9, 13, 24
Sensations, See Sense-data
Sensationalism, 12, 29, 126-127, 155, 158, 243
Sense-data, xiii, 5, 8, 9, 10, 11, 13, 14, 16, 26, 30, 103, 104, 106, 110-112, 121, 126, 127, 129, 142, 192, 193, 195, 199, 202, 206, 210, See also Sense impressions
Sense impressions, xiii, 5, 9, 12, 22, 23, 33, 127, See also Sense-data
Sense perception, 6-7, 51, 52, 199
Sensory appearance, See Sense impressions
Sharp, F. C., 258, 271
Sheldon, 189, 194, 194n, 195
Shepard, John, xxiv
Schopenhauer, 302
Sim Kovitch, 282
Smart, 24
Smith, Adam, 310
Smith, T. V., 232, 233, 237
Snow, C. P., 310
Social, the reality of the, 269, 270
Socialism, xx, 272, 273, 277-279, 279-289, 311, 334
Social realism, 254
Socrates, 272, 331
Solipsism, 73, 74
Spaulding, 54
Spinoza, 168, 237, 312, 327
Stebbing, 6n, 126, 158n
Stevenson, Charles, 259-260
Stout, 39, 145, 158n, 176
Strong, C. A., 5, 53, 55, 55n, 107, 133, 160, 181
Structure, See Organization

Subjectivism, 20, 29, 53n, 101, 223, 240, 241
Substantialism, 116
Supernaturalism, 103, 132, 133, 140, 167, 321
Swabey, 39

T

Taylor, 53n, 69, 73, 178, 183
Teleology, 49-50, 136, 185, 188, 190, 191, 193, 230, 256, 317
ten Hoor, Martin, xxi
Thilly, 138-139
St. Thomas, 164
Thomism, 28, 154, 163, 273
Tillich, Paul, 314
Time, 27, 32, 42, 68-72, 72-75, 87, 97-98, 100, 157, 169
Tory-socialism, 290
Toulmin, 230, 260, 261
Transcendence, xiv, 17-27, 74-75, 81-84, 128-129, 146-147, 154, 176, 206, 213, 214, 215-216, 218
Transcendental absolute, 26
Truth, xiv, 229-232, 232-239, 253-264, 322, *See also* Value

U

"Under the hat" theory of mind, xii, 19
"Under the skin" dualism, 20
Urban, xix, 240, 251

Urmson, 230, 261
Utopianism, 279-281

V

Value, xi, xix, xix-xx, xxv, 3, 136, 149-150, 229-232, 233-235, 239-256, 256-261, 269, 276, 304-305, 315-317, 318-325, 330, 332-333
Value transcendentalism, 149, 241, 246, 252, 256

W

Walker, 184
Ward, James, xxiv, 53n, 133, 202
Warren, W. P., xiii, xiv, 311
Watson, 189
Webster, 291-292
Wenley, xxiii
Werkmeister, W. H., xxv
Wesetermarck, 255
Weyl, Walter, 310
White, Morton, 13
Whitehead, A. N., xiv, xvi, 41, 48, 56, 151, 152, 153, 154, 155, 160, 172, 314
Whiteheadianism, 313
Wilson, Cook, 118-119
Witman, 294
Wittgenstein, 9, 17, 260
Woodbridge, xii, 54